BROKEN
CHILD

Marcia Cameron

BROKEN
CHILD

KENSINGTON BOOKS

KENSINGTON BOOKS are published by

Kensington Publishing Corp.
850 Third Avenue
New York, NY 10022

Library of Congress Card Catalog Number: 94-078681
ISBN 0-8217-4826-2

First Printing: February, 1995

Printed in the United States of America

Author's Note

My story is one of child abuse in the extreme, and the multiple personalities I created to deal with the pain. The cost of child abuse is a tale that needs repeating until every baby born is cherished and safe.

This book was written for neither notoriety nor sensationalism. All names but two have been changed to secure my anonymity and to protect members of my family. I am not a spokesperson for the abused or the mentally ill. I can only give my experiences. The tales of my abuse are as accurate as memory will allow, and the emotional reality is written as it exists.

This is a book of hope. It is an affirmation of my own hope for my continuing recovery from mental illness, and the hope that someone in a troubled state will read this and realize there are answers when life overwhelms. There are probably many roads to change. My journey was through the traditional psychiatric methods. My life is so radically different that I cannot help but say I believe in psychotherapy. Unfortunately, it took some negative experiences with the wrong therapists before I found Dr. Ira Steinman.

The names of Dr. Ira Steinman and Dr. David Leof are the

real names of the two psychiatrists who deserve recognition for being the remarkable therapists they are. Without them I would not be alive today.

My deepest gratitude goes to Dr. Steinman. If my life can ultimately be viewed as a success, then the success is his, too. He heals people not only because he is the consummate professional, but because he knows the art of sharing his humanity.

After five years of therapy with Dr. Steinman, I have integrated my many personalities, and have control over my need to dissociate. I never thought that was possible five years ago when I arrived at his office, having spent days in the cold wind walking back and forth over the Golden Gate Bridge, planning my suicide. The steel girders were icy and the water was dark, choppy, and inviting. Life was a splintered existence of voices, panics, unexplained behaviors, and pain.

Over and over during my first months with Ira, I begged him for drugs to help me die. I told him it was better to be dead than to talk about my childhood of pain. He wouldn't let me quit. He suggested I write all my thoughts, feelings, and experiences down on paper since I was emotionally zinging all over the place. I told him I couldn't write, I wasn't sure where to put punctuation marks, and he said that wasn't important. The point was that our only tool in therapy was language. The very process of putting my childhood into words gave the horror a chronology, an emotional texture and a framework in which I could reorganize myself from the wildly creative madness of multiple personalities to becoming one functional person. Maybe the greatest gift is that Dr. Steinman could look past my words and keep directing me with his language toward my newly integrating, more defined self.

This book is only a fraction of the hundreds of pages I have written in the course of therapy. I do not have textbook jargon or medical perspectives at my command; I have written only from a deeply honest internal viewpoint. A gallon of tears have sloshed over these pages, for my memories are still raw. I wish they would leave me, but they still stir in my mind and in my heart. Writing my story will be worth the effort if even one abusive parent reads this and seeks help. It will be enough if one more hurt human being feels there are answers to the inner pain. Maybe, like all authors, I am inspired to write, so, like footprints in the snow, someone will know I lived. Not well, but I am here.

Foreword

Broken Child is a chronicle of chaos, torment, fragmentation, and eventual healing, a patient's view of her life and a portion of her psychotherapy. It originated as Marcia's attempt to gain some distance from the overwhelming recollections and feelings she experienced during the course of her therapy, by writing about what she was going through between sessions. She brought in pages, sections, and then chapters, which we discussed in many different ways as an aspect of her psychotherapy.

Eventually, it became clear to us that she had written a compelling tale from which others might benefit. Her story is a testament to hope, persistence, and the benefits of intensive psychotherapy after even the most severe splitting of the personality into many personae.

Marcia's account of this portion of her psychotherapy with me is a reasonably accurate one, in spite of being filtered through her pain and frequent regressions. There is a good deal of evidence supporting her story of extreme abuse; many scars silently attest to her suffering. I believe the brutal childhood events Marcia speaks of are actual, for much has been corroborated by familial accounts and a physical examination by an independent physician.

Multiple Personality was the result of her perception of her tortured childhood and her attempt to evade pain by becoming other selves, whom she regarded as real. Her childhood maneuver to escape an overwhelming and intolerable situation led to what we call dissociation: pretending to herself that she was not the person to whom these terrible events were happening.

Marcia (a pseudonym) is a sincere, intelligent and engaging woman. Even though she was regressed, suicidal and frantic when she first came in, I saw the possibility for growth and psychological integration. From the first session, with her talk of doing things as "other people," it seemed likely that she was a Multiple Personality, that she had probably been severely traumatized early in life, and unwittingly fled that trauma by unconsciously splitting herself up into many imaginary beings. If this were so, I knew that I would have to recognize and integrate these beings, imaginary friends who never went away, into one person—often against Marcia's protests. I knew there would be suicidal crises, strong emotions, and intense pain. I hoped my care and therapeutic optimism would lead her through.

I sensed that supportive psychotherapy would be of little use to one so wounded. It seemed to me that reintegration could be best accomplished by a psychodynamic psychotherapy aimed at making clear to the paitent her history and the origin of her fragmentation. Through our psychotherapeutic understanding of previously unconscious factors, transference issues, conflicts and resistances, a framework would be built to limit the chaos and help her unify into one person.

The field of treatment of Multiple Personality has recently been subject to several factors that I believe are unnecessary and unwise: the use of hypnosis and the idea that a creative act of dissociation from pain is a viable alternative in adulthood.

I wonder if the emphasis on hypnosis, and techniques for its induction and use, prolongs the course of treatment. Therapists run the risk of becoming fascinated by the diverse personae that emerge during hypnosis and may worsen a patient's tendency to regress. It is very easy to miss the forest for the trees, to become mesmerized by the alter personalities and miss the crucial fact that this is a person trying to escape psychological pain through dissociation.

These patients are highly creative and imaginative, and spontaneously induce their own trances, switching from self state to self state—or, as far as they're concerned, from person to person. This lack of a central responsible core self is their difficulty; they don't want to accept their pain as their own. To hypnotize patients—to induce the switching—furthers their lack of a sense of responsibility.

This is a far cry from what I view as a much more patient-centered approach: holding the patient responsible, by building an understanding of the dissociative switching he or she does in an attempt to evade the deepest wounds.

Some hypnotists have told me that hypnosis only means using the patient's creative imagination in the course of therapy; by that definition I have no quarrel with those who hypnotize. My sense, though, is that hypnosis too often becomes the end, in and of itself, rather than aiding the patient in the resolution of a lifelong pattern of abdicating responsibility via dissociating from pain. I suggest instead getting the lay of the land rather quickly and attempting to integrate the different personalities, as I have helped Marcia to do.

In the same vein, I question the therapeutic position that it is reasonable for a patient to learn to live with many diverse personalities. A recent television drama and book leave the viewer or reader with the conclusion that to live with many personalities is a creative solution to childhood trauma. Such a conclusion is just the opposite of that presented in this book.

I believe it is the therapist's task to interpret the resistance to change, to go through the emotion-laden and transference-filled states that are bound to follow, and to continually interpret the material back toward fusion and integration into one personality. For a therapist to allege that many personae are a viable alternative is to concur with the fragmentation. In effect, it is to say that the therapist and patient do not possess the will or the emotional and psychological resources to weather reliving, understanding, and working through the trauma experienced by the patient.

———

It has been recognized for centuries that childhood traumatic events lead to later difficulties. Descartes wrote of this, as did the French "magnetizers." Later still, Janet and Charcot, from whom Freud learned a great deal, wrote of dissociation and the belief that psychological treatment dealing with unacceptable feelings and recollections could lead to the resolution of hysterical symptoms.

Interest in Multiple Personality and its psychological treatment in this country was strong until the 1920's, when psychiatrists began preferring the diagnosis of schizophrenia.

Whether this change in diagnosis and treatment habits had anything to do with Freud's decision to disbelieve his patients' accounts of physical and sexual trauma and conclude that patients were often fantasizing, rather than reporting actual traumatic events, is a question that continues to be evaluated. Suffice it to say that in the decade prior to 1926, many more cases of Multiple Personality than schizophrenia were diagnosed; between the 1920's and the early 1970's, the diagnosis of Multiple Personality fell into disrepute, and those psychiatrists who said they treated such patients were thought to be credulous and naive.

In the 1970's, with the publication of *Sybil*, and the work of Wilbur, Kluft, and Putnam, interest in Multiple Personality revived. Psychiatrists began to realize that this was not an extremely rare disorder, and that terrible child abuse nearly always underlay the patient's dissociation into other beings.

The interest in Post Traumatic Stress Disorder, secondary to the two World Wars, the concentration camps, and Vietnam, furthered our awareness of the severity of dissociation and psychological disturbance that may result in adults as a result of wartime trauma. The focus on child molestation and abuse over the last fifteen years has aided us in becoming aware of the all too prevalent reality of dissociation in children.

In the 1980's, Multiple Personality again became a recognized diagnosis. People with this disorder may have numerous physical complaints, loss of periods of time, amnesia, a history of physical and sexual trauma and neglect. There is a host personality and a number of alter or sub-personalities. There is frequent switching from one personality to another. Typically, each personality takes on a stereotypical way of being, acting, and occasionally dressing. There is no consistent thread of a life history; facts are made up when there is doubt as to what one did in an alter state.

Multiple Personalities may wake up as one persona after having gone to bed as another. Names are made up for each, inner dialogues are viewed as conversations between different people. Sometimes they know of some of the personae; sometimes the host is unaware initially of the others, which take on a life of their own.

The diagnosis of Multiple Personality is a valid one, but I do not believe in the existence of multiple personalities, I believe that people suffering from Multiple Personality disorder believe that there are numerous personalities. This is a very important point, since some therapists are espousing the notion that Multiple Personality is a viable life style. To my mind it is a form of disturbance and, as such, in need of decent integrative treatment by competent therapists, aiming towards the resolution of the personalities into one person with different aspects and feelings.

Multiple Personality is childhood dissociation gone wrong. A perfectly understandable attempt on the part of an intelligent child to remove oneself psychically from a situation one was stuck in physically becomes a snare in which the child, and later the adult, is trapped in a world of phantoms, composed of numerous personalities, each with his or her own feelings and ways of being.

I have treated a number of Multiple Personalities over the last twenty years, and am struck by how frequently they have been in a previous treatment which did not attempt to deal with and resolve the underlying dissociation into more than one personality. Certainly these people must act strangely, whether seen by psychiatrists or not. How can people so evidently disturbed remain so poorly treated?

Part of the answer to this question lies in the patient's desire to hide the dissociation from others. Often patients are in treatment for years before they trust a therapist enough to volunteer that they have amnesias, lose track of time, or were told by someone else that they acted very differently the last time they saw each other.

Another reason for the lack of sufficient treatment has to do with psychiatry's tendency during the fifty years from the 1920's to the 1970's to regard these patients as schizophrenic, and allegedly unable to profit from insight-oriented therapy aimed at resolving psychological conflicts through understanding. I strongly disagree with the position that deeply disturbed people can not benefit from intensive, insight-oriented psychotherapy.

Some therapists, when confronted with a patient as chaotic, regressed, and suicidal as Marcia was will adopt what is generally termed a "supportive" approach. By this is meant something akin to hand-holding, in hopes of doing little harm, and helping somewhat by offering reassurance and avoiding deep psychological issues. Medications are often used to deal with intolerable feelings.

Although this supportive approach appears to be a humane one, it often doesn't get to the bottom of the patient's difficulty. Such was the case with Marcia, as it is all too frequently with other deeply troubled patients across the varied spectrum of disturbances.

I advocate attempting to understand the origins of even the most disturbed patient's difficulty in a very common-sense way that includes looking at both the circumstances in which the difficulties first began and at the repeated pattern of defensive maneuvers that lock someone into a state of terrible discomfort.

With a Multiple Personality, a therapist must always keep in mind that actual traumatic events likely underly the split into different personalities, and be appropriately empathetic to the patient's hurt. From the first day that Marcia came in—fragmented, regressed, terrified, and suicidal—and began to recount even a little of her history, I found myself saying to her something that I'm certain most people would say to someone who told of such terrible experiences: simply, "I'm sorry for the pain you've been through."

More than any other patients, Multiple Personalities have altered self-images, and will frequently regress from their adult self to a younger self-representation. One grown woman saw herself in the mirror as a four-year-old little girl in a pink checked dress. Another woman would alternately see herself in her mind's eye as a fearful six-year-old or a crying infant. Marcia tells us how she would regress as she drove to my office, feeling herself grow both smaller and younger. She had to learn how to "think tall" and remain an adult in the face of her desire to flee to another personality or a younger self-state.

There are two prime considerations if one is to engage in a psychotherapy that may lead to lasting change. First, one must listen, understand, and, to the extent one can, make contact with the most wounded aspects of the self; this is the art—such as it is—of psychotherapy. As a therapist, one has to be open to experiencing and understanding all kinds of emotions for healing and change to occur in the patient.

Whether as a matter of personality or training, some therapists may not allow intense emotions to emerge, thereby aborting contact with the deepest levels of the person. Such an approach leaves the patient split within him or herself, convinced that his deepest feelings and essential being are too monstrous for the therapist, and consequently for others and himself. If such feelings are too much for the therapist, where does the patient put them?

This brings us to the second and most important point of doing therapy with all deeply disturbed patients, including Multiple Personalities: the necessity of making clear to the patient what is going on psychologically and in reality. Especially with the patient who is so disorganized, the therapist must provide a container for the regressions. This is done not only through the safety of the therapy sessions, for every patient should have this with every therapist, but through building a rational structure that explains to the patient what is happening psychodynamically. This is called interpretation, telling the patient exactly what is going on in the moment, in the transference replaying of past emotions in the present, and in the rapidly fluctuating self-states. Interpretation is like providing subtitles in a foreign movie, when the patient doesn't understand the language of his own psyche and behavior.

Interpretation slowly, sometimes infinitesimally, helps decrease patients' anxieties and terrors. The process is often time-consuming and costly, with halting steps of progress. Forward motion may be slow, with two steps forward, one and a half steps back the rule not the exception, as patients integrate issues that have plagued them over most of their lives. Families must be prepared to endure for the long haul, but such an approach offers the chance of lasting, not cosmetic, change.

Therapy itself may be extremely disconcerting to these paitents at times. In a Multiple Personality, it is necessary to bring into consciousness a terribly upsetting realty: these other people, known and unknown, are the patient's own creations. Such a statement from me may increase a patient's short-term disorganization, for as far as the patient is concerned, the other personalities, each with their own function, are other beings. To realize that I saw it quite differently was bound to make an already difficult situation even more difficult for a patient trying to hold on to an intrapsychic shell game.

It didn't take years of treatment for me to grasp the fact that Marcia had dissociated for most of her life. It is quite easy to see a person who is an unintegrated Multiple Personality fluctuate between different self-states, often going blank, closing eyes, changing breathing, or acting differently during the course of a session.

In Marcia's case, it took only minutes to understand that she was quite likely a Multiple Personality and several months to get enough historical material to understand some of the reasons for her dissociating into a number of personalities. At that time, feeling I had the lay of the psychological land—if not all the facts—I began the process of interpretation.

With Multiple Personalities it is important to take a history of each personality and to understand how they each began as an attempt to avoid pain or to derive comfort. As they are reintegrating into one personality, it is important to be alert to regressions, and to be available for a few moments here and there during the course of the day. Although Marcia felt she was a great burden to me, she was not. I view occasional phone calls to shore someone up as far wiser than rigidly adhering to the notion that patients have to "keep it together" between sessions. The minutes on the phone helped decrease Marcia's anxiety on two counts. First she felt grounded, knowing that I was there; secondly, my interpretive comments helped diminish her terror about whatever might have been going on.

Integration to a responsible self, one person able to deal with life, is the goal for any therapy of Multiple Personality. To the extent that the treatment helps the patient recognize that he or she has been many, it is extremely helpful. To the extent that the treatment aids the patient in monitoring his tendency to fragment and dissociate, it is very beneficial. To the extent that the treatment aids the patient in fusing into and maintaining one personality, it is successful.

Such patients have been through terrible and painful trauma and remain vulnerable to slipping into tremendous anxieties and regressions. As therapists and patients, it is important to recognize the Multiple Personality's frailty and strengths, and to be prepared to deal with his internal blackness. Most important for Multiple Personalities, even those who have been successfully treated, is the knowledge that he or she is only what we all are: one person with many aspects, hopefully integrated into one personality.

Marcia is on her way toward psychological reintegration. Her evident idealization of me is a relatively passing phenomenon, and not unusual; it was helpful in her process of change and transformation.

The satisfaction I take in this extremely evocative, powerful, and compelling personal story is due to the knowledge that the therapeutic process, when practiced reasonably competently, guided even this most severely disturbed person toward psychic well being and unity. I hope such an approach will work just as well on many others.

—IRA STEINMAN, M.D.
San Francisco

written in the second year of therapy
with Ira Steinman

PART
ONE

Chapter 1

I couldn't make the blood stop. It was everywhere, all blotched on hexagonal white tiles. I had been seeing it for several days—and hearing the voices whispering that I should die. I was trying to make the blood stop, but I was folded too far into the black place that lies at the back of my brain beyond the space of logic. In that black void there flashed the jumble of images that aroused the terror.

I got into my car to escape. As I drove, I turned on the windshield wipers to clear away the crimson blood that was sheeting across my field of vision. In my panic, I kept taking my hands off the steering wheel to wipe the blood from my eyes.

The road in Malibu Canyon twists and turns. I made the instantaneous decision. Enough. I could do no more, stand no more, be hurt no more. I unbuckled my seatbelt, closed my eyes, and pressed the gas pedal to the floor.

I remember going over the embankment, then turning, crunching, banging through bushes and rocks until my red Honda crashed into a boulder.

I have no idea how long I lay pinned to the steering wheel with the roof of the car pressing down on me. There were faces, shouting, then the fire department arriving with the jaws of life to cut me from the tangle.

When the paramedics tried to lift me out, I was screaming, "No! I'm waiting for the fire. I want the fire to burn me up!"

"Lady, you'll be fine. We're here. Relax."

I tried to fight them off, sobbing. "I want the blood to stop. I just want the blood to stop."

"You're not bleeding," said the paramedic. "There's no blood and no fire. You've been in an accident. We're here to take care of you."

I tried to get away from the hands that were prying the metal away from me. "Let me die. Just let me die!"

"Randy, get over here," one man shouted to another. "I think we have a head injury or a psycho."

As I lay strapped onto a board in the ambulance, I heard the sounds and felt the winding road but my eyes saw only the dark blood and the fire all around me. I closed my eyes and sank into the flames. The pain came later, along with the realization that I had been condemned to live.

Lying in a hospital bed in traction with the weights at the end of the bed threatening to rip my spine apart, I could only turn my head to see who entered the room, not that it mattered to me. In walked a tall, loose-jointed man with a square jaw and large, clear eyes. "My name is Dr. Williams. Dr. McLaughlin asked me to see you. I've been looking over your X-rays. You've had one hell of a wreck." This orthopedic surgeon pulled up a chair and propped his long legs up on the rung of my side rails. The slight jarring shot pain through my leg. In my floating Demerol haze I only vaguely understood what he was saying. "Smashed femur . . . need pins . . . factured lumbar . . . back surgery . . ."

Struggling through the pain and drugs to keep track of the conversation, I spoke the only thread of thought that was in my mind. My cut lips mumbled, "Please let me die. I beg you. When you operate just turn up the gas and let me die." Tears were running down my face, I struggled for breathe through my swollen, bruised nose.

Dr. Williams held my hand and whispered something intended to be reassuring. His words meant nothing. He leaned over and said, "Marsha, how did you get all those fractures I saw on the X-rays? You have many old calcified fractures—of your right shoulder, clavical, left arm, fingers, nose, and of your skull.''

"I don't know" was all I could murmur. Nothing made sense. The year was 1982, I was forty-one, and my mind was in chaos. All my adult life I had lived what I felt was a charade. I was the great actress playing a role, covering up for the missing hours on a clock, living with unexplainable fears and panics, fighting suicidal impulses, and battling depression. I had a childhood I kept trying not to remember. The worst of all was keeping from everyone the well-kept secret that inside my head lived a twin named Emily. This twin had a life of her own quite separate from my life. I had long ago constructed the belief that somehow in utero, in the first stages of gestation, my cells must have swallowed up the cells of my twin, rather like phagocytosis. We shared the same body, but not the same mind. We fought for control and dominance. I read stories of Chang and Eng, the famous Siamese twins, and felt nature had taken our attachment one step further. As a physical therapist, I had heard of surgeries removing tumors that contained hair and even teeth grown from misplaced cells. My logical mind had no other explanation for Emily. I hated this other voice, other self, and felt I was the ultimate victim of nature's whims.

I had read the book *Sybil* and other accounts of multiple personalities but absolutely discarded the idea that Emily and I could actually be the same person. It was an untenable thought. We did not like the same things, did not think or act alike. It is difficult to believe the elaborate lies a mind can construct to hold itself intact. I had made up the explanations for the unexplainable, yet doubts haunted me. I never told anyone of Emily for fear they would view me as deranged. The thought that I was crazy had often crossed my mind. Maybe I was truly mad and didn't know it. That didn't seem correct, either, because I thought I functioned well in life. I was smart. I'd been through four years of college getting a Bachelor of Science degree in Physical Therapy, I was married and had two teenage children. Crazy people weren't functional. Yet I knew of no others who had hours of the day they couldn't account for, times of getting in the car and not remembering where they had been. All my life I had to live being responsible for this whimsical, irresponsible twin. Emily stole things; stupid, glittery, childish things. She stole teddy bears, and I would have to take the blame when I got arrested. My humiliation was horrible as I was handcuffed and charged with shoplifting. I would cry silently, wishing the floor would open in a great cavern and I could escape in a leap to the center of the earth. The times I got arrested I would apologize profusely and make up blatant lies: "I'm sorry. I totally forgot to pay for this. My mind was on the dinner party I'm giving tonight." I would open my purse, usually having the money to pay, and always the gold Visa card. I was only prosecuted twice, but it was a deep, painful humiliation to have to take the blame for what I did not do. I was highly moral. I would never steal anything.

Emily was a slut. She went to boat docks and bars and slept with strangers. How many times did I find myself in the car, having lost time but feeling semen between my legs? My body would have the cloying scent of a man's sweat. I would only hope to get home to a shower before my husband, Dan, came home from work.

One of the reasons I didn't think I was a multiple personality was that I had read one personality is not aware of the other. I knew Emily. We had a dialogue in my head. We would argue and discuss things at length. There was often a power struggle as to who would have control. I was the stronger one most of the time. Emily seemed to have more power in times of stress and anxiety. Often when she took control, it wasn't that I was totally absent or had amnesia. It was as though I were locked away behind a shadowy veil and silently observed as she would take over. I was the helpless observer as Emily entered a bar and, with flirtatious animation, picked up a man. Her abandonment to sex was far more adventurous than my own. That is too kind a description. It was raw and base, and when Emily let me take over again, I would run to the bathroom and vomit from the shame of the experience. The occasions of total amnesia of events were more merciful. I didn't suffer over what I could not remember.

Emily and I threatened each other with death. Long ago I had resolved that I would be Emily's scapegoat. I would have to take responsibility for all that she did, since I was certain any explanations of a "twin" would get me locked up in a psychiatric ward somewhere. But with that sense of responsibility I felt if Emily ever did anything hurtful or sociopathic beyond stealing, I would kill myself to kill her. I lived with the fear of having to self-destruct to stop this terrible, impulsive, childish twin of mine who lived for the gratification of the moment with no thought for the consequences or obligations. I wept for a whole day when I saw Spencer Tracy in *Dr. Jekyll and Mr. Hyde*. I felt that was me, yet it wasn't me. Emily was sharing my body, but she was not me.

I had just had an abortion as a result of one of Emily's escapades. I had no clue as to who the father of this baby was, and Planned Parenthood had helped me one more time. Two hundred dollars, no questions, just the speck of life sucked out of me. I couldn't take it anymore.

"Don't ask me questions, Dr. Williams. Just give me something to help me die."

"You know I can't do that. Would you like to talk to a psychiatrist?"

I shook my head, causing a stabbing of pain. I was certain there were no answers. I didn't want to let anyone inside to the confusion in my mind.

I stopped begging the physicians for death. I wanted to die, but I was now in the get-well-health-care system. My next months consisted of surgery after surgery, physical therapy, patching up the broken body to get me well.

Emily remained quiet during the months of intense pain. I vacillated between depression at all I had done to myself and a sense of peace that with bandages and wheelchair Emily could not run. My days were accounted for. There was even a part of me that liked pain and a part of me that responded gratefully to being the patient, with nurses who touched gently and doctors who were kind.

Dr. Williams and I had formed a bond of some sort after that first emotional encounter. He was especially attentive. My internist and neurologist came and went from my room as though I were a leper, but Dr. Williams would put his feet up and chat a while. I looked forward to his visits. My medical background gave me the insight to ask him questions that drew him out. He began discussing his more distressing cases with me, talking about his own depression at being needed by too many people, and a marriage that was in its final death throes.

Saving an apple or a piece of dried-up hospital cake from my meal trays, I began offering him food and my cheeriest smiles. By the time I was discharged from the hospital we were Scott and Marcia to each other and had agreed to go to lunch somewhere together as soon as I was well enough.

My own marriage was in a perennial state of limbo. I fantasized and waited for Scott's visits. The clear sky-blue eyes and long fingers reminded me so much of my father. Even the mannerisms of the cocked eyebrow and ear tugging, as well as the brilliant mind and easy humor seemed similar. The fact that he was ten years older than I and looked so much like my father should have been a neon sign that told me I was looking for a replacement for my dead father. But all my life I missed the obvious. My inner confusion never allowed me to untangle even the most elementary of things, such as, doctors do not have affairs with their patients. There were no stop signs in my mind or my heart. I felt safe around a protective, dominant male. Scott listened to my depression and pain and still was warm.

It took three months after leaving the hospital before I was well enough to have the clandestine lunch with Scott. He seemed even more magnificent out of his white hospital coat, standing his full six-feet-two-inch height in a suit and a paisley tie. Shyness overtook me as I limped to greet him. I felt like the frog in the land of princes. The story was supposed to be the other way, but I did not feel like a princess, I felt like a barely liberated invalid, and this handsome man was all confused in my head in his role of doctor-father-protector-friend.

It always surprised me that men found me attractive, though I have blue eyes, even teeth, freckles sprinkled on my nose, and a well-proportioned athletic body. Scott was not my first affair. He was actually my third. I should have seen the pattern; all ten to twenty years older than me, all tall like my father, the protective, nurturing types who radiated self-assurance. All three men had said at various times they liked my childlike qualities. I didn't see it myself, but I remember my feelings were not a woman's feelings. I wanted to hold Scott's hand, to touch him, but I had no desire to be touched sexually. Each time the affair led to sex I felt disappointed, even somewhat betrayed, although I was an eager sexual partner. I would do anything for the feeling of safety. The look, the touch, the smell of a strong man quieted the eternal sense of unrest in me. I always lived as though I were a little lost fox, peeking out of a rock cave. I craved safety, security. I had married a man who was kind and gentle but could not make me feel safe or protected. We were two fragile beings wandering through an overwhelming world together.

For the next two years Scott and I had an intense affair. He was not even cautious. We had lunches in the hospital cafeteria, and quick sex on the examining table in his office while his staff was out to lunch. We flew in his plane to places like Big Bear for lunch, or Palm Springs for an afternoon swim in a sun-sparkling pool.

"Marcia, how did you get the scars on your legs?" Scott asked.

"I don't know." I tensed with the questions.

"How come you're afraid of matches and candles? I see you flinch when people light a cigarette near you."

"I don't know. I just don't like fire. It makes me feel sort of panicked," I answered offhandedly, as though I had no interest in my problems.

"I've noticed you're afraid of closed-in spaces. When we're at the hospital you always make us take the stairs, joking about staying in shape, but I remember when I insisted on the elevator and you pressed against the wall, looking white," Scott said.

"I guess I have a little claustrophobia," I answered, not wanting to let on I had an intense fear of being closed in. I always kept windows open and doors unlocked. Even crowded, stuffy rooms filled me with that familiar feeling of panic.

"Sweetheart, has someone hurt you?" Scott questioned.

"I don't think so," I lied.

"I'm normally against psychotherapy, but I think it would be a good idea if you went to a psychiatrist. You should have some answers to the broken bones, scars, and fears."

I didn't dare tell him about Emily. "I'll think about it," I lied again.

One Wednesday afternoon Scott drove me to Malibu to the home of one of his physician friends. The friend was gone and had given Scott the key. We had whiskey sours and looked out over the ocean. Slowly, gently, Scott made love to me on the big circle bed, with the western sun streaming in on us. His soft surgeon's hands and experienced mouth traveled my body, arousing me, only to have the familiar tension constrict me, keeping me from a climax. I thought it was a safe time of the month, so I didn't use birth control. At forty-three it hardly seemed that I would need it. I was wrong. I became pregnant with Scott's baby. My body was still in constant pain from my "accident," I was married, wildly in love with my physician, also in love with my husband, and the mother of two teenagers. Scott wanted me to have an abortion. He was adamant. I wanted Scott and the baby.

"Look, I've had kids already who are grown, and I screwed it up once already. My kids are on drugs and alcohol and not worth a damn. I won't go through it again," said Scott emphatically.

I was crushed that there was no promise of marriage, no joy at new life. I cried for days. Somehow I desperately wanted this baby. It was a love child, not just the consequence of Emily's running around.

I burst into tears in Scott's office, and his receptionist took me into one of the examining rooms to comfort me. She knew Scott and I were having an affair, so I sobbed and told her I was pregnant. She put her arms around me and said, "You should get an abortion. Scott will never marry you. He has gotten three other women pregnant before you." Stunned, I left the office shivering in shock. I was not special or unique—just one of his many affairs.

"Scott, have you really gotten three other women pregnant?" I asked when I saw him.

"Actually there have been four before you," he replied with great casualness, as though we were discussing an ordinary occasion.

"And you didn't think to get a vasectomy?"

"Hey, it's not my responsibility if a woman messes up birth control!"

I was seeing him with new eyes. All the romance, the feelings of safety that now seemed unsafe emerged to let me stand away from this handsome man and see a very flawed character. He was not offering marriage, condolences, or words of love; he was offering me money to have the abortion.

The promises of a someday together, the tender words, all had been a sham. I would have left my husband for Scott. Even though we were both middle-aged, I would have had his baby. I sobbed with the knowledge I was merely one of his flings, that the life inside me meant nothing but inconvenience to him.

I had the abortion and bled so profusely I had to go to the hospital. Grabbing my purse, I had driven myself to the emergency room with a towel stuffed between my legs. There were more lies trying to tell my husband the D&C they did was for fibroid tumors. That whole summer I was depressed. In August I went to the gynecologist and lied about abdominal pain and heavy bleeding. I asked for a hysterectomy. I didn't know why I lied to have surgeries. This had happened before. I lied about the abdominal pain in the past and had an exploratory abdominal surgery. Lying about acute pain again, I had my gall bladder removed. Now it was 1984, and I was fabricating tales about gushing blood with my menstrual cycle. In some ways the need for a hysterectomy seemed pressingly real, while part of me stepped back from the lies and questioned why I would do this to myself. There were no answers to why I chose pain. At the time I did know that I never wanted to be pregnant again, never wanted the humiliation of having my legs up on stirrups in a doctor's office, or the sadness that enveloped me like a shroud for weeks after an abortion, or the dreams of babies with sweet, tiny faces looking at me trustingly.

"At your age we will probably take your ovaries out, too," said the gynecologist. "You won't need them anymore, anyway."

My internal voices said, "Rip them out. Rip out all the parts." My words said, "Do whatever you think is best, Doctor."

I awakened in the recovery room to waves of nausea, pain, and the reassurance that all my reproductive parts had been removed. No more bleeding. No more pregnancies. No more abortions. I fell into my drugged sleep, grateful for the mutilation.

What I had not bargained for was the new state of menopause. I was given an estrogen replacement that made me break out in itchy hives. When that was stopped, the suicidal days and crying jags began. Emily was pressing me to end my life. Days became a blurry haze of tears and lost time. A new form of estrogen was started and I felt a bit better, but I was crying at every little thing.

With sleeping pills locked into my white fist, I thumbed through the telephone book and randomly picked the name of a psychiatrist from the Yellow Pages. I telephoned Dr. Naughton's office, and amid a torrent of tears told the receptionist that I was going to kill myself. She put me on hold for a minute, then in a kind voice told me to come see the doctor immediately. I went to my car in my bare feet, clutching the pills, and drove to Dr. Naughton's office.

A gentle-looking man of about fifty greeted me and invited me into his inner sanctum which smelled of old leather, had splashes of vivid green and brown, and deep blue carpeting. All I could do was cry and spew out my desire to die. I felt betrayed by Scott, sadness at the hysterectomy, and the certainty my life added up to hideous failure. There was a confusion of things I felt, but things I could not say. My fears, my panics, the Emily twin, the other voices in my head, had to remain secret. I feared the world of psychiatry even in my dark suicidal state. For fear of being hospitalized I tried to pull myself together and promised Dr. Naughton I would not kill myself until we had a few more sessions.

Just crying to a stranger did make me feel calmer.

The next day I went back for a forty-five-minute session. I felt self-conscious after having made such an idiot of myself the day before, but Dr. Naughton acted as though I had said nothing out of the ordinary. It irritated me that he kept asking me questions about Scott. I knew psychiatrists had to keep conversations confidential, so I was candid about my affair, but the seeming interrogation about my physician and where we made love seemed odd to me, as though we were discussing it for his fascination and not my pain. I was further put off by the discussion of how I would pay for sessions. I felt like screaming, "I want to fucking die and you wallow in irrelevance!"

I left feeling very depressed, fairly certain this man could not help me one iota.

I kept my appointments regularly once a week for about three months. We talked ad nauseum about Scott and the affair. Scott and I were still seeing each other for lunches and occasional afternoons, but he was no longer having sex with me. He said my going to a psychiatrist changed things between us. He knew I had told Dr. Naughton about us.

"Tell me about your childhood," Dr. Naughton said.

"I remember almost nothing before the age of eighteen when I got spinal meningitis and was in a coma. I'm certain I had a regular, happy childhood," I lied. I couldn't talk about what I knew.

"Marcia, I don't think a coma could wipe away a whole childhood. Try and think back and tell me about it. Just let your mind drift back in time."

I became agitated. Flaring in anger, I said, "How dare you tell me what I should and shouldn't remember! All this talking is pointless. We are not accomplishing one blasted thing with this drivel." I left his office. At home I wrote him an irate letter telling him therapy was useless, thanked him for his kindness and told him I would not be seeing him anymore.

For two months I continued to function erratically. Emily took over fairly frequently. I felt fragmented inside, detesting the lies to family and friends that I had to tell to cover for the events I missed, the times I was late.

In January of 1985, in a complete state of Emily takeover, I was arrested for stealing at the Broadway department store. With total amnesia of the event, I found myself in the manager's office clutching a large brown teddy bear that I had taken and walked out of the store holding. My sense of distress and copious tears must have moved the manager, for he let me pay for the bear. I now had an eighty-dollar bear, no self-esteem and the certainty I needed to find some answers to my life or I should just end it.

I went home and called Dr. Naughton's office. Surprisingly, he scheduled an appointment as though the lapsed two months had not happened. I still could not tell him of the stealing, the "lost" hours, the Emily twin, but I was willing to try more therapy.

"It seems I touched a raw nerve when I asked you about your childhood," Dr. Naughton said. "Do you think you are ready to face whatever it is that made you run from therapy?"

I wasn't sure, but I said a quiet "Yes."

My anxiety was intense at the thought of exploring what I was trying not to remember. It was as though for years I had been willing to add two and two and call it five, and now I was going to be forced to see what two and two really added up to. I wasn't stupid; as a matter of fact on a Stanford Binet I.Q. test, I scored close to one hundred and forty, but I'd been willing to live with a reality that didn't compute.

I lived with so many fears: fear of fire, closed in spaces, fear of thirst and hunger, and an intense fear of abandonment. I couldn't explain the scars on my body that marked me like Egyptian hieroglyphics, nor the X-rays of past broken bones.

When I was twenty-four I had reconstruction surgery of my vagina and clitoris. The doctor asked me when I went in for an examination how I had gotten the scars and adhesions. He didn't believe me when I told him I had never had a baby. He responded very conspiratorially that he would not tell anyone. I told myself I didn't know how I had been damaged. Dan, my husband, never pressed me for an answer even though he knew I needed the repair surgery.

There were so many things I couldn't account for. Even though I had elaborate and preoccupying explanations of Emily, I had no explanations for the memory lapses, the times when I knew I was doing bizarre things and using silly names. People recognized me as Muriel or Sophie or other names and I just played along, trying to fill in the blank spots. I agonized over Emily's behavior and spent endless time in inner negotiations with her working out schecules for "carcass time" as we both called it.

I even had a way of sealing off the things I consciously knew. I knew before I ever started therapy that my mother was mentally ill. I knew she had badly hurt me as a child. There were many specific events of abuse I remembered, even times she tried to kill me. I can't really explain how I could know things consciously yet remain completely distanced from them. I use the words "remember" and "memory" far too loosely. The more accurate word would be "confront." Committing myself to the process of psychotherapy was a decision to confront what I already knew but couldn't face. At the beginning my anxiety level was so high I wasn't certain I could do it.

I had spent such frantic energy in denying reality that I was rather like one who builds a sand castle at the mean tide mark, then decides to inhabit it. Instead of knowing the structure was faulty, all I could do was continue to shovel as the waves came. Starting therapy felt like I was being asked to give someone else my shovel. I had no idea we would end up leveling the whole castle.

Therapy proceeded slowly with the things I could remember, the family history that I had heard and the fragmented pieces of memory I was willing to share. I dug at the little threads of thought, like why did I hate the color yellow? I wasted therapy time talking about inconsequential things. Dr. Naughton told me I was avoiding real subjects.

As three more months of therapy passed, I was doing a great deal of crying about my physical pain. Finally, in one session I blurted out that my car accident had not been an accident, I had done it on purpose with the deep committed intent of dying. I cried for my physical pain, my lifetime of limitations, and I cried because I had failed to die and I was failing at living. The suicide attempt was good for a few more sessions.

Again Dr. Naughton brought up my childhood. Again he accused me of being evasive, of being entertaining, and of "circling." He used the term "circling" quite often, but I could never figure out what he meant.

Dr. Naughton often used terms I didn't understand. I felt as though I needed a degree in psychiatry to qualify as a patient. The first time he used the phrase, "It sounds like you are playing an old tape," I was really incensed. He used words like "transference" and "countertransference."

Every time we got close to childhood conversations I got aggressive and would attack him, spending a good bit of time being angry at him. I told him he had the emotional depth of a fruit fly. Another time I told him it was too bad he didn't have a throne since he loved to pontificate. He didn't buy into my anger, my witty conversation, or my evasiveness.

Slowly, in spite of my anger and my secrets, a bond grew in me with Dr. Naughton. I began to look forward to seeing him although I was nauseated and had diarrhea before each session. Often I had to leap up in the middle of a session and run to the bathroom. It took me months to get over the panic feeling as he locked the door when I sat down. I hated locked doors and the irrational desire to flee when I felt I was being confined. I always brought in a cup of coffee from his waiting room because my mouth dried to a desert parch in my high anxiety state.

About ten months into therapy, Dr. Naughton was going on a week's vacation and I would not have a session for two weeks. The old irrational panic rose in me. I couldn't understand my own anxiety. There were lots of people I liked who I didn't see for two-week stretches and it was no big deal. I began calling him on the telephone before he left. On the day he was to leave I asked him if I could come in for a few minutes to see him. He was kind enough to work me into his lunch hour.

"Do me a favor and bring me a sandwich when you come," Dr. Naughton said.

I made him a tuna sandwich and baked him a batch of cookies, as though this would be his last meal on the face of this earth.

I arrived at noon laden with food and leaking tears.

"Why are you so upset that I am leaving for a couple of weeks?" Dr. Naughton asked, while he munched on his sandwich.

Still crying, I said, "I don't know, I just am." Then in a torrent of tears, I said, "I feel just like when I was little, really young, about four, and my mother said if I laughed once more she would stop the car and leave me in the middle of the highway. I did laugh. I didn't mean to. She stopped and dragged me screaming from the car, leaving me in the center divider of the busy highway and told me I must never, ever cross the street, that I would have to stay there forever for being bad. I was jumping up and down, sobbing, 'I'll be good, Mommy. I won't laugh anymore. I'm sorry, Mommy. Please don't leave me.' I screamed as the car pulled away. My brother Bobby's face was pressed to the rear window and we were both crying as the car disappeared in traffic.

I cried and cried on that center divider for what felt like forever, then I sat down and, in deep desolation, sucked my thumb. Finally, a policeman came by and picked me up. He took me home in his police car. It was dark when I got there. My father was in the living room with my mother. Mom said, 'You are a very bad girl for running away from home. Go to your room immediately and I will come punish you.' "

Dr. Naughton said, "Didn't you tell your father or the policeman?"

"I couldn't tell anyone. I never told anyone or Mom would give me to the Gypsies."

Reliving the scene, I cried and cried. It was the beginning of remembering the locked secrets.

Dr. Naughton was very quiet while I cried. He looked at me with his steady brown eyes and said, "I think we have finally engaged in therapy."

That seemed like the most asinine statement when I was reliving abandonment on a street corner. My time was up, and I left him feeling angry that he didn't even acknowledge the event and overwhelmed with a sense of foreboding at what was creeping out of my locked-away memory.

The next months of therapy were exquisitely terrible. I had feelings of drowning in horror as I relived experience after experience. It was like an ugly tapeworm in my mind. Once I started pulling a segment out, it was attached to another segment of experiences. Sometimes the remembrances were explosive bursts of knowledge and others came in my quiet moments when, like a dog with a bone, I would chew on the pieces, commanding my mind to bring forth the locked secrets.

The memories did not come chronologically, nor even in order of the severity of the experience. There were little things I remembered and hideous things.

I did not relive the experiences casually. I was consumed, crying for months, and had intensely suicidal moments. Rather than recount the fragmented experiences as I lived them in therapy, I will give my story as I now know it to be.

Chapter 2

Aristocracy sometimes breeds its freaks. My mother, Gisela Brandt, was one of the aberrations of a long lineage that wound its way through titles, castles, the whispers of Hapsburg blood, and an uncle who was a raging schizophrenic kept locked in a back room of the family estate on the Rhine.

According to my grandmother, the family in Germany had wealth and position. Grandma Marie spoke fondly of her summer home, ski trips to the Alps, servants, and elegant parties. Apparently my grandfather was the family maverick. He fought often with his father. My grandfather was gassed during World War I and never fully recovered his health. In the 1920's, when my mother was small, she and her brother and sister were lavished with worldly goods but left to be raised by nannies. My grandparents were on an endless quest for medical miracles to help my grandfather's poor health, leaving their children for months as they traveled to spas and spiritual healers. My uncle has spoken of the perverted, sadistic tutor of their childhood.

In what was apparently a violent fight with his family, my grandfather decided to leave Germany with his wife and three children. His father swore to disown his son if he left for America. Disillusioned with Germany and particularly his own family, my grandfather arrived in America in 1936, when my mother was sixteen, to begin a new life. My mother often talked about how angry she was at leaving Germany and her friends. She was a committed Hitler Youth who marched in the streets and screamed in the rallies.

It was quickly evident that my grandfather was an aristocratic, but unemployable, dreamer. The family sank to an appalling lifestyle when the money ran out. Within a year, my grandfather died in front of his wife and children in a shabby apartment on the poor side of Los Angeles. My aunt has hinted that his death may have been a suicide, and I overheard conversations about my mother having to mop up the blood. With typical German pride my grandmother never let the relatives back in Germany know of the family's dire straits.

My mother spoke a beautiful tutor-taught English, so she immediately went to work as a receptionist in a doctor's office. Mother was beautiful, with huge, deep-set hazel eyes and hair that cascaded in pale-blond curls down to her shoulders. Her skin was almost translucent white, but her cheeks were always pink. Although she lived and worked in America, she stayed intensely loyal to Germany. Inside, she continued to seethe with anger at her father, who had taken her from her friends, home, and legacy.

My father, Frank, met my mother when she was nineteen and he was twenty-six. He was an attorney, a Yale graduate. My father was born to Jewish-German immigrant parents in California in 1912. When my father was eight, his father died of tuberculosis. My father told us of his happy childhood before his father died, enthralling us with stories of camping at Big Bear Lake when it was a two-day trip on horseback to reach the lake. He had Boy Scouts, a favorite jacknife he carved animals with, cookies made with gumdrops, and a sister he adored.

Everything changed for him when his mother remarried when he was ten. His mother, Bernice, married a Gentile, a Protestant, a rigidly strict disciplinarian. There was instant hatred between my father and his stepfather, Elias. Elias was a real-estate developer and the owner of a lumber mill. Although there was food and even luxuries for the family, the abuse began soon after Elias married Bernice. First came whippings with a leather belt and then a wooden board. All things Jewish were banished from the house. Grandma Bernice was forbidden to go to the synagogue. It broke her heart that her son was denied his Bar Mitzvah by her increasingly violent husband. In those days, according to the accounts of my grandmother, women did not think of divorce. She took care of her children as best she could and would drip tears of her own pain on to my father's welts.

When he was fifteen, my father ran away from home. He hitchhiked clear to New York, where he got a job cleaning offices for some lawyers. John Kendall, a high-powered trial attorney, befriended my father, inviting him to move into his big Long Island home, since his own children were gone. My father went to high school, living with the Kendall family. Although he was never formally adopted by the Kendalls, he took the family name and became Frank Kendall.

Mr. Kendall was generous enough to send my father to Yale in the 1930's when the whole country was reeling from the Depression. Dad studied extremely hard and graduated Phi Beta Kappa.

It was just after his graduation from law school that my father heard his stepfather had died of a heart attack. Rather than join John Kendall's firm as a junior partner, my father headed for California to be with his mother again and try to salvage Elias's businesses. The saw mill and paper factory had stood idle during the Depression and the main source of income for the family was the meager rents they could collect from the many apartment houses the family owned.

By 1938 my father had a law practice and was continuing to manage the real estate for his mother. The lumber mill had to be sold, much to my father's regret. He always felt if he had somehow managed it better the family would still own it. With money, a thriving law practice, and a WASP name, my father became a bachelor much in demand at debutante parties and social functions.

Daddy was handsome. As a child, I remember thinking he was the most gorgeous man in the world. He was tall, muscular, with long legs and beautiful long hands. His teeth were white and so perfectly even he could eat corn on the cob without leaving any kernels. His eyes were October sky-blue and his hair was thick. When it was freshly washed, it curled in ringlets, but he plastered it down with stuff that made it just wave.

My parents met in the doctor's office where my mother worked. It was instant mutual attraction. They began dating, and my father was proud of the stunning showpiece he had in my mother. He liked her innocence and naivete, since she had seen very little in her struggling years in America, yet she had the class and education that impressed him. She spoke six languages fluently, including English, with only a trace of an accent.

They married in six weeks after a whirlwind courtship, knowing very little about each other. Grandma Bernice, my father's mother, was crushed that they ran away to Reno to be married with no rabbi, and no religious service.

It came as a tremendous shock to my mother to find out after the wedding that she had married a Jew. It was so far removed from my father's concept of himself that he hadn't mentioned it. It was my grandmother, with her staunch Jewish pride, who had driven the point home. My mother, who carried the prejudice of the Aryan supremacy from her years in Germany, cried for days. To her it was an absolute betrayal on the part of my father. My dad could not fathom what the big deal was about.

I think that was the first clue for my father that Mom was not entirely normal. She sank into a depression after finding out he was Jewish. She barely ate or spoke to him. Things got better when she became pregnant. My brother, Robert Kendall, was born in February of 1940. He was a robust little blond baby who looked German, at least to my mother.

World War II was a time that separated my parents emotionally but not physically. My father worked with civil defense and my mother staunchly aligned herself with Germany. She kept close contact with her German relatives, who were ardent Nazis, even going to secret meetings in Los Angeles of German community members who supported Hitler's cause.

It was during this time, while my mother was pregnant with me, that she withdrew physically from any relations with my father. The German and Jewish gulf grew between them. Actually, my father looked at things from the standpoint of being a loyal

American. It was my mother who focused on his Jewish heritage.

My father had his first affair while my mother was pregnant with me. I was to hear about Daddy's affairs from Mom throughout my childhood.

I was born during the blackout just after the attack on Pearl Harbor in December of 1941. It was an emotional time for everyone and a harried time for my father, who was in charge of organizing the blackout at night for a whole city. He was not with my mother when I was born. I was a small six-pound, red-faced baby. Future disaster would spring from the fact that I looked like my Jewish grandmother.

When the nurse brought me in to my mother, she said, "This baby is not mine. This is a Jewish baby." In my childhood years I used to stand in front of a mirror and look and look to see what markings were on me that made me look Jewish. I never could see what mysterious thing I possessed that would make me Jewish. I had a prominent nose, but still of normal size. I never could figure it out. But Mom could. It took quite a bit of convincing before she would let me nurse.

According to my maternal aunt, my mother sank back into a depression after I was born. She didn't want me. When I was six months old Mother was sent to a hospital. I don't know what kind of hospital. I was abruptly weaned. My aunt moved in to take care of Bobby and me. The family story goes that I was a stubborn baby, refusing a bottle and not getting enough milk from a cup, so I, too, was hospitalized with malnutrition.

I have no further family information until I was three and my brother James was born in 1945. He looked just like Bobby. Much to the relief of everyone, my mother accepted him as a little German baby.

Again after giving birth, my mother became depressed. She stopped feeding us, or getting out of bed. Again my aunt came to care for us while my mother went to the hospital. I have sketchy, happy memories of the time with my aunt, and my father would tuck Bobby and me in bed together at night. Bobby and I were inseparable, sharing a room, giggles, and toys.

My earliest childhood memories are of that year when I was three. I remember Jimmy coming home from the hospital. I remember my mother's absence. I remember moving to our new big house in Santa Monica and the tragedy of no longer sharing a bedroom with Bobby. Even before the age of concrete memory, I have flashes of images, dark, ominous half-scenes in my head.

Our new house was huge, with seemingly endless big rooms. It was built at the turn of the century by a cattle baron. The floors were great expanses of mahogany held by square wooden pegs for nails. The hall walls were covered with red velvet paper, which I loved to touch. My father filled the living room with carved walnut furniture and Oriental rugs. Electric lights had been wired into the crystal-cut gas lamps that hung from the walls. The dining room had tall windows looking out on azalea plants and camelias that were two stories tall. I feared I would get lost in the huge house with its three stairways and never be found.

For the first time in my life I was without Bobby, who had begun kindergarten. I cried as he left for school. My whole world was Bobby, and I was afraid of the big house. I do not know if I was abused as a baby because three and a half is the age of my first memory, the beginning of the torture I remember.

Bobby remembers times when Mom hurt me when I was tiny, a time when she put me in the oven and shut the door, and a time of holding my hand over a boiling teakettle, but my first memory of abuse is the closet. I think I spilled milk all over the table, and in a rage my mother dragged me to the closet that was inside the closet under the front stairs. It was a small compartment, reached by a door behind the coats. It had seemed an odd, mysterious place to Bobby and me. We couldn't figure out why anyone would build a closet inside a closet. I vividly remember my mother struggling with my flailing arms and legs as I screamed, "No, Mommy, no! I'll be good! I'm sorry I spilled my milk!" She peeled me off her and shoved me into the blackness of that closet. I screamed and screamed, throwing my whole body against the door. My heart beat wildly in my chest. The blackness was encompassing. That was all there was. I felt I couldn't breathe. The certainty of being left and forgotten engulfed me. After the screaming came the exhaustion and the sniffling tears.

I have no way now of knowing if I was there for minutes or hours. At three and a half it seemed forever. I was terrified of the spiders that I thought lived in the closet. I was sucking my thumb in the bleakness of abandonment when my mother opened the door. I looked at her in defiance and said, "Just wait until Daddy gets home from work and I tell him what you did to me!"

My mother grabbed my arm, almost ripping it from its socket and dragged me up the stairs to my new bedroom. She threw me on the bed before leaving the room.

In a few minutes she came back with some big blue scarves. While I struggled and screamed, she tied my arms and legs to the posts of my bed. I remember her apron with the Tyrolean red-embroidered edges and her wild eyes that were looking at me but not seeing me.

In a stern voice, my mother said, "You are a wicked little girl. If you ever tell anyone about what I do to you I will give you away to the Gypsies. The Gypsy men will tie you to their wagons and they will hurt you and you will never see Daddy or Bobby again. You must never tell anyone that I hurt you." She took something and stuck it into what I now know as my vagina. White fire. I writhed against the kerchiefs binding me and screamed and screamed. "You must not tell, for this is how the Gypsy men will hurt you. They will take their big things and stick them inside of you."

When Daddy and Bobby came home I did not say a word about the closet or the experience in my bed. I sucked my thumb. I remember the blood in my underwear and the searing pain when I urinated. I held my urine until I thought I would burst and then cried at the stinging pain as I finally went.

Abuse breeds more abuse. I'm sure that for my mother it became easier as she did it. Severe punishment was dealt out for minor childish mistakes. I don't even remember what I did wrong. But the punishment stands out clearly in my mind.

I think I broke something of my mother's when I was dragged again up to my room, stripped naked, and tied with the blue kerchiefs with my legs spread-eagled so far apart that I thought my hips were ripping. "You're an evil little Jewish girl. We'll have to sew you shut so you won't use your wickedness." While I lay screaming, my mother took a needle and threaded it with black thread and leaned on me to keep me from wriggling. Her face had that angry glazed look as she hit me to keep me from thrashing against the restraints as I screamed. She sewed my labia together with the black thread. I could barely breathe as the needle went through me. The sewing seemed to take forever. Mom's elbow dug into my stomach as she leaned her full weight on me and she pinched my tiny parts closed for the stitching. She was growling out things at me as she worked. I don't remember anything she said, but as I saw her face over me, I knew she was someone else, someone I didn't know, someone who didn't know me. I vomited from the panic and pain, then I defecated on the bed. That enraged my mother further. She got scissors, cut the thread, untied me, then turned me over to lie in the vomit and beat me. She left the room with the bang of the door. Choking, and gagging from the trauma, I lay on a corner of my bed for a long time before I could move.

Numbness drifted over me as I sucked my thumb and wondered what I could do to not be wicked. I was sorry I was bad. I looked out the window for a long time, watching the clouds drift past my second-story window, and, like the clouds, I floated away from the pain. Maybe for a little while I could be a little bird and fly out in the soft breeze, then sit on a swaying branch of a tree and call to the other birds who would come snuggle me with fluffed feathers. Soon I was up in the very tiptop leaves singing happy songs with my bird friends. It was the beginning of learning to escape.

For seemingly no reason, Mom began pulling up my dress and putting her cigarette out on my leg. I would cry and beg her, "Please, Mommy, don't hurt me. I'll be good." Even one burn can feel excruciating on a small leg. I would stay far from her when she smoked.

I do not remember feeling angry with my mother. I remember feeling sorrow that I was bad. I thought my mother was beautiful and I wanted nothing more than to please her. I tried very hard. When she came home from shopping, I remember running to her with my arms outstretched and feeling the hurt as she sidestepped my hug. I learned not to touch her.

Getting tied in a dining-room chair became a frequent punishment for my minor mistakes. Mom would grab my hair, yanking
it, and say, "You laugh and are always happy just like Joan of
Arc. Everyone loved her, and they love you. You steal people
away with your laughter. I think you should burn up just like she
did." Mom would take a lit match and hold it up to my face. "I
will burn you and your skin will fall off your face and you'll be
ugly and you won't laugh anymore." She would hold the match,
or candle, or cigarette to the ends of my hair or along my arms
that were tied and unable to escape the heat.

The memories of abuse when I was tiny have the strongest
emotional intensity for me, since I hadn't yet learned the mind
trick of dissociating away from the pain.

When my father was around, or Bobby got home from
school, the abuse stopped. When Daddy was home, Mommy
would be nice to me, as though I weren't evil anymore. I was very
young when I figured out Daddy was safety. If I was in his presence or within touching distance I wouldn't be hurt. Dad was fun.
I got piggyback rides, we wrestled on the floor, and my favorite
thing was to snuggle in his lap when he read me stories. Daddy
returned kisses and he would blow on my neck and I would laugh
at the tickling of his whiskers.

Emily was my playmate who began in the closet, in the long
black hours of silence and imagination. I do not remember a particular day she arrived, but I have clear memories of her from
about the age of four.

"Your mommy doesn't like you very much," Emily said.

"She's your mother, too."

"No. Today I'll have a new mother. Lie down with me in this
back corner away from the stinky place and I will tell you about
our mother."

"Okay," I said, vividly seeing Emily in the blackness. My
friend had silky brown hair with shiny red highlights and enormous brown eyes that seemed to glow even in the blackness of
the closet, full of ideas and mischief.

"Our new mother has long fingers that will tickle our back,

and she will sing to us. Listen. I will teach you the song." And in the blackness she sang in a clear sweet voice, making up ballads. She thought of games for the two of us to play.

The closet became a more regular occurrence. Emily, my imaginary, escapist friend, became more real to me in the isolation of the long, locked-away closet hours. In the beginning she could do wonderful, spectacular things; she could fly, breathe under water, she could even dare to be angry.

One time my father went on a trip and I was put in the closet for what seemed an eternity. I banged my head again and again against the closet door. At first I screamed and cried, then, as time wore on, I sucked my thumb. I worried that I had been forgotten. I wet my pants. I was thirsty and hungry. I poked my fingers in my closed eyes to see the spots of color as a contrast to the absolute blackness of my confined space. I remember thinking my thumb had juice in it. My thirst was assuaged by sucking my thumb constantly. My stomach cramped and I doubled over in pain. Finally, I used a corner of the closet to defecate in and wiped myself with my wet underpants. I sat in the stinking black closet and waited and waited.

"I'm here," Emily whispered. "We can't stay here. It stinks. Let's go to the zoo."

"We can't go, we have to stay here."

"No! See the elephant over there reaching out with the peanut? Be careful not to get the slobber on the end of his trunk on you. Let's ask him for a ride."

"I have dibs on throwing the bread to the bears. I like the one that claps," I said, joining the fun.

"If you're gentle, the little monkey will come over to the bars and touch your fingers. Maybe we could go through the bars and swing on the tire inside with the whole family. I bet we can hang by our knees."

"Do you think the mother monkey will try to pick things out of our hair? I bet it'll tickle. She might let us hold her baby. Come here, Fuzzy. Let's call him that, because he's all soft. Baby things are always soft."

"Look! He's coming toward us. He likes us. Hold your hand out. Slowly. Oh, good! He's letting you pet him. He likes to nibble on fingers."

After hours of adventure we were back in the closet, cramped and thirsty. Emily said, "She's mean to leave us in here. There is nothing to do. It isn't fair that she put us in here. I'm getting really mad. You know what let's do? Let's go play with the ca-ca in the corner. It's soft and squishy. Let's put it on the walls and let Mommy know how mad we are for leaving us in here."

"No! We can't do that. She'll hurt us."

"I don't care. She might leave us here for ever and ever, until our skin falls off."

"Please don't get us in trouble."

Emily went to the pile of feces and picked it up in her small hands as I watched with my magic eyes that could see in the blackness, watched in fascination as she smeared and painted all over the walls, getting it in our fingers and hair, letting it cover us in angry satisfaction.

When the closet door finally opened, Mom let out an angry yell, jerked me out. "How dare you! What a truly evil child you are."

"Emmy did it, Mommy. I'm sorry. She did it."

"Now you're even a liar!" She beat me with a leather belt, making the welts burn, and shoved me back into the odoriferous closet.

Crying, I said, "See, Emily, being angry just makes it worse."

"It was worth it," she said, beginning our lifetime of differences.

I was in the closet so long, I remember lying on the floor drifting in and out of dreams of water. When the door was finally opened I was in a semiconscious state. I couldn't walk. Mommy picked me up and carried me to my bed. She was so nice to me, I think she was worried I was dying. She brought me a radio, chicken soup, and a melted cheese sandwich with the crusts cut off. I was too weak to eat, so she fed me.

I was getting alarmingly thin. I was four when the doctor decided I was malnourished because of all the infections I'd had and said my tonsils should come out. I went to the hospital. My father gave me a bear I named Pooh, although he was a teddy bear and not truly a Pooh Bear. I have a vivid memory of getting strapped to a table and looking at the man with a mask on his face and having it clear in my mind he must be a Gypsy and I was going to have the white-hot fire inside me again. I began struggling and screaming in a state of absolute panic. The doctor tried to calm me down by telling me, "I'm going to put a cloth that smells like orange juice over your nose and mouth. Just breathe deeply." The instant he put the cloth on my face, I knew he lied. It didn't smell like orange juice. Then everything went black.

When I woke up, only my throat was sore, and the nurse in white gave me ice cream to eat. I cowered in the bed and asked her where the Gypsy man was and when he was coming to get me. She laughed and said, "There are no Gypsies here. What you saw was a doctor." During my hospital stay Pooh Bear and I became inseparable. Because I was so skinny they kept me in the hospital for a few extra days. Daddy came every night, and all the nurses were nice. The doctor who had scared me and lied to me brought me a hand puppet and apologized for scaring me. The nurses rubbed my back and put lotion on me. One had beautiful red hair. I didn't want to leave the lady with the kind voice and gentle touch. I knew Mommy didn't want me to come home.

The year before kindergarten was a long nightmare. I lived in a constant state of anxiety and terror. Mom would grab my hand and put it over the cutting board and press the meat cleaver to the back of my fingers and say, "I'm going to cut off all your fingers and make pickles of them and then I'll give them to Daddy. They will be all crunchy and small. He won't even know he's eating your fingers." I sobbed as I stood there waiting for the big cleaver to come smashing down. Her eyes would dart around in an excited way as her tales of my intended torture got worse. The light would catch the green, golds, and brown of her eyes as she scanned a whole planetarium of intended horror in her mind. I was very small when I learned to recognize those eyes and know that all I could do in the presence of the wildness was endure. Screaming and begging did not help me.

I practiced getting dressed and playing, using only my thumbs. I got good at dressing and playing, pretending I had no fingers. I decided the hardest things would be fastening buttons and tying shoes. I worried about that for I was certain that one day Mom would cut my fingers off.

Mom's conversations when I was alone with her, while Bobby
was at school and Jimmy was sleeping, were increasingly sadistic.
She said, "I would like to cut you up and cook you with wine and
mushrooms and have a dinner party and serve pot roast of
Marcia." She took out cookbooks and read me various recipes,
then told me some new way I could be cooked and eaten. "I think
your bottom would look just like a pork roast if I surround it
with red potatoes. Your father isn't even a good Jew because he
eats pork. The trick will be that he's eating you." I sat quietly
sucking my thumb, feeling sad that the family would eat me. I
worried about what it would be like to be eaten and wondered if
Daddy would ever know it was me he had for dinner.

My mother talked to an angel. I was terrified of her when she
would speak with this terrible angel, for it told her I was evil and
wicked and should be punished. I guess this is evidence that my
mother was psychotic, but when I was little all I knew was that I
was petrified. Mom would begin pacing back and forth, or slamming things around, and begin jabbering to her angel. It usually
meant I would be hurt again.

I absolutely believed in the reality of the angel my whole childhood, way past the time I figured out Santa Claus was pretend. In
great detail my mother described the seven-foot-tall angel with
the enormous feathered wings that she kept wrapped around her
white gown, almost like a fur coat. Mommy said, "This is my
special angel that God has sent me. She's a Christian angel. She
knows about Jews like you. She'll be watching you for me. She
understands that you shouldn't have been born." My mother
could see her, and speak to her, and although she was invisible to
me, there were moments I thought I caught a glimpse of her.

There were many times I tried to talk to the angel. I would
look up, almost to the ceiling, and say, "Lady Angel, I'm sorry
I'm Jewish. Please don't hurt me. Please stop telling Mommy to
hurt me." But it was clear to me this was an angel that wanted me
dead.

It was like that the time Mom tried to drown me. I was in the
old pedestal bathtub getting my long hair washed. I was wriggling
and wimpering because shampoo was in my eyes. My mother was
talking to the invisible angel, and suddenly she grabbed me and

plunged me under the water. I remember looking up through the warm water at my mother's lovely face above me. Her big, clear hazel eyes stared down at me, and her blond hair touched the water. Her lips were pressed together as though she were holding her breath, counting the moments of my oxygen supply. I kicked and struggled and felt the panic of not being able to breathe. Then I melted into the black and the next thing I remember I was lying on the cold bathroom tiles, coughing and vomiting up water. My mother was muttering, "I wish I could kill you, you little Jew. You steal everyone away from me."

There is no one who understands hopelessness better than an abused child. There was no one to turn to, no place to escape. I lived with the terror of the Gypsies. Daddy would ask me how I got bruised or what the burns were and I would say, "I wasn't careful, Daddy. I'm sorry."

His nickname for me was Sunshine. He said it was because I laughed a lot and I filled his life with joy. I did feel joy with Daddy. I was safe when he was around. I would stand behind his big armchair when he relaxed and rub his thick neck with my tiny fingers. He smelled like Bay Rum aftershave, and no matter when he shaved he had a dark shadow over his skin. I would kiss and kiss him, feeling the scratchy whiskers on my tiny round cheeks. I painted him pictures and picked him flowers from the garden. I lavished loving attention on the only person who stood between me and annihilation. There were times I almost told him about Mommy. The white pain I had experienced between my legs during Mom's lesson of what the Gypsy men would do stopped me. There was an absolute sense of certainty that my mother would carry out her threat and give me away. I knew I wasn't wanted. I didn't know what I had done to be so bad. I did know Daddy loved me. He always touched and hugged me gently. He listened when I told him things, making me feel important.

He was a busy, successful man, and was gone a great deal. I remember the terror that would rise in me whenever I saw him take out his suitcase. It meant torture for me when he was gone. I would hang on his leg and sob, "Daddy, please don't go. Take me with you. I'll be good. Take me with you, Daddy."

"Sunshine, I'll only be gone for a few days. I would take you if I could. I'll bring you a surprise."

I would watch his car drive away in a state of abject desolation, waiting for the violence to begin again. Once when he drove off, I followed the car out to the street and stood on the sidewalk, and when a car drove up the street toward me, I stepped off the curb in the path of the oncoming vehicle. I don't remember consciously wishing to die, I just did it to escape the torture. The car missed me by inches and the driver got out and yelled at me. He told me I was a bad girl to walk in front of a car. I said I was sorry and slowly I walked home, to the house of horror, with nowhere to go.

There was the old pink enema bag I hated. Mom would strip off my clothes and put me in the empty, huge, old claw-footed bathtub in a crawling position. Then she would run the hot water into me while I sobbed in agony. "We must wash the wickedness out of you. You are an evil little girl."

"I'm sorry I'm evil, Mommy. I don't mean to be bad. Stop! Please stop! It hurts! I'll be good. I promise I'll be good!"

There isn't much room in a tiny body for water. The pain got so intense sometimes I would scream a wild animal sound as the water filled my insides to the agonizing feeling of explosion. Beyond my control, the water squirted out, making Mom angrier. I remember the brown water over my hands as I kneeled in the tub with the ornate gold faucets as she stabbed the enema tip further up my rectum. I learned to focus on the gold drain as I hunched in agony, pretending I was going down, down the drain into blue water, to a safe, big lagoon where I was free and swam with fish that played with me and blew bubbles in my face.

Emily couldn't help me in the moments of intense physical pain. No splitting or fantasy could take away the times of excruciating pain. It was at the ebbing of the intensity that I could focus away. "I'm not here. I'm not here."

Emily was more alive during the trapped, confined times. I remember being left tied up with the scarves in my bed, unable to wriggle or suck my thumb.

"Do you see the crack in the ceiling?" Emily asked. "Well, if you shrink tiny enough you can go out that crack with me. We can stand on the roof and probably see the park with the crawdad pond and the swings. Let's go swing clear to the top of the pole."

I had no question about the reality of Emily. My whole world was crazy. She did not need to make sense; she was escape. She could be a separate person, or she could be a part of me. There seemed very little distinction between our realities in the beginning. We were trapped, and we escaped into dialogues, into pretend freeflowing beings away from the boredom of confinement, the pain and the confusion.

After securely tying me so I couldn't wriggle or move, one of my mother's rituals was to take the ice pick out of the kitchen drawer and poke me only until it hurt, but never to puncture the skin. "We must be careful not to leave marks," Mom said. She held the ice pick in front of my eyes, moving it closer and closer, as close as my eyelashes, and she said, "I'd like to blind you. I'll poke out your pretty blue eyes and all the jelly will run out and you won't be able to see."

I felt my heart pound against my ribs as I visualized my eyeballs hanging out of their sockets. As I was being frightened, with no escape, the world would go black for me. I could barely breathe in the absolute void of the darkened world of my imagination. I thrashed and squirmed to be free, waiting for the final thrust of the ice pick.

Even as a tiny child I understood the concept of blind. I would walk around the house with my eyes closed so I could get used to being blind. I memorized where everything was in my room so when I was blind I could find my things.

This terror led to the creation of another split-away part of myself, a blind girl named Camille.

I have no explanation for how Emily began as a pretend playmate and slowly over time got incorporated into me, as though we were twins. It was an evolution of pain and imagination, one that I was not conscious of. It just happened. Yet there were other personalities, like Camille, who seemed to be created in moments of intense trauma. The fracturing of self was so complete that I had no knowledge of them. I would split so completely when I was being these personalities that I would experience it only as a lapse of time. My knowledge of the "others" came from what people told me I did when I was blanked out. It was as though there was too much pain to allow one person to survive, so my mind, in a desperate attempt to cope, created escape routes for the pain. I know now Camille was my attempt to deal with my terror of the blindness Mom kept threatening to inflict. If I were already blind, then there would be less anxiety at the ice pick poised inches from my blue eyes. "I am blind and I can find my clothes. I can walk without being able to see."

Bobby said, "You were really stupid last night. You were walking around with a stick, tapping everything, like that blind man we saw once at the beach. When I asked you what you were doing you said you were Camille, and you asked if I could take you outside before you died. I think you're just pretending to be the lady in the story Aunt Helen told us about when she baby-sat."

I had no memory of doing that, but as he talked I had an image in my mind of a beautiful, frail blond girl who liked pain, and was very sweet and kind.

It didn't upset me that I did things I couldn't remember. I was small and just accepted life for what it was. There was no constancy of life with my mother and there became no constancy in my mind as I struggled to survive my world of pain.

There were many nightmares, many nights I didn't sleep, nights when physical pain kept me awake, and nights when I lay still, listening to see if Mom would come in and hurt me one more time before I fell asleep. It wasn't until I was a little older that the abstract thoughts of my death played in my mind, wondering how she would kill me, what it would feel like to die. I never remember being afraid of death, but I was afraid of how much pain there was to dying.

I lived with pain. It was constantly present. Matches were put out on my skin, my hair was yanked, I got slapped or hit or slammed against the wall for the smallest mistake.

One day while trying to help set the table, I dropped the cream pitcher and it exploded in a spray of glass and cream. Mom dragged me up the stairs and tied me to the bedposts again. She left the room for what seemed a hundred years of awaiting the pain that she would be planning. Screaming couldn't save me. Knowing the pain was coming made my mind unable to escape. The focus away into the pretend, the oblivion, didn't work in the face of anticipated terror.

My mother came back with straight pins, the kind with the tiny balls on the end used for sewing projects. As I lay immobilized in my tied-up position, she took the pins and stuck them through my labia, as though I were a Thanksgiving turkey. I cried and screamed at the piercing pain.

"I should give you to the Gypsy men because you're such a bad little girl," Mom said as she stuck another pin through me.

She untied me and left the room with the pins still sticking through my little private parts and the end of the pins stabbing into my left thigh as I moved. I couldn't see the pins to take them out. I inched across the bed, getting stabbed harder with each move. I waddled to the bathroom mirror, which was full length to the floor. Sitting on the white hexagonal tiles, I saw the blood droplets spread across the floor as I pulled the pins out one at a time. I was crying in great hiccuping sobs. I was fascinated at the sight of my red, tear-blotched face and the sight of the pins sticking through me.

That night at dinner I couldn't eat, and I couldn't move when dinner was over. I was stinging down below. I put my head down next to my plate and just sat there. I don't remember what Daddy said to me, but I do remember him scooping me in his arms and carrying me upstairs. He took me to the bathroom and I almost couldn't breathe with the stinging as I urinated. I was fighting back the tears as I looked up at Daddy and saw him staring at the blood in my underpants. He said nothing. He carried me to my room and put my nightgown on me. I waited for him to ask me about the blood. Instead, he lay down next to me and tickled my back and snuggled with me for a while.

Later, lying in my bed unable to sleep from the pain, I heard my father shouting at my mother and my mother crying. I hoped he wasn't fighting with her about my being evil.

"I think she's angry with me because I'm bad," I whispered to Emmy.

"No, it's because you're Jewish."

"How can I not be Jewish?"

"Just be like me, just don't be Jewish. Just decide to be different from what you are. It's easy."

"For you everything is easy. You just make up whatever you want to be. Things don't work like that. When you get bigger you'll understand more." I was always the practical one, Emily the escapist. If reality didn't suit her she changed it. "I didn't mean to break the pitcher. I never mean to do bad things."

Emily said, "I don't really think it's just because you weren't careful. When Bobby breaks things he doesn't get tied up. It's because Mom hates you for being Jewish."

"Why aren't Bobby and Jimmy Jewish?"

"I don't know. Daddy is Jewish and no one hurts him. I think Daddy knows you're being hurt. That makes me mad. He should take care of us."

"No! Don't say that. Don't ever say that Daddy knows. If he knew he would take us away. It's because we've never told him."

When my father got angry with my mother it seemed only to escalate her abuse of me. The next day I was locked in the closet for the whole day. I was hit and burned several times that week. I remember all this because on the next Sunday, Bobby, Jimmy, and I were going to be baptized in the Presbyterian Church. My father explained how my mother wanted us all to be sprinkled with water so when we died we would go to heaven. Mom gave us several talks about Jesus, heaven, and God, who loved us.

I liked going to the beautiful church. We had attended fairly often, but usually I had to go to the Sunday school room and color and sing songs. I remember once I had been in so much pain from an episode with Mom that I lay on the floor in the corner while all the kids looked at me. The young Sunday school teacher came over and picked me up and held me in her lap and gave me graham crackers. I remember her paisley silk blouse against my cheek as I watched the Jesus picture on the wall. Jesus had curls just like Mom and he had angels, too. But in Sunday school they told me Jesus loved little children.

I liked being in the big church with the stained-glass windows. I stood very still while I was baptized.

After church we went to a party with my family at the home of an old lady. I don't know who she was, except that I remember she had saggy eyes, blotches on her skin, and big crooked teeth. She also had a swimming pool. The Sunday luncheon was held outside and I tried to be very quiet and good. The bruises on my back hurt. I walked to the deep end of the swimming pool while the grown-ups talked. Now that I was baptized I wanted to go to heaven. I remembered the Sunday school teacher saying, "Jesus loves little children." I knew Mommy didn't love me. Maybe Jesus wanted me. With my hair in ribbons, a Sunday dress, and Mary Jane shoes, I stepped off the edge of the pool into the deep end. I don't remember fear, just sinking down, down, turning and seeing my blue dress float around my neck. I took a breath of water—I was going to visit Jesus.

My father dove into the water with all his clothes on and rescued me. I came up coughing and choking. I was laid out on the side of the pool and Daddy pressed the water from my lungs. Instead of comforting me, he stood me up, turned me over his knee and spanked me. That was the only spanking my father ever gave me. All the way home in my wet clothes I sucked my thumb. Daddy was angry with me, Mommy didn't like me and even Jesus didn't want me.

Because my birthday was near the school cut-off date, there was discussion as to whether I could start kindergarten. I remember my sense of doom at the decision that I was so tiny and skinny that I should stay home the extra year. More closet. More pain.

In the fall, just before I turned five, a very happy thing happened. My father took my mother on a two-week vacation, leaving us with my Grandma Bernice. She was a twinkle-eyed, round woman with big breasts and a halo of snow-white curls around her face. She had been to our home on holiday occasions and we had been to hers, but I didn't know her well. My mother didn't like her because she was a Jew. I was intrigued at what she and I possessed that would make us both undesirable. I hoped she didn't know I was bad. I worried how she would hurt me. I resolved to be extra good and very quiet.

It only took a few hours with my grandmother to realize we were going to have fun. She giggled and had a tea party with us. She didn't yell at me when I laughed. She didn't even yank my thumb out of my mouth when I sucked it. She liked me.

Those two weeks were bliss for me. I got to curl up in Grandma's lap and hear old Jewish stories and tales of Germany where she had grown up. We baked cookies together and she taught me funny songs. She showed Bobby and me how to play cards. We played endless games of hearts while Jimmy toddled around.

We took walks to the park, pushing Jimmy in the stroller, collecting pretty autumn leaves and rolling holly berries along the sidewalk.

Bedtimes were my favorite. Grandma would lie on my bed with me and gently stroke my hair and sing me lullabies. She told me she thought I was a lovely, wonderful little girl. We whispered secret love things to each other and she rubbed her nose against mine. "It's Eskimo kissing," she said.

It was two weeks of paradise. I wasn't hurt even once, and no closet. Even Emily, who didn't like anyone, liked Grandma. We argued as to who would get to sit on her lap.

I was upset when my parents came home. I felt my heart would break as my father escorted my grandmother to the car. She kissed the tears dripping from my eyes and Eskimo-kissed me good-bye. I squeezed her as hard as I could, hoping she would know how intensely I loved her.

The vacation seemed to have helped my mother. She was nice to me for a few weeks. A big surprise was that she said I could take violin lessons from Mrs. Barsh, who lived down the street. My father bought me a one-half-size violin that had a beautiful tone. Daddy showed me how I could walk down the street to Mrs. Barsh's house. It was the first time I had been allowed to leave the house alone. It was a long walk from my house down the driveway through our orange grove to the street where I turned right, down past other big huge houses.

Mrs. Barsh couldn't walk. She had had polio and was confined to a wheelchair. She had a big beak nose, but a very nice smile and an infectious laugh. The three black hairs growing out of a bumpy mole on her chin fascinated me. I absorbed everything about her, since I had known very few adults. I liked her eyes, big and sea-green, that looked at me as though she liked me. My mother didn't drive, she had no friends, no one came to call and I was never allowed to leave the house. This was an enormous adventure for an almost-five-year-old.

Mrs. Barsh made the violin sing with the most beautiful music I had ever heard. Somehow the music touched the core of my pain-filled life and I sat at my first lesson with tears streaming down my face. I was overcome by the magnitude of the experience and the sound. "The violin sounds like it's singing and crying" was all I could sputter.

My violin lessons became the highlight of my life as Mom resumed the torture. I practiced my violin and lived for the approval of Mrs. Barsh, glowing with her generous accolades.

Music became an escape for me. My violin was the only thing I owned, besides Pooh Bear. Daddy gave me toys, but Mom would take them from me, throwing them in the trash or smashing them in front of me. Dad had given me the violin and paid for the lessons. I knew my mother would not take the violin away for fear of my father's anger. I fingered the beautiful wood and plucked tunes on it in my room.

I gave notes to my physical pain. Low notes were for the dull aches of things like bruises, middle notes were for the pain of holding the water of an enema, and high notes were for pain like burns or needles stuck in me. Often in my room I would make a melody of my pain, beginning at a particular point and working all the way around my body.

My view of the violin when I was tiny was not as an instrument I needed to master but a friend to keep me company. We had no television. I was not allowed to go out on the street to find friends. I desperately missed Bobby when he was in school. I had Emily, and the secret voices, but I was bored with them.

The terrorizing and torturing continued. I lived in constant physical pain. In one fit of violence, Mom threw me against the wall. Blood came out of my right ear and the sounds were as though I was standing in a long tunnel. By the time I was five, I don't remember screaming or fighting the brutality. It was part of my life. I expected to be hurt. I still tried hard not to provoke violence. No one in the world tries harder than an abused child.

"I must not talk loudly. I mustn't laugh. I mustn't run in the house. I mustn't spill things. I must never be angry" were things I told myself like a liturgy in an attempt to avoid pain.

What once was hidden, secret abuse became more open. I was hit and hurt in front of Bobby and Jimmy. They were never hurt. I was the sole, unlucky focus of Mom's anger and the brunt of the angel's wrath. But she began doing things like putting cayenne pepper in our food to see us cry. I remember little Jimmy shrieking as he tried to wipe the pepper from his tongue, and I saw Mom laugh.

At the Halloween carnival at Bobby's school we won little goldfish with the Ping-Pong balls that landed in the bowls. We brought home our three fish and were pleased with our new pets. Mom took the little bags and dumped our fish onto the kitchen floor. She stepped on them, squashing them flat. "We must not let things suffer," she said. That statement made no sense to me as I cried for my little fish.

Emily could lividly express the anger I didn't allow myself to feel. "I hate Mom! She had no reason to kill the fish. She has no reason to hurt us."

"Be quiet, Emily. If you do something you'll make her madder."

"I don't care!" She took the little smashed fish and smeared the guts around the kitchen counter.

She was bad and I got thrown down and kicked.

For Christmas when I was five, I remember being thrilled with the beautiful antique doll from Grandma Bernice. It was almost as tall as I was, with a porcelain painted face and real brown hair that curled. It had a lace dress and little buckle shoes. I loved that doll. I named her Sally and kept her next to my bed. In my loneliness for playmates, I played with her as though she were a real friend.

One day when Mommy was angry with me she tied me in a chair in my room, took a hammer and smashed in Sally's face.

"I wish I could do this to your face. You are pretty and everyone loves you more than me," said my mother. I sobbed as Sally lay in hunks of china bisque on my floor. The brown glass eyes still had the eyelashes attached as they gazed at me from the floor. Mom took Sally and threw her in the trash, leaving me tied in my room to mourn.

Dad asked me where Sally was and I told him I broke her. My fear of the Gypsies far outweighed my father's displeasure. "You were wrong to not take care of an expensive doll, especially since Grandma gave it to you."

"I'm sorry, Daddy."

Bobby and Jimmy had lots of toys and trucks and I got to play with them, but it wasn't the same as having my very own playthings.

Pooh Bear became very important after Sally had been destroyed. I used to talk to Pooh and tell him where I hurt, and what I was afraid of. I played pretend games with Pooh, and slept with him at night. I must have been about six when my mother took him from me one day and stabbed him with a kitchen knife, slitting out the stuffing of his belly, puncturing his arms and legs and cutting his face to shreds. In my child's mind it was a murder she was committing. Pooh was vividly alive to me and now he was dead. I sobbed and sobbed. I took his eyes out of the wastebasket and hid them under my pillow. I kept those eyes of my dead friend for years, putting them in secret hiding places.

I only had Bobby, Jimmy, and Emily. She became more real after Pooh was killed.

Bobby would bring me books home from his school and in the afternoons he taught me to read. It was easy. Then he taught me numbers and arithmetic. That was a cinch, too. I loved any attention from Bobby.

Mom would keep me in the closet now even when Bobby was home. She terrorized him into thinking I would be given away if he told anyone. She told all of us that I wasn't really her child, I was adopted. Bobby said that didn't make sense since we looked exactly alike and Daddy had told us about my being born during an air raid.

Bobby and I became closer with the open abuse. He would put Band-Aids on my burns, or sneak me cookies if I had my dinner plate taken away before I could finish. Often at night Bobby would come into my bedroom to check if I was okay. He was sure I was going to get killed, too.

There were nights when we lay in bed together, our little

blond heads touching, and talked of running away, but we had no money and no place to go.

"Something's wrong with Mom" was his explanation. "Should we tell Dad?"

"No, Bobby. I don't want to be given to the Gypsy men. Please don't tell."

The times of burns or painful enemas when I would scream really upset Bobby. "I hate her. She's a witch," he said.

Only Bobby and Emily were angry. I was too terrified of the repercussions of anger. Any sign of aggression on my part meant brutal pain.

I was a very allergic child, having bouts of asthma fairly frequently. Animal fur was an especially potent allergen to me. Mom gave me an Easter bunny once. I was thrilled at getting a present from her. I desperately wanted her to love me. She took the bunny and rubbed the soft fur all around my face tickling me with the softness. I began wheezing and that night had asthma so badly I had to be rushed to the hospital because I couldn't breathe. I felt confusion: joy at my mother giving me a fluffy bunny, upset that I was allergic to it, and devastation that my father would give away my new present.

My mother would take me to the pet store and let me hold kittens and bunnies, then would come the sneezing and asthma attacks. It took me years to figure out that her gesture was not a loving one.

The summer I was about to start school was wonderfully happy. Daddy took us camping in the High Sierras. Mom stayed home. We fished and cooked our meals over the campfire. We ate trout and pancakes, for that was about all Dad could cook. The four of us slept in a tent which made strange sounds when the wind blew, but we had Daddy next to us. He would put his big arm across Jimmy and me as we scrunched down into our sleeping bags. Being squished by Dad's arm was the loveliest feeling in the world. Bobby got to use Dad's gun and shoot tin cans. He whispered to me, "I would never kill anything, except maybe Mom."

That summer Dad gave me permission to cross the streets

near our house so Bobby and I could go to the park. Down the block and across at the corner lived an old, bent man with no front teeth. He sat on his front porch with his big green parrot and let us give peanuts to the big-beaked bird, who cocked his head and said, "Good-bye, I'm pretty." I thought being able to go with Bobby was the most wonderful thing that ever happened to me. We made friends at the park. They even let me play games. In one giant leap my world expanded beyond the closet and the pain. I could laugh in the park and not get hit.

I asked Emily, "Why don't you want to play with Bobby and my new friends?"

"Nobody likes me. I only want to play with you. Besides, no one believes I'm really real."

It was true. Bobby teased me unmercifully when I talked about Emily. Sometimes I would let her play, but I kept it a secret when she was there; I didn't like being laughed at.

Just before kindergarten was to start, when I was almost six, my mother, in a rage, threw me against the corner of the dining-room table, gashing my forehead. She taped the jagged edges together and as I sat crying, she said, "You'll have an ugly scar and everyone will look at it and know you are wicked."

The mark of evil was more humiliation than I could bear. I didn't want to go to school. I didn't even know for sure what school was, but I didn't want people to know I was wicked. I begged Daddy to let me stay home forever. I cried and told him I didn't want anyone to see my scar. He said that was ridiculous, that it was just a little scar and with time it wouldn't be red anymore.

The next day, Daddy brought me a little cut red garnet in a tiny velvet box. "There is a place called India and women who are princesses wear stones like this in their foreheads. They cut their head, just like you and decorate themselves. They think it makes them special. I think your scar makes you special."

It was always the double message. Evil. Special. Wicked. Princess. I felt better about the scar but still felt shy.

The first day of school I walked around with my hand over my forehead. The new children asked me why I had my hand on my head, but I was quiet and sucked my thumb. At recess one boy pulled my hand away and said, "Oh, just a scar." I was relieved he didn't gasp and acknowledge how bad I was. After that, I began to play.

I instantly fell in love with my teacher. She had a sweet face full of happy smile lines, gray hair, and wore bright clothes. I began to follow her around everywhere. I was her willing slave for any school project. Already knowing how to read and write made me an instant success. I could tie my shoes and tell time, too.

Mrs. McDonald liked me. She would let me sit on her lap sometimes, and she called on me to help with the other kids. I tried to kiss her whenever she leaned over and I held her hand whenever she let me. One day after school, lingering as usual, I asked, "May I please be your little girl? I will be very good and quiet. Please take me home with you."

"Why, Marcia, I would love to have you as my little girl, but you have a mother and father who love you very much and they would miss you."

I couldn't tell her about my mother, for there was always the fear of the Gypsies. I said very quietly, "I'd like to be yours." I stood very close to her, fingering the soft folds of her dress, struggling against my desire to hug her hard.

I remember walking home from school slowly, feeling the rejection and not wanting to return to my home. Daddy loved me, but he wasn't home often.

Soon after that, my mother hit me and broke my nose. Going to school with cotton packing stuffed up my nose and a big bandage across my face made me terrified someone would guess Mom had hurt me. The idea of being saved never seemed an option; it was the fear of Mom's retribution if anyone discovered the truth that had me terrified. I made up some kind of lie. It was hard to breathe with the bandage, but I loved the colorful look of my eyes going from red to purple to green.

One day, in the desperate hope that Mom would love me more if I were ugly, I took her scissors and cut off my eyebrows and eyelashes. I don't know why I honestly thought she would be glad. It was a great surprise to me to get beaten by Mom. Dad was angry and Mrs. McDonald said it was a dumb thing to do. I sat in the classroom as everyone howled with laughter at me. I just sucked my thumb.

It wasn't until I began school that I noticed the fragmentation of time. I could be sitting in my little circle of classmates, with my hands folded, listening to a story of Babar, and the next thing I would be aware of was the teacher saying, "Marcia, just what do you think you are doing?"

In my hand would be chalk and I would be standing at the blackboard in front of wild drawings, with the whole class snickering at me. It was the regimentation and accountability for my actions that made me realize I wasn't like everyone else. I just sort of drifted away and did things I wasn't aware of. It was devastating, because I wanted desperately to be liked.

Chapter 3

The first thing I did when I was introduced to the school library was ask for books on blindness. I had been terrorized by the threat of being blinded so often that it seemed imperative to me to find out all I could. I found a book about Braille and color coded the clothes in my closet. I taught myself to eat as though my plate was a clock and the hands pointed to the food. Bobby and I practiced with "Meat at nine o'clock, peas at five." In my mind it was an earnest game.

Even at six I knew something was alarmingly wrong with my mother. I didn't have labels like mentally ill, I just knew that other people did not treat me as she did. In a deep aching way I wanted her to love me. Even the slightest of smiles or the occasional soft touch was enough for me to fantasize that maybe if I tried harder she would love me. I can't explain the intense loyalty I felt toward her. Partly it was fear, and partly I loved her because she was my mother. She was the beautiful queen and I was her adoring servant leaping to her every command.

I felt very proud on Valentine's Day when I brought Mom my plaster of Paris plate with my hand print on it and a big red yarn loop for hanging it up. It had been an important project at school, and I thought my mother would know how much I loved her when she unwrapped the white wrinkled tissue paper. I had wrapped, unwrapped, and rewrapped it dozens of times, fantasizing an enveloping hugging scene with Mommy. I dared to lean against her shoulder, standing next to her as she sat at the kitchen table and opened the paper. I shyly reached up and fingered her soft curls that cascaded down to her shoulders and touched the blue flowers on her dress.

Without saying a word, she lay the plate on the table, then got up to go to the back porch. She reentered the kitchen with a hammer and a big nail. My heart soared with joy that she was going to hang my handprint on the wall. Instead, she came over to the table, picked up the plate and placed a few newspapers under it. Then, looking right at me and not saying a word, she placed the nail in the middle of my plaster palm and brought the hammer down hard. The plate fractured into white hunks. The symbolism of her act was abundantly clear to me. I shrank back against the kitchen wall, the tears coursing down my cheeks as white as the plaster.

Some things I accepted. Because I was evil, I must be burned, cut, hit, and locked up. Yet other things, even with my life of abuse, I innately knew to be wrong.

Once when I was five, and a cousin was visiting, I remember my sense of alarm that Mom made us take baths together while she sat on the lid of the toilet watching us and directing me to do things to him. She sat there in her cotton print dress with the round collar that always had the diamond circle pin on it and commanded me to pay attention to what German boys looked like. She peeled Pippin apples as she sat there. Once she got a big kitchen knife and held it to me and forced me to suck the little boy's penis. He squirmed and laughed. I don't remember what Mom said, but I remember feeling what we were doing was wrong, especially since she threatened me with the knife.

When I was six, the Kendalls, who had sent my dad to college and law school, came from New York to visit us. I remember how excited Daddy was about the visit—cleaning, planting flowers, giving us instructions on how to be polite. They were wonderful

people, even asking Bobby and me to call them Grandpa and
Grandma. Mr. Kendall had a loud laugh and wore a big gold
watch, which hung on a long chain, tucked into his pocket. Mrs.
Kendall had hair that was a white-blue color and so thin I could
see her pink scalp peeking through. They brought the boys trucks
and me a beautiful doll, which of course Mom later took from
me. That was a glorious week. We went to restaurants and the
zoo with them. When they left, Grandpa Kendall pressed six silver dollars into my hand, one for each year of my life. Bobby got
eight, and Jimmy three. We marveled at our wealth. Dad and
Mom had never given us money, even though we knew we were
rich compared to other kids at school. We had lots of clothes. I
even had jewelry. My mother made me wear a pearl necklace to
school with my expensive dresses, saying, "If you look nice no
one will know I have to punish you for being wicked." Looking
nice was some kind of necessity. I had all kinds of pretty dresses
and shoes, but no money and no toys or possessions that were
mine. This money seemed a fortune. Bobby and I talked for days
and days about how rich we were and all the possibilities of our
newfound wealth. I knew I couldn't spend mine because Mom
would take away whatever I bought.

"Maybe we should bury the money in a jar in the backyard,"
Bobby said. "It could be our escape money if we want to run
away."

That is what we did. Digging deep into the dark dirt, we put
our treasure of fourteen dollars under the lemon tree and told no
one. It was our secret.

I felt my heart would break when kindergarten came to an
end. I cried for days that I wouldn't see Mrs. McDonald anymore. Cutting and gluing had been fun, music was wonderful, but
Mrs. McDonald was my fantasy mother. She spoke softly, she
laughed and smiled a lot. She liked me. I humiliated myself once
more before school let out by begging her to adopt me. I fantasized about what it would be like to be her daughter and the fun I
would have. More than anything I craved affection. I wanted to
be kissed and hugged and cuddled. I wished I could sit on Mrs.
McDonald's lap and pat her breasts and bury my head in her soft
neck.

Summer meant the loss of new friends, the loss of Mrs. McDonald, and more violence against me. My increasing awareness that I lost hours in a day came when I was six. I could be locked in the closet and be there the whole day and it would only seem like minutes. Though not aware of any conscious effort to do so, I learned to go away from the intolerable.

Bobby had taught me to hold and play with spiders so I wouldn't fear them in the closet. He was upset when I got locked up.

"See, spiders are nice, they only tickle you when they walk on you," he said.

No longer fearing the spiders helped, but the closet had a stench from all the times I had to urinate, when I could not hold it any longer. The blackness was absolute. There was not even a ray of light, nor any sounds in the closet behind the closet. It was abandonment at its worst. I was certain I would die of thirst or shrivel in hunger. I worried that Daddy would not know how I had died. Often I worried that no one would remember I was in the closet and I would be left to die. I wondered if bones were really white like I'd seen in pictures of skeletons. How long would it take to become just bones, and where would my skin go? I wondered if my skin would look like the potato I'd found at the back of the cupboard that was all shriveled. I wondered if I would get squishy like a rotten apple, or all hard and wrinkled like the dried potato.

There were times when I felt sad for my own death, which in my own mind seemed a certainty. Other times I just apathetically accepted the fact that one day soon I would be left to die in the closet, or that Mom would kill me.

I would lie on the floor of the closet and my fears and thirst would get drowned out by the voices that would talk to me, saying lovely, escapist, imaginative things. Emily split into life in my mind, suggesting we have a tea party or play house. In those games, our mother was someone named Sophie. She was warm and gentle, a good bit like Grandma Bernice. She didn't mind being Jewish, and in our parties we had big slices of egg bread, beautiful twisted loaves with sesame seeds on top, served with sweet butter and homemade boysenberry jam. There was a giant pot of English tea which we drank with milk and sugar out of thin, dainty teacups. Sophie liked number games. We giggled as we made up puzzles of numbers to add and subtract. She liked singing songs, too, German and Hebrew ones, while she danced little dances in our dark, cramped space under the stairs.

Somewhere in my deprived existence Sophie became another personality, a nurturing, Jewish, maternal woman. She loved domestic things like cooking and sewing. She became the part of me that would whisper reassurances, affirm the value of being Jewish.

My panic escalated when Bobby was gone. He was my one assurance that I would be found! At eight, he was allowed to go places on his bicycle, and sometimes he left for the day. Whenever he could, he tried to take me with him because he knew what leaving me meant. I became the tag-along with Bobby and his friends.

Bobby and I decided to make more money for our treasure jar. We opened a lemonade stand at the end of our driveway. Dad was pleased at our enterprise and he said he would buy all the sugar and paper cups. We had several lemon trees on our grounds, so we went into business right away. Some of the neighbors who stopped were surprised to find out children lived in our big house, since they had never seen us before. We met the Jamisons, a Baptist family who lived four houses down. They had a ten-year-old daughter, Susie, who became my friend that summer. She would stand on the curb and flag down cars, in which sat potential customers for our lemonade stand. Susie was the one who introduced me to the full-blown concept of hell and damnation. Her parents took me to a Holy Roller-type church service, where, with great vividness, the pastor described flames licking at the feet of the wicked and unrepentant. I didn't know what "sins" were, but I knew from my mother I was evil. Now I had the added worry of hell when I finally did die. After the service, Susie introduced me to the pastor, who asked me if I had been saved. My only answer was "No," for my idea of "saved" was for someone to take me away from my mother.

"We will pray for you, child," said this scary man, who put his hand on my head and proceeded to invoke the Holy Spirit to enter my heart. I was terrified, thinking he was calling on some magical power to strike me down. I waited for Mom's angel to appear with a sword. When I didn't die, I was a bit relieved.

I lived with a great deal of anxiety at being Jewish, being evil and bad and being always hurt. I bit my nails, sucked on my braids, and at six still sucked my thumb. Mom painted my thumb with Tabasco sauce, but I would wash it off and suck it anyway. I needed my thumb. I tried hard to stop sucking it, but I couldn't.

"Big kids don't suck their thumbs," said Bobby.

"Pull that thumb out of your mouth," my father demanded.

But I needed the juice in my thumb, and the reassurance I felt when I sucked it.

First grade brought another happy time, and another teacher I loved. Miss Simpson had huge brown eyes, was very young and enthusiastic about everything. When I kissed her, she kissed me back. She let me play my violin for the class and told me I was a very talented person.

The academic work of school came easily for me, but in first grade I was distressed that if I didn't pay attention my mind would slip away somewhere. Emily didn't always want to stay in a desk at school. I got in trouble for wandering around the class-room when I didn't even know I had done it. That was to begin my lifetime of covering up and apologizing for my "twin."

I could feel my little cheeks grow hot and pink as the teacher said, "For goodness' sake, Marcia, you're out of your seat again. Can't you sit still and pay attention like the other students?"

I whispered, "Emily, stay in the desk. I don't like to get in trouble." Out loud I said, "I'm sorry, Miss Simpson."

"It wasn't me," Emily said. "It was one of the others. You always blame me, just because I'm the one you know."

"Well, you're the one that always does the bad stuff."

The year was also punctuated with happy times spent with Grandma Bernice, new friends, a longer day at school, and the realization that I got approval for being smart. But there were days when it was agony to sit still with my bruised bottom or my little-girl parts that had been hurt by Mom.

My seventh year was terrible. Mom and Dad fought a great deal and Dad didn't come home many nights. Mom said Daddy was having sex with another woman. Mom began talking frequently to her angel and getting more violent with me.

Mom would strip me naked, tie me to my bedposts and rub my clitoris with cold cream, making me feel all warm and nice down below, then take a broom handle or wooden spoon and jab it inside my vagina, saying things like, "I'll have to teach you how to use your little Jewish cunt."

I never told anyone I was Jewish. It was as black a secret in my mind as the abuse.

"We must be careful now that you're in school not to leave marks," Mom would say as she would take long needles and stick them deep into my foot. She began to lock me in the closet on some days right after breakfast. I was highly distraught at missing school. She would write a note saying I had been sick or had had an asthma attack. I was very tiny and underweight for second grade, so the teacher accepted it. Occasionally my black and blue marks were questioned by teachers, but I would make some excuse, such as I was always banging into things.

Fritz and Frieda added stress to my life. From my earliest memories, they were part of my childhood experience, and as real to me as Mom's angel. Mom would sit at the edge of my bed while she had me tied to the bedposts and tell me over and over about Fritz and Frieda, the elves who lived in the big basement of our house, in their own tiny home behind the furnace. They were her German Heinselmenchen, which according to folklore are the elves who come in the night to work and help people, but Mom had ownership of these elves. They were malevolent creatures with big eyes that watched me from their invisible hiding places and would tell Mom if I was doing anything wrong. They could hear me wherever I went and would report even the slightest infraction of the rules to her. As a child, I could hear them breathing behind the curtains and hear their tiny footsteps following me. At vulnerable moments when Dad was putting me to bed, I considered telling him about Mom, but I knew Fritz would scurry to her on his tiny felt shoes, and I would be murdered even before Dad could pack a suitcase.

Just as I tried to talk to "Lady Angel," I used to try to negotiate with Fritz. I wanted him to know I was trying very hard to be a good girl. Whenever I was lucky enough to be given candy or something special at school, I would save some for Fritz and Frieda, putting little stashes of things at the bottom of my bed to try to win them over. When they didn't take my offerings, I thought it was because they didn't like me because I was Jewish.

Bobby and Jimmy were terrified of Fritz and Frieda, too. Bobby and I would sometimes agree to meet inside the closet to whisper to each other if we had important things to say, or we would print notes to each other about Mom. We decided that elves can't read, or if Fritz could, it would only be German, for that is the language Mom spoke to him.

It became clear in my mind, at age seven, that Emily was my twin. She was no longer the freeform, pretend playmate of the closet. She was a distinct person, separate from me, with definite likes and dislikes. We had lengthy internal dialogues, even arguments. Our relationship was still one of friends, but her anger, her willingness to do things that got me into trouble, was upsetting. When I told people about Emily, they either said I was lying or pretending. We had the awareness that we shared the same body but not the same life. Emily was prettier than I was. She refused to be Jewish. We began to get favorite clothes, our own set ideas of how to do things, and individual preferences. I simply accepted my twin, my loss of time, with the same willingness that I accepted the abuse. It simply *was*.

Linda Franklin became my best friend. She was small like me, had brown braids, buck teeth, and a bubbly, sweet personality. The days I got to go to her house after school became the jewels of my memory. Mrs. Franklin was the sweetest woman I'd ever met, next to my Grandma Bernice. She was tiny, walked as though she was floating, and smiled constantly. She spoke in a soft, lilting way. At least two afternoons a week I went to Linda's after school. I liked Linda, but I *worshipped* her mother. She played games with us, let us brush her long hair, taught us jump-rope tricks, let us play dress-up in her tiny clothes and put on her makeup.

Linda begged me to let her come to my house, but I never did, giving excuses like, "My mother isn't well."

I thought I would unravel with excitement when Linda asked me to spend the night at her house. We giggled all the time and Mrs. Franklin let us have a special tea party with her best porcelain dishes and gave us little chocolates. She let us finger-paint in blue and green and red on big rolls of waxed butcher paper. At bedtime, Mrs. Franklin let us talk until late at night, then she came into the bedroom and sat with us.

"You girls will have to settle down now," she said. "Maybe if I rub your backs you will relax."

I winced as she touched my bruised back. "What's the matter, Marcia?" she questioned as she pulled up my nightgown, turned on the light and gave a gasp.

"Marcia, how did you get all these black-and-blue marks?"

I was frozen in mortification. "I can't tell you" was all I could whisper.

Mercifully, she let it drop. But she did say if I ever needed to talk to her about it, she would be glad to help me. I shyly mumbled, "Thank you," but the imprint on my brain of the white fire-pain kept me silent.

Mrs. Franklin went out of her way to be sweet to me. I was invited over often. She baked cookies with Linda and me. She made me feel very special, as though my presence thrilled her. She oohed and aahed over my pictures from school, and my good report cards. Linda seemed perfectly content to share her mother and little sister with me. Her mother must have talked to her, for there was never any badgering on Linda's part to come to my house.

Over the years, Mrs. Franklin went to all my school functions, made me Halloween costumes, and took me dozens of places with her family. She was my almost-mother.

One day I threw my arms around Mrs. Franklin and expressed my undying love. "Could you adopt me and could I be your little girl?" I asked as I kissed her. Unlike the rejection that had come so flippantly from my teachers, Mrs. Franklin sat me on her lap and looked at me with serious, thoughtful eyes. "There is nothing in this world I would like better than to have you be my little girl. Unfortunately, it isn't easy to take a child from someone else. The law says you belong to the parents you were born to. Next to my own two little girls, I love you more than any other child. I wish I could be your mother."

All the way home, kicking a rock, I felt depression in a profound way. The concept of ownership had never crossed my mind. My mother didn't love me, or want me, but she owned me like a dog or a cat. There would never be an escape or another mother. I was exhausted to my core with the terrorizing, the physical pain, the isolation of the closet. Mrs. Franklin couldn't take me. Grandma Bernice couldn't save me. Daddy was gone all the time.

I picked at my food and didn't sleep at nights. My frail weight dropped even lower. I mentally drifted in and out of time frames.

When Daddy came home, he was alarmed at how I looked. "Sunshine, you're getting so skinny. You must try and eat."

My teacher asked me if I was all right.

That summer between second and third grade, my dad took time off from work and took the three of us children to the beach for a few weeks. Grandma Bernice came to stay with us, too. She stuffed me with goodies, and in the joy of not being hurt, I began to eat and play again. Daddy took us swimming. In the early-morning hours we went shell hunting and walking along the edge of the waves, kicking at the clumps of seaweed that hid the treasured cowrie shells and abalone. At sunset we fished off the rocks, with the surf surging and spraying us as it hit the rocks. We let our perch swim in the tide pools. Grandma Bernice enthusiastically cooked the fish we caught.

Grandma told me stories, lots of them about wicked stepmothers and witches. She fingered the scars on my leg in an unconscious way while she told me about Hansel and Gretel. She never talked directly to me about the scars, but somehow I knew she knew more than she could say.

Bobby, Jimmy, and I got brown and hardy in those weeks of fun. I even stopped sucking my thumb in the daytime, although I still did at night. Emily was content and quiet. We piled on Dad at night in a heap of laughter and wrestled on the floor. Grandma Bernice hugged and kissed us constantly. Bobby, at nine, thought that was mushy, but I could tell even he liked it. We teased her because she didn't like the sand and worried about getting freckles from the sun. We would swim until we were cold, which was hours, then we would flop on the hot sand, roll around, and later build elaborate lopsided sand castles.

Driving home, Bobby and I were desolate. We discussed whether we should tell Dad what was really happening at home. Again, I was the one who talked Bobby out of saying anything. My fear of retribution by our omnipotent mother was profound.

In August, Dad rented a mountain cabin at Lake Arrowhead. With great anticipation we packed for our week's adventure. The road seemed endlessly twisting as we made our way up the mountain. We stopped and looked out over the city of San Bernadino and the blue mountains beyond.

We arrived at the lake and drove around part of it, until we came to a private driveway. We bumped along on the dirt road and there in the middle of the pine trees was a beautiful two-story home; not at all the cabin I imagined. Inside, there were stuffed animal heads on the wall, a huge fireplace, and everywhere the glow of beautiful golden wood. Bobby, Jimmy, and I slid around on the polished floors.

For a couple of days we had a great time fishing with Dad and hiking in the woods. Then he called his office and I felt my heart stop midbeat when he said he had to get back to Los Angeles to do a deposition on a case. I knew what his leaving always meant. Again I clung to him, begging him to stay, the terror alive in my mind. Panic rose as I watched the car disappear in a cloud of dust.

For a day everything went well. We swam in the lake in front of the lifeguard, while Mom read a book.

The evening of the next day Bobby and I got rather wild and were wrestling about. I accidentally bumped the table which held the kerosene lantern. The lamp went crashing to the floor, spilling the burning kerosene in a trail of flames. Bobby and I shouted, "Help! Fire!" Mom beat the fire with a blanket and put it out, but it had blistered the beautiful polished wood floor.

Mom was livid at me, not Bobby, never Bobby. She grabbed me and shook me so hard my teeth cracked together and I bit my tongue. I could taste the blood and feel the sharp pain.

I don't remember the words Mom yelled at me, but I acutely

remember being dragged outside, way out into the thicket of trees. Mom took the rope that had tied our suitcases to the top of the car and slammed me against the trunk of a big tree.

"Stand still," she commanded as she began tying the rope around the tree and my torso. I dared not move or cry out, fearing what would come next. It was twilight and the woods seemed scary as the shadows made giant shapes of dark and light.

Mom finished tying me. My arms were free but my face was resting on the rough bark, my body was pressed tightly to the tree. I only had shorts on and it hurt my legs.

Mom was yelling at me and began to beat me with a tree branch. I gasped with each stinging whack. I tried not to scream for fear of having her hurt me worse.

Instead of untying me, she said, "You can spend the night tied to this tree to think about how wicked you are. If you cry or scream I'll come out and hurt you worse." She turned and left me tied so tightly I could barely breathe.

My tongue hurt, my back hurt from the beating, my legs were getting poked by the little knots of the pine. Any normal child would have screamed and wailed. This cabin was far from any other cabin, up its own private road, but still I thought of shouting at the top of my lungs for help. From experience I knew I could not. I did not dare cry out. It was unthinkable; Mom would hear me.

My sense of abandonment was the most intense I had ever experienced, as the sun set and the trees turned from shadows into black, frightening shapes. I sobbed quietly, my nose running, the sniffles going down onto my T-shirt. My heart beat fast and every sound in the woods got amplified a thousand times. I couldn't see or hear anyone in the cabin. I was alone—terrifyingly, frighteningly alone.

The mosquitoes came out in full air force battalions as the night got blacker. Fortunately, I had my hands free to swat them as they droned in on me, but I couldn't bend over to swat at my legs. I could feel myself turning into mosquito meals.

The pain, the trauma, and the length of time made me have to urinate badly. I held it as long as I could, until the half-moon rose above the trees. Finally, out of desperation and cramping, I wet, the warm stream of urine running down my legs and into my Keds tennis shoes.

The terror mounted in me as I began worrying that bears would smell my urine and come and eat me. I cried in my fright and my breathing was in fast gasps as I waited for a bear to swipe at me with a clawed paw. I heard a thousand noises and felt beetles walking on my skin. Every sound was ominous in the blackness, the trees looking huge and threatening in the pale moonlight.

I got cold, bone-chillingly, teeth-chatteringly cold. I was tiny and the elevation over five thousand feet. I was in pain. I was cold. I was terrified and forgotten.

"I will not stay here" was my thought as Emily sprang to life.

"Let's leave," Emily said. "Tonight we'll go to the moon."

I concentrated on the friendly face of the moon above me. Emily mounted a winged eagle and the two of us flew to the moon that night. We found a river of warm milk and underground houses, all cozy and warm with adorable moon men, who played with us and fed us Snickers candy bars with extra peanuts that were set in tiny bowls carved from green moon rocks.

I know now that is dissociating from reality, but as a child it was survival. It was escape from the inescapable.

I do not remember any more of the night, but the next morning when I was untied, I crumpled to the ground. My legs would not work. I was numb with cold and immobility. Mom had to carry me into the house. I had my arms around her neck and could smell her Fabergé cologne as she held me. I wanted to kiss her cheek, but I did not. It was enough to be held, if even for a moment.

When third grade started, Mom bought us a beautiful black German shepherd puppy. Of course I was allergic to the sweet little animal. But I couldn't stop playing with it, even though I wheezed constantly.

My mother got angry at my asthma and I further enraged her by doing something—I don't even remember what. I do remember being dragged up to my room again and tied to my bed with the blue scarves. "You're an evil child. You have stolen your father from me."

"No, Mommy! I've never taken anything. I promise I haven't stolen anything."

Again the ice pick was poised over my eyes and stuck carefully, just until it hurt, on my face and slowly down my body. Mom's conversation got crazier and angrier. She took the ice pick and began raking it up and down my labia and clitoris, cutting me, then stabbing at me. She poked it over and over into my tiny vagina and into my rectum. I screamed blood-curdling screams of agony. I was sure she was killing me. When she stopped, she was crying, one of the few times I saw her cry, and she was talking to her angel as she left the room. I lay with blood running from my wounds. I couldn't get out of bed for a week. Mom never said she was sorry, but she took good care of me, bringing me snacks and books and things to play with. She even brought in her jewelry box for me to look at.

My body healed faster than my mind. To have the pain again after the freedom of the summer with Dad was too much. I couldn't even escape into fantasy. I was deeply depressed.

My asthma continued. Daddy came home from his mysterious "trips" and took me to the doctor, who emphatically said, "If this child is to stop having asthma, you must get rid of the dog."

Mom sat me down, looked me piercingly in the eyes and said, "The whole family has decided we would rather keep the puppy than you. You'll just have to learn to live with asthma because King is more important than you."

I went up to my room, still wheezing, and lay on my bed. The stains of the ice pick experience were still on my covers. I walked out on the balcony overlooking the cement driveway. The only thought in my mind was a compelling need to escape. "Let's leave," Emily said.

"I wish I could fly like you. I would fly away. No one loves me, no one wants me."

"It's easy," Emily said. "Just flap your arms real hard and you'll go up, up into the sky. You're right. No one loves you, except maybe Bobby."

"Will you help me fly?"

"Sure! I'll go with you. We'll never come back. Maybe they'll even be sad we're gone."

I climbed onto the railing of the balcony, looking up at the sky. I do not remember consciously choosing to die, merely to leave what I could not tolerate anymore. I stood on the rail flapping my arms, determined I would fly away. I took a giant leap off the rail and plunged head-first from the second-story balcony. I felt no fear as I fell, merely a fascination that flying didn't work.

I have no idea how long I lay crumpled on the driveway. I drifted back to time and place with Bobby shouting and crying over me, "Don't be dead, please don't die."

The next memory was of my mother yanking me up and the piercing, electric pain that came from the broken arm she was pulling. I could hear the bones crunching.

Bobby made a sling out of a towel, as he'd learned to do in Boy Scouts, and went with me to the hospital. Both bones in my left arm were broken, so I got a cast up to my shoulder.

It wasn't until I lost consciousness later that night that they discovered my fractured skull and brain concussion.

The doctor told me to curl up in a little ball for a spinal tap. He was amazed I didn't even whimper when he stuck the needle in my back. I wondered where else he would stick needles, or if he would tie me up. In just a few moments he said he was done, and he said he was sorry he had to poke me, that I was a brave, good girl. It seemed an odd message, for when Mommy stuck me she always said I was bad or evil.

I kept vomiting from the concussion and the doctor told me to lie flat in bed and not wriggle. Nurses brought in sand bags to put by my head and body, to keep me from moving. Terror rose in me at what would come next, but they talked gently and brought me a Popsicle.

I never did tell anyone I had jumped off the balcony on purpose.

I missed three months of the third grade because of the accident. A good portion of the time was spent locked in the closet. Mom would give us breakfast and Dad would go to work, Bobby and Jimmy would leave for school, and Mom would order me into the closet. I would try to smuggle bits of food into my clothes, for there was no lunch in the black stinking space under the stairs. I would hide long string to play with, or rubber bands, anything minutely small that could be a distraction during the long claustrophobic days. If I was caught hiding anything, I was beaten. My greatest escape was my imagination. Emily's and my game-playing became wonders of creativity. We could play a whole game of checkers on an imaginary board, in total blackness. But even then there were endless hours of boredom and anxiety that I would die unnoticed in the closet. My arm in the cast ached and my headaches were fierce.

I think it was about this time that Sunshine came into being. She was a very young personality, who sucked her thumb incessantly and didn't want to grow up. She was the personality who got me in trouble at school by scribbling on the blackboard and printing letters in big scrawly print with her left hand, all messy and wrinkled.

When I finally returned to school, everyone knew their multiplication tables, everyone except me. It seemed as though life had gone on without me and I was overcome by shyness and the humiliation of not understanding the classroom work. At recess I ran from the playground and hid in the bushes. My teacher found me and commanded me to return to the room. It was a horrible year. The teacher was strict and very intimidating. I got F's in arithmetic and cursive writing on my report card. I was used to A's, so I felt deeply ashamed. I didn't tell anyone that I was unaware of time for long stretches and that it was Sunshine doing the work. I had the sensation of being dragged into invisibility somewhere far away and gray. I didn't know why I wasn't like everyone else, but I had been laughed at when I tried to explain Emily, Sunshine, or Camille.

Mrs. Franklin tried to make me feel better by saying, "Of course missing three months of school would put you behind, and your teacher was a very inconsiderate woman for giving you F's."

My asthma continued all through third grade because Mom wouldn't get rid of our puppy. I loved King, but didn't like the wheezing. I had many nights of sitting up in bed struggling to breathe.

"You know Mom is keeping King on purpose just to make you sick," Emily said. We shared the same body, but she never had asthma; at least she always acted like it was only me.

"I love King."

"Then you're stupid!"

"It's not his fault that he has soft fur."

"Of course not! It's Mom's fault for keeping him. Mothers are supposed to take care of their kids."

It was about this time that Emily began stealing, usually tiny little objects, things people wouldn't notice were missing.

Daddy took us to Chinatown, out to a family dinner, and in the little gift shop that smelled of sandalwood incense, Emily stole a tiny carved ivory man, and a little carved deer, both less than two inches high. I blanked out the theft, but when I found them in my pocket later Emmy told me she did it.

"You shouldn't steal things!"

"I can if I want to," Emmy said. "Mom takes everything else from us."

I felt humiliation for being party to a crime, but secretly delighted to have something to play with.

Emily stole other small items once she figured out how easy it was—little pieces of chalk, jacks, and a tiny rubber ball. They were our first possessions. We were smart enough to figure out how to hide our secret stash. I took a thick white sock and put our treasures inside, then folded them to look just like an ordinary pair in the back of the drawer.

At the beginning of summer I went for a happy week to Grandma Bernice's house. She took me to a concert at the Hollywood Bowl and I saw the play, *Peter Pan*. I clapped for Tinkerbell until my hands got sore. Grandma Bernice rubbed my hands with her lavender hand lotion which she retrieved from her huge handbag right while we were sitting in our seats. Then she brought my hand up to her lips and kissed the palm. "I'm glad you love fairies, too," she whispered.

I held up my other hand to be kissed as I smelled the lavender. "But I don't like elves," I whispered back.

When I got home, my mother was almost incoherent in her tirades about my father and his other women, Jews, and her hatred of me. My father had left on a business trip to Washington, D.C., for two months. Mom announced that for the whole time he would be away she did not want to see my Jewish face. I was locked in my room, not to see or play with anyone for the next two months. Desolation overcame me as I sat in my huge, beautiful room with its wooden floors, a wool area rug with lovely big pink roses splashing the edges, a desk and chair, a walk-in closet filled with clothes. There were no toys, no radio, nothing to play with, except my secret little cache of items in the sock drawer.

After the warmth and fun of Grandma Bernice, the isolation was unbearable. Hours dragged by in merciless succession. For days I lay on the big four-poster double bed and looked at the face made by a crack in my ceiling plaster.

Occasionally I cried, but gradually my imagination came to my rescue. There was Emily, who could escape the room. There was Sophie, the imaginary mother, who could think up wonderful stories, which were always about mothers who loved and wanted their children. She seemed to have a limitless number of creative games to suggest. She made a pretend oven of the desk, where truly delicious meals were baked, then fed to the two-inch-high ivory man we named Yen, the only Oriental word I could think of. There was Sunshine, the small child, the needy self, who I took care of. Joey was the one who played the daddy. He was young and Jewish. He could be angry like Emily, and in the long days of isolation he etched his initials into the desk in dozens of places with a nail file. There were others who I do not remember.

The saving grace was a full-length mirror in the bathroom connected to my bedroom. I danced in front of the mirror and shifted from one personality to another, carrying on long conversations, seeing the different images, different faces smiling back at me. The long isolation was reinforcing the dissociation, but for me at that time it was salvation; I was being entertained and saved by my companions.

I saw the sunrise casting pinks around the room and the next thing I would be aware of was a cold dinner sitting on my desk and the sky growing dark outside. Those were the lucky dissociative days; lucid days were harder, seeming to drag on forever. I missed my friends and my violin. I missed Bobby the most.

Mom would come at mealtimes, unlock the door, say nothing to me and leave me a plate of food, then relock the door. I will eternally remember the sound of the dead-bolt being jammed into its lock on the outside of my door.

Bobby never forgot me. He would sneak up when Mom was

busy and send me messages under the door. We played hangman, passing the paper back and forth under the door. We played tic-tac-toe. Comic books were smuggled under the door and I avidly read every one he could bring me. Bobby taught me Morse code by tapping on the door. We could whisper to each other, but we dared not talk aloud and get caught.

From my room I looked into the orange trees, so Bobby climbed clear up in the tree nearest my room and flashed me Morse code with a mirror reflecting the sun. He smuggled me drawing paper and pencils. I spent many happy hours drawing, then hiding my pictures from Mom under my bed.

Mom had learned to drive that year and she had gotten her first car. On the days I heard the car pull out of the driveway, taking Bobby and Jimmy with her, I felt the intense sensation of abandonment. No games, no meals, only my split-self playmates.

Maggie, our Irish maid, had worked for us for years, but she was a nonperson to me. She knew of the violence. She had seen me get burned, she had walked by me tied in a chair. She long ago had told me, "Get away from me, child. I'm sorry for what goes on in this house, but I have six children to feed and I need this job." She could hear me scream or pass on by the closet as though I didn't exist. She was one more adult who looked into my child's eyes of pain and turned away. On days Mom left the house, I hoped Maggie would come to my room, but she never did.

I stood by the hour with my face pressed to the window in the hope of hearing Bobby or Jimmy play, or of seeing a bird fly into the trees. As summer dragged on, Bobby got bored with the under-the-door games and he would ride off on his bicycle. I felt like screaming and flailing my fists at the locked door, but I knew that would just get me hurt. I thought of my school friends playing jump rope and swimming and I would lie on my bed in the hot room and weep.

One of my other personalities (I don't know which one) began to pull my hair out. Whole sections on the front of my head became bald. I don't know why I did it. I was upset when I looked in the mirror, but still I kept doing it.

It was a very hot day when I stood at the window in my endless wait. Then I took a crayon that Bobby had smuggled me and I wrote in bold print on the window: PLEASE COME TO ME. I left it on all day hoping someone would come. Late in the evening, Bobby tapped on my door and whispered, "What did you write on the window? It's backward. Do you want Mom to come hurt you?"

I rubbed it off with an old sock. I was upset when I realized you have to write on glass backward for anyone to read it from the other side. It was like I had sent a flare into fog. I returned to Bobby, who was lying on his stomach by my door. He passed me a note which said, "Don't give up. I love you more than anything. Shall I go to the police?" At the bottom was a picture of the two of us hanging from the ceiling by a rope with a noose around our necks and our tongues hanging out.

"No, don't do anything to make Mom mad." I always talked him out of his rescue ideas. We couldn't fight Mom, Lady Angel, and Fritz. We both cried, and Bobby slid his fingers under the door. He had bitten his nails down to the quick, and even had raw red spots where he had gnawed at the cuticles. His ravaged hands were like a love sign to me. I lay my face down on his fingertips.

Hunger cramped my stomach, for often there was no lunch. I gnawed all my pencils and erasers, and guzzled water from the bathroom sink. In the last month, when Bobby had gone to play with other friends, out of hunger and desolation I began peeling strips of my wallpaper off the walls. At first I tried to peel the white strips between the pink flowers, then in anger I peeled great swaths off the walls and chewed the hunks of paper. The dried paste tasted sweet. After many days of doing this, I became very constipated. Finally, I lay on my bed and whimpered from the pain of the stomachache. After a few days of not touching my dinners, Mom came and talked to me. It was our first conversation in weeks. She saw the missing wallpaper and was angry I had eaten it. She figured out my problem and brought in castor oil and gave me a hot soapsuds enema while I sobbed in agony. Even that didn't work, so she lay me on the bathroom tiles and broke up the cemented paper in my rectum with her finger. There were no words of sympathy as I wailed and bled.

After that she began bringing me lots of food, realizing I was down to a weak collection of bones. I must have looked horrible with my skinny body and bald spots, for she let Bobby bring me dinner. He wasn't allowed to leave until I finished all my food. That was a saving connection to life. Bobby sat on my rug with me and played jacks while I ate during his turn. He even began bringing rich malts and chocolate bars. I think Mom panicked, realizing if I died in the room, she would go to jail.

Just before Daddy returned home I was let out of my room. I was weak from lack of exercise. Mom sat Bobby, Jimmy, and me down and told us we could not tell anyone, especially not Daddy, that I had been in my room for being so wicked. She put terror in our hearts and minds at even the *thought* of telling. She said Fritz and Frieda would be watching every minute. We all took Mom's threats seriously.

Mom had my room rewallpapered and put a lovely lace canopy over my bed. My desk was refinished and she hung a lovely oil painting of the ocean over my desk. My summer looked as though wiped away, but my many selves remembered.

Dad came home and said he was shocked at how skinny and pale I was. Mom said I had been sick all summer, and that I had singed my hair on the gas burner while I was making popcorn.

Dad took all of us, including Mom, on a camping trip to the High Sierras. I was too weak to keep up the hiking, and even Dad was a bit disgusted with me.

Dad made me wear a blue tennis hat to cover my ugly head, which had scabs from where I had pulled the clumps of hair so hard that my scalp had bled. We stopped at one campground. The only time Mom was cruel to me there was in the outhouse. She grabbed me by the back of the neck and shoved my head deep into the stinking latrine hole and said, "I wish when I was pregnant with you I'd have come here and let you be born here." The swill at the bottom left a lasting picture in my mind.

By age nine I was becoming aware of the control Mom had over her own violence. It was calculated, for when Dad was home she would talk sweetly to me and never hurt me. Daddy was the safety for me. Hope would well inside me when Dad was around. Mom braided my hair gently, spoke nicely to me, acted as though I was special. Time after time in my affection-starved existence the hope would begin to sprout in my mind, only to be cruelly dashed again and again.

"Where were you this summer?" Linda asked when we began fourth grade. "Bobby said you were sick and your mother said you were spending the summer with your grandmother. I missed you! Your hair looks awful! What happened to you?"

"I did go see my grandmother, and then I was sick. I burned my hair in an accident." Always the lies.

"It won't take too long to grow bangs where you burned your hair. You look like you went through a lawn mower," Linda giggled.

Miss Dunne was a pleasant fourth-grade teacher, although rather ineffective. She was from the South and moved and spoke slowly, barely able to get her huge bottom between the desks, but she was fun to be around.

We got to oil paint in school, and Miss Dunne asked us to paint a picture of children playing. I painted a big picture of children playing hide-and-seek in the orange trees. To finish the picture I painted in the big window pane in a cross over the picture. When Miss Dunne asked me what the bars were for I became deeply embarrassed. My concept of children playing had been as the viewer from my room.

When I brought the painting home, Mom was livid. She shook me, saying, "Don't you know this is another way of telling people about what I do to you? You are a bad girl." She took a kitchen knife and held it over my fingers, threatening again to cut them off and make them into pickles. Then she took the knife and cut up my painting. I hadn't meant to tell anyone. I never painted again.

Not long after that, someone gave us a slab of venison to cook. This great hunk of meat was lying on the big butcher-block table and Mom was carving the meat off the bone. For no apparent reason she grabbed me and pulled off my blouse and lay me on the table in the blood next to the meat. My arm touched the wet meat. I could smell the blood in my hair. Mom took the knife and held it in front of my face. She said, "You sing and you laugh and you have stolen everyone from me." I didn't have the faintest idea of what she meant. She got crazier and went to the back porch for a rope. The idea of getting off the table while she left the room was not even a thought. Self-preservation no longer existed in my head. Enduring was all I knew.

She came back with the rope and tied me up to make "pot roast of Marcia." She pretended to carve off my arms and legs. "I will give King your shin bones to chew on. I will cook you in the big Dutch oven with onions and mushrooms and your precious Daddy won't even know he is eating you. I will tell everyone you ran away. No one will even know you are dead."

Her face had the faraway crazy look that meant talking with her was useless. Then she took the knife and cut deeply into my right breast. I cried and screamed, begging her to stop. Blood poured out into my armpit. The torture seemed to last a year. There was deer blood in my hair and my own blood ran onto my clothes. My blood mingled with the blood on the table as I twisted and screamed. I didn't know if Mom was going to finish killing me. Looking down, I saw the gaping wound and my blood oozing out. Mom continued to slowly, graphically touch me all over with the knife and tell me all the things she would do to me.

Slipping into a state of shock, not from blood loss but from terror, I think it was one of the few times I lost consciousness, or maybe I just dissociated and consciously left to a safer place.

Later, Mom took me to a doctor I had never seen before and he put stitches in my chest.

It was about a week later, as the stitches in my little flat breast were getting itchy, that Emily came angrily to life and said, "You just lie there and let her do things to our body."

"You know Mom just hurts us worse if we don't lie quiet."

"Well, I don't have to be nice. You're the nice one. I hate her."

As I watched, an observer from a distant place, Emily, my body, my hands, picked up the raw liver that Mom had soaking in a bowl of milk in the kitchen. Emily picked up the cold, slimy, dark organ and in ever intensifying anger began smearing the bloody liver on the counter, the walls, the kitchen table on which I had lain and been cut. She smashed the liver around and bashed it until little purple-red globs stuck on the walls. The liver was ruined and the kitchen a disaster. I was frightened at what Emily had done. Hours later Mom found me hiding under the dirty clothes in the hamper. She dragged me crying into the kitchen, where she put my finger in the nutcracker and squeezed it until I heard the bone go crunch.

Dad put his foot down about King because he was home enough in the fall to see the severity of my asthma.

While Dad was at work, Mom got the dog in the living room and fed him strychnine inside ground meat. She made us sit and watch King writhe around and vomit and finally die. It seemed as though we were forced to watch for hours. Mom kept saying "We mustn't let things suffer."

She explained to Bobby and Jimmy that it was my fault we had to kill King. As I was sobbing in my room later, Bobby came in and said he knew it wasn't my fault. "Mom's crazy. She could have given King away. He was a beautiful dog. I hate her guts."

Bobby could always express the anger I never could.

Jimmy was just six and didn't talk to me for a long time. He believed I was the reason King had to die.

True to our code of silence, Dad knew nothing of the murder. He assumed we had given King to someone. He brought home a little black kitten because we were all so dejected after the experience. He said it had to be an outside cat and for me not to hold it. Jimmy perked up a bit having an animal to play with.

One day Mom was backing the car out of the garage and I saw her face as she deliberately ran over Bootsie the kitten. It screamed in pain as its back legs were crushed. It tried to drag itself forward. Mom said, "Oh, dear. We mustn't let things suffer" as she put the car in first gear and ran over Bootsie again, killing her this time. Jimmy cried for days.

The big pewter nutcracker became a very disabling form of abuse. Most of the time it just flattened my finger, leaving the imprint of the metal teeth, but occasionally I heard my bone go snap and I knew my finger had been broken. Twice in the fall of the fourth grade I had broken fingers on my right hand. Mom would splint the finger with a Popsicle stick and bandage it, but writing in school was nearly impossible. It ruined recess, too, for it was hard to play games with broken fingers.

Miss Dunne asked how I broke my finger.

"I fell off my bicycle." Again the lies.

"You certainly seem to hurt yourself often."

Looking at the ground to keep from bursting into tears, I said, "I'm sorry. I'm just not very careful."

"You better slow down. You do things too quickly."

"Yes, ma'am, I'll try."

Sitting in school was always an agony with the bruises and inflamed private parts. I used to dread urinating at school because sometimes it burned so much I couldn't breathe or walk for a few minutes.

I was just turning ten at Christmastime in fourth grade, and I had accomplished what I considered to be the supreme feat of my life. For his birthday, just before mine, my dad asked me for one present—that I stop sucking my thumb. It was the hardest thing I ever did. For nights I couldn't sleep. My mouth felt desert parched. There are no smokers more addicted to nicotine than I was to the security of my thumb. It had been juicy when I was thirsty, provided comfort in the closet, reassurance after the brutality.

That day, decorating the Christmas tree, I was feeling happy and proud of myself because Daddy acknowledged the gift, the effort I'd made for him. I was singing and rearranging the balls on the tree. Mom came in and said, "Stop that annoying singing." I stopped, then forgot about it and began singing again in my clear child's voice. Mom went to the fireplace and picked up the poker. She lunged at me with it, but thrust it harder than she meant to and the sharp end impaled me in the side.

I crumpled in pain in a ball on the floor, certain that she had at last managed to kill me. Blood was spurting from the hole in my side.

Mom quickly got a towel, packed it in my side and carried me to the car, laying me on the backseat. She cried on the way to the hospital. "Marcia, baby, I am so sorry. I don't know why I do the things I do to you. I don't know why I can't love you. I'm sorry."

Rather than threaten me, she begged me not to tell Daddy or the doctors she had caused my injury. Of course I lied, saying I'd fallen on the poker.

A piece of my liver had been cut, so I had to stay in the hospital over Christmas. Daddy came every day, staying even into the nights. He looked pale and haggard. He would stroke my head and bring me surprises and read me stories.

Christmas in the hospital was a happy time with carolers, little toys on the food trays, and cookies. All the nurses were very gentle with me. My doctor questioned my story of how I fell on the poker. I cried and said, "I don't want to talk about it."

The self of me had been fragmented, split into compartments to hold the pain and anger. With all its intelligence and creativity, my mind had found a way to save me. But what was survival for the child was not a functional way of life for the adult. I had become a multiple personality.

Chapter 4

Putting experiences into words as I have done in this last chapter puts structure, sequence, a kind of rational overview to events that were not at all that way. How can I adequately describe terror? How can I put into words what some of these events were like in my internal self? I write as though there was a cohesive, sane thread running through my existence when there was not. It was external and internal chaos. Even as I write, I am aware that I am writing as my Marcia personality remembers it. Emily would write a whole different book. Her tale would be of rage at being locked up, being hurt. She would write how she hated everyone by the time she began school, trusting no one, stealing pencils and milk money from other students' desks. She would stand defiantly in front of the principal and deny that she stole the teacher's watch during recess.

She was the designated Guard personality, the one who had an internal radar for danger. She could read every gesture, every twitch of an eyebrow on Mom. She ran outside to the trees, or hid in the garage at the merest hint of Mom's rising anger. Emily was crafty, clever, and totally self-serving. She would only save me because our bodies were the same.

I write with love and attachment to many. Emily loved no one. She had a job that she learned early: survival. Cheat. Steal. Lie. Manipulate. Be cute. Smile. She was a human coyote who learned to survive where other life forms wither away.

In her anger Emily could escalate the abuse from Mom. A deliberately sassy walk, an ever so quiet mutter of words, a deliberate smashing of a plate. Not often, for survival was her chief role, but enough, just enough to convey "I hate you back" to Mom.

I write as though I remember a time when she was not there. I really do not. From my earliest memories that sink into dark murk and feelings of anxiety, I shared life with Emily. She was my playmate, my friend, my enemy, my protector—as I was hers. Control slid with fluid ease back and forth between us. I imagine conjoined twins learn the same sort of interactive relationship. There were agreements and arguments on who got body time. This sounds vastly complex, but compared to my outside world of unexpected, horrific violence this was not a stress. Emily was comfort. I got secret satisfaction at her rage. She did what I was too terrified to do. She was aggressive while I was sweet.

Emily had two big passions—eating chocolate and playing hopscotch. From my earliest memories I can see her—us—jumping on one foot. She jumped on all the designs of our huge living-room carpet. She hopped upstairs and downstairs. She hopped in the closet. I think the hopping might have served as a release of tension; I don't know. I would get so tired and Emily would still be hopping, hopping.

I was the braid chewer and Emily was the hopper. I would gnaw endlessly on the ends of my long braids. There was juice in the hair, just as there was in my thumb. When they finally dried, the ends would be all stiff. My teachers would yank them out of my mouth, saying it was disgusting, but it was a pain-relieving and calming habit.

Emily was a more twitchy, nervous person than I was. Mom would slap us for her grimaces and rhythmic twitches.

I thought it was truly horrible that Emily liked pink. We had a pink dress that I would only let her wear on Thursdays. That was pink day. She also liked a silver dog pin she had stolen and kept insisting we wear, making me nervous the police would find out. Emily didn't care about things like jail. She would jay-walk across a busy street. I was the kind who would wait at a corner for a green light.

She was bolder than I was, saying what she thought more than I did. People liked her even though she didn't really care if they did or didn't. I always cared. I wanted desperately to be loved. Emily was louder and funnier, with an irrepressible sense of humor. She said things at school that made everyone laugh. It embarrassed me when she caused my classmates to turn and look at us, but she liked attention. Sometimes she would say or do something on purpose to humiliate me or draw attention to me, for I blushed fairly easily. It was really weird—Emily never blushed. She took delight in my flaming pink cheeks.

Emily was far more calculating. She liked the attention she got from being cute. Even in grammar school she knew how to hug people, or touch their hands in a way that would have them be warm back. I never was as daring, except once or twice with teachers. I shrank from touching, always afraid that contact would mean pain.

Emily loved to decorate our school projects with drawings and doodles. She took pens and drew flowers around the burn scars on our legs. She would color a clown face on a big black-and-blue patch on our thigh or some other hidden body area. She stole a pink pencil and colored our toenails pink.

She loved cosmetics. Every chance she had, she put them on. Halloween was always her favorite holiday, since she could wear lots of makeup. She always wanted to be a princess or a lady, creating the image with rags stuffed in one of Mom's old dresses to make it seem we had breasts. I always wanted to go in a pirate outfit, or a ghost costume. We used to fight about this, but she always got her way, so every year we'd wobble around the neighborhood in high-heeled shoes going trick-or-treating.

I always wanted to have a long neck like Audrey Hepburn, because once I heard my dad say how he loved her long neck. Emily always wanted big lips. She deliberately pushed ours out to give a full, pouty look. She took pomegranate juice and stained our lips red, or took the watercolor brush and painted on red lips, telling me not to lick the color off. In third grade she swished the thick red poster paint and colored us a deep crimson. I got in trouble for that. I also was punished for her habit of eating the sticky white library paste at school.

She loved to play dress-up games, probably adding to our dissociative abilities. She'd smuggle clothes out of Bobby's closet, or use Dad's or Mom's clothes and concoct hilarious outfits where we would be someone else. She could invent great escapist stories as we pranced in front of the bathroom mirror.

The movie *Lili* with Leslie Caron made a big impression on both of us. After that we played for weeks with puppets made out of socks and we danced and twirled in front of the mirror by the hour. In the movie the unloved little waif found love. All our fractured selves fell into the magic of that story.

Any movies, books, fairy tales, or television shows we saw at other children's houses became fuel for our imaginative play. We invented and reinvented ourselves. In the end of our pretend dramas I found love, and Emily found adventure and excitement far from the confines of the closet.

It surprises me that I am the one who survived as the stronger self, not Emily. She was angrier, more extroverted, more manipulative, the headstrong, impulsive one, prone to dominating me and in communication with the other personalities. I hardly knew the other selves. I almost never talked to them. What I knew is mostly what Emily told me, and I filled in the lapse spaces of memory with what friends told me I did. It is only now that I am integrated that I am recovering memory of what the others did or were. Just as the memories of abuse surface, the memories of my others are becoming my own.

I certainly wasn't dissociating all the time, for then I would have been rendered nonfunctional. Stress, pain, terror, and isolation, were some of the things that made me shift into other selves.

I was very tiny when I began filling in the blank spaces, the inconsistencies. Not being able to account for minutes or hours of time, finding myself in different clothes or geographical locations, was just an accepted part of my life. I became very adept at scanning the scene and putting together what the others inside had just done or said.

I would feel bewildered at moments coming back to dominance after a time lapse, and was always the one who was left picking up the loose threads of life. Emily and the others simply existed and acted out their own little roles while I was left to explain to people or apologize for what my body had done while I was not there. I was very young when I figured out no one believed that Emily had done things, or Joey or Sunshine. They laughed at me. I learned to simply apologize. "I'm sorry, I don't know why I did that." I knew inside it hadn't been me, but it was easier just to look at a teacher or a school friend with my big, innocent blue eyes and just say, "I'm sorry." I was forgiven for a multitude of sins because part of me was gentle and cute.

My behavior was erratic because my many selves didn't connect with each other. Because of the continual social confusion, we all agreed to try to cooperate. I was the one who seemed to constantly be trying to organize the others.

We all learned very early on to stick by "The Code." When I was very young I'd learned about the Boy Scout Code of Honor from Tim who lived down the street and played with Bobby. He had patches and badges, and I was enthralled with the idea of having a code of honor. I made Emily talk to the other selves; we made some rules, such as that they had to call themselves Marcia in public. They weren't allowed to hit or bite even when they were angry. Sunshine wasn't allowed to suck her thumb in public and Camille wasn't allowed to be blind in the street. The list was long. Emily was the code keeper.

Emily and I were definitely the two main personalities. There was always a dialogue in my head, from my earliest memories. We would discuss taking turns. She liked arithmetic, so I would let her do all the math in school. Most of the time when Emily was using our body it was as if I were the distant observer, watching as though a gauze curtain had been dropped over me. I would shrink tinier and tinier. Away, far way, through the shimmer of white gauze I would see and hear, but I would not participate. I'd watch from my small safe space as she did bold or angry things. Sometimes even with Emily I would disappear, just gone, ceasing to exist for an increment of time.

Maybe you've been driving a car, stopping and starting and turning yet five miles down the road you realize you don't remember anything you've just done. The mind went elsewhere. I'm certain dissociating is like that.

There was comfort in the closet to have another voice, a playmate. Emily began as a friend. I liked her when we were little, even admiring her spunk and anger. There was a satisfying expenditure of emotional and creative energy dealing with the other selves. None of it was conscious choice, merely a way of organizing chaos and horror. At the time it was a sane way to survive an insane mother. It was putting structure to my inner world, which held no safety in my outer world.

It is only now that I am less crazy that I can look back at my mind before and try to communicate what it was like to be split into different selves. It was continual nonequilibrium. It was like being caught in an avalanche of snow and rocks, where the turning, churning, never stops. It was a life with no grounding, no soft center, no inner quiet.

Life had the feel of a carnival room with crazy mirrors. Everywhere there were distortions, lack of orientation, an unrelenting sense of anxiety. But whatever my inner distortions were, they were nothing, truly nothing, compared to the abuse.

There are no adequate words for what it was like to lie in bed at night and wonder if this was the night Mom would come in my room and plunge a knife into me. Stepping out of bed in the morning, feeling the pains as I moved my battered body, I'd wonder if this was the day my eyes would get poked out. I'd check my room and closet feeling the urgent need to keep it memorized for the time she finally blinded me. The endless stress of survival— the hunger, the bone-chilling cold of the closet in winter, the thirst in summer. The eyes that must see the coming danger at all times. The small hands that must always be careful not to spill and the feet that must not be noisy or bump things. The ears that listened to every nuance of sound in the big house. I resolved my death. I drifted away from the terror. Multiplicity is a way of numbing what is more horror than the mind can deal with. It's a way of organizing the mixed messages. I was Daddy's Sunshine. I was Mom's Jewish child meant to be tortured and killed, for Jews were meant to die. I was good. I was bad. I was isolated for endless hours. I endured unrelenting physical pain. It turns the mind into a hodgepodge of vibrant disarray.

Dissociation is a form of self-abuse, when one puts feelings and actions out of the realm of conscious choice. Emily even liked pain. I remember one time she took a needle and thread when I was a teenager and sewed black cross-stitched X's on the soles of our feet. I pulled them out later with tweezers. She stuck needles in our nipples and wove pink thread around and around them.

I imagine schizophrenia isn't far removed from dissociation, when one reorganizes reality to reach some new way of finding a sense of safety.

There is a certain safety in multiplicity. There is emotional satisfaction, too. I was horrified to watch Emily steal or Joey hit people, but there was pleasure, too, at seeing them brave enough to do what I never could. It was like going to the movies and watching the Terminator level a room of bad guys. There was so much inside pain, I let the pain find expression in the actions of others because it was inconsistent with what I could accept doing. I accepted public blame, but I never felt guilt for what the others did.

As a small child my multiplicity was not upsetting to me, but as I became a teenager I was very upset and humiliated by my others.

Keeping friends, interrelating with people when my behavior and intactness were so variable, was a stress that made me retreat from any social life. I functioned, but it is only now that I am finding some predictability in my life that I know the enormous stress multiplicity produces.

What is merely unacceptable acting out for a child is truly humiliating as an adult. I had a self called Closet Baby who would sometimes wet her pants in grammar school. Once she came out when I was marketing as an adult, loaded baby bottles and rattles that she wanted in the shopping cart, and urinated on the floor at the check-out counter. There were times as an adult when all I could do was burst into tears of shame, leave, then not ever return to the place of my humiliation.

Adults are expected to have control over impulses and feelings. I did not. Even when I was small I tried to find a way to control my inner group—hence The Code.

Joey was the worst offender at breaking The Code. It seemed there was always trouble when Joey came out. I couldn't talk to him like Emily could. I was always trying to piece the story together later. Joey would fight. In second grade he jumped on the back of the class bully, a boy named Red, who tripped kids as they went to their desks and squashed sandwiches. Joey pummeled him with our fists, giving him a bloody nose and black eye.

When he was out he wanted to be a boy and even told the teachers after one fight that he was Joey, not Marcia, and spit on her. Later, when I was in detention after school, I felt deeply ashamed for what he did and had to listen to the teacher lecture me about hitting, spitting, and even lying about who I was.

"Marcia, you make no sense at all. One minute you can be sweet and cooperative. The next you can be an aggressive, angry child. Your schoolwork is unpredictable, too. You turn in beautiful, neat papers one day and scribbled, messy ones the next. You must try harder. What is wrong with you. Are you unhappy?"

"No. I'm fine. I'll try to be better."

Joey liked sports of all kinds. He liked messy things—clay, mud, spitballs. He rejected all things feminine.

Joey was obsessed with the idea of being hungry. He sometimes stole food out of other kids' lunchpails, since Mom sometimes sent us to school with too little. After school he picked through the trash barrels when no one was looking and smuggled half-eaten apples or thrown-away sandwiches in our lunch box. He stashed food in every crevice of our bedroom he could find. Ants became a problem in our room, especially when he put jelly sandwiches under our shoes or underwear. I remember being angry at Joey when I had to shake ants off my underpants before putting them on in the morning.

Joey was a very oral person. Not only did he like food to the point of obsession, but he was probably the world's best bubble gum blower. He was passionate about bubble gum. He picked it up off sidewalks, out of trash cans, stole it, coerced friends out of it. He could chew three pieces at a time, sometimes four. He kept stashes of chewed, hardened bubble gum behind the headboard of our bed and under our desk at school. It took only a little while to get it soft again. He sneaked a stack of chewed wads of gum in the closet so when we had our interminable hours there he could practice and practice. I didn't like that because my jaws got sore and Joey didn't care that the huge bubbles popped and got stuck on my eyelashes and eyebrows.

Joey was proud of being Jewish. When he looked in the mirror, he saw the strong Jewish face of the grandfather he'd seen in pictures on Grandma Bernice's bedroom wall. He wanted to be very tall and wear glasses on his big nose. No one but Grandma Bernice ever talked about Jews. Joey knew very little, but what he could find out he clung to.

Someone gave me a Beanie and Cecil hat when I was about six. Joey took the little helicopter blades off the top and used it for a yarmulke. Alone in our room when I would unbraid my hair, Joey would come out and put a twisted tendril of hair in front of his ears and tuck the rest of the hair up under the cap.

One holiday a big box came from Germany. One of Mom's relatives had sent it, and in the bottom of the box was a beautiful candle with little wax chickens and roses on it. Joey took the candle and hid it in our room. On Hanukkah Joey lit it and put on the beanie cap and draped a little shawl he'd made from a strip of an old sheet over his shoulders. He made up his own little prayers and chants in jibberish or singsong words. He didn't even know what being Jewish meant, but in his heart he was a good Jew.

He was also a very angry Jew. He hated Mom. He was angry at Dad for being a Jew and never, ever talking about it. When he grew up he was going to be a rabbi with a beard and chant wonderful things in a temple.

He coveted Bobby's BB gun. Joey liked the idea of revenge. He played dark, violent death games with the little clay figures he made. He took great delight in helping Bobby put a cherry bomb in an anthill and blowing it to smithereens. Sophie was angry. She got upset when Joey wanted to kill things.

Sophie was Jewish, too. She was born old. From my earliest memories she was an old woman. She was a nurturing self, a gentle, kind care-giver. Sophie loved cooking and tea parties. She loved making food look beautiful on plates, like a lovely picture. She enjoyed preparing food for Joey who was always hungry.

She adored plants. She took care of daffodil bulbs in the backyard and checked them every day to see how high they had grown. She planted vegetables in secret garden plots behind the orange trees. One summer she grew and ate a whole patch of her own carrots, which she watered with a heavy sprinkling can.

Sophie grew sweet potatoes held up with toothpicks in glass Skippy peanut butter jars. She enjoyed seeing the stems trail down to the floor and search for light. She always identified with those potato plants, how the leaves always knew where the window was. Sophie always knew where the window was, too. She was always looking out, waiting.

She was a melancholy self. Death was the constant theme for Sophie. She thought about it, worried about it. She was into global grieving. She cut out pictures of starving Jews behind barbed-wire fences from *Life* magazine. She kept the pictures in the bottom drawer and on regular occasions would take the pictures out and rock back and forth, back and forth, crying, studying the bony faces to try to understand the reason behind all the suffering.

Every animal Mom killed was a trauma for Sophie. After the dead pets were buried in the backyard, Sophie would go and dig them up at regular intervals to see what stage of decomposition they were in. When she dug up King with a shovel a few months after he was buried and found he had no eyes anymore, she covered him back up and rocked back and forth on the mound of dark dirt and mourned. Mourning to Sophie was sort of a Hopi Indian chant she'd seen in a movie once. It was just the right sort of sound for grief.

She dug Bootsie back up and put her in a shoe box. Sophie didn't even care that Bootsie's body was all squashed from the car and her stomach wasn't even there anymore. Sophie wrapped the kitten in a soft cloth and would bring her out from under the bed and rock and pet the soft fur. I was the one who had to throw the cat away; Sophie would have just kept petting and petting it.

She put our favorite white rat that Mom killed in our blue lunchpail wrapped in Kleenex. Sophie took the rat out of the lunchpail every day after school and held the stiff little creature in her hand and softly stroked it with her index finger. It began to stink in the lunchbox and made my sandwiches taste peculiar. I dumped it in the trash can at school. Emily said Sophie was all upset about it.

She picked dead things off the sidewalk to carry around—beetles, spiders, long worms that had drowned after a heavy rain. She would put the worms in my coat pocket. I always jumped at the cold, slimy feel when I reached into the pocket because I wouldn't see Sophie do it. Her obsession with dead things really made me angry sometimes. Joey would stomp on worms or snails, Sophie would pick them up, I would step over them, and Emily would hop around them in circles.

Camille was very sweet and quiet. Some of my most humiliating moments have been when it was Camille's turn to have the body. It was next to impossible to explain to anyone why I was seen running into things or feeling my way through the sightless world of Camille.

"I was just playing a game," I lied to whoever confronted me with my unusual behavior.

"You are the strangest child," said one teacher. "You are like quicksilver the way you change constantly. Sometimes I don't understand you at all."

Camille was a perfect victim; docile and apathetic to the world. More than anything she wanted to be loved. She thought if she didn't cry or protest when we were being hurt that maybe, just maybe we would be loved. Camille loved Mom and Dad— and nearly everybody. She was wonderfully heroically blind.

This personality really made Bobby and Jimmy angry. "Stop pretending you can't see," demanded Bobby. "You're acting really stupid."

Camille organized our drawers and room to function in her blackened world. She knew the number of steps from one room to another and that there were eighteen steps down the back stairway.

She was lovely and frail, with tiny little wrists and a long neck. Camille would count the steps into Mom and Dad's room when they weren't around and go in Mom's closet and sniff the Wind Song cologne she always wore. She would feel in Mom's drawers for her folded sweaters and hold the cashmere to her face and bury her nose in the soft armpits to get the smell of Mom. She stood in the darkened closet of the very person who had stabbed her eyes out and sniffed the body smells of the mother she wished would hold her. She yearned for softness. She liked the feel of Mom's real silk blouses. There had been nothing soft in our room since Pooh Bear was killed.

She would count the precise steps to the bathroom and pat herself gently with Mom's Yardley bath powder, feeling the soft powder puff against her skin. Then she would wash it off, certain of being beaten for touching anything that was Mom's.

Camille would go to Dad's closet and feel all the nubby jackets, the tweeds and woven wools, and smell the wonderful aroma of him. She even liked the stench of his weekend socks thrown in the back of the closet.

For a while Dad smoked a pipe, and Camille sniffed the tobaccos in the can and sucked on the bitter pipe end. She liked the idea that what was in his mouth was in her mouth.

There was no anger in Camille, no survival drive. She was perfectly content to be blind or to die. It made no difference to her. She didn't deal with concepts of fair or right and wrong. Life simply was as it was.

She liked strong flavors in her mouth. She sucked bay leaves and cloves from the kitchen cupboard and sucked on cut lemons. She felt her way outside and sucked the drops of nectar out of the honeysuckle flowers, standing still so the bees wouldn't sting her and breathed in the fragrance of the flowers through her nose in long, slow breaths. Camille found pleasure in the midst of blackness.

Sunshine was six. No matter how old I got, she stayed six, and a very immature six. She wanted bears, soft, fuzzy ones she could cuddle. She spoke in a high little kid voice and she liked the dark closet. Sometimes she would go into the closet and sit in the blackness and be very small, nearly invisible. She wasn't a big problem when I was young, but as I became an adult, she was deeply embarrassing. She sometimes took over when Emily was running wild. She would emerge when strangers were making love to Emily and make everything even more confusing. Emily would pace and scream at how Sunshine screwed everything up.

Sunshine was a nest builder, with blankets and pillows and shiny trinkets. She was attracted to sparkles, like a blue jay. She decorated her tiny arms with glittery bracelets and kept stashes of fake diamond jewelry, hiding them in pillow slips. She had the terrible habit of biting herself and sucking on our arms and leaving big purple marks. I used to get angry because it was hard enough in school to hide Mom's abuse, let alone Sunshine's.

It's extremely difficult to explain away regressed behavior as an adult. It was far easier to cover for Emily's flirtatious, promis-

cuous behavior; at least it was accepted more readily in the adult
world than a young child's voice asking a man if she could suck
his nipples for a while. Sunshine was like one of those cats that
didn't get nursed long enough. She always wanted to suck things.
She was trusting and innocent and never saw danger.

Closet Baby wasn't even a real personality. She was a very tiny
child who only longed and felt. She wet and cried and curled up
in a little ball. Sometimes she needed to come out and get in a
crawling position and rock back and forth, just trying to stop the
pain with a rhythm. She'd lie with her chest on the bed and her
legs drawn up under her and her rear in the air like a stink bug on
alert and rock her bottom back and forth. She'd rock until she
became so small she was invisible. She rocked until she didn't see
the blood anymore. She rocked until she was just a breeze flowing
through the room. A speck. A molecule. An atom . . .

The personality who means the least to me is Muriel. I don't
know when she came into being, or why. She was very rarely
around when I was a child. She came out more when I was an
adult. I didn't like her. She was condescending to the rest of us
and rather bossy. She was also an outgoing, loved, funny person.
She was English, and so very proud of having parents who were
artists.

She did have some good qualities. She had zest for living; she
actually *liked* life. She loved the cultural things—classical music
and beautiful paintings. She liked to take a day and wander
through an art museum.

Keeping Muriel from taking off on an adventure was a problem. She loved to travel and see new things, meet new people. She
was the flamboyant, people-loving, cultured lady. She knew fine
wines and could tell exactly what spices flavored a new food. She
craved new sensations, new sights, new sounds. Every room she
entered she collected a new friend. She felt disdain for my limited
world with my many fears and panics. She dressed boldly on her
outings and was drawn to French cafés and strong coffee. She was
fearless, for her childhood had been happy and secure. She talked
endlessly about her family in England and the shopping sprees
she had shared with her mother in London.

Joey couldn't stand her. He thought she was phony, with all
her interest in Van Gogh and Brie cheese with fresh garlic and

pine nuts. She collected obscure bits of knowledge to sound intriguing to strangers. She had a wealth of statistics, and if in doubt she made them up. She was entertaining before she was accurate, the story far more important than the reliability.

Everyone loved Muriel. She saved my life at some social functions. She was the perfect cocktail party guest with her big smile and effervescent trivia sprinkling the conversation.

Unfortunately, like Joey, she broke the Code of Honor, feeling she was above the system of rules for the plebeians she was stuck sharing space with. She deeply complicated my life by introducing herself as Muriel to people and giving my phone number to strangers. Not just men, but charity organizations asking me to help with fund-raising, or women she had charmed in shopping malls who called to invite me over.

Muriel liked to help people and spread cheer. There was one period of time in my early twenties when Muriel took over a great deal and decided to explore Christianity. She got baptized four times in different churches, once in The Church of Christ by immersion. The small church congregation had a special coffee reception for her after the service. Later Emily came out and asked the pastor if he wanted to fuck her. I pieced all this together when the pastor came to my house with a Bible and said he would pray for my soul, for I was a wicked sinner. He asked me if I was a virgin and got me so confused as to what was going on, I cried and told him to leave my house. I begged Muriel to stop the escapades.

Joey was furious at the baptisms since he was the devout Jew. He went into a synagogue once and, in talking to a rabbi, found out he wasn't even a Jew since his mother was German. He rejected that information and dug the beanie hat out of a drawer and with a blue felt pen drew the Star of David all over his body. Standing in front of the mirror with blue stars everywhere, he could see his circumcised penis between his legs.

There was as much conflict between Joey and Muriel as there was between Emily and me. Joey was always angry, Muriel cheerful and enthusiastic.

She was terrible with money, running up excessive purchases on our one credit card. As an adult I never accepted a card with a credit limit over five hundred dollars for fear Muriel would go on a spending spree.

She was wonderfully generous, giving every last dollar in our purse to any beggar who approached her. On cold winter days she gave her coat and sweaters to old people who didn't look warm enough to her.

One Thanksgiving, when I was married and expecting my in-laws for the holiday dinner, Muriel boxed up the roasted twenty-pound turkey and all the trimmings and drove it to the shelter for abused women. She was the light-hearted giver, and I was left to face the consequences of serving barbecued hamburgers to all the family, since it was too late to cook another turkey. This just added strain to my relationship with my husband's family. Their assessment that I was odd was very accurate.

As an adult Emily was the personality who stressed my life the most with her stealing and promiscuity. I felt ongoing, deep humiliation over her exploits. Sophie wandering through cemeteries, or Sunshine lying in the closet with mounds of blankets and stacks of glittery bracelets were nothing compared to finding myself with a half-drunk man in some motel that smelled of old cigarettes and room freshener, with flashing lights blinking on and off past the filmy windows. I hated that more than anything my other selves did. Young boys. Old stinking men. Guys with beer guts so big they could barely have sex.

She liked speed. Everything had to be fast. Fast sex. Fast cars. Fast music with a strong beat. Roller coasters. Carnival rides. She found an adrenaline high could made the pain stop. Why she didn't become a drug abuser I don't know. Maybe because I could alter reality without chemicals.

Before I'd even gotten a driver's license, Emily stole a big green car with the tail fins flaring in back. Someone had left the car keys shimmering on the floor mat. Emily drove on the freeway to Long Beach where she rode roller coasters until her money was gone. She returned the car in the dark to where she'd stolen it.

At seventeen she flirted herself into a job as a topless dancer in Hollywood, but the job only lasted until the second night, when the owner asked for her proof of age.

She talked friends into escapades in high school. She went

with two friends to Skid Row in Los Angeles just to see what it was like and another time to Pershing Square to see the old Chinese man they'd heard about who had curling fingernails about a foot long. They found him and shared cigarettes with him just to see how he could manage with the long nails. Emily was never short of ideas.

We had different sets of friends, which was extremely difficult to juggle. We didn't like the same people. Emily smoked in the bathrooms at recess and I never did. I liked science and tried to be a good student. I loved the library. Emily loved the football games and school assemblies.

My behavior swings did not go unnoticed. I knew I was often the topic of conversation among my peers—I was "a head case." I confided in no one. Only Bobby and Jimmy knew about my other selves. They could tell which one was out. Jimmy especially liked Joey because he'd go outside and play baseball with him. Bobby really liked Emily because she was lots of fun. The secret of the many selves was as safe with them as the abuse. We all lived in a world that made no sense. As I became an adult we stopped talking about my many selves. The shifting attitudes and behaviors were then just part of their view of who I was. The integration of my many selves into one whole was slightly upsetting to Bobby, who sees how much I've changed. He liked my more flamboyant aspects! In the incorporation, some characteristics of the others have become part of me, others haven't.

What deeply embarrasses me now is how I was willing to maintain a structure built on self-deception for so long. Now it seems logical that there is no way one body of a given sex and chronological age can house other selves of varying sexes and ages—and even claim different parents!

Everyone is capable of inner dialogues, like when you're considering buying a car and list the pros and cons, or when you have conflicting feelings about anything. My true mental illness is that I honestly believed the others were real. Now, that is crazy! I made an inner comfort zone as a child, a set of characteristics and attributes that I labeled and identified as separate entities in order to deal with ongoing trauma.

The other day I said to Dr. Steinman, "I must have been a

little nuts." He smiled and said, "No, you were a lot nuts. Now you're just a little nuts."

I also feel embarrassed at looking back at decades of an elaborately maintained self-deception. The mental illness is that I was willing to forego holding up my thoughts, beliefs, and behaviors to any external reality that would let me examine myself.

It's difficult to sit down and write a book and expect anyone to believe that I could go to college, be married, have children, function on a basic, though erratic level, and maintain this insanity. I feel like Edgar Allan Poe taking pen in hand, expecting anyone to find credibility in this account when I am clearly the unreliable narrator. "Believe me though I am quite mad . . ."

It's very easy to see now that all the "others" were just pieces of me, rather like a jigsaw puzzle that gets badly put together by a child, the extra pieces just tacked on haphazardly around the edges. But most children grow and learn how the puzzle actually fits together and will rearrange it to make a whole picture.

For me the inner threat was so monumental that I was willing to die, or run, or maintain a rigid denial of reality to keep from dealing with the memories and pain. I was willing to live life like a screwed-up puzzle because the threat to the lopsided structure was too great.

It is of no consequence to me whether anyone believes it's possible to be a multiple personality. All I can tell you is that there was more safety for me in a pretend structure than the real world; safety to the point that I would overlook scars on my body, time lapses, humiliation, erratic behavior, criminal behavior.

I would not have given up my mental illness if it hadn't been my perception that suicide was the only other alternative. To give up this ridiculous cling to madness has been the most difficult journey of my life, for I have had to claim all the pain and memories I had so carefully divided and subdivided. I had risked functioning, relationships, my actual safety for the safety of the frantic diversionary tactics of multiplicity.

Now that I am a singular person it is difficult to acknowledge the glaring stupidity I was willing to live with my whole life. Multiple personalities make for great movies but the real pain and pathology seems lost in the drama.

Chapter 5

"Why isn't she hitting us?" Emily asked.

"I don't know," I whispered back. "Maybe she's waiting for a special time to kill us."

"She's probably waiting for Dad to leave town."

At first I thought it was only because I'd been in the hospital that Mom wasn't hurting me. When I had come home after being stabbed with the poker, there was a hero's welcome for me. Linda came with her mom, the first time ever in my home. She marveled at the beautiful house I lived in.

But in the night I could hear terrible fights between my father and mother. I could even hear my name in the shouting.

I don't know what transpired between them, but I do know a miraculous thing happened. At the age of ten, the physical abuse against me stopped. I was hated, I was psychologically tormented, but I don't remember ever again being physically hurt by Mom.

It embarrassed me the way sometimes at bedtime Dad would take off my clothes and turn me around and look at me. He never asked me anything, he would just look at me intently, then blow on my neck, pat my fanny or tickle me. He stayed home more, and was the one who put us to bed at night. When the light stayed longer in the evenings, we played baseball outside and kick-the-can in the street.

For the first time in my life, I wasn't in pain. I must have eaten better without the constant hurting, for I began to plump out. I was no longer the tiniest in school.

Dad said I could join the Girl Scouts with my friends. Linda and I had a good time learning to tie knots and making crafts. When Mrs. Franklin became the troop leader, I couldn't even concentrate in school on the Tuesdays we had the meetings. I was jealous, though, sharing Mrs. Franklin with my other friends. I glowed with pride when the troop voted that I carry the banner in our local parade. Dad even helped us at our pancake breakfast.

There was a terrible scene at our house when Dad fired Maggie, our maid. She begged and cried, and Mom cried. In a commanding voice Dad said things about her "guilt of silence." I ran into the orange trees and hid from the emotional confrontation.

Daddy hired Ruth, an attractive middle-aged woman, to be our maid. Bobby and I decided she must be expensive since she spoke well and dressed elegantly. She wasn't as good as Maggie at cleaning, but she was sweet. She let me help cook things in the kitchen. When we came home from school, she was there with us until Dad returned from work. If he was late Ruth stayed with us, acting as if it was no inconvenience at all.

Mom cried in her room a great deal. She hardly spoke to us.

Bobby said Ruth had probably been hired by Dad to make sure Mom didn't hurt us. I still wasn't sure what Dad knew, for he had never asked me, but it did seem that Ruth was more body-guard and nanny than maid. We were certain of our guess when Dad hired a cleaning lady to come once a week to vacuum and scrub.

We began to feel safe with Ruth around. Bobby and I didn't even care that Mom was in her room all the time. One day we could hear her sobbing behind the door. Ruth couldn't comfort her. At night Dad couldn't get her to control her crying. Daddy took her to a hospital. She was gone several weeks. To have full rein of the house without Mom gave me a delightful sense of freedom. I could run in the great expanse of hallway. Jimmy and I slid down the great carved bannister. We jumped down the laundry chute from the second floor to the first. I took a flashlight into the horrible closet and saw for the first time what it looked like, without fear of the door swinging closed behind me. We even played with the intercom system and shouted in the living room just to hear the echo. Emily said not to trust this new freedom.

Ruth was never affectionate or playful, but she was very tolerant toward us, and she cooked us wonderful meals.

We were secretly disappointed when Dad said Mom was coming home from the hospital. She arrived looking thin with what looked like burn marks on her temples. Bobby asked her about the marks and she said it was from electric shock treatments. That sounded terrible to us and we felt sorry for her. At least she wasn't crying anymore.

Ruth had given us permission to hear the radio while Mom was away. We were sure that the radio would go back to being forbidden. It wasn't, for Dad bought each of us kids a radio for our rooms. We listened to *Sky King, Sergeant Preston,* and *Gunsmoke.* I thought I would die laughing over Edgar Bergen and Mortimer Snerd.

The summer before fifth grade Bobby and I flew to visit our other grandmother, my mom's mother. She didn't want us to call her "Grandmother," but "Marie." She had visited us before, but we had never been to her house, which was in San Mateo, just south of San Francisco.

Marie frightened us. She was very formal and proper and Bobby and I instantly knew we were going to hate the visit. We became the model children, turning into the quiet robots we had been trained to be.

We rode the trolly cars in San Francisco, walked on the Golden Gate Bridge, and went to the zoo, but it was an ordeal. Marie had her meals exactly on the dot of six. Lace doilies covered the arms of all the chairs and sofas, and if we didn't sit quietly and carefully they would slip off. She never laughed and she had no toys or games for us to play with. However, she did own a television, and every night she let us watch it. Having never seen it before, we were intrigued, but quickly became bored. We would rather play baseball outside.

"Now we know how Mom got crazy," Bobby whispered to me in the night.

"She never even smiles," I observed.

We were thrilled to go home and find Dad waiting for us. "Go get your things. We're going to the beach for two weeks with Grandma Bernice." Mom stayed home with Ruth. That was pure joy.

In fifth grade someone gave me two pet rats and a cage. I took very good care of them. Dad said I could keep them in the garage. Before long the two rats produced a family and I had about eight rats, much to my delight. Jimmy and I would play with them after school, making houses and runways out of blocks for them. We would lie down and let them crawl all over us, and I giggled in the middle of my sneezing attacks.

One day in a fit of anger Mom came to the garage with a big soup kettle filled with water. She put my rats in the water, to the wailing protests of Jimmy and me.

"Rats are filthy animals that carry diseases," she said. "We must kill them quickly."

"I'll find another home for them if I can't keep them. Please don't kill them! They're my friends!"

Mom held a lid that was smaller than the soup kettle. When all the rats were swimming around with a panicked look in their eyes, she grabbed my braids and pulled me over to the kettle. "You mustn't let them suffer. Press the lid down in the water and they will die quickly."

"No! Please, no!" I was sobbing. Jimmy was crying and ran from the garage.

Mom forced the lid down on the rats for a few seconds, then raised the lid up. The rats were all wet, sputtering and uselessly pawing at the slick sides of the kettle. "You mustn't let them suffer," she said as she plunged the lid down again. When she raised it, a few of the babies were dead, but the bigger rats were swimming. She made me take the lid and I felt the icy cold as I plunged the lid deep in the water. I held it down a long time, not wanting to see the panic in the rats' eyes. When I finally lifted the lid, they were all drowned.

I hated my mother at that moment.

"Let's kill her, plunge her face into ice-cold water until she turns blue and dies," Emily's voice screamed in my head.

Mom left the garage.

Jimmy wanted to play with all the dead rats. He kept crying and I couldn't stop crying, either. We found a shoe box and buried them outside next to Bootsie and had a funeral service, marking the grave with a little wooden cross.

There were so many crosses at the gravesite. Mom had cooked a bunny in the oven that Bobby had been given. There were crawdads we had caught in a pond that she dumped in our bathwater, swimming all around us until they died in the heat. There was the baby bird that we dropper-fed since it fell from its nest, and Mom threw it on the kitchen floor, saying, "We mustn't let things suffer." *We* suffered. After the rats, I never accepted any more pets. I didn't want to love anything and have it get killed in front of me. There had been too many tears and too many little dead things I had lovingly wrapped for burial. We had a funeral service memorized because we had said it so often.

Death was a preoccupation when I was young. My death had seemed real and repeatedly imminent. Mom had made me sit still in a chair time after time and read Bible verses to me. They were usually the scariest ones about hell and unrepentant souls. I feared God and I feared death, somehow having gotten the message that because I was Jewish I wouldn't get to go to heaven, yet at Sunday school they talked about Jesus loving little children, and being baptized was a way to heaven.

Just after the death of my rats, I was invited to church with a friend one Sunday. It was communion Sunday and the pastor was talking about the bread being the flesh of Christ and the wine being the blood of Christ. I sat spellbound in horror as all these nice people symbolically ate and drank Jesus. Tears were rolling down my face. How often had Mom talked of cooking and eating me? "The recipes of Marcia," she called it. I identified to such an extent with the symbolic eating that I was upset for days. Poor Jesus, no one loved him, either.

By the age of eleven, at the end of fifth grade, I was maturing at an embarrassing rate. I grew taller than everyone else and developed full breasts and pubic hair. My body had been violated to such an extent that I felt no sense of possession over my physical self. I was intrigued, yet distanced from the new things that were happening to me. Bobby no longer came in my room to lie in bed with me and Daddy never let me cuddle with him anymore. He stopped lip-kissing me; instead, I got pecks on the cheek. The hatred Mom had for me left me alarmingly vulnerable to new messages. I needed the love and assurances of Bobby and Dad. It was disorientation to be changing so quickly. At school I drifted, still doing well academically, since that took zero effort, but feeling detached from everything in my life.

I stopped all the young childish efforts to be lovable. I didn't try to charm my teachers or cultivate pretend mothers. I was numb from hopelessness. Even though the physical abuse had stopped, instead of flowering I was somehow deadened by the constant messages of hatred for me.

I still felt the yearning to have Mom look at me and throw her arms around me in delight at seeing my face. I craved her love. In spite of all the abuse, I still loved her. I wanted desperately to see her eyes glow with love for me. By eleven I knew it wasn't ever going to happen.

Dad's physical aloofness with me upset me. He never explained things, he would just say, "Big girls don't do that." I didn't want to be a big girl if it meant separation from him.

One day I saw a movie with a mushy kiss, and that night I came on to my father in the same way the starlet had in the movie. I pressed my new firm breasts against Daddy and kissed him full on the lips. He grabbed me by the shoulders and shoved me away from him. "Don't do that, Sunshine," he said gruffly. "That is not the kind of kissing daughters do with their fathers." He walked from the room abruptly. Silently, I cried. I did not want to grow up. I didn't like the new isolation that my body was bringing me.

I began finding myself under my bed at odd times with my thumb in my mouth, clutching a small soft blanket that Grandma Bernice had made, regressed to Sunshine.

I was happy to be going to Girl Scout camp as soon as school was out. I packed all the necessary things and sang with Linda all the way to the mountains on the big bus. "Ninety-nine bottles of beer on the wall, ninety-nine bottles of beer . . ."

Once at camp, Linda and I got separated into different groups. I was in a cabin with talkative girls and one girl who had false teeth from an accident and kept flicking them in and out. I was filled with apprehension. New situations always overwhelmed me with anxiety. Everything was okay for the first couple of days, and then on the third morning I went to the outhouse, the kind Mom had shoved my head in, and when I wiped myself there was blood on the toilet paper and blood on my underwear. I was deeply alarmed that something was wrong but decided I would wait and see if the bleeding would stop. Awhile later I got stomach pains and the blood was pooling in my pants. It seemed clear to me that somehow in the hiking I had ripped open the ice pick wounds, or some other damaged place. I couldn't tell the counselors or anyone that I was bleeding because then I would have to tell them about Mom. The silence would be even unto death.

"See," Emily said. "I told you Mom would find a way to kill us. Here we are a million miles from home and one of the stab wounds has opened up. We're going to die and I don't give a shit."

"You shouldn't use words like shit. Besides, how do you know we're going to die. We never have before."

"With luck we might."

"You always want to die," I said.

"That would be better than what we've had so far."

The bleeding continued into the next day. My jeans were getting stiff with blood. I changed clothes and stuffed toilet paper in my underpants. It was the scratchy kind of tissue paper that made more of a mess of the blood than absorbing it. I prepared to die. I lay on my cot and told the counselor I was sick. By the next day of skipping meals and lying on my cot in a sleeping bag that was damp with blood, the counselor insisted I see the camp nurse. I cried and said I couldn't. It took two counselors to wrestle me from my sleeping bag. I was crying. They stood me up and gasped at all the blood caked on my clothes and my legs. With tears running down my cheeks in shame, I said, "I'm dying, but I can't tell you about it."

"Are you sure you're not menstruating?" my counselor asked.

"What's that?" I responded in total innocence.

"You're eleven years old and you have never heard of men-struating?"

"No," I said. "What is it?"

The counselors started laughing and laughing, then got serious as they saw my distraught face.

They explained it to me, brought me to the camp nurse to make sure their guess was correct, then helped me shower and borrowed some clean clothes for me. They gave me a box of sanitary napkins and showed me how to use them. It was a relief to know I wasn't dying, but I felt humiliated by this new condition of womanhood. I hid the box from the girls in the cabin and would sneak the Kotex under my shirt to the outhouse. The counselor had said all women menstruate, but I was fairly certain she was lying. My mother and grandmother had never talked about it. None of my friends had ever mentioned it, but then again I didn't have many friends.

When I was sitting next to Linda at the campfire, I asked her in a casual, oblique way if she had ever heard of menstruating. "Sure," she said. "But we don't have to worry about that yet. It happens when we're twelve or thirteen."

"Oh," I said, not divulging my womanhood even to my best friend.

When I got home, I told Mom and Dad. I don't remember Mom's comments, but Dad was pleased. "Well, my little girl has become a woman."

Mom bought no provisions for me, so twenty-eight days later I was unprepared for it happening again. Mom never did buy me Kotex. I had to ride my bicycle to town and go in the drugstore and buy my own supplies. The first time I had to pay for Kotex I thought I would melt into the earth from embarrassment. I would often give Jimmy my allowance, which I started getting at age ten, to go to town with me and pay for the pads. Since he was ignorant as to what he was buying, he thought it was a great way to make money. He didn't even know that in my mind he was saving my life.

"Let me make one thing clear," Emily said. "I'm not about to have blood coming out of my body."

"It's not like we have a choice," I said.

"I don't like blood. It reminds me of the things Mom stuck in us, like the firepoker."

"Well, I hate it, too, but we'll both have to get used to it."

"Not I." Emily would purposely take off the pad and I would find myself at school with bloodstained clothes and the teacher whisking me to the nurse's office where Mrs. James would give me pads and a talk about menstruation. My cheeks would flame red in embarrassment.

Sometimes in the middle of the night Emily would take off the Kotex and I would wake up a sticky mess.

Mom never did acknowledge my cramps, which at times were terrible. I got no sympathy. Once when I was doubled over from cramps at Linda's house, Mrs. Franklin put me in her bed with a heating pad on my stomach and brought me mint tea with honey in it. The attention made me love her all the more and ever aware of the hole in my life.

About a month before Halloween, the topic of discussion at school was who would have a Halloween party at their house. One boy said, "Marcia, your house is huge and scary, why don't you have a party? None of us have ever been there."

Ice water ran in my veins at the thought of bringing my friends to my house. I had never had a birthday party. Dad had taken me to the movies, and one year he took Bobby, Jimmy, and me to the circus for my birthday, but I had never had schoolmates over. Mom was too unpredictable.

My school life and my home life were as isolated from each other as I could make them. My other states of being, the lapsed memory times, where I had to lie to make up for what I did not remember, isolated me even further. My life had become a juggling act of lies, and I certainly didn't share my secrets with the kids at school. Even walking home by myself I would feel the foreboding as I turned down my street. The big house with the dark, pain-filled secrets. We three children let no one into our world of terror.

Another friend piped in, "That's a great idea, to go to Marcia's house."

The group momentum upped the enthusiasm and the pressure.

I wished death before exposing my friends to my other life.

"I can't have a party," I muttered.

"Of course you can. You have the biggest house in town. It'll be great!"

Even Bobby heard from a kid at school that everyone wanted a Halloween party at our house. The more I objected the more intrigued my friends got about the house.

I asked Dad and Mom at dinner if I could have a Halloween party. Dad said, "Sure."

Bobby said he would help me make a haunted house.

Mom said nothing.

I went ahead and invited my friends, telling them it was a costume party and to be prepared for a haunted house. I sounded enthusiastic, but it was false bravado. I lay awake at nights wondering how Mom would act. My only hope was to have Dad stay home and help with the party. He said he would certainly try to be there.

Bobby and I spent two weeks working on our haunted house. We put streamers over the doors, and blue lights, and borrowed a skeleton from a weird high school boy Bobby knew. From a book in the library Bobby got the idea of everyone sitting around in a circle while someone recited a tale about a man being murdered and cut up and his parts passed around the group to be touched. In the dark we would pass bowls that had hard Jell-O for the liver, macaroni for brains, peeled grapes for the eyeballs, and so forth. Bobby was very enthusiastic about this night of horror. He said he would help me and would recite the tale while everyone sat in a circle in our huge living room. Dad found us a record of Japanese music that sounded properly scary.

Mom helped us by buying refreshments and the ingredients for our witches' tale.

When the night finally arrived, I was a wreck. Mom was too quiet. The house was ready, but at the last minute Dad had to leave town for a big meeting. Fear rose in me; my safety was leaving me.

All my friends arrived in various hilarious and goulish outfits. It doesn't take much in sixth grade to set off group silliness. Bobby took masterful command of the evening. He was held in reverent awe by the girls, and respect by the boys. In eighth grade he was almost six feet tall and his voice was beginning to change, or at least crack when he spoke.

The haunted house tour was a smashing success, with friends getting pushed in the absolute blackness down the laundry chute and into the secret corridors that paralleled the hall upstairs. We marched everyone into the deep cold cellar to Bobby's moans and groans.

After refreshments, Bobby commanded everyone to sit in a big circle. Mom had been out of sight the whole evening, but she said she would bring us the bowls of Jell-O and grapes at the appropriate times. Bobby blackened the room except for the coals glowing in the fireplace at the end of the living room.

In a low whisper Bobby began his tale of horror. When we got to the parts of the body that were to be passed around, the boys got loud and the girls shrieked appropriately in horror. A couple of the boys laughed. "Ha ha. This is just a peeled grape, not a real eye. This isn't real brains."

"I'll bet this is Jell-O," one boy said with bravado.

"I dare you to bite it," said another.

Just then the lights turned on and everyone began to scream. In the bowls were real brains, liver, eyeballs, a pancreas, and other cow parts. Blood was all over our hands and some kids had blood on their costumes.

Mom had gone to the butcher shop and without telling us had exchanged our fun parts for the real animal anatomy.

The girls were jumping and screaming at their bloody hands. The boys were trying to be brave. Bobby saved the day by laughing and shouting, "I fooled you! I fooled you! Happy Halloween!" He acted like he had pulled off the world's best joke. Some of the boys began to laugh, but the girls were all upset and tried to race to the sink to wash the blood off.

I wanted to die. My worst fears of Mom destroying my party were realized. Now my friends would know the world I lived in. I was certain no one would ever speak to me again. The party broke up immediately. I have no further recollection of the evening, since I dissociated from the trauma to the self-hypnotized safety of my imagination.

The next day I feigned illness, feeling too humiliated to go to school. Bobby came home and said all the kids were talking about the wonderful Halloween joke. I felt forever in Bobby's debt. He was enraged about what Mom had done. "She ought to be locked up somewhere. We are lucky no one found out she's wacko."

"She just did it because she hates me," I said quietly.

"She did it because she is sick in the head," Bobby answered. "I hate her guts."

The next day when I went to school, the furor had died down. Class was back to normal and my friends all made comments to me about the party, but at least they spoke to me. I had been certain I would be ostracized forever.

Sixth grade seemed like a long, awful year. My teacher frightened me because her way of controlling the class was to shout and pound desks with her fists. I would cringe, waiting for the physical violence that never came. In class I would lose track of time, drifting in and out and trying to guess what I had done, or Emily had done during my escape from reality. I felt out of sync with the kids in the class, who were getting caught up in their first boy-girl relationships. I was embarrassed by my height, my figure, and the boys who got crushes on me. I didn't know how to deal with the attention I was getting. I was voted president of my class because all the boys voted for me, saying I had "great knockers." A 36C bra in sixth grade was a point of deep humiliation as far as I was concerned.

Emily liked breasts. "These boobs aren't half bad," she'd say, strutting in front of the mirror in our room. After a bath she would twirl our breasts, singing fast songs and enjoying the jiggling. She wanted to wear tight sweaters, and wiggle when she walked. She liked the attention that embarrassed me. She began demanding "Body-time," as she called it. We had mostly been willing to share our body, but as it changed we did not share the same self-concept.

Roller-skating was my passion. Linda and I skated every afternoon after school. One especially great place to skate was near the Catholic Church, which had long expanses of slick sidewalks, some weaving through a beautiful rose garden.

Pedro was the Mexican gardener at the church and we waved to him as we skated at breakneck speed through the garden or twirled on the big cement squares. After a while, Pedro became our friend.

One day he showed us a photograph of his young sons. It surprised me that he had children, for he seemed timelessly ancient with his almost white hair and deeply lined mahogany face. I was fascinated by the sweat that puddled in his forehead grooves. He leaned hunched over on his hoe until the priest passed by, then he moved quickly, no longer walking old.

He would invite Linda and me and whichever other friends were skating with us to come visit him in the greenhouse in back of the church. He would sing and play his guitar and teach us Mexican songs. I would watch, mesmerized by his left hand, which was missing part of a finger, as he pressed the stump to the strings.

Emily was aware of how he looked at us. She would move provocatively around him on skates, grabbing a piece of his shirt in pretense of falling down, or skating quickly toward him, pretending to be unable to stop, crashing gently into him so he could feel her breasts. "Stop it!" I would say.

"Don't be such a spoilsport. I'm just having fun."

One day I went skating alone and Pedro was there pruning the roses. We talked as I skated around showing him my tricks. He invited me to the greenhouse, and I went with no sense of trepidation. He was my friend. We sang some songs and Pedro kept moving closer and closer to me, then began speaking softly in Spanish. His eyes got really funny and glassy, and he pulled me to him.

"Oh! You are a beautiful woman. I love you," he said as he kissed me on the mouth. He tasted of old cigarettes. I tried to move away from him, feeling a sudden revulsion and sense of betrayal at what my friend was doing.

"Stop, please stop," I protested as he began unbuttoning my blouse.

"Let me see your beautiful bosoms."

"No! Please, no!" I said as he pulled my blouse off and with a quick flick had my bra undone.

He buried his face between my breasts and was murmuring to them and kissing them.

I was in total confusion. He was my friend and he was acting strangely. What he was doing felt nice, but it felt wrong.

He stood up and pulled down his pants. That moment gave me my first sight of an erect penis. I was horrified. It seemed huge and brown, and he began pressing me with it. It hurt. All the alarms went off in my head for he was no longer touching me gently. He had me pinned to the wall and was pulling at my shorts. His body seemed all around me. He smelled and he gazed at me with the same look of nonrecognition that my mother sometimes got. I was a mass of confusion; man, Gypsy, torturer, friend. What was this man? His penis was rubbing between my legs, then pressing, pressing to get inside me.

It was fear that made me yank myself free of Pedro. I grabbed my clothes and raced out of the greenhouse. He was swearing and lunging at me, but he couldn't chase me, since he had no pants on.

I was nearly naked as I raced away and hid in some bushes to put my clothes on. I felt dirty all over and was shaking. I didn't know what had happened, but I felt sure that I had done something wrong. I had been raised to assume I was bad and always guilty.

When I got home, I ran to the bathroom and took a bath, washing and washing as though it would strip away the confusion. I knew almost nothing of sex; my parents had not told me anything, although I did know a little from school and seeing dogs mate. But there were so many things I didn't know. Would it hurt the way the broom handle hurt me? Would it rip me inside like the ice pick? Weren't people supposed to be married to have sex?

My whole life was a mass of secrets, so this became just another episode tucked into my wall of silence. I wanted to tell Dad, but I didn't know how. He had told me never to be alone with a strange man, never to take rides or candy from strangers, but Pedro wasn't a stranger, he was my friend.

Abruptly, I gave up roller-skating at the church. I couldn't tell Linda what happened. I didn't know how to tell her.

A few weeks later there was a big commotion. One of the girls I skated with had been beaten and raped by Pedro. It was a violent attack and my friend, Virginia, went to the hospital.

Guilt descended on me as I heard adults talking about the sick man who would hurt a child that way. I was sure if I had told someone, maybe Virginia wouldn't have been hurt. I felt responsible.

The police came, handcuffed Pedro, and hauled him off to jail.

I missed him. I wished I'd had the chance to talk to him and have him explain to me what he did to me, and why. Another part of me was relieved to never have to see him again.

Virginia came back to school, and everyone whispered about her, which made me feel worse. I wished I could be brave enough to tell her she was not alone, but I couldn't.

My near rape left an impression on me, but I had been mutilated and tortured so often that this episode was more confusing than traumatic. I had been violated repeatedly and violently to the point that I held no concept of ownership over my own body.

I had effectively relinquished all rights to even the most basic sense of self. I tuned out my near rape just as I did my other abuses.

Sixth grade dragged on interminably. I felt abandoned by Dad and Bobby, upset at the boys at school who were pestering me, and depressed at Mom's continual psychological abuse. I must have dissociated, for I had no memory of a span of time and found myself hours later in my bed with a brain concussion and scraped-up knees. My vision was blurry and I kept vomiting.

Bobby said, "You deliberately rode your bike in front of a car. I saw you."

"I don't remember doing that."

"Are you trying to kill yourself?"

"I don't know. I truly don't remember doing anything. Please don't tell Mom or Dad."

"Do you think I would? Haven't I always taken care of you? You scared the hell out of me today."

"I'm sorry, Bobby."

I missed a week of school listening to *Mary Worth* and *My True Confessions* on the radio, waiting for the headaches and my vision to clear.

I wondered if Emily had chosen to die. There were many things about myself I didn't understand.

Grandma Bernice got sick during my sixth-grade year. Congestive heart failure was the label the doctors gave. Her breathing was labored and her feet and fingers were a deep purple-blue. As soon as summer arrived, Grandma Bernice moved into our home. Dad had picked her up and packed her suitcases, insisting she was too sick to live alone. My mother gave her my bedroom, thinking it would upset me, but I was thrilled to have Grandma stay, even in my bedroom.

Dad hired a nurse to take care of Grandma, but within days my mother had fired her. Another nurse was hired, only to be fired again.

Grandma Bernice's health deteriorated rapidly. Fluid began collecting in her abdomen and ankles. The doctor made a house call and let me stay in the room while he aspirated some of the fluid to help Grandma breathe. I told the doctor I would take care of Grandma Bernice. This kind old physician told me how to put the nitroglycerin tablets under the tongue, how to bathe her in bed. Probably because my mother wasn't there he spoke to me as though I were an adult.

Grandma Bernice became bedridden within a week of coming to stay with us. She lay in my big four-poster bed, looking tiny and frail, except for her big stomach. She ate almost nothing.

My mother never took care of her at all. Without the nurses, who were fired, or Ruth, the maid who was on vacation, the nursing care fell to me. Daddy was angry at Mom for firing the nurses and said I was too young to take care of Grandma, but I begged to be allowed to do it. Dad, out of desperation, agreed. He had an extra bed brought into the room for me, so I could sleep next to Grandma, in case she had chest pains or needed anything in the night.

Grandma was weak, but for the whole month of July we giggled and she told me stories. She told me how babies were born and what it was like to be a mother. She kissed me and stroked my hair as I lay in bed next to her. When I look back at that month I realize it was she who was taking care of me. We were like two lone travelers on a secret journey, sharing each other. I don't remember anyone else during that month. I don't remember leaving her to go play. She was filling my loneliness with her loving. She told me how wonderfully well I did things for her, always praising me and extolling my virtues. I never remember her complaining, even when she had to struggle to breathe.

I bathed her, brushed her hair, and brought her meals, which she hardly touched. She perspired a great deal, and every evening Dad would come and help me change her sheets and we would sit her in a chair and Dad would join our ongoing party.

The only time I got banished from the room was when the rabbi came to visit Grandma. She liked to talk with him alone.

In August, Grandma had some violent chest pains and got acutely worse. She lay in bed panting for air, barely able to speak or move. She no longer ate. She drifted in and out of sleep and we didn't giggle together anymore. The doctor came and said he would respect her wish to die at home; she never would consent to go to a hospital.

No one asked me about my feelings or if I could cope with Grandma. Ruth was back but made it very clear that she was not hired as a nurse.

The doctor showed me how to regulate the oxygen, how to turn Grandma in bed and rub her back so she wouldn't get sores. I remember the loose skin that was paper thin as I rubbed it. She was too weak to get up to go to the bathroom, so I brought her a bedpan. None of this seemed alarming to me. I adored Grandma Bernice. She was my whole world that summer.

She tried to prepare me for her death. She whispered her gratitude and love messages to me. Even too weak to eat, she would pat the sheets for me to come lie on the bed next to her. Her eyes cherished me. Her fingers touched me lightly. She told me she was going to die but that her life had been full and now was finished. Her only sadness was in leaving me. She said she knew Mom hadn't treated me well and it had broken her heart. As she said that, I thought how little she knew of what I really had lived through. Even in death I could not tell her, but I wept, and with a shaking hand she wiped the tears from my face. She kissed my eyes.

I was lying in my bed next to Grandma when I heard her breathing change. It was a slow, rattling breath. I went over to her and turned on the light. I couldn't rouse her; she was in a coma.

Life was confusing after that. My father's sister, who had almost never come to our house, arrived. The doctor and the rabbi came, too. Dad sat by Grandma's bed with his sister and I felt like an outsider. I wanted everyone out of Grandma Bernice's and my room. She and I belonged together after two whole months of sharing every waking moment. She couldn't die.

It took Grandma two days and two nights to die. Dad banished me from the room and I sobbed as I lay next to Bobby. I was angry to be sent away and angrier still to be losing what I felt was a big piece of my life. I loved Grandma with an intensity that was in proportion to my deprivation and my need. I thought my heart would break.

I cried the whole day she died. Mom said she was glad Grandma was dead. "She was just an old Jew," she said. I wanted to kill my mother at that moment. My heart was breaking with the grief.

I don't even remember her funeral, or if there was one. I was dissociating from the pain of the loss of Grandma.

I'm not certain if I dissociated more easily as I got older, or if I remember it more clearly, because in adulthood time holds a definition that it doesn't have when one is young.

Emily seemed an active, angry part of my life after Grandma died. She wanted to run away from home. I didn't know where we could go.

In seventh grade my good grades began to slip in direct relation to the time I was no longer in class. I would drift away mentally to my neutral escape place, or Emily would force me to ditch school. The classes were fifty minutes, then on to a new class and new teacher. All the change seemed threatening to me and opened up ample opportunity for splitting myself and running from the pain I held inside. It was pain beyond losing Grandma Bernice. It was the pain of being unloved by Mom, the pain of telling lies when I didn't know where I'd been or what I had done, the pain of feeling an outsider to the world to which my friends belonged.

It was about December when Dad noticed how alarmingly thin I had become again. He had also received a notice from school about my absences. It was a sunny Saturday and Dad said, "Let's have a special day, just the two of us."

"I would love that, Daddy," I said as I scurried to get ready. I put my waist-long blond hair in a ponytail with a ribbon. I hated my hair that Mom yanked and threatened to burn, but Dad loved my thick blond hair, saying I reminded him of the Rapunzel story. He would tease, "Rapunzel, Rapunzel let down your golden hair."

I was in high spirits when we drove off together. Dad took me into Los Angeles for breakfast at an elegant restaurant, then we rented a rowboat in MacArthur Park and took our coffee cake crumbs in the boat to throw to the ducks and geese.

Dad seemed in a thoughtful mood as we paddled around. We talked about Grandma Bernice and how much we both missed her, and how much I hated school. I couldn't tell Daddy about Emily or that she was making me ditch.

Finally, Dad looked me squarely in the eyes, with a penetrating gaze. "Sunshine, tell me what Mom has done to you."

Instant panic rose in me. "I can't, Daddy," I pleaded.

"Yes! You can talk to me. I want to know the truth, the real truth."

I began crying. "I can't tell you. Mom will give me away to the Gypsies. She said I'll never see you again if I tell you."

"Don't be ridiculous, of course she can't give you away to the Gypsies. How can you believe such a stupid thing?"

"You don't know what Mom is like. You just don't know."

"She hurt you sometimes, didn't she?"

"Please don't make me tell you, Daddy."

Dad took my hands and cupped them in his big hands and said, "I mean it. I want to know, and I absolutely promise you Mom can not give you to the Gypsies. I wouldn't let her ever give you away."

I thought of how much he didn't know and was crying harder. "Daddy, you'll be mad."

"Sweetheart, for God's sake cut this out and just answer my questions."

I was disintegrating under the persistent interrogation. Too much pain had been held in for too long. I was certain there would be a major act of revenge if Mom found out I had talked, but I launched into my tale.

I told Dad about the closet, the summer locked in my room, the times I was tied up, and graphically told him about the pins, the needle and thread, the ice pick. In my tears I spared him nothing. I was oblivious to him as he sat staring at me in the rowboat. I was bubbling forth the horror of my life all the times he was away.

Suddenly, there was a choking sound, and I focused on Daddy. Great tears were rolling down his twisted face. Our eyes met and held. He got up from the seat opposite me, the boat rocking precariously. Kneeling on the floor of the boat, he put his head on my lap and hugged me tightly, sobbing great, wracking, noisy sobs. His tears were getting my legs all wet, and I tried to comfort him by stroking his hair. I remember the stickiness of his hair oil. It took an eternity for him to gain control. He cried, "I didn't know. I didn't know. My poor baby. My precious baby."

Later, when he stopped crying and was blowing his nose on the big monogrammed handkerchief he always carried, he said, "Why didn't you tell me before? How could you suffer this much in silence?"

"Daddy, if you tell Mom I told you, she'll hurt me. You just don't understand." Now I was crying again and alarmed at the enormity of what I had done.

Dad almost suffocated me in his intense hug and said, "I promise you, you'll never be hurt again. Forgive me, my baby."

I didn't know why he wanted me to forgive *him*, he had never hurt me, and I knew he did not know the omnipotence of Mom's powers. I felt terrified rather than reassured.

We sat in silence, both distractedly looking at the ducks following our little boat. Dad got oddly withdrawn. I worried he was somehow angry with me.

When we got home, Dad burst into the house. He told me to go upstairs and pack all my things in a suitcase. He yelled to Bobby and Jimmy and told them to go pack their stuff. I went upstairs totally mystified and anxious that I had done something terribly wrong in telling Dad. Then I could hear the shouting, crying, and crashing noises from my parents' room. The words were muffled behind closed doors, but I knew a violent eruption in our lives was taking place.

Dad threw our suitcases in the car and ordered Bobby, Jimmy, and me into the car. We weren't certain what our fate was to be. Without even saying good-bye to Mom, Dad squealed the tires, racing out of the driveway. We didn't dare speak. None of us knew what was going on. Dad took us to a beautiful hotel, with a swimming pool and a television in the room. When we were in the room, Dad sat on the bed with us and said, "Kids, we're leaving your mother. I should have taken you away years ago. I had enough evidence and clues." He broke into great sobs again. Brokenly, he said, "Why couldn't you have told me? What must she have done to all of you to keep silent as you have done? I'm sorry. I'm sorry."

We all hugged him and then all four of us were crying.

Jimmy was crying because he didn't want to leave Mom.

"It's my fault," I said. "I didn't mean to be bad."

"Marcia, there's nothing you could have done to deserve what has happened to you. Your mother had no right to do what she did to you."

The next day while we were in school Dad went apartment hunting. We moved into a big beautiful apartment that already had white furniture in it.

There was no feeling of elation at leaving Mom. We felt confused, upset, and responsible. Dad tried to rally our sagging spirits. He played baseball with us and took us out to get hamburgers and malts.

"When are we going back to Mom?" I asked over dinner.

"Never" was the adamant reply.

It was a big concept. No Mom. No house. No abuse. Belief in my safety did not come quickly. I kept expecting Mom to burst through the door and drag us home.

Dad forbade us to call Mom or let her know where we were staying.

Ruth remained with Mom, so the care of Jimmy and the cooking fell to me. I thrived on being made to feel important. Dad was a good cook and we had laughter-filled evenings as the two of us cooked and figured out how to do laundry.

My heart sang with pleasure as I walked the mile home from school, knowing there was no hostility waiting for me. I gained weight rapidly in my new environment and my clothes no longer hung in bags on my thin frame.

Dad must have made a real effort to cut back on business to be with us. For the first time in our lives he came home regularly for dinner. I don't remember any trips, although on a few occasions when he was late he had a very beautiful woman named Louise come stay with us. She wore gold bracelets that jingled as she moved her arms. She wore lots of makeup and smelled heavenly. Sometimes she was there when Dad was home, and even though we kids liked her, we felt jealous. I was crushed when I saw him kiss her. We were very nice to her even though she was the intruder because she tried so hard to be nice to us. She bought me my first lipstick and took me shopping for my first pair of high-heeled shoes. We all laughed uproariously as I wobbled around on my white heels. Even though Louise looked like a movie actress, we discovered she had a silly, fun side.

When summer came, I was very self-conscious about the burn scars on my legs. Louise showed me how to put makeup over the scars, so I could wear bathing suits and shorts. I knew she knew about Mom by the way she acted. She spent time talking girl-talk with me, telling me about dating, kissing, and getting married. Louise made me feel grown up. She showed me how to curl the ends of my long hair and pile it high on my head. We went to Chinatown and Dad bought me tortoiseshell hairpins.

That summer before eighth grade when I was thirteen was rapturously happy. I don't even remember thinking of Mom. We hadn't wanted to see her and Dad didn't make us. The few times we *had* seen her, it was tearful and emotional and Jimmy was upset for days afterward. Unlike Bobby and me, he had mixed loyalties and missed Mom and our house. But by summer we felt free to swim and play and ride our bikes around town. Linda could come play at our apartment and even spend the night.

We went to Baja, California, camping on the west side near Scamon's Lagoon. The four of us slept in a hot tent and washed in the ocean. We caught lobsters and abalones and bought vegetables from the Mexicans. It was a long trip on the potholed road but a trip that will always live in my mind as the epitome of joy. I was stung by a jellyfish, overly sunburned, stuck with a fish hook, but every moment was fun with Dad. He made everything an adventure. Bobby speared a halibut and Jimmy learned to skin-dive with us. The four of us would take our masks, snorkels, and spears around the rocks and seaweed gardens and catch our dinner. It was a magical fairy land under the sea.

I do not remember Emily during those happy times. What lives in my mind are the campfires, the stories, the interesting Mexicans, and my elation at no longer being tormented. I was loved. I could feel it. Dad constantly communicated it to us. He never spoke of Mom, or the abuse; it was as though we were all beginning a new chapter in our lives.

Bobby, Jimmy, and I were very close. We had lived through hell together, so we looked out for each other as survivors do. We never fought. Jimmy was sometimes a pest, but Bobby and I tried to include him when we did things. He was cute, with a freckled nose and white-blond hair.

Summer went too quickly. I resented the tight saddle shoes and the new skirts for school. I wanted to camp forever.

In the apartment house there was no place to practice my violin, so I stopped taking lessons, but Dad let me take tennis lessons after school. I was a natural athlete and I learned quickly. It was about this time that boys became a priority in eighth grade. I began to enjoy the unidentifiable power I had over boys, but I always had to contend with Emily for control. It was hard to convince her to butt out of my friendships. She had her own friends, but Roger was my first boyfriend. He would walk me home from school and take me to the local ice cream parlor for malts.

My self-confidence was growing by taking care of Dad and my brothers. I was getting lavished with praise and encouragement from Dad. My grades were good. I was not ditching.

Christmas was terrible that year. We had to see Mom, and it was a traumatizing, tearful event for Bobby, Jimmy, and me and ended in a shouting match between our parents. I was so upset to be back in our old home seeing Mom that I ran to the bathroom and vomited. Sunshine wanted to find the closet, the stinking hole where we had spent hours and hours of our life and retreat into the dark womb of the forgotten and the familiar. Emily wanted to take a kitchen knife and plunge it into Mom, just the sight of her filling Emily with rage. I was miserable knowing how much I still wanted Mom to love me and that she never would or could. She greeted the boys with hugs and enthusiasm and was merely polite to me. I didn't want to even be near her or the house and remember the rejection and pain.

In January, Dad invited me out to dinner, just the two of us. He bought me a grown-up looking dress and took me to the Brown Derby restaurant. We ordered prime rib and there, sitting one table away, was Clark Gable. I was too embarrassed to ask for his autograph, but I felt like a princess in an enchanted kingdom that night. Dad even let me have a glass of wine and he toasted me: "My beautiful daughter who will always be special to me." Dad said I could keep the candle that had melted down as we ate.

I remember feeling how much I loved my father as I sat jiggling around on the seat of the car on our way home, holding his huge hand, feeling safe.

He often did spontaneous, fun things with us. We would go out to the movies on a school night if we got our homework done. We went out to eat in restaurants when we didn't feel like cooking. The local hamburger joint became a favorite, and Bobby and I could choose songs on the jukebox, usually Teresa Brewer songs.

Dad was bigger than life to me. He was the savior, not just the father. I'm certain there is no love more intense than the love an abused child has for the "safe" parent. I worshiped him. I studied everything about him and worked to please him.

A sense of humor began to develop in all three of us children. We had been oppressed by Mom so long we had to learn how to laugh. Dad made a big effort to make life fun and funny. Our fun was no longer play-acting to cover the pain and abuse, it was genuine.

Dad was as excited as a kid when he got a Cessna airplane. We lived through his blow-by-blow accounts of his flying lessons.

It was in February 1956, just after I turned fourteen, that Dad decided to take the plane on a business trip with a friend, who was also an attorney. I remember how enthusiastic Dad was about his big legal case and his airplane as he scurried around packing.

I resented having the woman Dad had hired come live with us

while he would be gone for a few days. I felt I was a grown woman, certainly able to stay with Bobby and Jimmy without the intrusion of a babysitter. I had tried to argue Dad out of it, but he insisted we not stay by ourselves. I was grumpy and barely kissed him good-bye. I wanted a turn to fly with him. Bobby suggested he ditch school and go on the trip, too, but that didn't work with Dad. No deal.

I don't even remember the name of the nondescript lady who stayed with us, or the dinner she fixed, but I do remember going to bed and worrying about the news of a big storm. It was the middle of the night when I awoke to a knock at the front door. Without even putting on a bathrobe, I walked to the door and opened it. There stood two policemen.

"Is your father's name Frank Kendall?"

"Yes," I said, "but he isn't here now, he's on a trip." Then I saw their faces. Instant alarm shivered through me.

"May we come in?" the young blond officer asked.

"I guess you can." I opened the door to let them enter. "What's wrong?"

"Is there an adult here?" the dark one asked.

"Just a minute," I said, going to the babysitter's room and knocking. She came out looking sleepy.

"I'm sorry to tell you there has been an accident, a plane crash. There were no survivors. Frank Kendall is dead."

I screamed, "No! No! You're lying. My daddy can't be dead. You made a mistake!"

The blond policeman came over and put his arms around me as I began to shake violently, and the reality of what they said sank in.

Bobby and Jimmy heard my sobs and came into the living room. It was three in the morning and Bobby and I clung to each other and cried and cried. Jimmy was numb and refused to believe it. The babysitter made everyone cocoa as if for a tea party. The police officers awkwardly took the cocoa and I sobbed, "How can you sit and drink when my daddy is dead?"

I began to get hysterical and one of the officers gripped me firmly. "I'm sorry, kid."

The babysitter said, "You'll have to see their mother," and gave the policeman Mom's address.

"We will have to take you to your mother's house now," said the blond officer.

"No. We'll stay here alone," cried Bobby.

"Sorry, we can't do that. Go get your stuff."

Time, space, and reality all started to crumble in the next hour. It was as if everything was slow motion and I was outside my body watching it all from a distance.

We were put in the police car and we drove away from the apartment with the white furniture, freedom, and laughter.

My mother screamed when she heard the news. She began sobbing and babbling, then the policeman called a doctor. At five in the morning, the doctor came and gave my mother a shot and me a pill, which made me sleepy. The morning seemed like a long drawn-out play. Neighbors and friends arrived as the news was broadcast on the radio and television.

I never thought about school. It was as though all of life went in limbo. By noon, reporters were at our home, people were bringing casseroles, and my aunt was pressing us for details on the funeral service.

My only thought was, "Daddy, Daddy, I need you. You can't be dead. Oh, Daddy, please don't be dead."

There were discussions among the adults as to who would identify the body for the coroner. The plane had flown into the storm and ice had formed on the wings. The airplane had hit the mountain and exploded on impact. I listened in horror as I heard someone say they were trying to get enough body parts together to make a positive identification.

"Oh, Daddy. Please don't be in pieces. Don't be dead."

I drifted from intense pain to numbness and back to intense pain over the next few days. I don't remember eating or sleeping or even what anyone else was doing. My world was gone. The safety was gone. I was back in the house of torture with Mom, and there was no Daddy.

The memorial service was horrible. There was no body, so there was no casket, just flowers at the altar and a couple of hundred people talking to me and grown-ups crying. I felt disconnected from everything. All the adults who said they loved my father, my daddy. I thought, "How dare they say they loved him. He belonged to me. I belonged to him. Daddy, didn't you and I stand in the very center of the universe?" I hated all those people, people who had looked past my pain of a lifetime, people who would say nice things and leave me with my mother.

After the service, a couple of Dad's cousins took us to a movie. I sat in that movie about a carnival and marveled that somewhere in the world people laughed.

I wanted to die. This is my first memory of wanting to be dead. That night after the carnival movie I got down on my knees by my bed and I prayed to God, "Please let me die. Let me be with Daddy. I can't live without him." I was back in my old room with the memories of two whole months locked away from the world. Without Daddy I couldn't imagine what life could be, except pain.

When I awoke in the morning to the sunlight streaming in through my flowered curtains, I felt abandoned by God. There could not be a God, I decided.

I think I must have dissociated, for I have no memory of doing it, but I hacked off my long blond hair. I cut it angrily and radically to a few short inches. Daddy had loved my hair. It was thick and golden, and Mom had tormented me with it for as long as I could remember.

When I returned to school in a few days, everyone gasped at my hair, and mumbled apologies about my father's death.

"My God! What did you do to yourself?" asked my Russian science teacher.

During lunchtime he put me in his car and drove me to a beauty shop where he paid for me to get a decent haircut and a permanent. I was so far removed from reality that I didn't care what people whispered about me.

It was less than a week after Dad died that Bobby left. He left in the night, with no note, no good-bye. When I went to his room, he was gone. I looked outside under the orange tree and there was an empty hole where our treasure jar was buried. It had about fifty dollars from our years of adding to it.

I threw myself on my bed, sobbing in anger and abandonment. Why didn't he take me? Where had Bobby gone?

It was at this moment of indescribable loss that my Joey personality resurfaced into domination. He was fourteen, but he was big and strong and very angry. He went into Bobby's room and smashed it to a pile of rubble. The baseball trophies, his radio, his stacks of old comic books and sports magazines were demolished. With Bobby's big hunting knife Joey slashed the sheets and gutted the mattress. He put on Bobby's clothes and boots, stomping through the house and terrifying Jimmy, who watched it all.

Joey was the one personality in me who was capable of violence. It was the rage of years of torture. This Joey-self liked loud music, baseball, masculine things. He never grew past the age of fourteen. He stayed locked in the angry emotions of abandonment.

Mom seemed as broken as I was. She barely noticed Bobby was gone. I expected great outbursts of abuse and violence, but there were none. She stayed in her room and talked to her angel. She read the Bible a lot and prayed. She didn't fix dinner or go marketing. When the casseroles were finally gone, I asked her for money for food and she handed it to me, with no questions or directives.

Out of necessity I took over the household duties. Jimmy began coming to me for things. I tucked him in bed at night and we would hug each other and both of us would begin to sob all over again. We grieved at the loss of both Dad and Bobby.

Mom made us look at the photos of the plane crash. She shoved them in my face, saying, "This is what happened to your precious father." There in the snow were airplane parts and pieces of bodies. There was a close-up of Daddy's red Pendleton shirt and a head with no face. I ran from the room sobbing.

I developed a great anxiety that I had no face. I would have to touch my face to see if it was there. Dozens of times a day I had to check in a mirror to see what I looked like. When I wasn't touching it, or seeing it, I was certain my face was a blank piece of flesh.

It surprised me that when I met people they did not gasp at my appearance. I knew that I did actually have a face, but the moments of certainty that I didn't continued for almost thirty years. Until in therapy I remembered the photograph of my beloved father without a face.

———

A persistent nightmare haunted me. Night after night I would have the dream that Daddy had crashed in the snow, but instead of exploding into fragments, he lay wounded in a snowbank. I dreamt a woman found him and dragged him to her mountain cabin. The woman's daughter helped nurse Daddy back to health in this hut. The girl was pretty, with blond hair and blue eyes, and as my dad got better, they laughed together. The warm scenes played in my dreams of this charming woman and her sweet daughter captivating my father with their charm. Night after night I would wake up, dripping with perspiration and crying because Daddy had chosen another family, another little girl. I would clutch my pillow and sob in my sense of abandonment.

One part of my mind clung to the belief that Daddy lived. There should have been a body to see, a white hand to touch farewell. It was vibrant life one day, then the emptiness of policemen at the door. I wondered what I had done to make him want to leave me. I grieved that I had not been enough, that another girl in another place was now his child, sharing the intimate conversations and the silly fun.

I fantasized an expedition into the mountains to the plane crash. Maybe he had crawled into the woods and was waiting to be rescued. When I presented the idea to Mom, she hauled out the pictures again, forcing me to see arms and pieces of red flannel shirt, my dad's favorite shirt, lying in the snow.

Losing Bobby, too, was intolerable. Every day I waited for a letter from Bobby, but none came. My best friend, the sharer of the abuse years, my comforter, had abandoned me. I did not understand it. I felt angry that he left me. I wanted to escape with Bobby. He should have asked me, I would have gone. Without Bobby to help instigate a plan, my thoughts of escape died. There was Jimmy to care for. I had no money, no place to go. My years of silence had conditioned me to believe I was alone in the world. I did not know there were alternatives to Jimmy and me being the chattel, the possessions of a deranged mother.

Grief followed me through the days and nights. I cried constantly. I stopped menstruating. Grief was like standing alone outside at midnight and losing the belief there would be a morning. I have fragmented memories of the rest of my eighth-grade year and the summer. It was a long drought of the soul, when awareness and growth stops and endless waiting takes over—to see Daddy's or Bobby's face, to feel a hug, to share the mealtime hilarity and own once again the safety.

My life became a fragmented existence of personalities ready to take me from the pain. I still do not know them all; to me they were just missing hours out of my day, the time when the hands of the clock could just leap forward, and I would be in a different place wearing different clothes.

I put my violin away in the top of my closet. The music in me was dead with Daddy. He had loved the sweet music I played for him. My violin belonged with him. I never played again.

I do remember Mom insisting that we trade bedrooms. "Your father loved you the best. You should sleep in his bed."

I had mixed feelings about moving into the huge master bedroom suite, with the big fireplace and walk-in closet. It was a relief to leave my room, the room of so much torture and childhood pain, but I didn't feel any closer to Daddy sleeping in the bed my mother had shared with him.

By summer Mom was coping better with life. One day one of Dad's friends came over and sat talking to Mom a long time. He called me in to listen to what he had to say. "I'm sorry to be the bearer of bad news, but you know Frank had invested heavily in many ventures. The biggest purchase was the lumber mill in Tennessee. He borrowed against his life insurance and this house. Unfortunately, since his death, several of his business ventures have failed without his brilliance at the helm." He turned to Mom. "With the power of attorney you gave me, I have sold his law practice and the failing businesses, but financially things look bleak. With the small income you will have from now on you can't afford to keep this big house. We'll have to put it on the market."

"Absolutely not," Mom replied. "This is my home and I refuse to leave it. I will find a way."

Mom did have the capacity to function and come to grips with things. She figured out the mortgage payments and what money she needed to raise. She put an ad in the newspaper for boarders. Ruth, our housekeeper, was terminated.

I thought it was a terrible idea to have strangers in this god-awful house. All my life I had kept people away from my house and Mom's erratic behavior.

Very quickly we got three boarders. Jake was an elderly widower who had no children, well into his seventies, with a delightful sense of humor. I had to be careful before asking him a question, for the response could make me late for school or an appointment.

Viola, or Auntie Viola as she asked us to call her, was an arthritic older woman, probably in her late sixties, who walked with a cane and complained about nearly everything. She smelled of Ben-Gay and rose petals, which she kept in little sachet bundles in every drawer. She had tried living with her daughter, but it didn't work out. Her children banded together and answered my mother's ad. Auntie Viola had a little stiff black mustache, and bags under her eyes. She scared me a bit.

The biggest mistake Mom made was taking in Beth as a tenant. Beth was sixteen and went to high school in our town. She had been kicked out of a Swiss boarding school and was on probation at the high school. She smoked, bleached her hair, and bragged about her sexual escapades. Her parents were some sort of missionaries, but I decided they couldn't love her very much to have left her in the care of my mother. I'm certain no one in town would have given my mother a letter of recommendation.

Beth was angry to be left with us, and let it be known she would not lift a finger to help.

Mom, out of spite, demanded that Beth and I share the master bedroom. I was terribly upset at that decree.

The first night with Beth sleeping next to me in Dad's king-size bed was horrible. She demanded the side my father had slept on. I needed space for my grief and was overcome by the prospect of sharing a room with this tough girl.

During the night I discovered something worse—Beth was a bed wetter. I woke up to the feeling of dampness creeping under my legs.

Beth apologized as we got up to change the sheets and told me she didn't know why she did it, it was a big problem in her life. I didn't feel sorry for her. I was angry that my father's bed was defiled in this way. I was angry at her presence in my home. Grabbing my pillow and a blanket, I went into Dad's closet and curled up on the floor, holding his leather slippers in my arms, and cried myself to sleep.

For months I slept in the closet, wishing for nothing to do with Beth, and wanting to be near Daddy's clothes which Mom never took out of the closet. In the mornings I would strip the stinking-wet bed and start the laundry. Even Beth's cigarette smoke couldn't mask the clinging urine odor.

I could not manage to be more than barely civil to Beth, who had been dumped by her own parents. She was flunking all her classes in school, and I felt contempt for her as she gave me detailed descriptions of her promiscuity. She would beg me to come out of the closet and sleep with her. One night I capitulated and climbed in bed, building a sheet dam between us so I wouldn't get wet in the night. She asked me if I had ever had sex and I said no. She began to graphically explain it to me and then told me I was beautiful and she would like to show me what sex was like. I didn't have any idea what she meant when she came over to my side of the bed and put her leg over mine. Then she kissed me on the mouth. I leapt out of bed in disgust. I took my pillow and blanket and went to sleep in the basement of the house, which was as far from Beth as I could get. It was cold and hard on the cement floor, but it was a place I could cry myself to sleep.

Mom did nothing to help with the boarders. At fourteen I had to cook for six people, do the laundry and the cleaning. Jake was amiable to everything, but Viola complained about my cooking efforts. She would hover in the kitchen giving me lessons. At the time, I resented her, but later I was grateful for the tutelage.

Jimmy burned the trash in our incinerator out back and tried to take care of the orange trees and yard. At night we would visit for a while. It was a big leap to go from having a maid and a gardener to being the only one, out of six people, who worked.

"Don't you feel like Cinderella?" Jimmy asked.

"I never thought of it, but I guess you're right, only there isn't any Prince Charming."

"Well, we have the mice," Jimmy said. "Only they are more

like big tree rats. They are coming into the basement somehow."

We were infested with the big rats. They walked around the house as if they owned it, raiding the kitchen at night. Mom finally called the exterminators when Viola threatened to move out.

"I'd rather have the rats," Jimmy said.

"So would I," I giggled.

Letters to Germany were coming and going. One day Mom said to me, "How would you like to go live in Germany? My cousins want to adopt you."

Panic ran through me. Life was awful, but at least it was familiar. I knew Mom's relatives were Nazis. "Please, Mom, don't send me away to Germany!" I begged.

Later that day I sneaked into Mom's room and found the letters on her desk. Only one letter was in English and it talked about raising me as a good German and keeping the bloodlines pure. Obviously, my mother never told them I was half Jewish. Lying on the desk were passport papers and other documents. I was distraught by the possibility of leaving my school, Jimmy, and maybe never seeing Bobby again.

In one of the few assertive things I've ever done, I wrote a letter to the cousins who knew English, begging them not to take me, that I was half Jewish, all American, and had no desire to be German. I told them I would hate them if they made me go.

"Good for you," Emily said. "It's about time you did something assertive. Tell all those Nazi relatives you'd rather be dead than eat sauerkraut with them. Tell them you'll burn their house down."

I don't know if Mom ever found out I wrote to my cousins, but after the next letter arrived from Germany the subject of my leaving was dropped.

It depressed me that even with all I was doing to keep the household going, Mom wanted to get rid of me. I would never be loved by her. It seems odd that by fourteen I wasn't immune to the rejection, but I wasn't. I seemed to have an ever-renewing capacity to be hurt. I was pretty, I was an A student in school, I was running the boardinghouse, and still I wasn't enough, never could be enough for her.

All the loss and longing got focused on Mr. MacMurray, my ninth-grade English teacher. He was tall, enthusiastic, had a sense of humor, and his face crinkled when he laughed. It was during the early rains in October when my year-long obsession with him began. Rain came pounding against the classroom window and all the kids in the English class had to eat lunch in their homeroom. I sat at my desk lost in the storm, reliving what it must have been like for my father realizing his plane was going to crash. I sat with tears rolling down my face, and the bell rang to go to the next class. All the kids filed out of the room and I was lost, far away on a mountainside looking with my mind at bits and parts of Daddy. Mr. MacMurray came over to me and pulled up a chair.

"You're having a hard time, aren't you, Marcia?"

I didn't answer, I could only nod my head through the tears.

He took my hand and gently pulled me to a standing position, then put his strong arms around me.

Feeling the first human contact since Daddy had died, I dissolved in a flood of tears. I cried and cried and he simply held me. I got tuna fish on his shirt.

I missed my next class as Mr. MacMurray spent his office hour talking to me. My grief bubbled forth and he simply listened quietly. He encouraged me to get involved at school, inviting me to join the tennis team he taught.

I did join the team, getting passionately involved because it meant being near Mr. MacMurray. He spent time talking with me after class and tennis. He was enthusiastic about my natural athletic ability. Occasionally, he gave me a pass from my fifth period art class to come visit him in his office. We would sit and laugh and talk and sometimes I would cry.

One day in January, just after I turned fifteen, I began to cry, and he pulled me to him and held me again. Then I leaned my face up to him and kissed his cheek. He looked at me a second and then returned the kiss to my upturned mouth. That was my first adult kiss. Immediately afterward, he said, "I'm sorry. That shouldn't have happened." I was sad he apologized because it was one of the loveliest things that had happened to me.

It embarrasses me to think back to the ardent attachment to him I had that year. He let me call him Keith when we were in private. I wrote him love poems and baked him cookies. I dressed to attract him. At fifteen, I looked at least eighteen, and I never was young-girl silly. I had lived through too much to ever be light-hearted. Our conversations were adult and, on the whole, revolved around him. I was the captivated listener to his every word.

The attraction was strongly mutual. When I professed my undying love, Keith said, "I'm twenty-six. That makes me eleven years older than you."

"That isn't too much. Can't you wait for me until I'm eighteen?"

"When you're eighteen you'll have forgotten all about me. You love me because your father died and you're lonely."

"That's not true," I protested.

After tennis games I would hang around as long as I could to be with Keith.

The real problem started when Emily took over. In my trance-like state I watched as she stood next to him, fingering his tie, pressing our breasts against him, feeling his growing erection. Emily liked her power. She was never shy. She put her hand inside his shirt, kneading his strong back, then wrapping her two legs around his one and wiggling to let him feel her receptive warmth. The kissing grew from soft lips to open mouth, hungry exploration. Emily sighed as he cupped her large breasts in his hands and squeezed the nipples gently.

Later, I said to Emily, "You mustn't do that. It's not nice."

"Of course it's nice. You like him, don't you? I'm just trying to help you. You're too shy."

"I love him, but I don't think teachers are supposed to love students."

"I'll help you. Without me you'd never get anywhere."

One day in late spring I got a note to report to the principal's office. I didn't know why, for my grades were good and I never missed school—I loved every moment of it, because at any time I might see Keith in the corridors, and always in the treasured English class.

The principal ushered me into his sterile-looking room and offered me a chair opposite his desk, which was lined with pictures of his children.

"Marcia, this is a delicate matter, but I want you to be honest with me. Have you been seeing Mr. MacMurray away from the school?"

"No."

"We know he has been giving you passes to get out of art class to see him. What have you been doing in his office?"

"Just talking," I said, feeling a growing sense of alarm at the intense face staring at me from across the big desk. "He has been helping me with my problems. We talk in his office. That's all."

"Has he touched you in any way?"

I couldn't tell the principal we had been holding hands and occasionally kissing, and I certainly couldn't tell him about Emily. There were a few times with Keith I had no memory of, so I wasn't sure what Emily had done. "No, he has never touched me."

"That is not what I have heard from the P.E. teacher and members of the tennis team. You told one of them you loved Mr. MacMurray."

"I do," I said simply. "He is a wonderful person and he has done nothing wrong." My face flamed scarlet.

"Thank you, Marcia. That will be all."

Keith was noncommunicative and said I couldn't have any more passes to visit him. He became brusque with me, which tore me to pieces. I wrote him pleading letters and tried to waylay him in the halls.

I heard two other teachers talking about Mr. MacMurray, saying he did not get his teaching contract renewed for fall and that the school was fortunate he didn't already have tenure. Slinking down the hall, I hoped his dismissal had nothing to do with me. No one said anything to me about it.

The last month of school dragged by like a thousand years. One of the last times I saw Keith he let me stay after school in his classroom. We sat on the floor, under the blackboard, leaning against the wall. He took my hand and gently played with my fingers.

"I'll never stop loving you, even if you don't let me see you," I said.

"You'll forget all about me soon."

"Don't say that. I love you," I protested.

"I'm leaving for the East Coast as soon as school lets out. I hope you go on to high school and grow and learn."

"I'll wait for you forever," I said.

He leaned over and brushed a curl off my face, put his hand behind my neck and kissed me softly, lingeringly. "I'll remember you," he said.

That was the last time I ever saw him alone. There were final exams and the ninth-grade dance to prepare for. I told all my friends how I would save the last dance for Mr. MacMurray. By this time all the kids at school knew I was in love with him. My nickname was "Pet" because I was the teacher's pet. I thought it was a wonderful compliment. Other girls were jealous because Keith was definitely cute, with blue eyes and pink Irish cheeks.

The evening of the dance arrived and I had to go with Robin, a ninth grader with big feet and bad breath, but he was the first one who asked me. He was my admission ticket to seeing my true love, who was going to chaperon the dance.

I was already at the dance when Keith MacMurray entered with a slinky, overly made-up woman of at least twenty-five. The boys at the dance all talked about the gorgeous lady with him. I thought she looked like a hooker. Keith asked his date to dance and gave me an "I'm sorry" look across the dance floor.

I fled upstairs to the restroom where I sobbed my heart out. Ninth graders love a crisis and my friends rallied to this one.

"He just brought her here to prove to the school he doesn't love you. Teachers aren't supposed to fall for their students," said one friend.

"He's tacky," said Linda.

"He just wants to hurt you so you'll get over him because he knows he has to leave soon," said another friend.

All of our crying and dithering disrupted a good portion of the dance.

One girl cut in on Keith while he was dancing with his date and gave him an earful about how he was breaking my heart.

I never danced with Keith. He left early and the evening went on and on. I finally dried my eyes and was forced downstairs by my hovering friends to the waiting Robin. He seemed oblivious. It was midnight when Robin's father drove me home and Robin gave me a shy, wet goodnight kiss. It was awful after Keith's kisses.

School was out and another lonely summer began. Keith moved away and the gossip died. I never got a letter from him. He was wrong about one thing—I never did forget him. It might have been wrong for a teacher to get involved, even in a minor way with a student, but for me it filled an enormous need. He was a friend to talk to, a human being who offered solace to my life without Daddy and Bobby. Even now I wonder what became of him.

My relationship with him increased the antagonistic relationship I had with Emily. I felt she was somehow to blame for my losing Keith. She was aggressive, and I was deeply humiliated and angered by her.

Jimmy and I got our first letters from Bobby a year after Dad died. First I was relieved he was alive, then I felt anger at his abandonment of us. He was in Massachusetts, as far from California as he could get, working as a lobster fisherman. Other than some frostbitten fingers, he was fine. I wrote him long letters after I had an address.

I was in a dark funk as summer vacation began when I got my first phone call from Bobby. I could barely breathe with the joy of hearing his voice.

"Why did you leave without saying good-bye to me?" I had to know.

"Because you would have made me take you and I didn't even know how I would survive. I just knew I had to leave," he said. "I would have killed Mom if I had stayed. I hate her for what she did to you, to all of us. There is no way I could go back to that house after Dad died. I knew I would kill her and end up going to jail for the rest of my life."

"I miss you, Bobby."

"I miss you, too. I don't know when I'll ever come back. Maybe when you finish school you can come here."

"Write me lots and call me often," I shouted as the operator cut us off.

He was alive; that was the most important thing.

I never loved Jimmy like I did Bobby. He was my brother, but he never was my friend as Bobby had been. I guess the fact that I had to play the mother role with Jimmy changed our relationship. I was the one who checked his homework and mended his clothes. I kept Dad and Bobby alive for him by talking about them.

In that summer before high school Linda and her family moved to Pennsylvania. The idea of saying farewell to Linda and Mrs. Franklin made me cry for days. I spent night after night at their house and helped them pack. It became so emotional for Linda and me that Mrs. Franklin called my mother to invite me to leave with them and stay for a month in Pennsylvania with them. Mom agreed to let me go. I was ecstatic.

We drove across country, and saw all the sights, like the Grand Canyon and, detouring north, Mount Rushmore. The sights meant nothing to me compared to being with the Franklin family. It was a happy month. When it came time to leave them, I thought my heart would break. Linda and I exchanged lockets of hair and bought silver friendship rings at an Indian reservation, swearing our undying love for each other. We have never lost touch with each other. I still have my ring and Linda's hair in my jewelry box. Mrs. Franklin has never forgotten my birthday and we still write each other.

The airplane trip home was my first flight. After Dad's accident, I was terrified by the experience. My heart pounded, and when the plane hit some air pockets I got sick, more from fright than the motion. No one was at the airport to greet me. I sat on my suitcase for about an hour, then telephoned home. There was no warmth for me as there had been at the Franklins'.

"Take a taxi home," my mother said.

Jimmy was glad to see me and Jake seemed rather high-spirited about my return. Auntie Viola was never enthusiastic about anything.

Good news awaited me. Beth had gotten pregnant by God knows whom and her parents were arranging for her to go to a home for unwed mothers. Her parents were nasty to my mom, but I didn't care. I thought her misfortune was one of the most wonderful things that ever happened to me. I didn't even say good-bye to Beth when she left. I made it a point to be out of the house.

The big king-size bed was too permeated with urine to be re-deemable. With sadness, I watched the men from Goodwill carry my father's bed and clothes down the stairs. I tried to retrieve his slippers and a couple of his shirts, but Mom refused to let me keep anything. I stood at the top of the stairs looking at the boxes, filled with all the parts of my father's life, disappearing from my life. Tears streamed down my face. Mom commanded the men not to give me anything—his awards, his cuff links, even his pic-tures were being given away. I flew down the stairs begging for a photo of Dad. The man with the box handed me three. Mom tried to grab them from me and they got wrinkled. I screamed, "I hate you! You're glad he is dead. You want me to be dead, too."

I ran up the stairs to my room, slamming the door behind me. Daddy's things were gone, his lingering scent was gone, he was gone.

Emily came intensely to life with the anger and as I watched helplessly, she took a razor blade and slashed the wallpaper of the bedroom to shreds. I was incapable of anger, it had been terror-ized out of me, but Emily could be richly angry.

Emily screamed in the voice of a demented soul, "I hate the damn witch. She has wrecked our life. She hates me and I hate her. I want her dead, not Daddy. I hate him for dying. I hate all the pain inside. I hate everyone! I hate!"

I don't remember what punishment Mom dealt me for the slashing of the room. It was probably additional household chores, but it left little impression, for I felt I was doing every-thing already. I was a damn slave. If it hadn't been for Jimmy, who needed me, I would have left home like Bobby. Every part of my being screamed, "Run, leave this place!"

As I began high school, I had more incidents of dissociating. Emily was a problem to contend with. She did flamboyant and hostile things, things I would never do. She stole things, little trin-kets. I remember finding them in my room and feeling depressed as Emily laughed at me because I was a prude. I could miss an hour or two out of a day, time that just disappeared from the clock, and have friends tell me of the hilarious things I had done that I couldn't remember. Emily was the instigator behind spray painting the initials of our high school on the entrance of our rival high school and putting red dye in their fountain. I was mortified by the celebrity status I achieved among my peers for something I have no memory of doing. I never got caught.

"Marcia, I can't believe you got on top of Ron's car at the drive-in, doing that wild dance and unbuttoning your blouse. Did you hear the guys yelling for more? I can't believe how gutsy you were," said Judy.

"Tom says you went all the way with him in his car after the dance, but don't worry, no one believes it because you're so sweet. You sure seem changeable, though. You can dress differently and act differently. Sometimes I don't even know you," said my friend Vivian.

Felix said, "You're really weird. Sometimes you come on to me and act all sexy, then other times you seem really shy. First you get mad at me for not kissing you, then when I do, you get all upset and cry. Sometimes I think you're a nut case."

"I'm sorry, sometimes I do things I don't remember."

"Come on, baby. In Algebra you said you wanted to do IT, now you're acting all frozen and shy."

"Please, I'm sorry. Let's just go home."

"Jesus! Hot, cold, hot, cold. You could make a guy go crazy."

Probably one secret to my success at hiding the twin-self was that I was a driven achiever, always striving for the A's, being polite and nice to teachers. No teacher would have thought me capable of Emily's escapades. I suffered over the dual roles my body took. I was shy and deeply embarrassed to hear of the things Emily did. She was clever. Long ago she learned to call herself Marcia in public to keep her identity a secret. To me it was an act of treason and betrayal. I hated this twin with the irresponsible, angry nature.

Sometimes Emily smoked cigarettes and later, after she left, I would resent the rotten taste in my mouth and stale smoke smell lingering in my long hair and my clothes.

My high school years were fragmented between school, home, friends, Emily, and the other dissociative pieces of myself. My memory lapses were frequent, possibly out of acute embarrassement at what I did, or was told I did. Even now, a good bit of those years is locked away from memory. I know I was still a virgin in high school, but I don't know if Emily was.

After Beth left, Mom took in a mentally retarded boarder named Herb, who was in his early twenties but functioned at about a six-year-old level. He was sweet-natured but drove me crazy with his constant talking—he repeated everything he said over and over. He slept with Jimmy in his room.

I did all the cleaning, marketing and cooking. Jake used to help Jimmy out in the yard and sometimes helped me vacuum the big house, but it was a big load for a teenager.

It was during my sophmore year that I decided an escape would be for me to get a scholarship to college. Sometimes it would be two in the morning before I could sleep, because with dishes, laundry, and ironing it was often ten o'clock before I could begin my homework. After falling asleep in class a few times, a boy at school sold me some "uppers" to keep me awake. I began to use amphetamines to keep me going. It made my swings between the wild Emily and the studious Marcia even more of a roller coaster.

I had friends in high school and was in with the "in crowd." My acceptance was based on the flamboyance of Emily. Even though I was popular, I was distant from people, effervescent and cheerful in a crowd but not daring to get close to anyone because I knew I couldn't trust what Emily would do. The less I was with people, the less I would have to explain. My Marcia side felt out of place with everyone. I had a home I couldn't bring anyone to, no money, hours and hours of housework, and a driving need to excel at school.

There were some happy times in high school—slumber parties, dances, pep rallies, and beach parties. I loved sports and played on the varsity hockey team and won a trophy for our school in tennis. But there were times of agony over my erratic behavior, the time lapses I couldn't explain and the lies, the constant lies I told to hold my fractured life intact.

———————

At the end of my junior year, our family finances were in dire straits. Mom accepted an offer for our big house.

Looking back, I don't know why I wasn't overjoyed at the move, but I found it hard. Jake gave Jimmy his pocket knife and he gave me a beautiful amethyst crystal which I still have today. We all cried as we parted, even the crotchety, complaining Auntie Viola. Herb followed us from room to room as we packed boxes. Over and over he kept saying, "I'll go with you." Jimmy and I tried to talk Mom into letting Herbie come with us, but she said no. We weren't sure who would help Herb comb his porcupine hair or make him his favorite cookies. It was a sad parting. I had taken care of them for two years. Jake and Viola went to a retirement home and Herb went to a board-and-care facility for retarded people.

We moved into a small single-story home set way back from the street in a grove of olive trees. My new bedroom was a bright atrocious yellow, with barely enough room for my bed and desk. Leaving a room that had a fireplace and canopy bed brought a mixture of feelings. The old house was the last thread holding me to Daddy and Bobby's memories. It was also the house of torture and hard work.

"Fuck this house!" Emily said. "This place is a monument to pain. Fuck Mom. Fuck this house and all its memories. Fuck life!"

Mom had control of the money and paid the bills. It was a challenge for me to budget the food money so we wouldn't run out. Often we did reach the state of empty cupboards and Mom would berate me for my squandering money, which I did not.

My senior year was a splintering of functional and nonfunctional behavior. I was in the honor society, school treasurer, and a homecoming princess. No one knew Emily was stealing from the student body funds while I was treasurer.

"Please, Em, I beg you, please don't take the money. We have a responsibility. Don't get me in trouble."

"I won't get you in trouble. We're clever. We can make phony entries, no one will know."

"But it's not honest."

"To hell with honest, we can take what we want to. We never have any money. No one gives a shit about us."

"But I don't want to steal."

"Then don't! I'll do it for us. I'm definitely the more helpful twin."

"I think you're awful!"

"Tough shit! I want to go buy some makeup."

I was hauled into the vice principal's office when Emily passed out the answers to an exam. She had broken into the U.S. History classroom after school and stolen a copy of the test.

"Marcia," he said, looking at me through glasses that made his eyes seem about three yards farther away than his face. "Why would you cheat when you are a student body officer?"

"I'm sorry, sir. I guess I just want to be liked." Inside I was screaming, "It's Emily! Stop her! Make her go away and leave me alone. I hate her for tormenting me."

"Well, don't do anything that stupid again or we will have to remove you from office."

"I'm sorry."

One early Friday morning before school started, my Joey personality came out and broke into the biology lab and set free all the white rats that were kept in cages for the nutrition experiments. Two boys in my class saw me and asked me what I had done and why I had men's boots on. I told them I wasn't Marcia, that my name was Joey. Later I faked some excuse about taking too many uppers. The teachers never found out but some of the kids started calling out to me, "Hey, Joey!" I was humiliated that Joey had acted outside of "The Code."

The big sister of one of my friends loaned me a formal gown with puffed sleeves and sequins for the homecoming float I would ride on during the football game. I remember feeling like a phony as I sat waving from my float, thinking of the scars my gown covered and the disjointed life I lived. Rather than enjoying the attention, I felt embarrassed by it.

It was at the Christmas dance that Brent and I became friends. We danced nearly every dance together. I thought he was handsome, with wavy hair, and a dimple in his chin, and he was the quarterback of the football team. We began to spend every spare moment we could grab together. We talked mostly about trivial things and our college futures. I had applied to eastern colleges, hoping to get as far from home as possible. Brent was going to U.S.C. on a football scholarship.

It was difficult for me to let Brent begin to get close to me. I did not know how to have a relationship with someone who really wanted to get to know me. On one hand, I ached for closeness, on the other, I was terrified by it. I begged Emily not to interfere with my relationship with him.

The relationship had progressed to the hand-holding and kissing stage and the beginnings of deeper conversations when in the spring of my senior year I came home from school with an agonizing headache. I decided I was getting the flu and went to bed. Mom was sitting in her rocking chair, going back and forth, muttering and knitting as she often did, oblivious to my comings and goings. I spent the next day in bed burning with a fever and feeling the intense headache and stiffening of my neck. I knew I was seriously sick but didn't think to call a doctor. When you're sick you stay in bed, I thought.

It was Jimmy who found me sometime that evening in a deep sleep that he could not rouse me from. I never heard the ambulance, nor was I aware of being checked into the hospital's intensive care unit. I was in a coma, with spinal meningitis. My amphetamine-weakened system was in collapse.

Chapter 6

Coming out of the coma, at age eighteen, was like struggling to awaken when one would rather turn over and continue a dream. Sounds invaded the dense, sleepy fog in my brain. I felt hands touching me, turning me, sometimes hurting me. I cannot pinpoint an exact moment of consciousness. I am not aware of suddenly opening my eyes and being alert. It was a slow invasion of the here and now into my dream state.

My first memory is seeing a roomful of doctors standing around my bed. I saw the sea of faces, but I couldn't grasp the words they were saying. It was as though they were speaking a foreign language. I *was* acutely conscious that I lay uncovered and my hospital gown was pulled way up as one doctor tapped my arms and legs, then shone a light in my eyes. I turned my head from the invading light and reached down to pull my gown over me. I was surprised that my arms and hands felt as though they belonged to someone else. They made jerky, spastic movements. I felt oddly disconnected from myself and watched in hazy fascination as my hands fluttered.

The doctors hovered around me, commenting on my condition, and one doctor tried to talk to me. I tried to say something but I couldn't think of the words. I lay on the crisp white sheets and gave a wan smile, feeling confused and tired. Nothing made sense. I wasn't sure where I was. I didn't know who the doctors were. Later, I learned I was in a hospital in Los Angeles, in a teaching facility filled with student nurses and medical students. I had been in a coma for ten days. I woke up to a tube in my nose that felt huge in the back of my raw throat, and I had a catheter hurting my bladder and pinching me when I moved. My head ached terribly. I had trouble focusing my eyes. The light seemed glaringly bright. It was easier to close my eyes and drift back into sleep.

People kept talking to me in loud voices and shaking me out of the tranquil sea of nothingness. I resented waking up. It was a harsh reality of strange tubes and sounds that made no sense. I have no idea how long I lay in the peaceful twilight state, neither here nor there. Time was disconnected. My dreams were punctuated by the invaders.

Gradually I became more aware. It bothered me that words floated by me as if in slow motion. Some words I grasped and others just slipped on by. I couldn't make my wishes known. I wanted the tube out of my nose, and someone tied my hands with gauze to the bedrails since I tried to pull out the invasive tubing. Being tied up set off an alarm in my brain. I wanted to get out of the bed and escape whatever this place was. I remember struggling against the arm restraints as I tried to get out of the bed. Instead of words coming out of my mouth, it was just odd sounds. I couldn't find the words. In frustration I kicked my feet and began to cry. I didn't know what had happened to me. Where were my words? Why was my body jerky and disconnected? I needed answers, but no one spoke to me as if I were a person.

Then at long last there was eye contact with a young red-haired man in a white coat. He was shining the light in my eyes again and tapping me. He smiled and spoke to me, looking me intently in the face. I couldn't answer. When I tried, more foreign sounds came from my mouth.

This kind-faced man pulled the tube out of my nose and offered me a sip of ice water. The cold felt wonderful on my raw throat. He showed me things he wanted me to do, like touch my finger to my nose. I tried to do what he asked but my hand acted like a palsied ninety-year-old hand. It embarrassed me.

As the days passed, I began recognizing bits of conversations; connections were coming back. I was too shy to speak because everything was still fragmented.

My catheter was removed and the nurses began bringing me a bedpan at regular intervals. Sometimes I would need to urinate badly, but because I couldn't speak I would just lie quietly feeling the pressing fullness until I was remembered. Sometimes the cramping pain of needing to void lasted for hours when I was forgotten by busy nurses.

Some of the nurses were brusque and hurried, others seemed gentle. One nurse who was very round and black seemed especially kind. She would talk softly to me the whole time she bathed me or made my bed. With big, soft hands she would rub my back. I wanted to talk to her, but I couldn't.

The group of doctors filed in again and the head doctor came to my bed and pulled me to a sitting position, then stood me up. My legs felt like rubber hoses connected at my hip. I fell into him. I felt deeply, terribly ashamed and embarrassed in front of these strangers. They talked about me as though I weren't there. I didn't understand all their words, but I understood that they were not addressing me, they were discussing me as if I was an object, a specimen to be analyzed. Couldn't they see the tears in my eyes?

Physical therapists came in and worked my muscles every day. They had me lifting little weights and gave me a big weighted spoon to eat with. Mealtimes were a humiliating and sloppy experience. My hand could miss my mouth just as easily as hit it. After being a tennis champion, the spastic movements seemed a horrendous degradation.

I have no way of knowing how long it took for there to be visible improvement. The aphasia, my problem with words, cleared fairly quickly, but I was too shy to try and talk. I couldn't bring myself to stammer and halt over elusive words, so I chose not to talk. During this time my world was a feeling, reactive place, not one of cognitive thoughts, yet Emily and the others were still in my mind.

One curious result of the meningitis was a wonderful forgetfulness of the first eighteen years of my life. It was not true amnesia, just a willingness to let my past lie behind a blanket of fog. I recognized all the people I knew. I remembered Dad's death, and Bobby. I knew Mom was crazy and that I'd been hurt, but details, specific events, were clouded. I suspect now that the forgetfulness was one more form of dissociation, since I had no desire to know. I asked no questions of family or friends to fill in the blank places. Looking back at my whole meningitis experience, I wish I knew how much of the damage was hysteria, with my mind needing one more avenue of escape, and how much was physiological damage.

Mom came to the hospital to see me, and in my groggy state I barely acknowledged her, yet I felt an intense anxiety at her presence.

Brent, the boy I had been dating for two months, came with Jimmy to visit me. He walked in wearing his letterman's jacket and carrying a box of See's candies. Jimmy had been to see me in the hospital before, but this was Brent's first time and he looked like he was standing in the middle of a road waiting for a truck to roll over him. His face went as pastel green as the walls when he saw my hands reach jerkily for the box. He and Jimmy got silly with the bed controls trying to cover their discomfort. I was painfully aware of the bedpan the nurse had placed on the bedside table and my long hair that was in uncombed tangles. Jimmy and Brent kept up a rapid dialogue about sports, then began throwing ice cubes at each other from the pitcher by my bed. I closed my eyes and pretended I was falling asleep. I didn't even try to talk to them. Brent never got close enough to touch me; he stayed at the bottom of the bed. As soon as they could, they both fled. Brent said, "I'll come see you again soon," but he never did.

His visit threw me into a depression. I lay in bed wanting to die. I had nothing to hang on to. My sense of self had been overturned in a short time. At a self-conscious age I had suddenly become a physically dependent freak. I didn't know how to deal with it. It's not as though I had any solid core of self to call upon. There was no united family behind me pulling for my recovery.

My complete apathy to my very existence must have been

viewed as brain damage by the medical staff. They spoke to me in monosyllables, if at all.

I was moved out of the I.C.U. into a hospital room with an old woman. She looked shriveled and parchment white as she lay quietly.

My nervous system was so raw from the meningitis, every sound and light was painful. The noise from my roommate's TV would make me cry. Her visitors coming in and out, as well as the intrusion of the nursing staff and housekeepers, jarred me to the point of screaming. I wanted escape. Emily rescued me from the hospital room. We would leave on our trips of fantasy.

One day the old woman seemed to take a turn for the worse. She moaned a great deal and would crash into the side rails as she tried to turn in bed. In my damaged state, her decline only meant further harassment to me. I was not capable of compassion for the suffering of the noisy stranger.

One night she began coughing and choking. I didn't know what was going on, but I knew she needed help. I fumbled with my maverick hands for the call button. The nurse came, in an eternity, to find my neighbor in bad shape.

"Code blue," said this nurse into the intercom. At eighteen I didn't know what that meant, but within minutes a whole bunch of people were in the room. They pushed my bed against the wall to make more room. I heard an odd variety of sounds and conversations. In the end they pulled the sheet over my neighbor's face and left the room. I wanted to know if she was dead, but no one came and spoke to me. In a while a nurse and orderly came and they zipped the woman into a plastic bag. Then I knew she was dead.

I relished the new quietness, sleeping deeply for the first time in weeks.

An odd young man in a white jacket began visiting me in my room. I didn't know if he was an orderly or a medical student. It didn't matter which to me. He brought me cups of ice cream, and never said much as he stood and stared at me. He had short hair, acne scars and wore glasses. I didn't like him, but there was nothing I could or would say to him during those strange nonconversational visits.

One night I was sleeping and was abruptly awakened by a hand being clamped over my mouth. The hospital was quiet, it must have been the middle of the night. I felt startled and confused. No one ever gave me treatments at that time. Something clearly was wrong. Then I recognized the guy with the acne-scarred face. He spoke in a loud whisper. "If you yell for help I will kill you. Do you see this syringe? It's full of narcotics and I'll kill you if you don't lie quietly."

Terror rose in me as he took off my hospital gown, exposing my body in the shadowed darkness. He held the syringe with a long needle in front of my eyes. Even on an unconscious level the old experiences I'd lived through filled me with dread. I lay absolutely still, just waiting to be his victim. The creep put my hands in the hospital restraints. I did not even struggle. I felt the panic, but torture was familiar to me.

Slowly, he began kissing my body, playing with my breasts, licking, sucking on me, then biting me as he worked his way down my torso.

"You have the face of an angel and a body that is driving me mad," he murmured. "But you're like all of them. You're all alike."

I didn't know what he was talking about.

My body was experiencing pleasure and revulsion as he touched me and kissed me in ways I'd never been before.

Suddenly, he seemed to turn angry, and he lifted up a tongue depressor. "Open your mouth," he commanded. I opened my mouth and he wedged the wooden stick sideways between my back teeth, prying my mouth open. I felt the panic rise, not knowing what he was doing or why he was angry with me. He was breathing hard as he pulled down his pants and began rubbing his penis along my abdomen and breasts. He turned my head to face him and he stuck his penis deep into my pried-open mouth. I gagged and couldn't breathe. He jabbed in and out and around, suffocating me, gagging me, hurting me.

I moaned and struggled in the restraints. My nose began to run, and tears sprang from my eyes. Catching my breath was uppermost in my mind.

Just when I thought I would pass out from lack of air, he ejaculated in my mouth. I choked and sputtered as warm semen squirted down my throat. As he withdrew his penis, I vomited, coughing and choking to get air.

The man untied my hands, put my gown and covers back on me without saying a word, then pushed my head into the vomit and left the room.

I lay in the slimy mess a long time. I didn't call for a nurse, I just slipped away to my fantasy escape place.

I came back to reality when a nurse found me and said, "My goodness, you've vomited and you never even called me."

She cleaned me up and ran warm water over my long blond hair to clean it. She changed my sheets and gown, but she couldn't take away the memory of the night.

The obvious question is, why didn't I scream or shout or fight? The answer lies in my years of torture—to resist was to be hurt worse. I simply learned to endure.

He came several more times to have oral sex, vaginal sex or, if there was any activity in the corridors, just quick, harsh fondling.

"Your beauty drives me wild and you're not even truly here with me," he said. I'm sure he saw me as a brain-damaged object.

I lay awake at nights waiting to see if the door would open. My life was valueless to me, existing in a damaged state and waiting to get hurt again.

The man in white had bad breath, and on the two occasions he climbed on top of me for sex his body odor gagged me. I hated him, but I did not resist. He no longer needed syringes or restraints. I merely lay there hating him, willing myself away as he did what he would do.

Emily hated him with a passion. She devised ways of killing him, taking pleasure in thoughts of dismembering him, beginning with his damn invasive penis. She wanted to carve him up slowly and listen to him scream. I remember the thoughts in my head were hazy and inarticulate, but my emotional self and my emotional duality was intact. I was as aware and sensitive as an anemone in a tide pool.

I wasn't like Emily. I worried I would get pregnant. I had been a virgin, at least I think I was, and I knew very little about the facts of sex. I wasn't even certain if oral sex could cause pregnancy.

I have no way of knowing how often this happened to me. It

was probably only a few times, for this *was* a hospital, but the anticipation and the horror of it mushroomed.

I hardly ate. I didn't try to talk or watch television. I simply lay there and let my mind escape when it could. I had the warm, quiet places in my head where I could leave the hurtful reality. I simply became one of my "others," and, like the Good Witch of the North in *The Wizard of Oz*, could enter my magic bubble and float into the fluffy cloud-filled sky, and in Technicolor imagination, look down on the Munchkins playing in the fields of flowers.

In retrospect, it's curious that Emily spoke before I did. The first words in my head were hers.

It was the Marcia-self who was hurt and confined and failing to recover.

Emily was strong and well and full of passion for life. "I won't stay here. I hate hospitals and I hate being raped. I'll get that guy, I'll get all guys. I don't ever want to be an adult if this is what the world holds for us. I'm never going to grow past eighteen."

She didn't. Emily never got older after those rapes. I had birthdays and grew older, but she stayed a teenager. Of course this wasn't logical, but being a multiple personality isn't logical.

One night the creep came in my room again and stripped me naked. He pulled me to the bottom of the bed and propped my legs up. They flopped apart, exposing my private center to his eyes, then his fingers. He had his pants off and was standing at the end of the bed rubbing his organ around on my pubic hairs. Suddenly, the door of the room opened and there, standing with a look of consternation on his face, was an intern. He said a "God damn it" as he flicked on the light. In a split second he gave a roaring noise and literally threw the rapist against the wall. He was yelling and hitting him, then hauled him out of the room. There was a big ruckus in the hall. The intern came back into my room, saying over and over, "I'm sorry. I'm so sorry." He put my gown on me and pulled me up in the bed, putting a pillow under my head. He brushed my hair from my eyes and I winced as he touched me. "I'm sorry. I'm so sorry. He won't ever bother you again. I promise you that. Why didn't you scream? Damn! That shouldn't have happened!"

There was a great commotion of nurses, doctors, then a policeman, but I responded to no one. I just watched everyone from
my far away hiding place.

The next day my room was changed and I had a roommate.
None of it mattered to me. My apathy was profound. The nurses
and doctors seemed overly nice to me. My doctor gave me a pel-
vic exam, and shortly after that I began vomiting bright red
blood. The drugs and stress had given me a duodenal ulcer which
bled. There were barium milkshakes and enemas, X-rays and an
ice-water-in-a-tube procedure of some kind to get the bleeding to
stop. Little glasses of milk and Malox were brought every hour,
and a steady delivery of Jell-O and custards.

A bladder infection turned into a raging, painful kidney infection. My immune system was reflecting my mental state. I didn't
care if I lived or died.

I probably would have died if it weren't for two people—the
red-haired doctor and the large, nurturing black nurse.

This doctor came and sat on my bed and picked up my hand
and squeezed it.

"Marcia, I am so sorry for what has happened to you with the
meningitis, and I know of the rapes. You have been having a rotten time, but I don't think you're as brain-injured as some people
think you are. I think you're very depressed. Will you try to talk
to me?"

I turned my head to the wall. Instead of leaving, this kind man
kept on talking to me. He told me how he was a resident and was
overworked and had hardly seen his wife the past month. He
spoke to me as if I were a special friend of his, as though he
needed this confidential conversation with me.

Tears began to roll down my cheeks as I paid attention to him.
It was the first time since the meningitis that anyone had truly
spoken to me as though I were a human being.

I turned back to him and he saw the tears.

"Marcia, even though it may be difficult for you, please try to
talk to me. I know you can understand me. Take it slowly. I have
time. You don't need to be embarrassed. Do you have any brothers or sisters?"

"Yes. I have two brothers," I said slowly in a croaky, unused voice. It was the first time in the weeks since the meningitis that I had spoken, and I did it surprisingly well.

This doctor, named Roger, was thrilled. He said, "Hurrah, you can talk!"

"But I forget words," I said slowly.

"That's okay. It will come back to you. You're doing beautifully."

"I want to die," I stated flatly.

"I can understand that" was his understanding reply.

"What has happened to me? Why can't I walk?"

In slow, simple sentences Roger explained about meningitis and what a high fever does to brain cells. It was the first time anyone had bothered to explain my mysterious symptoms. He gave me hope of recovery.

"You have had some brain injury from the meningitis, Marcia, but you'll recover quite a bit of what you've lost because you're young. You'll need to work hard to recover."

"I don't want dancing hands," I said, unable to think of the word "jerky."

"Your muscle control will come with time and effort."

"Will I walk normally instead of falling over?"

"I'm sure you'll walk again. You have good reflexes in your legs."

This was the first hope anyone had given me.

Roger squeezed my hand and said, "I'm so very happy you can talk. I'll come see you every day. I'll help you get better, but you have to try."

This was the conversation that brought the light into my darkness. I could talk, haltingly to be sure, but I *was* able to communicate and Roger hadn't made fun of my efforts.

True to his word, he came every day, encouraging me to talk and eat. The bland ulcer diet did nothing to stimulate my interest in survival. Roger used to eat the custards off my tray as we would chat. I got the feeling it truly mattered to him that I get well. He was genuinely enthusiastic with each step of progress.

Annie, the black nurse, was part of my cheering section. She was thrilled when she found out I could talk.

"Honey child, you'll be well in no time," she enthused as she worked my arms and legs.

Roger and Annie were the only two people I would risk speaking with. My shyness over my halting words was acute. Gradually, the other staff members encouraged me to try to talk.

I learned to maneuver in a wheelchair and began sitting in the halls just because I was lonely. The medical students and nurses all were friendly. The ward seemed a friendly place.

Some of my high school friends came to visit and brought me a beautiful flowering azalea plant. It was an awkward visit, for it brought home to me anew what a different world I had entered, a fun house full of trick mirrors. Life was all distorted.

It thrilled me to have the azalea to give to Roger. He had been complaining about not having enough money for things. He was touched by my offer of the plant for his wife. With him I wasn't self-conscious. He could get me to talk and smile. I was coming out of my shock at the damages.

Every day was a regime of activities—physical therapy, speech therapy, occupational therapy where craft projects were devised to help me regain the motor control in my hands. I made odd things out of clay and sewed things in big, ugly stitches, but I felt I was a part of this hospital family.

Annie even brought her daughter in to visit with me. She was about my age, and I felt jealous she had a mother like Annie who could touch gently. I had been so traumatized by the meningitis that it made me feel very young. I craved the nurturing touch of Annie. Every evening she turned me over and with large, soft hands rubbed my back with lotion, working out the tension knots, then slowly, lovingly, rubbing and tickling me.

Just when I was beginning to show some progress and was getting comfortable with the hospital routines, my mother came and told me she was taking me home. Roger strongly objected. The other doctors told her I wasn't ready to go home, but Mom was adamant. She checked me out of the hospital against the doctor's orders.

I sobbed as Annie hugged me good-bye.

"This ain't right, child. You shouldn't be leavin'."

We hugged for a long while and she stroked my long hair.

Roger was livid. "I'm damn sorry that we can't stop your

mother from taking you home. I'm so proud of how well you're doing. Let's hope you keep progressing at home."

"Thank you, Roger, for being my friend." I got his white coat soggy with my tears.

Mom brought me home without a wheelchair or any equipment. I was fearful of what she had planned for me. She acted strangely. I wasn't sure how I would manage at home.

When our car pulled into the driveway, I felt anxious, knowing this was not a good plan. Mom had Jimmy come out to the car and together she and Jimmy half carried, half dragged me into the house. Instead of elation at getting liberated from the hospital, I felt a sense of foreboding and worry that physically I could not cope with my life at home.

Jimmy and Mom plunked me on my bed in a heap, then put pillows under my head.

"Mom, I need to get a wheelchair. How will I get up to go to the bathroom?"

"We'll have to see about that, dear."

"I'm glad you're better, but you still can't walk," Jimmy said. "What are you going to do here at home?"

"I don't know, Jimmy," I said, beginning to cry again.

"Mom's been talking to her angel. She's getting weird again."

"God, I'm scared," I said.

After dinner, Mom ordered Jimmy out of my room. She pulled up a chair by my bed. "I need to talk with you, Marcia. God has commanded me to help you die. You have been suffering enough. My angel will give me the strength to see us through these trying times."

"Mom, I'm getting better. I can talk again. My legs will get better, I'm certain of it."

Mom ignored me and rose from her chair and came and knelt by my bed in a praying position. She folded her hands and began to pray, "Dear Jesus, I give you this child. Please take her from me and end her suffering. Forgive her for her sins and her wickedness. She is ready to come to you, Lord."

I wasn't sure what Mom was planning, but I was frightened. Even without full memory of the past I knew she was crazy and had hurt me. As terrified as I felt, I also became passive.

"Marcia, what I'm doing is an act of Christian kindness. You will be with our Lord soon."

She stood up, bent over me and kissed my forehead, "Goodbye, Marcia." She walked out the door and I heard the lock click in the latch.

I went to sleep that night, baffled by the whole farewell scene and suspicious that Mom would come back to the room and try to kill me. Nothing was improbable with Mom.

In the morning I needed help getting to the bathroom, which was beyond the locked door. I heard Jimmy leave for school. I shouted, "Mom, I've got to use the bathroom!"

There was no answer. I waited all morning. About noon I began to cry with the realization something was very wrong. I had been abandoned and I feared it was deliberate.

I crawled from the bed and pulled myself along the floor to the door. I turned the knob. It was securely locked from the outside. Mom must have put a lock on the door; there hadn't been one there before.

I banged on the door and shouted. No one answered and no one came. I had to go to the bathroom desperately. Just as in the childhood days of the closet, I pulled myself over to a corner of the room and relieved myself on the floor. I was crying.

All day I waited and no one came. Finally, I heard Jimmy return from school.

"Marcia," I heard Jimmy whisper outside my door. "Mom has the door locked and she won't give me the key. She says it's time for you to die."

"Jimmy, she's crazy. Can you get me help?"

Jimmy began crying and I didn't understand what he said.

In the hospital I had been on several types of medications. The sudden withdrawal from all the drugs made me shaky and nauseated. Perspiration wet my sheets in the heat of my room. There was a summer hot spell and my room was baking from the sun that hit the big windows.

By night, thirst was uppermost in my mind. The drug withdrawal made me vomit on the floor. I just leaned over the bed and watched as I retched onto the carpet. The taste of it intensified my thirst.

That night I could hear Mom in the hall outside my door,

talking to her angel and praying to God. I called to her, but she just continued her vigil.

By the next day I was dissociating, escaping into my dream states. My apathy from the years of abuse overcame me. Instead of screaming or breaking windows for help, I lay like a limp, lifeless doll, awaiting my death. I didn't care. I wanted it to come quickly.

Another night came and went. I heard Jimmy yelling and crying.

By the third day the urine and vomit had turned my hot room into a hellhole. My wrinkled sheets felt like mountains on my perspiring skin. I drifted in and out of fevered sleep. Thirst. It was the supreme drive. There is no hunger when thirst is acute.

I wished for the power to die. I wished Emily could take me away. There was a cacophany of voices in my mind. Joey was angry. Camille was glad we were dying. Sunshine, the small child, was passive. She had waited a lifetime to be taken care of.

It was sometime during the course of these days that Muriel came into existence. She was a mature personality with a calm, rational mind, who seemed to handle crisis well. She spoke in soothing tones to the group of us. I think she is the one who felt the desire to live. Sophie didn't care if we died. She kept babbling on about the concentration camps, being totally useless. "Stop this right now," said Muriel. "We are all thirsty, but we will make it out of this room. Why, when we recover I will take you on the loveliest trip to England to meet my parents. You'll especially love my mother, such a dear, sweet lady, who smells of lavender and wears her sensible shoes while she paints watercolors of the countryside. She was born in Wales, you know." Muriel did have a tendency to talk in endless enthusiastic streams.

I have no idea how many days and nights I lived through in that hot yellow room. I felt surrounded by a sea of yellow. Yellow walls, yellow urine, yellow sheets. Yellow was hot. Yellow was pain.

I was drifting in and out of consciousness, resigned to my impending death, when I heard Jimmy banging on my door.

"I've called the police, Marcia. Hang on. I'll get you out."

I heard shouting in the hall. Jimmy's voice was angry and Mom was yelling.

When the police arrived, Jimmy had a butcher knife and was holding Mom against the wall. He was crying and threatening to kill her. Incredulously, the police believed Mom's story that Jimmy had gone crazy and attacked her with a knife and that I had been very sick with the flu and she was about to take me to the hospital. Mom was set free and Jimmy was sent in a straightjacket to the mental hospital. No one believed his story about Mom and he was kept for two months and given a whole series of shock treatments. He lost a semester of school. My mother's sister even went to court to try to get custody of Jimmy at this point—and lost at the hearing. I was too sick to be involved, but my aunt has all the documents. Jimmy said they never even let him testify.

The fact that Mom could get the police to believe her shows again how violent abuse is so far from the minds of normal people that they can't perceive it where it exists. It also shows that Mom was calculatingly evil. She was not so crazy that she couldn't lie and carry on a believable conversation. With clear, light eyes she could look a person in the face and lie. I was too close to death to hate her then, but I do now.

The ride in the ambulance is just a blur in my mind: the needle stabs over and over trying to find a vein to begin an IV, new sounds, new faces as I arrived at the county hospital. After a few days of hydration and medical care, I was transferred to a large rehabilitation hospital outside of Los Angeles.

Intense self-consciousness overtook me as I was deposited in a large room with three other young women. It had all been too much for me, the upheaval of leaving the hospital and Roger and Annie, the days and nights of abandonment in the hot room, Jimmy struggling and screaming as the police subdued him, my acne-scarred rapist, the sights and smells of a county hospital. I lay on my new bed in a strange new hospital with roommates looking at me and I couldn't even answer. I curled up into a little hump in the bed, wanting to be invisible. There was no grounding, nothing solid or secure to my existence. Even my own body had betrayed me, my beautiful eighteen-year-old body that was scarred by abuse and rapes and no longer obeyed commands from a brain that had been fried by fever.

I have read remarkable survival stories about people's enormous will to live to survive all odds. I survived just because my body kept breathing. There was no fight or spunk in me. I lay in this new hospital numb to my core. There were no tears left to shed, no reason to walk or talk. My depression was easy for the medical personnel to zero in on. Everyone was extremely kind to me, but insistent that I eat and move around.

My roommates were a lively group. One girl had been in an auto accident and had severed her spinal cord, one had lost an arm and was learning to use a prosthetic hand, and one was recovering from an aneurysm that left her paralyzed on the left side.

I was shocked at the physical disabilities all around me. I was not unique, just one of many. It lessened my self-conscousness. Babs, the girl in the bed next to me, was the one who was paralyzed. She was twenty and had been in college. Her boyfriend was killed in the car crash. I couldn't believe that she could be so outgoing and friendly with all that had happened to her. She would lie in the bed next to me, reading all the funny things out of the *Reader's Digest*, giggling and looking adorable with her round cheeks and dimples. One secret of her ability to conquer, I decided, was that her family came to see her constantly. She had a mother who came every day, bringing us cookies and pizzas. Her sister, in beauty college, came and washed our hair and gave us exotic hairdos. She loved tinkering with my thick blond hair since it was almost to my waist.

Mom came to see me in the hospital, but I refused to talk to her. I didn't want to see her ever again. Her visit filled me with the dread that she would try to take me home, but she did not. I never allowed her to see me the whole time I stayed in the rehabilitation hospital. Just thinking of her filled me with anxiety.

Emily said in that eternal inner dialogue that if Mom ever tried to take us out of the hospital she would kill her, or me, but she would never go back.

Mom called one day to see if she could come, and in a dissociative rage Emily threw stainless-steel basins and bedpans around the room with great crashing sounds. Emily screamed and howled her rage as I lay watching from a distance.

A nurse came with a shot to calm me. The next weeks I alternated between Emily's rages and Marcia's depressed passiveness. The staff thought I was reacting to my disability and had a psychologist come talk to me about my anger, which I denied having; I didn't dare tell him that it was Emily who was angry. We had silly talks about coming to terms with my disability and working to get well. For a while I was put on Valium and Emily calmed down. I still could lose hours of time as Emily escaped the strangeness of the people and place. Gradually she became subdued as I grew more comfortable with the hospital and its staff.

My native curiosity began to bring me out of my shell. I began to make friends, wheeling down the corridors. For those who could navigate, mealtimes were in a dining hall. It was a jolly social time, all of us soon ignoring other's disabilities.

Babs and I had plenty of friends and attention, since we were both young and cute.

The rehabilitation regimen was grueling. One of the hardest things for me was reading. The words on the page looked like squiggles on a Chinese scroll. I had to learn to read all over again. "See Spot run. Run, Spot, run." It was humiliating at eighteen to be struggling with a large-print primer and blocks with letters on them. Spelling, writing, and reading left me shaky with the mental effort.

Swimming still felt as natural as breathing. My large muscle skills were good. Swimming toned up my weak muscles, and my bony body got back its athletic look.

In physical therapy one day, waiting to use the parallel bars to practice walking, I was sitting in my wheelchair in an old blue sweatshirt and pants. My hair was braided down my back and I had no makeup on. I looked at the bars and my heart gave a little jump. One of the handsomest men I had ever seen was rhythmically swinging his heavily braced legs between the stretch of bars. He was perspiring from the exertion of a few short steps. He was tall and black-haired with chiseled features and a cleft chin. He had sky-blue eyes like my father, large and fringed with curling dark lashes. A small scar on his cheek gave him a rugged look. His naturally dark skin gave him a suntanned look, a stark contrast to most patients, who turned pasty white in the hospital.

For the first time I felt interested in something beyond the perimeters of my own arms and legs. I regretted looking like a slob at that moment.

As the man twisted and heaved himself into his wheelchair, I applauded his efforts. He turned and gave me a big grin.

Instantly I felt embarrassment that it was now my turn to try to walk. I had no leg braces, just jerky, spastic leg movements. I fell often. I wished this handsome man would leave so I could avoid making a spectacle of myself.

The physical therapist, oblivious to my shyness, wheeled me to the beginning of the bars. "Okay, Marcia, let's go."

Shakily, I hoisted myself up, my cheeks flaming red as I realized this gorgeous guy was going to stay and watch me.

"A fellow gimp," he said, grinning.

My inattention and embarrassment made my poor coordination worse. I clutched the bars and felt certain I couldn't walk.

"P-p-please go away," I stammered.

"Hey, what's there to be shy about? Aren't we all in this together in this godforsaken place?"

"Let her concentrate," said the physical therapist. "This is work time."

"Aren't you going to introduce me?" the handsome stranger said to the therapist.

"Marcia, meet Sandy, one of the world's surfing greats. Sandy meet Marcia, one of our newcomers."

We exchanged greetings, and then with great effort I walked the length of the bars, fighting for balance and smoothness.

"How lucky, not even any leg braces," Sandy said. "You'll be dancing before you know it."

After I was done on the bars, we wheeled our chairs over to a corner of the big room. It amazed me how quickly Sandy got me talking. I was so interested I forgot to be self-conscious at how labored my speech was, pausing to search for the elusive words. I'm certain I was more fluent than I felt.

Sandy was twenty-six, eight years older than I. It intrigued me that a man would take the time to talk to me. We laughed and joked like old friends in a matter of minutes. As I laughed, it struck me as odd to hear my laughter; it had been months since I had laughed.

Sandy had broken his back, severing his spinal cord, in a motorcycle accident in the desert. "It's ironic that after surfing in
some of the biggest waves in the world that I bit the dust in the
desert," he said.

We commiserated with each other on how life was shitty and
complained about the rehab process. The friendship began easily
and progressed as though it were the most natural thing in the
world.

Babs had met a guy named Eric, who had lost a leg in a boating
accident. We would sit around in our wheelchairs and play cards.
It was hard for me, since my memory was still playing hide-and-
seek, causing me to lose track of the cards that were played.
Sandy said as long as I laughed and we didn't play as partners I
was a welcome addition to the group. I was the only one too uncoordinated to shuffle the cards. Eric joked, "For real entertain-
ment, let's see Marcia shuffle."

"You're rotten, you gimp," I laughed. I had evolved to the
point of seeing humor in our situation.

Sandy played the guitar beautifully. A whole group of us
would sit around in the evenings singing folk songs.

We pulled pranks on each other, jamming the wheels of our
chairs, hiding leg braces, having food fights. We became a rowdy
fun-loving bunch, drinking wine that was smuggled in by relatives. We were a happy world of outcasts.

Reality intruded when we would get taken in vans on an outing. Suddenly, we would turn into a group of cripples and be the
objects of stares and whispers. Sandy would get morose and noncommunicative. His black mood would last for two days after an
outing. Babs and I were less depressed by our circumstances.

I was envied by the group because my legs were progressing
well. I learned how to use crutches to walk. Eric and I could race
around on crutches and Babs and Sandy were stuck in their
chairs. Sandy could use crutches with full leg braces, but since he
had no feeling from the waist down, it was precarious and dangerous for him to try.

Sandy was thrilled for me when I mastered crutch walking. "I
always wanted a woman I could look up to," he said from his
wheelchair.

"Now I can get closer to you," I said, navigating my crutches right up to his chair, losing my balance and falling on him, my crutches flying in every direction.

I sat in his lap, and after the laughter subsided, he looked at me and kissed me. It was my first romantic kiss since Brent in high school. It felt wonderful with Sandy.

Romance grew rapidly. I thought he was the most perfect human being I had ever met. We spoke intimately, sharing the secrets of ourselves.

I tried to tell Sandy about Emily, and the lost moments, the voices. He listened intently and said, "You can't have a twin inside you. That just doesn't happen. What's probably wrong is brain damage from the meningitis. That'll get better, just like your walking and your other injuries. Don't worry about it."

I dropped the subject. I couldn't tell him she had been there all my life. It's curious I forgot much of my childhood abuse, but I remembered Emily clearly. She was unexplainable.

"Em," I whispered. "I really like Sandy. Please, I beg you, please stay away from him. You've always had all the guys. You know more than I do. You'll wreck it for me if you come out."

"If I give you Sandy, then you'll have to give me my own body-time."

"Even better would be for us to have a transplant and you get your own body."

"Sorry, toots. It doesn't seem to work that way. Will you let me have some time?"

"Okay, if you just let me have Sandy."

"That's a major favor. I'd like to see his balls. Fucking with a cripple might be fun."

"You are the most incredibly disgusting person in the world! You don't even know what love is all about."

"There's no such thing. If you let yourself get close, you'll just get hurt. There's no one you can trust. No one. Just grab the kicks while you can."

"Em, I'm really sorry for you."

One night after lights were out in the hospital I went to Sandy's room and sat on his bed as we whispered. He pulled me down next to him and tried to touch my breasts. Panic rose in me. I jerked away. "What's the matter, sweetheart?" he questioned.

Most of the touching I had ever known was painful. I didn't know how else to react. In confusion I told him about my rapes in the hospital. "Oh, my poor baby," he said as he hugged me gently. "I'll take as much time as you need, but you need to learn to be touched."

I could handle kissing, but that was about all. It took day after day of Sandy setting the mood of loving safety before he could even touch my breasts or fondle me. Like a frightened deer, I would stand still and then move swiftly away. My heart would race from the anxiety and the stirring of new feelings.

One night we went outside and sat alone in the little garden area, watching the stars. I was on Sandy's lap. He began kissing me, then he fumbled for my bra and unsnapped it. He pulled it out from under my shirt and slowly lifted up my shirt, exposing my breasts in the moonlight.

I sat frozen with anxiety as Sandy said, "You are perfect. You're gorgeous." He put his mouth to my nipple and gently kissed and sucked on it. I felt the mixture of panic and pleasure. One part of me wanted to leap up and the other part of me felt the sharing of sensuality and love.

Sandy took my hands and showed me how to caress his neck and back.

It was a tragedy for Sandy that his accident had rendered him impotent. To me it was a gift. I could feel secure that the hurtful penis would not be jammed into my mouth or into my terror-tightened vagina. I liked the safe, gentle touching. I felt cherished.

We had wildly happy times. One day we decided to go to the Los Angeles zoo. We got a pass to go out of the hospital for a day and took a bus to the zoo. I was walking with crutches, which was a big mistake. By the time we got to the first animals, I had blisters forming on my hands. My legs became uncoordinated from the exertion of walking a long way. We sat on benches next to every animal exhibit. We came to a slight incline and my legs gave out. In exhaustion I sat on Sandy's lap with my crutches on top of me. Neither of us could move. Some nice man pushed the wheelchair until we were on the level again. Then Sandy, with his huge, strong arms, said he could navigate and thanked the guy. We rolled slowly along, Sandy unable to see where we were going with me on top of him. I was laughing as I gave him directions.

We were so intent on looking at the people and animals, I forgot to mention to Sandy we were heading down a slope. Sandy swore as we picked up speed down the incline, with me awkwardly blocking his view. We crashed into a grass embankment, throwing both of us out of the chair. We lay in heaps on the grass and howled with laughter until tears went down our cheeks. The chair was tipped over, my crutches had gone flying, and we were in a tangled mess with Sandy's catheter bag leaking all over us. We just lay there too convulsed with laughter to even untangle ourselves. People came running. Soon we had a small crowd staring and offering us help.

The laughter and the exertion rendered me totally useless. I couldn't even get up. I just lay like a rag doll, giggling. Sandy was the first one to recover his sense of propriety and directed two strong young guys on how to pick us up. Sandy sobered at the realization of the spectacle we created. When I was set on top of the wheelchair, we had to ask for help to get pushed out of the zoo. A guard had to call a taxi to get us home. We both had to be lifted like babies into the taxi.

When we got back to the hospital, we fell into a deep sleep from the overwhelming exhaustion of the experience, but later that night, when we told Babs and Eric, the story grew in hilarity and drama. We were young and in love and the world be damned.

The very next week someone put a large gorilla poster from the zoo in Sandy's room with the scrawled message, "Ya wanna dance?"

Sandy's brother had an apartment, and one day he came and said he was going to go on a short trip and handed Sandy the key. Sandy said to me, "Let's escape this place and we'll cook a real meal, not this reconstituted Purina we're served in this dump."

We made elaborate plans and had Babs's sister pick us up and drive us to the apartment. We waved good-bye to her and realized as she was driving away that the apartment was up a flight of stairs. By this time I was using only a cane and could navigate the steps quite well. Sandy had to leave his wheelchair at the bottom and go up backward, using his arms to hoist his body up. We rummaged in the kitchen and, true to his word, Sandy's brother had left us steaks and potatoes and even a chocolate cake. Without his wheelchair Sandy was useless as a cook, so I fixed us dinner and we ate a candlelight meal, toasting each other with cheap Chianti wine. It was special to talk, just the two of us.

I washed the dishes while Sandy sat and watched me, marveling at how well I could move now. I no longer was dropping things or moving spastically. We had both been in the hospital about eight months. My progress had been rapid. Unfortunately, Sandy's only progress was to learn to function with his permanent disability. I was racing toward recovery. I could eat with ordinary utensils and my speaking and reading skills were progressing.

"Come here, beautiful," said Sandy as I put the last dish in the cupboard. "Let's go into the bedroom."

With total comfort in our relationship, Sandy swung himself from the chair and pulled himself along the floor, his legs dragging lifelessly behind him. I limped on my cane after him. He pulled himself up on the bed and panted a bit from the effort. I sat on the bed next to him. He unbuttoned my blouse and pulled it off me, flicking away my bra.

"Please take off your clothes. I want to see all of you," Sandy said gently.

Instantly I felt shy. I hadn't been naked for a man since my first hospital days after the meningitis. "I have scars," I whispered.

"How did you get them?"

"I don't know. I have no memory of my life before the illness, except for bits and pieces." I knew more than I could tell him.

"Let me see," said Sandy.

I undressed awkwardly, in the full bedroom light. Sandy leaned up on his elbows and looked at me. He pulled me onto the bed next to him and caressed my naked body.

"You're beautiful," he said. "You do have scars, but they don't take away from your beauty. You must have had a big accident when you were little."

"I don't know" was my evasive reply.

"Help me take my clothes off, please."

I pulled off his shoes, socks, and pants. Sandy asked me to empty his catheter bag after he disconnected it. It was the first time I'd seen him without clothes and I thought he looked wonderful. His legs were atrophying, but his chest and arms were rippling with the compensating muscles.

I lay still in my ever-present state of alarm as Sandy touched and kissed me in ways I'd never been touched before, pleasure ways, sensitive ways. I froze when he touched my clitoris.

He enveloped me in his arms and said, "My sweet, hurt lover. I won't ever hurt you, don't you know that? I love you, Marcia." He took my hand and kissed the end of each finger.

"I love you, too," I replied. I kissed him all over—his face, ears, and neck.

Our passion grew as our hearts bonded together. Suddenly, Sandy was crying. "God! I can't do it. I love you and I want you and I can't do it. I thought maybe, just maybe I could."

"I don't mind, truly I don't," I assured him, meaning every word of what I was saying.

"God, Marcia, why does it have to be like this? I want to be able to make love to you," said Sandy through his sobs.

I felt magnificently close to him that night. I had known so little emotional closeness in my life that I felt my heart would burst from the aching wakefulness of letting another person close to me. Our pain brought us together and love held us tight, sharing the losses and the joy.

We stayed together the whole night and I let Sandy explore my body as I awakened to what a loving touch meant. I never climaxed; there was too much anxiety bred from wooden spoons and rapes. But just to be able to lie comfortably and be pleasurably explored seemed a gift.

We were late to physical therapy the next day and with good humor got in trouble for being AWOL from the hospital.

Over the next few months we were together as much as we could be.

I was nineteen in the summer of 1961 when Jimmy came to see me with the exciting news that Bobby was coming back to California.

"That's great news!"

"I wonder if he wants me to live with him?"

"That would be a good idea," I said.

I knew Jimmy was living at a friend's house since he got out of the hospital. He was angry his memory was still poor after the shock treatments.

"I'm never going back to that shrew," he said.

"I don't ever want to go home again, either," I said. "I'm not a child, so she can't force me to come home."

"I hate her guts," said Jimmy.

"Tell Bobby to come see me as soon as he returns. I've missed him so much."

The thought of where I would go and how I would live worried me, since I knew I couldn't stay in the hospital much longer. I was a success story for them. My recovery had far exceeded all expectations for me.

Two weeks later, Bobby arrived at the hospital. I hugged and kissed him, cried all over him, and hugged him some more. He was gorgeous and tall and looked like Daddy. He was a man at age twenty-one. I hadn't seen him for five long years. So much had happened to both of us that in one way we were strangers, yet in another way we were the inseparable siblings that trauma had welded together at a young age. Our love for each other was vibrantly alive. We talked for two hours trying to capture all the missing years for each other. Jimmy had told him already of Mom's attempt to murder me. "There is no way I'll let you go back home to Mom," said Bobby.

"What if the three of us get an apartment somewhere?" I suggested, then paused. "But what will we do for money?"

"That's one reason I came back to California. I got a letter from Dad's friend telling me that when each of us turns twenty-one we get twenty thousand dollars left to us in a trust fund by Grandma Bernice."

"You're not kidding?" I squealed. "That really does mean liberation from Mom for all of us. Yeah!"

"I've even talked to the trust officer to see if the money could be used for you and Jimmy to go to college and they agreed to release the funds for education purposes. As soon as you're ready to leave here, why don't you try college?"

I blushed, not wanting to tell Bobby I was at a sixth-grade reading level. Time would tell what healing would still take place.

"Oh, Bobby, I would love to come live with you and Jimmy. I've missed you so much."

"Great, then it's settled."

I thought my heart would explode from the pleasure of seeing Bobby again. The added news that I had money for college opened whole new doors of thought. Sandy and I had focused solely on recovery and what we could do in the here and now. We never spoke of the future; it was as though the walls of the institution owned the perimeters of our beings.

Sandy, in his usual generous-hearted way, was happy that I had some goal to work toward and a plan for when I was well enough to leave. His parents were eager to have him return home and live with them a while, giving him time to decide on a career or college. Sandy had not gone to college; he had been a carpenter and surfer. The accident ended his life as he had known it.

It was almost a year to the day that both Sandy and I were ready to leave. My recovery had been truly remarkable. I still walked with the cane for balance, but I had regained most of the use of my arms and hands, I spoke beautifully and was reading fairly well. I felt my mind was growing in alertness. I no longer missed pieces of conversations.

Eric had left the hospital long ago, but Babs, Sandy, and I cried for days at the prospect of breaking up our group. All of us were fearful of what life held for us. Babs and Sandy were joined to their wheelchairs for life. I was the lucky one, getting to walk out a nearly functional woman.

Our last night, the whole hospital had a party for us. We three had been a hub of social life in the pain-filled institution. We had found joy in the microcosm.

Late that night, Sandy and I went outside. "I love you so much, Marcia. I'm afraid it will never be the same when we leave here."

"Of course it will," I said, full of confidence. "What we have found isn't related to place or circumstance. We'll love each other forever."

"I hope you're right. If all goes well for us on the outside, will you marry me?" he asked.

"Of course I will. I love you more than anyone."

We announced our engagement before we left. We were cheered and congratulated and we promised to come back to visit. We felt we were leaving a family.

Bobby picked me up in his old tan Volkswagen. This time it was a happy feeling to not have to load in a wheelchair or crutches.

"Mom is angry we're going to live together."

"Good," I said. "Let her stew. I don't ever want to see her again."

We drove to Bobby's apartment, and Jimmy was there, all packed to go off to Princeton University, having gotten a scholarship. That scholarship was an enormous achievement, for he had made up the missing semester and graduated with honors with his class. His success was partly due to a wonderful physics teacher who had become a mentor and friend after he got out of the hospital. Mr. Feldman had become almost a parent to him while I had been in the rehab hospital. Although Mom retained legal custody of Jimmy after the court hearing, he mostly lived at the Feldman's house. Little round Mrs. Feldman even took care of Jimmy when he got his wisdom teeth pulled over Easter vacation. Their two young sons played endless games of basketball with Jimmy and their whole family stood up to cheer at his high school graduation.

Bobby, Jimmy, and I sat in the shabby apartment with the blotchy carpet and ate a mound of fried chicken and drank Coors. We talked all night about the future—the past was too dark to explore. I couldn't remember most of it and Bobby told me I was lucky I couldn't remember. A sense of foreboding kept me from pressing him for details of our past.

Mr. Feldman, Bobby, and I took Jimmy to the airport and hugged him good-bye. He left without even a farewell to Mom.

Sandy came over in the hand-controlled car his parents had bought for him. He was depressed by their overly solicitous manner and the way his old friends reacted to him. Our conversation was maudlin at best.

I felt guilty because my challenges seemed exciting to me. I got to cook and clean and figure out what I could and couldn't do. I lost my balance vacuuming, I still had to make grocery lists so I wouldn't forget things, but I was doing well. My progress could be charted almost daily in a forward momentum. I learned to button buttons and have legible handwriting. My reading ability was only up to simple novels.

I registered for two courses at the local junior college. I was determined to try.

My first day at college was exciting and traumatic. I felt intensely self-conscious, as though I had been on a long voyage that no one in the class had shared, and I was different from all the eager eighteen-year-olds. I was almost twenty and my life had been so different from theirs. I felt I fit in better at the hospital.

Taking notes was a supreme effort in concentration. By the time the two classes were over, I was drenched in perspiration from the effort. My arms and legs got shaky just from the stress.

That night I felt very discouraged. College was not going to be easy. There would be no kind therapist saying, "That's okay, just try it again tomorrow."

This was college textbooks, lectures, and exams. I almost quit, but Bobby and Sandy both encouraged me to keep trying. "One day is hardly a test," said Bobby.

Each day was less frightening and easier than the day before. I never talked to anyone for the whole semester; I just went to my classes and returned home, shaking from the mental and physical effort.

That semester I got an A in Psychology and a B in English 1A. It was a milestone considering the zombie I was at eighteen. Sandy took me out to dinner to celebrate, but things were on the decline between us. As I was progressing and achieving, Sandy was slipping ever deeper into self-pity and depression. He wasn't working or going to college. He was drinking quite heavily and hanging around a pool hall and bar. I loved him intensely, but I was hurt he wasn't trying to build a life for the two of us.

One evening he arrived at our apartment on a motorcycle. In a half-drunken state, a friend had tied his legs on the bike and turned him loose. How he arrived at my house alive I don't know, but he crashed into the curb and fell over on the bike unhurt. I was angry. "How dare you risk your life and the lives of innocent people!"

"My life isn't worth shit," Sandy said drunkenly.

I hauled him in the house and sobered him up with coffee.

The more I recovered, the more Sandy mourned his losses.

"I love you too much to have your life tied to a cripple," said Sandy.

"Damn it! I love you. I'm sorry that your legs don't work, but it doesn't make me love you any less."

"You deserve a husband who can make love to you and give you children."

"We can adopt, and you know sex isn't important to me. Being with you is all that matters."

"You'll resent me with time. It'll tie your life to this damn chair, too."

"Sandy, I don't know how to make you believe I love you more than anyone in this world. You're so full of self-pity you don't see what we have together. I don't care about your legs, but I do care about your head and what you do with your life."

I kissed him and he was unresponsive.

We continued dating for a whole year, but it wasn't with the laughter, joy, and passion we had in the hospital. Sandy remained sullen and depressed, drinking more, not even trying to get a job.

I finished another semester of college, again only taking two courses but getting A's in both. Sandy came over to help me celebrate completing my finals. I had been practicing my big surprise, finally being able to walk without my cane. I made him a spaghetti dinner and was quivering with the excitement of my new victory. I greeted him, using my cane, then said, "Watch this." I put my cane down and walked across the room with only a trace of a limp and twirled before returning to him with a smile on my face.

Instead of being happy for me as he usually was, his face held a somber frown. "Don't you see that this divides our worlds? You're beautiful and healthy. You deserve all the fullness of life now that you're well. You can't have that with me. It's finished between us." He turned and wheeled out the door. "Good-bye Marcia, I'll always love you."

Sandy refused to answer my phone calls or see me. I cried the whole summer. I lost my best friend and none of the reasons he gave me made sense to me. I had loved him so deeply.

Chapter 7

That summer without Sandy, Emily was wild and seductive. The splitting of selves seemed to be an ever-widening gap. I didn't like what Emily was doing. She wanted to hurt the world back. "Let's fuck and laugh" was her response to my introverted, shy self who grieved the loss of Sandy. She spent most of the summer taking over, going to parties with Bobby's friends, smoking pot, screwing. I felt humiliated by all she did.

Going back to college in the fall helped calm the upsetting dissociating I was doing. I enrolled in three courses and decided I would aim for a degree in physical therapy. I'm not certain whether it was the happy memories of the rehab hospital or if it was because pain was the only thing I identified with, but I felt I had a new goal in life, to help others.

The next two years of college have blurred in my memory. It was a time of exhaustion, driving my mind and body to ever new limits. I was accepted at UCLA, in spite of my limitations, to study to become a physical therapist. What used to come easily now came at high cost. College textbooks in physiology and anatomy, chemistry courses, took me hours more studying than they would have before the meningitis. I used every learning technique

I could think of—outlining, note taking, tape recording lectures. The harder I worked, the more my concentration improved.

I enjoyed college.

In an anthropology class I met a cheerful, spunky girl named Diane. Sitting next to each other in class, we became friends over the semester. One day she brought in a flier from the counseling center advertising a trip to Europe with one of the professors. "Let's go together," she said as I read it.

"I'll have to see if I can scare up the money for the trip, but it sounds interesting. I'm worried I might be a drag, though, because I'm still recovering from an illness called meningitis. I get pretty uncoordinated when I get tired."

"You seem fine to me," Diane said. "You walk well."

"Only when I'm rested. If I don't stay within my limits I also get a bit mentally confused and forgetful."

"I don't believe a word of that," Diane said. "You're getting an A in this class and you seem really smart."

"Thanks," I said, "but four years ago I couldn't walk or even write my name. I'd like to claim I was a medical miracle, but it has taken an incredible amount of work to get to this point. Are you willing to go on a trip with someone who may fall down a flight of stairs, or get lost because I can't figure out a map?"

"We'll put bells on your shoes, so you won't get lost, and I'll walk up stairs behind you with my hand on your back for balance."

"You're really serious about wanting me to go?"

"Hey, I'm not totally unselfish. With you along I'll be certain to meet European men. Every guy in this class has the hots for your body."

"You exaggerate," I said, laughing.

Diane wasn't pretty, but her personality made her sparkle. She seemed to genuinely want me to go on the trip with her.

I asked Bobby what he thought of the idea.

"It's a great plan," he said. "It's about time you forgot Sandy and lose the mental picture you have of yourself as an invalid. You'll manage beautifully on a tour."

"What if I get too tired and get klutzy?"

"Then you'll just have to learn to live with the embarrassment. You can't put your life on hold for a body that sometimes gets maverick."

"That's easy for you to say, you athletic hunk. I'd give anything to play a game of tennis again."

"Don't slip into Sandy's mentality. Look at all you can do now."

"That's right. I think I can go to Europe!"

Diane and I left in July with the tour. We were twenty students eager for adventure, and we went sightseeing all day and partied until late at night. We met students in every country to drink and talk with.

Diane was a perfect traveling companion; nothing upset her. She woke up cheerful and stayed sweet in the rain and in train stations and was kind to me when my legs gave out. In the Alps I got parked by the group near a barn of dairy cows when my legs refused to climb. Everyone treated me with humor and kindness.

Often I would be the one putting drunk friends to bed. With my questionable coordination, I never drank unless I was in a secure place where I couldn't make an idiot of myself. Besides, when I drank, all my other selves got crazy. I did even better than I expected I would. I felt I had passed over some imaginary threshold into the world of normal. I needed some consideration at moments, but I didn't feel I was a drag on the trip. I was part of the camaraderie.

I shied away from the one-night relationships one often has when traveling. The group labeled me, "ice princess." Obviously, Emily behaved.

Diane didn't need my help meeting men. In Scotland, she met a man with red hair and freckles who looked just like her. They fell in love, and a year later she returned to Scotland to marry him.

In Czechoslovakia, just outside Prague, we went into a little Jewish synagogue. I had never been in one before and was filled with a sense of confusion. On one wall was carved the names of all the Jews from that village who had died in concentration camps during the war.

Douglas was the only one on our tour who was Jewish, and there on a section of the wall were the names of his grandparents, his aunts, and an uncle. I put my arm around him as we all began to cry in that tiny synagogue that was darkening in the late-afternoon light. It was odd, but suddenly I felt jealous that he belonged to something, to a history. Was I Christian or Jewish? My German half belonged to the side of the perpetrators, my Jewish half had names somewhere carved on a wall, or lying in unmarked graves. I felt devoid of heritage. There was a longing in me to enter a church or a synagogue and have a feeling of homecoming. Home for me was just a tacky beach apartment I shared with Bobby, with wicker furniture and cheap posters decorating the walls. I had no history, not even a childhood I could remember. As Douglas wept for the relatives he never knew, I wept for being free-floating in time, unbound by heritage or closeness.

A week later when we were in Athens, bumping along on a tour bus, I got violently ill. I assumed it was a tourist dilemma as I rushed off the bus to vomit. All that day I felt sick, with ever-intensifying abdominal pains. That night I lay in my hotel room, skipping dinner and perspiring with a burning fever. By morning, I knew I was more than just stomach-flu sick. I was rushed to the hospital and had emergency surgery for a ruptured appendix. Diane was sitting by my bed when I awakened.

"You're going to be fine, Marcia."

"I feel awful," I moaned.

"You're going to have to stay in the hospital a while because your appendix burst. The tour is almost over so you can fly home as soon as you are well. I wish I could stay with you, but I've got a summer job I have to start."

"I'll be okay," I said, feeling uncertain.

The whole gang came the next day, filling my room with flowers and fruit and hugging me good-bye. "We'll see you back home. We'll have reunions of this adventure."

My fever continued to climb and I was put on antibiotic IV's. I had peritonitis. The pain was excruciating. As I began to recover, I could only stare out my window to Athens below me, with the blue Aegean Sea in the distance. No one spoke English. I was given nothing but white rice and tea.

At night I would lie filled with the old fear of having the rapist enter my hospital room. It wasn't a rational fear, but the isolation and pain made my mind play crazy games. I lost time again, and when I came back I had my hands tied to the siderails. Being tied up made me really panic, and I lay in the bed crying. A young doctor came into my room and said I had pulled my IV out of my arm and had thrown things around the room. He was the first English speaking person I had talked with. He said my fever had made me act strangely. I knew it was not the fever, but I was grateful for the excuse. I relaxed a bit knowing someone spoke English.

I was treated very well during the two weeks in the hospital. The doctor even took me to the airport when they arranged a flight home for me. They pulled the drain for the infection out of my stomach the very morning I was to fly home. My incision still hurt on the long flight from Athens to California.

It took me a month to recover.

When classes began in the fall, I was happy to see all my friends from Europe. It had been a time of growth and fun.

Sitting in a speech class one day, I met one of the student teachers. Daniel Cameron was instantly likable. He was handsome in the English way, with pink cheeks, fine features, and blue-gray eyes. At five feet ten inches, he seemed taller, because of his muscular frame.

My nervousness in speech class was obvious, so Dan kindly offered to help me. We struck up a friendship right away. He had finished his master's degree and was working as a teaching assistant until a high school teaching job opened up for him. He invited me to a local coffee house to hear a poetry reading. Those were the days of espresso, folk music, and unrhyming poems. We both got to laughing over the intensity of the coffee house scene, and decided to go to the beach to feed seagulls. We walked in the wet sand, talking about European history. He was very nonthreatening, almost boyish, with a dimple when he smiled.

Over the weeks we spent many hours talking and laughing, but I barely thought of him as a man or a date. He was just a comfortable friend. It was on about our eighth date that Dan kissed me. I was taken aback, for I hadn't thought of him that way. There was no electricity or passion or deep sharing as there had been with Sandy. It wasn't love, it was familiarity I was feeling with this man.

Over the next six months we continued to date, doing fun things, "regular couple" things like seeing art exhibits at the museum and the planetarium at Griffith Park. We were boringly ordinary in our conversations and activities.

One weekend we drove to San Francisco and did all the regular tourist stuff—Lombard Street, Fisherman's Wharf, and the Presidio. That night, Dan said, "I love you. Will you marry me?"

It took me by surprise, and I startled myself by saying, "Yes."

We still had never had sex; in fact, we touched very little. That night in our hotel room Dan made love to me. The earth didn't move. I felt affection for him, but there was no deep intimacy. Lying next to him, I thought how little he really knew about me. He knew about the meningitis, but I had never told him about the rapes, nor could I introduce him to a mother who almost murdered me, or share with him a past I only partially remembered. He never asked me how I got my scars. There was so much we didn't talk about. Life was things, facts; the focus was on the here and now.

Emily shouted, "For God sake tell him about me! Are you going to spend your life with someone and not tell him the truth about us?"

"And what is the truth? What are these voices? Who are we really? I don't know how to explain us."

"I don't want to get married. Living with you is strain enough. To wake up to old-mister-solid-citizen-teacher sounds ghastly. Let's just screw around and skip the domestic bullshit."

"Just face it, Em, we never have wanted the same things. I want to get married and have babies. I think I even love Dan."

"How many times do I have to tell you love doesn't exist. It's only in the movies."

When we returned from San Francisco, I went to Sandy's house. I insisted I see him, refusing to take no for an answer. I hadn't seen Sandy for two years, but my heart leapt at the sight of him. At first the conversation between us was strained, but it warmed in minutes.

"Sandy, I'm engaged to marry a man who is an English teacher, but I still love you."

"Does he have legs?" asked Sandy.

"God! Is that all you ever think of? I'm here to tell you I've never stopped loving you, and if you give me any sign or hope I won't marry Dan."

"Do you love him?"

"It isn't what I had with you. We had it all."

"You live in a fantasy world. I can't even afford a wife. I live on disability payments."

I realized this conversation was useless. Sandy was chosing to throw away the earth and the stars. "Doesn't it matter that we share each other's very souls?" I whispered.

"Don't you know it's because I love you that I won't marry you?"

"No. It's because you don't love yourself. Good-bye, Sandy." I left crying. I shed so many damn tears for this stupid man who let a wheelchair come between us.

With Dan there was laughter and good conversation and a mellowness that was comforting. I should have held out for intensity, but I learned from Sandy that kind of closeness hurts too much.

I had just graduated from UCLA when I married Dan in June 1965, in a small church wedding with his family and mine. Bobby gave me away during the simple ceremony. Jimmy wasn't there. He had only come home once since he went to Princeton. Mom acted pleased that I was capable of "catching a man." We flew to Hawaii for our honeymoon. It was a happy week of blue water, snorkeling, drinking rum drinks with orchids, and being the dutiful tourists. Dan was a patient, gentle lover, but he was not sensual or masterful. I tried hard to respond. The play-acting began on the honeymoon with my being the responsive, enthusiastic sex partner, when inside I felt anxiety. I had heard about orgasms and I knew I wasn't having them, but I tried to make sex pleasurable for Dan.

I had thought on our honeymoon I would talk about the real, deeper things in my life with Dan, about what it was like to be disabled and fight back to health, about the rapes that traumatized me. Most of all, I thought I would explain Emily. How could I be married to a man and not explain that sometimes, especially when I was upset, I could vanish away somewhere and my twin would take control of my body, a twin I was ashamed of, for she could be angry or hostile or seductive or steal things. I knew I had to tell Dan, but the time was never right. The conversations never went to the deeper level. My sense of guilt grew with every day I didn't share the secrets.

I never meant to cheat Dan. I wasn't trying to be dishonest, I just didn't know how to be any different. I didn't know how to trust or be close. I didn't know how to open the doors to the pain and let him in. There were secret places in me that even I couldn't face.

When Dan came up to me and touched me when I wasn't anticipating it, I would flinch. When he spontaneously hugged me, my first reaction was to stiffen.

Dan said, "My neighbor once had a dog that he whipped. The dog always shied away from being petted. There is something about you that reminds me of him."

"Thanks a lot," I said.

"No, I'm serious. Have you ever been hurt by someone?"

"Dan, I should have told you before we were married that after I had the meningitis and was just out of a coma, I was raped in the hospital." What I couldn't tell him was that it had been multiple, terrorizing times—oral, anal, hurtful sex. I also couldn't tell him of the dark, fearful, snatches of memory that haunted me.

Dan responded in his usual unemotional way. "I'm sorry that happened to you. Let's go out to dinner tonight."

The issue was dropped.

When we returned from our honeymoon, a stack of wedding presents awaited us in our little apartment in Venice Beach. Dan's parents gave us a thousand dollars to buy furniture with, and my mom gave us a gun. I knew it was just one more way of letting me know she wanted me to die, but didn't respond when Dan said, "That is a really bizarre wedding present. Your mom is sort of strange."

"She *is* weird," I agreed. I wanted to tell Dan of the week in the yellow room, but words wouldn't come.

We had just gotten home from Hawaii when Dan got his acceptance to flight training school in the Air Force. "I'm going to be a pilot! I made it! I've always wanted to fly a plane." Within days, he left for Pensacola. I joined him after I got everything in our apartment packed up and in storage.

Florida was fun with Dan. We went to the ocean as much as possible, and even though his training was grueling we saw each other often. I lived in a little white house off-base.

We had not been using any birth control since we got married, but Dan said, "It looks like I'll be going to Vietnam when I get my wings. Maybe we should put off having a family until I return."

I burst into tears. "Please don't go. I beg you, don't go."

"It's my chance to fly," said Dan.

"But that is how my father was killed. I couldn't survive a knock on the door in the early morning."

"I'm not going to die. I'll come back to you."

At Dan's urging, I made an appointment to get a diaphragm from the base doctor.

The examination seemed to take a long time. The doctor would touch me one place, then another, asking me if it hurt.

When the exam was over, the doctor peeled off his gloves and said, "Mrs. Cameron, come into my office for a minute."

He closed the door behind us and said, "Somehow you have been very badly ripped inside by a past pregnancy. Your cervix is badly scarred and your clitoris is completely bound by scar tissue.

"I've never been pregnant, Doctor."

"Of course you have, but we don't need to tell your husband if it is a family secret."

"No. I mean it. I've never been pregnant."

"I can't think of anything except a birth or badly botched abortion that could scar you in the way you are scarred. You need reconstruction surgery. Sex can't be very pleasurable for you with those scars. Your clitoris is badly mutilated. Besides helping you enjoy sex, we need to fix your cervix so you can have a baby someday. With the external damage I'm seeing, we can only hope internally you are functional. I'd say there is a possibility you may not be able to carry a baby to term."

I left feeling deeply upset. The idea that I might not be able to have children filled me with sadness.

I told Dan that surgery was scheduled to fix something wrong with my female parts. He mercifully asked me no questions. I did tell him the doctor wasn't certain we would have children.

"Of course we will, and they'll all have your blue eyes."

Dan drove me to the hospital and stayed until I was out of surgery. Again there were questions as to how I had been so badly damaged. I honestly didn't know, but I felt great anxiety at the questioning.

Dan was thoughtful and gentle, waiting for me to heal before having sex. I was hoping for his sake that the surgery would transform me into an orgasmic sex kitten. No luck. Sex was no longer painful and my clitoris did have feelings of pleasure, but nothing could change my underlying anxiety. It depressed me. Somehow I was lacking as a woman.

My depression didn't last long, for Dan got his orders to Vietnam. We didn't want to waste a moment. Looking at his boyish face sleeping next to me, I realized how precious he had become to me. We didn't know how to communicate well, nor did we understand each other, but a love was growing. The days before he left, he was wracked by fever and chills from all the vaccinations. We packed up our stuff and I got ready to return to California.

Dan had barely been gone when I missed my period. I knew I was pregnant. I waited another couple of weeks before I wrote him the exciting news. It was wartime, I was alone and suddenly I felt connected to something. A baby would keep Dan alive forever.

Dan wrote back that he was excited, too, that I certainly had proven the doctor wrong with great alacrity.

I began working at the Veterans Administration Hospital in the physical therapy department. I related to the men with disabilities; I had been there. Seeing the amputees and brain-injured patients we got from Vietnam filled me with dread that Dan would return to me injured, or not at all.

Sometimes I'd have to leap up in the middle of a session with a patient and throw up. I had terrible morning sickness.

At night I went home alone to my apartment. Bobby had gotten married, Jimmy was still in the East at college. There was no one I was close to. I tried to see Dan's parents, but I felt shy with them. I would bake brownies or cookies and send love packages to Dan. I would also bring cookies to the men in the hospital.

One evening when I was about four months pregnant, I stayed late at the hospital because one of the floors was having a party and I had no reason to go home. There were friends of patients there, too, and some had been drinking. We all laughed and joked. The beers I drank made me woozy, and Emily came out for a while. The next thing I remember it was midnight and I was one of the last to leave, feeling nauseated and headachy.

The parking lot was very dark, and I walked clear around the unlit side to the employee parking area. I heard footsteps behind me. Just as I found my car at the far edge of the lot, a half-drunken man from the party came up to me.

"Hey, beautiful. I saw you looking at me up there. You want to go out with me?"

"No, thank you. I'm on my way home for a good night's sleep."

This man, who had been flirtatious and funny at the party, suddenly seemed menacingly huge. I fumbled for the keys to my car. He loomed over me, pressing me against my car.

"You can't tell me you're not interested. You came on to me, you made it pretty clear what you wanted."

"I'm sorry, it must have been the alcohol." Damn Emily.

He had his hand on my shoulder, pushing me back against the car.

"Please don't hurt me. I'm pregnant."

"The hell you are. You have a gorgeous body." He leaned down and with beer breath kissed me on the mouth. Revulsion shot through me.

"Please let me go," I pleaded, struggling to get away from his body that was suddenly all over me.

He ripped at my clothes while I struggled against his massive frame. Panic rose in me. I had lived through this before. I bit him as hard as I could and began hitting him.

"Bitch. You damn bitch."

With giant hands he grabbed my arms and slammed me against the car. With one hand across my neck and shoulders pinning me, he took his other hand and beat me. He knocked the wind out of me, and I felt a hard hit to my abdomen.

Suddenly, the fight went out of me. I became the abused, hurt child again, just waiting for more pain. I drifted away from my body, and watched myself from a distance getting hit again and again. Then my silent body was down on the pavement and this animal ripped off my pants and his pants and raped me in the dark parking lot.

I don't know how long it was before I was found. I was dissociatively drifting away. "I am not here. This is not happening. I will be somewhere else."

From a great distance away I felt myself getting lifted onto the stretcher and heard the ambulance sirens. "I will find a warm, safe place to hide," the voice inside said. I drifted beyond the cramping abdominal pains, the operating room, the lights, the hands and voices. I was choosing not to be part of the scene.

People were trying to rouse me, speaking to me, shining lights in my eyes. My voices said, "Don't go back. You don't want to know. Stay in the void, in the nothing where it is warm and safe. There is no safety in the other world."

I don't know how long I floated away from reality. Reentry was awful. There was an IV in my arm, and pain radiated from every inch of me. It hurt to breathe and move. I was black and blue all over.

"Is my baby all right?" I asked the doctor, who was a stranger to me.

"I'm sorry, you lost the baby. It was a little boy. How can we reach your husband or a relative?"

I was crying, holding my stomach. The little hard pouch was gone. There would be no more butterfly wings of life. My baby. My son. Dan's son was dead.

I cried for the loss of his life and I cried for my guilt. I hadn't screamed or run or truly fought. I had slipped into passiveness, just as I had in the hospital years before. I let my baby get killed. I didn't know if Emily had done anything to provoke the attack. She probably had. I hated her.

I chose to go away again. I left the doctor and the hospital and the pain. I could hear myself crying from the faraway place. I felt the needle in my arm and the doctor talking to me from a distance.

Every time I came back to the here and now I couldn't deal with it. There was nothing to trust. No one to hold me. No connection to life. Dan seemed as far away and as unreal as everything in my existence.

In a lucid moment I remember sitting in the bed holding the pillow in my arms, as though it were a tiny baby and I was sobbing, "Daddy, Daddy, why did you die? Don't you know how much I need you? I need you to take care of me."

The doctors sedated me heavily. I'm certain they thought I was a bit crazy. They were right.

The hospital sent a telegram to Dan, but he was in the war zone and couldn't get leave. He sent me a beautiful telegram saying he loved me. I cried for myself, for Dan, for the son we would never know. I cried for the trail of pain that followed my life.

My body mended faster than my mind. I was in the hospital for two weeks, probably more out of the staff's concern for my mental state than my physical condition. When I was not dissociatively escaping, I was curled in a little ball crying and leaving my food trays untouched. When the doctors alluded to the possibility of a mental hospital, I pulled all the fragmented parts of me together to let them know I could cope enough to be released.

I went home to my apartment and felt the overwhelming loneliness of the isolated world I lived in. I didn't even contact Dan's parents. I didn't know what to tell them. I took a leave of absence from work. I stayed in bed and just stared out the window. I wanted to die, but I didn't have any actively suicidal ideas, I merely ceased existing in the here and now, letting the voices within me speak, letting the self-hypnotic escape routes save me from more than I could deal with.

Bobby dropped by after work one day and was alarmed at how skinny I had gotten. "You're not eating," he accused. He packed a bag for me and led me to his car. "Hey, we've been through worse," he said. "You'll snap out of this depression staying with us."

He was right. Bobby and his wife Nancy were fun to be around, laughing and joking, keeping me from slipping away. They made me eat and get dressed. I must have stayed a couple of weeks, imposing on their generous hospitality.

Going back to work was helpful. Other's problems seemed greater than my own, forcing me to pull myself together.

Just when I was beginning to rally out of the depression, I got a package in the mail from Mom. In it was a large butcher knife and a note saying she was sorry I had lost the baby. The message was clear. I threw the box on the floor and stood there crying.

Emily went on a rampage, stealing dozens of things from department stores. I was depressed Emily was out of control, doing what I would not do. It wasn't until years later in therapy that I figured out she was the anger I could not express, but at the time I felt deep humiliation at her stealing. I returned articles that had the stores' tags on them. Emily took the knife Mom had sent and cut up an upholstered chair in my living room. I not only had my own grief, I had an angry twin to worry about. It was a ghastly couple of months of crying jags, lost hours, and stolen objects before the tempest inside began to quiet.

Dan got R&R leave and sent me a plane ticket to meet him in Hong Kong. My spirits gave a flicker of elation at the thought of seeing him again.

Our meeting was awkward, almost as if we were strangers. It took us a Peking duck dinner before we began to feel intimate with each other. We had a happy ten days, neither one of us discussing the war or our lost baby. We talked about China, my job, the sights we were seeing. Dan bought me a beautiful gold-and-jade necklace and gave it to me before we made love slowly and sensually on the ornately carved Chinese bed.

When I returned home, it was a happy surprise to be pregnant again. I had barely healed from the rape and new life was beginning again.

Pregnancy filled me with joy. I liked my work and I began to make friends with the staff. I was less lonely.

In my sixth month of pregnancy I had to quit work. The doctor was worried about an "incompetent cervix," with the scars and surgery I had had. I was relegated to bed rest at home. The days dragged slowly as I worried about Dan getting killed and worried if I would have a normal baby. My secret fear was that the fever of the meningitis might have hurt my ability to make a perfect baby. I had written of my fear to Dan, but his response was, "Of course our baby will be normal." He refused to discuss my maudlin "What if . . ."

I resolved that no matter how many fingers and toes or brain cells it lacked, I would take care of it and love it.

Emily's voice hounded me. She did not want a baby. She said, "Neither of us knows how to care for one."

She was right. I was certain I was lacking the instincts of motherhood. In the months of bed rest, awaiting this bundle of love, I read every book I could find on child rearing. I didn't just read the books, I memorized sections. Anxiety coursed through me, nagging that I would not be adequate.

By my eighth month my balance was thrown off by my big stomach, and I had to use a cane and walk carefully to avoid falling over.

I was cooking dinner for myself one evening when the labor pains began. I was alarmed, for I was four weeks away from my due date. As I rushed around packing a suitcase, I knew for certain this baby would be dead and once again I would be huddled in a hospital bed all alone. Images of flames engulfing a tiny corpse made me crazy with my anticipated grief. I became convinced this would be a dead Jewish baby. I was crying and crying all by myself and began grieving and throwing things around the apartment.

I dissociated and have no recollection at all of going to the hospital, or the delivery. The nurse said I was riotously funny when I arrived by taxi, in the bearing-down stages of labor, amniotic fluid leaving a trail behind me, cheerily telling everyone, "I need to reach Mumsy and tell her seven lords a–leaping will soon arrive." I guess Muriel was the one who went through the delivery for me.

Kevin was just over four pounds, but perfect in every way. Bald and red, I thought he was the most beautiful baby I had ever seen.

Milk engorged my breasts as I watched Kevin through the window in his tiny incubator. Every day of waiting to take him home seemed an eternity. In two days I got to go home, but the hospital kept Kevin for two weeks, until he reached five pounds. The nurses dressed him in a little blue knit outfit for me. He was beginning to grow eyelashes and looked like a little doll.

The first few days and nights were horrible. Kevin cried to be fed every two hours around the clock. I had rampant insecurity.

Emily said, "I don't want to be needed. I don't want you to wake me up in the middle of the night. I refuse to help take care of a red, crying creature."

"I don't know what to do with him, either. Maybe you can help me."

"No way. I've seen its yellow shit. I don't want any part of this mother stuff. Ask Sophie. She knows all about babies."

I said to Emily, "As long as I am taking care of Kevin, if you ever take me away and leave him alone or if you hurt him in any way, I will kill you. I know I'll die, too, if I kill you, but I'm totally serious."

"All right already, Little Mother. You can have the squirmy little beast. You have my word I won't hurt him or take you away."

Over and over, in a litany, I said, "A mother's touch should be as gentle as butterfly wings." I had the fearful thought that I would hurt this baby.

Maybe my fears kept me on guard, but I was a good mother. I touched gently. Times when I got frustrated I used an old rocking chair and would rock and sing. If Kevin cried too much, I cried, too.

One of the nurses I'd met while I worked had a baby the same time I had Kevin. We became friends and I went often to her house, surreptitiously studying everything she did with her baby. I absorbed every gesture, every word. We walked our babies together and took them to the zoo before their eyes could even focus.

Kevin was deeply satisfying, even though I was insecure. He seemed wise, with his tiny face peering trustingly at me. He was a cheerful little soul.

As the weeks went by, my confidence grew. Cuddling him seemed natural. I didn't know why I was so fearful I would hurt him. I decided if I made any mistakes it would be that I would hold him too much, love him too much. It seemed imperative to me that my baby never know the feeling of abandonment. I even brought him in bed with me at night, frightened I might not hear him cry.

My hands had not fully recovered their dexterity, and I worried I would stab Kevin with the diaper pins. My own fingers got stabbed regularly. I walked slowly with him for fear I would lose my balance and fall. I had viewed myself as normal until Kevin arrived and my slight limitations seemed monstrous now that my baby's survival depended on me. My hearing loss, which had not handicapped me, frightened me when I realized I could not hear Kevin cry from another room. There were little things and big things to contend with by myself.

I was overjoyed when I got the telegram, in September of 1968, telling me Dan was arriving home. He was alive!

I greeted him at Travis Air Force base with Kevin, who was six months old. At last we would be a family.

Kevin looked like Dan, with round pink cheeks, and big gray-blue eyes. He was a tiny little baby, weighing only about fourteen pounds at six months because he was born prematurely, but he was a gurgling, grinning character. He liked Dan right away.

Dan was the one who found the transition to instant fatherhood a bit traumatizing. His first decree was that Kevin was not allowed to share our bed. He put Kevin in his crib. I tried to let Dan take over as father, but I was so upset at Kevin's banishment that I burst into tears and went to sleep on the floor next to Kevin's crib in case he cried in the night. It took a few nights and a large measure of my crying to resolve the issue that we were now a family. Somehow Dan had to find his place in our lives, however tightly Kevin and I were bonded.

After the first difficult adjustment weeks were behind us, we entered a happy, contented time in our lives. Dan got a teaching job in a town north of Los Angeles. We made friends in our new community and I felt secure for the first time in my life. We bought our first home, a tiny wood-and-glass house with a vaulted ceiling and a giant oak tree in back.

When Kevin was about eight months old, I asked the pediatrician, "When do babies learn to have a bowel movement on their own?"

"What do you mean?" he asked.

"When will Kevin have a bowel movement without my having to stick a Q-tip or thermometer in his rectum to make him have a BM?"

"My God! You don't need to do that. You shouldn't do that! You could hurt him. Babies go all by themselves. They don't need any stimulation."

"I'm sorry. I didn't know," I said.

"Have you been doing that every day?" he asked.

"Yes. After his breakfast."

"Well, stop immediately."

"Do babies need to be flushed out with enemas?" I almost whispered it.

"Heavens, no. Where did you get such strange ideas?"

I know now I was just repeating what had been done to me without my even knowing it was wrong.

On Kevin's first birthday I discovered I was pregnant again. Dan was thrilled.

My pregnancy was difficult, with bleeding and premature labor pains which the doctor stopped with alcohol dripped by IV into my veins for a few days. Then I was ordered to bedrest. With Kevin toddling around, it was nearly impossible to lie in bed, but I managed until labor began two weeks before my due date.

Little Cynthia rushed into the world, ripping my already scarred cervix, but arriving tiny and perfect.

Coming home from the hospital, I felt the burden of taking care of two babies and feeling like a trussed turkey with all my stitches. The first few weeks are a blur of tired memories. My stitches got infected, Cindi had colic, Kevin demanded attention, and Dan seemed oblivious to the stressful confusion. I hated his aloofness to my need at that moment. Dan was always kind and polite, but he didn't grasp situations of need, as though his mind couldn't encompass anyone but himself.

After a routine got established and my body healed, I entered the loveliest period of my life in spite of being neurotic. My Emily voice quieted. It was as though nursing Cindi I was nurturing some deeply starved part of myself. I breast fed Cindi until she was two and a half, and stopped only because Dan finally demanded it.

"For Christ's sake, Cindi unbuttons your blouse in public for a snack! You're going to have breasts you can tie in a bow if you don't quit being a dairy cow to her."

"But I love it. I love her."

"Well, try hugging instead of nursing, and give the kid a cup. Make it silver. Make it a Bugs Bunny cup—anything, but quit nursing!"

I had excessive fears about everything. I worried about my children's nutrition, never feeding them store-bought baby food. I made all my own and pureed it in my blender. I feared poison in Gerber jars.

Dan's and my worst arguments were about Kevin and Cindi. I plugged shell night lights in their rooms and always left the door open. I didn't ever want my babies to know blackness or closed doors. I kept our bedroom door open too.

Dan said, "Can't we please make love with the door closed? They will be perfectly fine by themselves." He would shut all the doors, then I would get anxious, cry, get out of bed and open all the doors.

Usually Dan gave up trying to deal with my fears and let me have my way, since there was so much anxiety connected to my thoughts.

I worried about fire constantly. I had the image in my mind of Kevin and Cindi being enveloped in flames. Every room in our house had a fire alarm on the ceiling, which I tested weekly. I constantly replaced its batteries. I asked an electrician to check the wiring in our house to make sure it was safe. Dan was angry when we got the bill. He was angry, too, when I called the fire department to check on the smoke I smelled. I did this several times, but it was always imaginary or from a neighbor's barbecue.

When the children were about four and two, I began my treks with them to the ophthalmologist. I was convinced they were going to be blind. I went about every six months, hovering next to the chair while my squirming youngsters got checked. Finally, the ophthalmologist got cross with me. "Your children have perfect vision. You need to stop worrying. Don't waste my time or yours." I waited another six months and took them to a new doctor just to make sure the other one wasn't wrong.

I had several episodes of blurred vision and one period of time when I lost my vision completely for a few days. Dan took care of the kids and drove me to the ophthalmologist who said he couldn't find anything wrong with my eyes, but he proceeded to order a whole battery of tests to rule out a brain tumor or multiple sclerosis. He sent me to a gruff old neurologist who told me he thought it was hysteria. I never went back to him, nor did I call the psychiatrist's number he had written down for me.

It is fortunate that my children were born with noisy, irrepressibly inquisitive, outgoing personalities. No one was going to keep them from joyously careening through life. We read stories together and every day took long walks through the fields past the houses and fed horses and cows. By four they could both read, and libraries were always our favorite journey.

Dan became involved in coaching the soccer team after school and singing in a barbershop quartet. He was always kind and gentle to the children, but he didn't feel the joy I felt in parenting, nor the apprehension. My babies were my whole world, and my world had many fears from the childhood I did not remember. When they skinned knees or had fevers, I became unglued. Maybe the lack of involvement I read into Dan's actions was merely adult, calm logic.

When Kevin and Cindi began preschool, I volunteered to help. I couldn't bear relinquishing them to anyone else. I didn't trust other people with my children, especially not women. I was like a clucking hen.

During those first days of mothering, I rarely dissociated. From what I have read about abused children becoming abusive adults, I feel a welling of gratitude that somewhere way inside I absorbed my loving father and my Grandmother Bernice enough to pass on the loving. It didn't come easily. I lacked maternal instincts. I was filled with fears, panics and insecurity, but my mother heart was loving.

Unfortunately, simply loving is not enough. No matter how hard I tried, or how good my intentions were to be a good mother, I failed. My children were thriving, but as time went on, the stress and my fears began unraveling me. I became more erratic in behavior; I couldn't keep a constant exterior because there was no constant interior. There was the driving, black, unexplainable pain. There were the voices, always the voices, and there was Emily. . . .

Chapter 8

"Fuck this scene," Emily said. "I can't handle this domestic bullshit. I never wanted to be saddled with little brats that drool, slobber, and cry. I'm outta here."

"No, Emily. Please don't take me away. At least give me time to get a baby sitter."

"I'll give you exactly an hour to get one. I don't give a shit about the rug rats."

"I hate you. You'll steal something. Please don't take anything."

"Time's ticking. Get the sitter while I go change clothes, real clothes, not the jeans and baggy sweater you wear. Let's flash our stuff. Let's let it pop out and jiggle."

The war would rage between us. I would demand control until I could safely leave the kids.

As the car backed out of the driveway, the struggle would be over. Emily would flick on the radio to blasting rock, stop at a signal light and get out the makeup case, put black pencil lines around our eyes, blue shadow above, and silvery pink frosted lipstick on our lips.

The Marcia-self receded further away, as Emily acted like the seventeen-year-old she was. A tough cookie. She would drive to the gas station and buy cigarettes, then squeal the tires leaving the station, off to a fun time.

She liked to bowl. In the next town there was a big alley with lots of lanes and a bar next door. The men that hung out there liked cheap talk and tight ass.

"Buy me a beer?" Emily would slink provocatively onto a stool.

"For you, honey, I'll buy all day," some beer-gut man would say. "Hey, babe, are you selling your stuff?"

"Honey, if I like you, it's free. Show me a good time and I'll give you something to remember later." Emily would lean over the bar, pressing her arms together just enough to let the breasts round up, out of the low-cut tank top. She would take long, slow drags on her cigarette and exhale with her head tilted up, so the smoke would rise up to the red-lit beer signs above the bar. She would drink. Not much, but she would down the first couple of beers fast.

None of my selves drank much. We learned when we were very young that we lost all control of who would come out with alcohol. The fracturing selves could get dangerously chaotic.

Emily liked disco dancing, country-western dancing, those penny arcades where for quarters she could play table hockey with lonely sailors. Not all escapades led to sex, but there were numerous times after dancing up a sweat, she'd strut into a hotel with some stranger, and after checking in as "Emily Jergens," she would go into a room, the dead-smoke, green-bedspread kind of room. She liked the name Emily Jergens. The Jergens was after the lotion she carried in her purse, the little trial-size bottles. She would beg to be rubbed all over with lotion by the anxious men, who were all too eager to comply.

Emily wanted pleasure, but she wanted pain, too. She would try to talk whatever partner she was with into tying her up with his belt, or pulling her hair hard. Some guys wanted no part of kinky sex. A couple of times the men realized that Emily was "a bit off," as one man put it, and left. More than once she was hurt.

Emily had a thing for eyes. She always began sex by kissing the man's eyes with her large soft lips, the lids, the brows, then lightly running her tongue across the lashes, then sucking the lashes.

She liked ears, too, biting, penetrating with her tongue.

She always began gently with the face before sex escalated into wild passion.

"Do it to me hard, baby. Bang it! Slam it! Hurt me! Do it to me!"

She was an angry lover; biting, scratching, mock-fighting, slapping, then varying it with provocative kisses—oral, genital, licking, sucking. She was a hurt, uninhibited teenage self. She did not know tenderness. She knew animal sex, mutual usury. If the sex was rough or hurtful enough, occasionally she would reach a climax. The orgasm would often switch who was in control. I can't explain it; it was as though her energy dissipated and the Marcia-self was back in command.

My sense of degradation was enormous as I would get up from the bed and step into the shower with the tiny paper-wrapped soaps and scrub and scrub trying to get alcohol smells, stinking-man sweat smells, the Clorox-scented semen off of me.

It was hard to reenter the room with some man I'd just made love to but had no desire to touch.

"Please take me back to my car."

"What's the matter, honey, don't you want to see my big fella again? He's ready for more action."

"No. Please let's leave now. It was great, but I've just got to get home."

"We can do it slower, gentler this time. Come on to bed. It's still early."

"I can't. I've go to get home to my kids."

"Oh, great! I fucked a mother. You sure as hell don't act like a mother."

"I'm sorry. Please let's just go . . ."

"You sure did a fast change, red-hot hell cat one minute and quiet little mouse the next. You're a weird one."

The Emily face had been scrubbed off in the shower and the back-combed puffy hair was back to straight-combed and I would head for home, filled with sadness.

"Mommy, Mommy, we missed you," little Kevin said throwing his arms around me, smearing me with grape jelly. His warm little-boy smell was ambrosia after the hours away.

––––––––

Emily liked shopping malls. She would dress with less flair and flash when she went to a mall. "To rip off a store you have to look nondescript" was her explanation as she would put on one of my dresses, subduing the makeup, putting my gold hoop earrings in her ears. The clothes didn't make the person, she could be Emily in my clothes, and I could take back over, dressed in hers. But we both knew whose clothes were whose.

When Emily looked in the mirror, she saw a tall teenage self, a brown-eyed, tilt-nosed lithe woman of five feet ten. She actually saw her reflection differently in the mirror. She saw her breasts as voluptuous; tools for her hobby. I viewed mine as scarred appendages that were for nursing babies. We walked differently. Emily had light, slinky steps; I had a regular athletic walk, with no major hip-swaying. She could walk into a room and know she was a coveted sex object. I always felt timid entering a roomful of people.

When I looked in the mirror I saw my blue eyes and average, five-foot-four stature. We were complete opposites. Emily was angry; I was sweet and gentle. She was wild, and I was shy; polar opposites in disposition. She was impulsive and irresponsible, even bordering on sociopathic.

"Fuck the world. It needs fucking!"

We spoke with different syntax. I don't use words like "fuck."

"Let's go rip off something from Nordstrom's."

"Please don't. I'll buy you whatever you want."

"That's not the point, toots. Let's hurt back. I remember what you haven't a clue about. I'll tell you, Little Mommy, it's a screw or be screwed world. Let's have some jollies. Let's go."

"I hate you. Why don't you go away and leave me alone!"

"It doesn't work that way, dry cunt. We're stuck with each other. It's my turn, so nyah, nyah."

"I don't want to get arrested."

"You won't. I'm clever," she said.

"No. You're stupid. You got us arrested last year."

"Hey, that's nothing. Look at all the stuff we ripped off."

"Why? Why would you do that?"

"I got to hurt them back. All of them. All the faces that never saw us. All the faces that turned away."

"I don't understand what you're saying. Let me buy what you need."

"Sweet cheeks, you couldn't buy what I need with a million dollars. Besides, I don't want even one buck of Dan's moola. I'm too good to take his money."

Emily would walk demurely, unobtrusively through the crowds at the mall. Sales and pre-Christmas rush were best. She could spot the mirrors that were two-way security glass. She knew the rotating glass lights were often hidden cameras. She knew to get another customer between her and the camera and slip something into a pocket, or the big shoulder-bag purse. She could hide jewelry in her hand and pretend she was reaching for a Kleenex and drop the earrings in the bag as she let out a sneeze and then blow her nose with the Kleenex she retrieved from the bag. She could take a silk blouse off a hanger, fold it up into a tiny ball with one hand while seeming to be pawing through the rack with the other, then slip it into the purse.

Later, at home, I felt grief when it was only me with my mound of contraband. I never kept it. It wasn't I that had stolen it. I either wrapped it up and returned it, saying I'd found it in the parking lot, just left it somewhere inside the store, or if I'd been totally unconscious of the theft, not knowing which store it came from, I would give it to charity. There was no victory in being a successful thief. Over the years I stole items worth thousands of dollars.

There were so many things Emily and I didn't share. She didn't menstruate. I'm the only one who had periods. She didn't feel pain. She refused to acknowledge it. Even when I was in bed with the flu, Emily could get up out of bed and leave for the day, oblivious to the sore throat, or fever and chills. She had a pain blocker in her part of the brain, I think. I could be miserable and she wouldn't feel it.

Well, I don't think that's entirely right. We had our separate pain. She liked some pain. When life's stresses were crushing down on me, Emily would take over, and sometimes when the children were napping, or later when they were in school, Emily would go lie on Dan's and my big king-size water bed. She had odd rituals, ones that I didn't understand, but observed from my trancelike out-of-body perspective.

She would lie on the bed, pulling off all the covers and flop down on the sheet, stark naked, wiggling to get the water rocking. She spread strips of torn blue cloth over our body, draping and sometimes tying it tight around the ankles. She wrapped the blue cloth around our neck. She would bring out the box from on top of the closet, the one that held some of the knives Mom had sent me. There was also an ice pick and some wooden spoons and spatulas.

Emily would set the water in the bed into a slapping, rocking motion as she would begin to masturbate. As the pleasure began to build, she would begin hurting herself. She would take a knife and hold it over herself, poking it deeply, but not cutting herself, all over her body. Poking. Jabbing. She'd pick up the ice pick and hold it over her face, bringing it closer and closer to her eyes, then slowly, painfully press it into her skin, not stabbing, just pressure to the point of pain. She would spread her legs far apart and poke the inside of her thighs, the abdomen, then the clitoris that responded in alarm to the cold, harsh metal pressing against what should have been the pleasure center. She would chant to the rhythm of the rocking bed:

You Jew, you Jew,
You wicked little Jew.
Your cunt sucks,
While men fuck,
You Jew, you little Jew.

This pain, this pain,
This pain is not the same.
This pain pricks,
Like Mom with sticks.
This pain is not the same.

During these bizarre, self-hurting rituals Emily brought things to bed to stick in her vagina. One favorite thing was a large, refrigerator-cold peeled cucumber. She would rub it around her stomach, over her legs in seeming sensuality, then jab and jab it hurtfully, deeply into her vagina, our vagina, my vagina.

The self-hurting felt good. Like everything else, it made no sense. There was no orgasm that I remember during these times, merely the build-up of sexual pleasure and then escalating abuse. Once in a while she would pierce the skin, but most often it was just the momentary feeling of pain.

One summer day when it was very hot outside, Emily lay on the big bed, rubbed ice cubes around herself and stuck the ice into her vagina, holding it there in exquisite pain until it melted and ran out onto the sheets in a puddle.

At these times when I was there, yet not there, I viewed Emily as another being. I viewed our body as the eighteen-year-old, long-legged body. Even the concept of exterior self changed. I did not understand Emily's need to hurt herself.

On one of those ritualistic occasions she brought candles into the room, pulled the curtains, and in the shadow-sprinkled darkness took a needle and thread and sewed big X's into the bottom of her feet, going through the thick summer calluses, into the tender part of her feet. She passed the candle under the soles and watched the black stitches and the trickle of blood in fascination. I don't remember any pain. It was her pain that day.

Emily gave us gonorrhea.

After a visit to the doctor, and after a culture, he called me into his office. "I'm sorry, Mrs. Cameron, but you have gonorrhea. I am sorry for all the ramifications to this, because you're married. You will have to take antibiotics and your husband will have to take them, too. Whichever one of you has had other partners, they will have to be told as well."

The walls seemed to be pressing in on me, the air becoming dense. "Do I have to tell Dan?"

"Of course you must. You both must have the disease at this point. You both need treatment."

I took the prescription for antibiotics and folded it four times into a tiny square of failure.

I left, hating myself and hating Emily.

That night I handed Dan a pill. For what it would do to our marriage I thought it might as well be cyanide. "You need to take this. I went to the doctor today and he said I have an infection that maybe was passed on to you. We both need to take antibiotics."

"What kind of infection?" asked Dan, popping the pill into his mouth.

"Oh, I don't know, something to do with one of my ovaries, some woman kind of thing."

"That's strange. I hope you get better soon."

Nothing more. No inquisition. No divorce.

"The man's a total idiot," Emily shrieked.

"Be glad," I said. "I want this marriage. He doesn't deserve to be hurt."

"Of course he does. All men deserve to be hurt. Aren't we all hurt? Isn't that what this whole fucking journey is about?"

"For you, it seems to be," I said angrily.

She seemed to be actively working against me and my life, making me feel I was a victim.

Scabies was another gift from Emily. I think it was a trucker she caught it from. They shared some Coors and tinsel dialogue in a bar, then screwed in the bed in back of his truck cab right at the side of the road. She did it several times with him, lying in the cramped quarters listening to cars go by on the highway.

It wasn't long after that the itching began. Unfortunately, the whole family got it before it was diagnosed.

Cindi got the itchy dermatitis and scratched herself red. The idea of little mites burrowing into my children filled me with despair. I stood Cindi's little body in front of me in the bathroom, smearing her with the prescribed lotion, and cringed at the lesions and oozing places where she had scratched herself raw. This was failure.

Emily laughed and sang out, "The itsy, bitsy spider climbed up . . ."

"Shut up, Emily. I hate you! I wish we were both dead."

"Do what you want with us," she said. "I wouldn't give one lousy buffalo nickel for either of us."

There were clothes in my closet that were not mine, and not Emily's either. There were jewelry and wigs in little stashes in my drawers and I did not know how they got there. In the back of my walk-in closet was what seemed like a little nest. There was a soft yellow blanket all folded up, a baby's bottle, and a teddy bear. More than once I would rally from my blanked-out time and find myself in the blackness of the closet, curled in a small ball with my thumb in my mouth. Once it was Cindi who was shaking me. "Wake up, Mommy. Wake up. Why are you on the floor?"

As if back from a distant land, I struggled to orient myself to time and place. "I think I just like to nap in the closet." More lies. It was Sunshine in the closet. She was just six, with her front teeth missing. She wanted to find a safe place, away from all the pain. More than anything, she wanted a daddy.

The closet had secrets to tell me, but I didn't want to know the secrets. There were some vivid-colored clothes in the back, like a bright blue suit with a paisley scarf. There were lots of scarves in my drawers, bits of rope, scissors, an ice pick, makeup I never remembered buying. There was one whole shoe box filled with nail polishes, which I never wore, but would find myself wearing after one of my blanked-out times.

One really odd thing was the way my closet was always organized by outfits and colors. Pants hung neatly together, then blouses, and next the dresses. Blue was always on the far left, then green to golds, then browns to blacks on the right. No matter how I would put things in my closet, seemingly at random, they would, after one of my time lapses, end up straightened and color organized.

There were Braille labels on my drawers and in the bathroom, little sequences of felt dots by the handle of the drawers. I didn't know what it meant, but I didn't take them off because I felt they were significant.

Again it was my children who told me about Camille.

"When you walked around the house bumping into things and said you couldn't see, you told me not to call you Mom. You said to call you Camille. I don't like it when you pretend you're not my mom," Kevin said.

"You keep feeling my face with your fingers to see if it's really me," said Cindi. "I don't like it because you don't laugh when you pretend to be blind."

Kevin said, "That's a stupid game, Mom. Who wants to walk into stuff and not see?"

It's difficult to explain to anyone the rigid denial of reality that went on in my own head. Nothing made sense. Time could be steady and linear, or it could be lapses. I didn't question it, at least not often. When I did, I felt a deep depression. Nothing about my life made sense. I grew up in a world with no order or logic or safety, and I perpetuated the random chaos inside myself. All of life made no sense, so the important thing was covering my tracks, my episodes of odd behavior, with lies that could at least hold the external structure of my life intact.

"Hello. May I please speak to Muriel?" asked a stranger's masculine voice on the telephone.

"I'm sorry, there is no one here by that name," I answered, feeling the dread of this familiar kind of dialogue, but choosing denial.

"Muriel, I recognize your voice. It's slightly different, but I know it's you."

"I'm sorry, but I think you're mistaken."

"What's the matter? Did I hurt your feelings or offend you in any way? We had such a great time yesterday. You certainly were the life of the party. You were a regular Auntie Mame. I don't think I've laughed so much in years. Let's go get a cup of coffee together," said the baritone voice, trying to be inviting.

"I'm sorry I can't. Really! I'm not Muriel."

"Whatever you say, but thanks for the fun afternoon yesterday. Good-bye."

Over the years I got a fairly clear picture of the extroverted, flamboyant Muriel, who could walk into a room and captivate attention and men with her comedic, gregarious ways. She wasn't a cheap lay, for the men who called always sounded like proper gentleman. She'd be likable, I would think, but that's as far as my thoughts went. I did not have any memory of her. As far as I was concerned, she was some theatrical person passing out my phone number around town.

"Mommy, why do you call me meine liebling?" asked Kevin. "When you sit in the rocking chair, you cry and cry and you don't even hear us talking."

"I'm sorry, I guess I'm just sad sometimes. Don't you ever feel sad?"

"Yes, but I don't change my name and do silly things," said four-year-old Kevin. "You call yourself Sophie when you sit in the rocking chair."

"I do? I'm sorry."

"You scared us when you put Cindi in your lap and squeezed her real hard, then you took your clothes off, Mommy, and you wanted her to suck on your breasts. You said you wouldn't let them get your Jewish babies and kill us."

"Oh, God! Kevin, I'm sorry. I don't know why I get weird sometimes."

"Are we Jewish?" asked Kevin.

"Only a little bit. It's nice to be Jewish," I said, not believing it.

"Then why do you cry when you say you are Sophie and you talk about Jews being dead?"

"I don't know, Kevin. Sometimes I do things I don't remember."

"I know. Something's wrong with you. I remember what I do."

"I'm glad, sweetie. Please tell me when I do things that frighten you. I don't mean to, truly I don't."

"I know, Mommy."

Dan brought home a bassett hound puppy when the kids were about three and four. We all enjoyed Freddie, even though he was stupid. His brain could probably have been interchanged with that of a chicken without any noticeable effect. He had a good heart, though. One day when he was about a year old he tugged his leash out of Kevin's hands and ran out in the street in front of an oncoming car. I heard the screaming children and howling dog from inside the house. I went out to find Freddie flopping on the asphalt, unable to get up. He was bleeding out of a giant hole in his abdomen and his intestines were like sausage links on the street. The man that hit him was standing over him crying. The kids were sobbing, "He's bleeding. He's hurt."

I have no memory of the next events. The very next thing I heard was the sound of the .38 pistol going off. It was me holding the just-fired gun, and Freddie was dead from a bullet through the back of his head.

Over and over again, five-year-old Kevin theatrically demonstrated for me the accident and how I had come out of the house saying I was "Joey" and that we mustn't let things suffer and I'd put the gun up to Freddie's head and killed him. The kids had endless discussions as to whether the car killed Freddie or if I did. I tried to make them understand, but even I was shocked that I could load and fire a gun so effortlessly. I was an ongoing mystery to myself.

One evening Dan and I drove to Santa Barbara for a quiet seafood dinner. We sat at a pink-tablecloth-covered table and were quietly sipping our wine when I happened to make eye contact with a man across the room, the sort who would come to an elegant restaurant in a plaid flannel shirt, open at the neck, revealing his T-shirt. He was sitting with a young, pretty woman. He raised his beer glass as though to toast me, then my heart stopped. He was one of Emily's afternoon escapades. He kept watching me through dinner, so that I hardly remember eating.

When Dan and I were on our coffee, the man got up from his table and came toward us. I wished for instant death from a giant wave, a tsunami, that could sweep me out to sea.

"Haven't we met somewhere before?" he said with a friendly smile. "My name is Sam Kingsly."

Dan stood up and held out a hand, "I don't think we've met. I'm Dan Cameron, and this is my wife, Marcia."

"Maybe it was somewhere in a crowd, it's just you both look familiar. Sorry." He chatted a few minutes and went back to his table. The way he smiled at me, I knew he remembered.

The next morning the telephone rang. "Hello. Is this Marcia or Emily?"

I froze. It was the man from the restaurant. "Hello," I squeaked into the receiver. "This is Marcia."

"This is also Emily," he said.

I didn't argue. I never tried to explain Emily. Who would believe me?

"I think we're sharing a secret, aren't we?" Sam said. "I have a feeling this is something you'd just as soon your husband didn't find out about, right?"

"Please! Don't call here. I'm sorry about what happened."

"I thought you might want to meet me over at Motel 6 this afternoon."

"No. Please, I can't."

"If you don't, I'll just have to have a little talk with that husband of yours."

"Please don't. I'll meet you just once if you promise not to tell."

"Three o'clock, babe. Bye."

We met and it was the Marcia-self there feeling deeply degraded and uptight.

"What's the matter? You were a hot whore last time."

The more ardent he got, the more frigid and tight I became. He got rough, angry, and screwed me, then got out of the bed and left in disgust.

A few days later, he called again. "I think it should be worth about a thousand bucks to a lady like you to have me keep your secrets."

"I don't have a thousand, truly I don't. Dan's a teacher and we have two little kids."

"Don't give me the dedicated PTA mother kind of bullshit. I'll take jewelry if you haven't got cash. I'll give you two days to fork it over. I'll meet you at Denny's Restaurant on Tuesday at ten in the morning, or I'll call Dan. Got that? Bye."

I walked around the house crying. There was no way I could come up with money without Dan finding out. I had two rings that together would add up to about a thousand dollars. I hatched a plan to stage a robbery.

I farmed the kids out to a sitter, saying I was going shopping, but instead, drove home and broke into my own house, smashing the glass of the sliding back door and ripping the screen. I made the bedroom look ransacked, turning drawers out on the bed, taking the cash out of Dan's drawer, and stealing my own rings.

I picked up the kids from the sitter and drove home to pretend to the children and neighbors we had been robbed. I called the police, paced and gnashed my teeth in the agitation due a violated suburban homeowner.

Dan was more upset about the door and screen than the fifty dollars and my rings.

I was so upset by the whole event that I cried continually, not eating or sleeping.

On Tuesday, Emily and I argued about who should go to the restaurant.

"Look, sweetness, you shouldn't mess with guys like this. It's my turf, my fucks."

"You'll just make it worse," I protested. "You'll probably make love to him again."

I won the internal argument, but I was in a disintegrated, disheveled state when I got to the restaurant. I had intended to be emphatic about this being a one-time-only blackmail or I would call the police, but when I handed him my favorite ring, a black pearl in the free-form gold setting, I burst into tears. "Don't do this to me anymore," I blubbered. "All I want to do is die." I threw the rings at him and crashed my way out of the restaurant, bumping into busboys and shoving people at the door.

Later that day, I lost time again, and when I came back I found my finger deeply gashed and my own blood dripping from my bathroom mirror. My blood spelled the words, "Help me." No one did. I wiped it off with Windex before Dan came home from work. At least the creep, Sam, never called again.

By the time Kevin and Cindi began grammar school, Dan and I were drifting apart. He was a workaholic, preoccupied with his teaching and sports teams. My friendships were superficial. I went to PTA meetings and interacted with neighbors and other mothers, but it was not meaningful to me. The core of me was locked away, fighting myself and my fears. My functioning was crippled by my panics.

One neighbor invited us to dinner, and the candles burning on the table loomed up so ominously that I could barely speak throughout dinner.

Women who tried to become friends found me distrusting. I held people away. How could I have friends when I had to leave an area when someone lit a cigarette, or shut a door behind me? My life was filled with fears I couldn't explain and nightmares that made me prowl the house like a caged jungle cat.

In times of stress, such as after the time Dan yelled at me for something, I would dissociate. I could disappear for hours and find myself on a street far from home.

There were only a few times when I left the children unattended, but it did happen. Usually I had enough control over my "others" to make arrangements for the kids when the voices would begin to press me to leave.

One day, Dan was furious at me for turning his underwear bright pink when I put a red dress of Cindi's in the wash. It was a small thing, but Dan attacked my ability as a homemaker. We yelled at each other and he stormed out. One minute I was crying and the next thing I knew it was about three hours later and I was sitting in my car in the next town. I called my neighbor to go watch my children until I got home. I made up some feeble excuse, but I was devastated that I had lost consciousness of myself and left my children. It made me cry for days that I was an irresponsible mother and that I was capable of these unaccountable lapses of memory.

The two friends I stayed close to were Babs, my paralyzed friend from my days in the rehab hospital, and Linda, my childhood friend. Both had gotten married and Linda had four little dark-eyed boys. Neither lived in my town, but we wrote, phoned, and got together once a year or so. Both friends knew me well enough to know I was "nuts," but they kept being my friend. It was Linda who first used the word "dissociative" to me. She told me once that she thought I was a multiple personality. "Marcia, how could you not be, with the mother you had?"

I changed the subject every time they suggested I go to a psychiatrist.

One episode in 1976 definitely should have sent me to a psychiatrist. Kevin was in third grade and Cindi in first. A package arrived in the mail which I eagerly opened, since I hadn't been expecting anything. Inside were photographs of King, the dog from my childhood, a card with the faces of white rats pasted on it, and a large knife. The package was from Mom. She did things like that once in a while. I hadn't seen any pictures of our dog since I was a child and it triggered an anxiety attack that left me unable to breathe.

Shortly after that, Jimmy called me from New York. His life was in crisis to the extent that Dan and I jumped on the next plane to go see him. Jimmy had graduated from Princeton and got an MBA, but was unable to work or maintain relationships. We stayed with him a week, and during that time Jimmy talked about many things that I couldn't deal with, things I was frantically running from. Dan was able to get help for Jim, but his crisis created one for me.

By the time I arrived back in California, my thoughts were very disjointed. I went through Halloween with Kevin and Cindi, functioning like a zombie. Seeing Jimmy again after several years brought forth images, flashes of scenes, and emotions I couldn't identify. I saw blood on the walls and floor again. I was hallucinating and hearing voices.

The pumpkin was still at the front door and a bowl of trick or treat candies were on the kitchen counter when I went into the kitchen and turned on the gas oven. I shut the doors to the kitchen and put towels under the cracks. I had to tinker with the oven to figure out how to get the gas to flow without the fire. I unscrewed the little appliance light. While I was doing that, I was imagining flames and seeing a baby. I was seeing King flop around the living room after he was poisoned. I looked in the oven, and in my crazed state it seemed safe and dark and warm. It seemed like a place where the voices would be quiet, a place where all time would be accountable time, a place without blood on the floor.

I got on my knees and lay my head on the oven door. In my mind at that moment I had no husband, no children, no rational thoughts. I do remember looking up to the poster-paint pictures of Kevin's taped to the refrigerator, and from that angle I was the small child looking up and the oven was the tunnel to climb into to get away. I had to get away.

The next thing I knew Kevin was coughing, crying, and clutching onto my neck. "Mom, what's the matter? There's gas in here. It stinks like gas. Why is the oven open?"

I was groggy and calm. I staggered into the living room and flopped on the sofa. Both children climbed on top of me. "Mommy, are you sick?"

"A little. I was cleaning the oven and I guess the gas made me sick." The weight of their little bodies made me feel I was being pulled back from my tunnel.

"You shouldn't turn the oven on when you clean it," said Kevin.

"You're right," I said. "Do me a favor, kids. Don't tell anyone I did that today. Daddy will be mad that I wasn't careful. Let it be our secret."

Cindi said, "That's okay. We know how to keep secrets."

I was asking my children to live with lies just as I had lived with lies. That made me more depressed. There was also a look of uncertainty in Kevin's eyes. At age eight he no longer trusted me, because I was unstable. He had the world pretty well figured out and he knew there were missing puzzle pieces to his mom.

It took a few weeks for the voices in my head to stop and the depression to subside. The children and I didn't discuss the oven scene anymore, but both Kevin and Cindi were affected by it. Kevin began acting up at school and became argumentative at home. I had broken the trust that I would be there for him. It was as though he tried to be as obnoxious as possible to see what I would do. Cindy began to wet her bed every few nights and raced home from first grade every day, refusing to go play with friends or even play by herself outside. It took several months before either one of them resolved the trauma I had inflicted.

It was Dan who helped them heal. He noticed how upset they both were. It wasn't his way to talk with them about feelings, but he became an involved father, doing lots of things with the kids in the evenings. He and Kevin spent hours playing baseball together on the weekends. He built a beautiful bird house with Cindi. For years it hung in the tree outside, dancing its garishly painted colors in the sunlight and attracting only the bravest of birds.

The fact that I had never had an orgasm with Dan added to the stress of our marriage. When he began making love, I would freeze up. I didn't mean to. I didn't even know why. I liked the gentle caressing part of lovemaking, but not the passionate part, and I hated my clitoris touched. It filled me with anxiety.

Living with me could not have been easy for Dan. I was neurotic, though I tried to be inconspicuous about it. The beach bonfire with the teachers at his school filled me with panic, but I just quietly walked down the beach, away from the group, feeling the need to touch my face to see if my skin was still there.

There were dozens of things that made me feel isolated and different. I couldn't find the gaiety inside that I saw in others. I laughed but it felt hollow, as though the core of me was a dark, deep place.

Physical pain plagued me in a kaleidescope of symptoms. It seemed as if I was always going to doctors, having tests run and being told there was nothing organically wrong with me. I would go to different doctors and felt pleased when they would do exploratory surgeries. I had three abdominal surgeries that seemed to calm the voices for a little while. I sought pain, not knowing why.

Physicians I consulted for my symptoms suggested I undergo plastic surgeries for my scars. I eagerly submitted to the knife to have the scar on my breast, my nose, and other scars repaired to fine little lines. Since Dan's insurance covered the surgeries, he expressed pleasure over my scar removals. I had the burn scars planed on my legs. There was the haunting thought in my head that maybe I wasn't having the repairs to look better but for the pain they inflicted.

Only occasionally was I questioned by doctors about the scars. No one suggested psychiatric care.

Emily said, "God damn it! Why do you have to be carved? Leave our body alone! You just want us to lie in bed forever so I can't leave."

"Maybe if I have surgeries, you can't screw around. Maybe if I'm lying in bed with stitches, you can't steal things."

"That's a tacky way of dealing with our relationship," Emily said.

"We don't have a relationship. We have mutual torment."

My next-door neighbor, John, became my friend. He was an attorney, like my father, and, like the other men in my life, he reminded me of the father I had loved and lost. John was fifteen years older than I, and effused paternal caring. Our encounters began as all neighbors do, with borrowed and lent tools and garden supplies. I never sought an affair, just as I never chose so much of what ran my life. Like an amoeba reacting to my environment, I gravitated toward warmth.

John was attentive and kind, fixing Kevin's bicycle tire, pulling a wood splinter out of the paw of our dog.

To say I was innocent in beginning an affair would be a lie; I dressed for John, baked him goodies. He was married, but his wife was an ambitious career woman who was never home. What began as clandestine lunches turned into an encompassing affair.

What I longed for most in life was safety. When John held me it was the feeling I had with Daddy. Inside I craved holding, touching, grounding. Dan couldn't give me that, he was too insecure. John was enveloping and almost dictatorial, making the small hurt child in me feel at peace.

For two years I lived for my moments with him. Sex to me was the barter for the feeling of safety. Our relationship was anything but safe, with sex in my own bed with him while the children were at school and lunches in dark, quiet restaurants. I thrived on the feelings of being taken care of, while in reality I endangered my own marriage. We were not very cautious.

The affair ended abruptly when John accepted a partnership in a law firm in Phoenix. Our farewell was passionate and full of promises, but we both knew it had ended for us.

"Look who's had the easy beaver," Emily taunted. "Your substitute daddy left you like all men do. No one stays."

"He loved me. I know he did."

"There's no such thing as love. It's use or be used. I swear to God, you haven't learned much in this life."

"At least I don't have sex for sport."

"You wouldn't know what a fun time was if you were standing in the middle of Mardi Gras."

I dissociated frequently in my grief and sense of abandonment when John left. Emily took over and I found myself in places I would not have gone, doing things I would not have done. I hated myself for the shattering of my own accountability.

John was the first of several affairs. It wasn't that I was unhappy with Dan, it was that he couldn't quiet the part of me that was the crying, hurt child. He was too sensitive, too gentle, too destructible himself to make me feel safe. Without even knowing why, I gravitated to the strong males, the ones with a commanding presence and paternal warmth. My need was more compelling than my guilt. The various parts of me were so far removed from each other that I could make love to a man at noon, shower, fix dinner, and make love to Dan at night. It was different needs, different pieces of me, so I felt no conflict. It never was a need for sex—I never had orgasms. I became the giving, sensuous lover for the security of being held. I could captivate men with witty conversation and I invested a good deal of time and energy in pleasing them. I learned about their hobbies. I cooked their favorite foods, gave them back rubs, was the pleasure-giver sexually. There was nothing I wouldn't do making love, since it was merely the implement to bind them to me. I was smart and pretty enough to establish relationships easily.

With a completely opposite style, Emily continued her escapades, usually triggered by emotional upset or stress. It is difficult to describe the degradation that I felt over Emily.

"Please, Emily, I beg you. Don't take me away," I pleaded.

"I have to get away from the spineless yokel you are married to. I have to leave the brats. I can't be needed. I've got to split."

"I beg you, no, please don't make me leave. I hate you!"

"Look, sweetness, I need to go fuck with someone. Your goddamn life is too confining for me."

The war between us would rage to exhaustion. I grieved over the lapses. It was no minor effort to cover my tracks, living with lies.

"I'm sorry, kids, I needed to go shopping."

"Dan, do you like my new hair style? I thought it might be fun to be different."

Having a difficult time finding any meaning to life, I enrolled in night courses at the university near us. Depending on who was in power, Emily or me, it was an avenue for meeting people to suit all needs—pot-smoking students for Emily and kindly professors for me.

One semester I took an art history course from a Dr. Simon. He was a tall, gangly, beak-nosed professor who loved to use his power to victimize his students. He seemed ruthless in his attacks on a couple of rather bumbling students. One girl regularly was reduced to tears. There was deep hatred in me for anyone who made another person a victim. His abuse of his position became intolerable. With cold, callous calculation I set about to teach this professor a lesson. I went up after class and turned on my charm. I brought him coffee at the breaks, captivating him with my knowledge of Flemish art and peppering my conversations with information such as the compounds used for pigments during the Renaissance. I studied obscure tidbits of information about varnishes and egg-yolk based paints to make him think I was a real art history buff. I got A's on his exams. I invited him out after class one night and engulfed him in attentiveness. This ugly creep was like putty. He began leaving notes on my desk and calling me at home, even though he knew I was married. I told him I would go out with him. It was near the end of the semester when I went to coffee after class with him. He suggested we go to his house. He was almost groveling in his eagerness to get me into bed. I let him try to set the mood with brandy and soft music and enjoyed the whole scene.

"Marcia, you're so beautiful. Your eyes are an enigma of clear blue innocence and the pain of someone who has seen too much." He was struggling to be profound. He moved closer toward me on the couch, touching me.

"Not here, Allan, let's go into your bedroom. I want you. Your brilliant lectures in class have made me crazy wanting you."

"I can hardly pay attention to my lectures when I see you looking at me. I've never had a student like you. You're a ripe, full woman." He kissed me.

I followed him to his bedroom hung with garish abstract modern art and Batik hangings. His room was as repulsive as he was. I let him undress me and fumble with my clothes, nervous as a teenager as he took off my shirt and bra.

"You have gorgeous tits," he said, leaning down to kiss them.

He lay down on the bed, letting his erection stand at attention in the dim light. "God, I need you. Come lie on me."

At that moment I turned hard and cold. Triumph was at hand. "I wouldn't make love to an ugly man with a tiny dick," I said, and began putting my shirt back on. He rose up with a look of horror on his face.

"Professor Simon, I just wanted you to know what it feels like to be a victim. You have enjoyed giving this feeling to so many others. Good-bye."

I turned and walked out of his house, slamming the front door behind me. Victory was not sweet, it was awful, leaving me feeling dirty and degraded, too.

There were a few more classes before the final exam. Dr. Simon was subdued and not at all vitriolic to those he had previously singled out to humiliate. We never spoke again. I got an A in the course. He probably didn't dare try to change my grade.

If anyone had asked me why my life was fragmented between being a good mother to my children and a woman who had many affairs, I wouldn't have been able to answer. I even loved Dan. The fears, the panics, the things that drove me made no sense to me. I did know that a good portion of my problems stemmed from my mother. Even though I had a disjointed memory of my childhood, just hearing her voice on the phone filled me with deep anxiety. Every birthday and Christmas I got knives from her. Dan always got a gun at Christmas. Over the years we accumulated an interesting collection. I would open the box to a new Sabatier knife and weep. Having Mom call me to complain about her health or ask me about the children could reduce me to tears. Dan should have been angry at the messages Mom sent. I wanted him to get irate and throw the guns back in her face. I wanted him to do what I could not do. I quietly lived with the rejection and split off from the feelings to let the Emily-self run.

One day after Emily took control and stole a wallet while I was shopping with the kids, Kevin said, "Mom, you shouldn't steal things. You tell us it's wrong to take things, but then you do it."

I wanted to blurt out that it wasn't me, couldn't be me, but I said, "I don't know why I sometimes do bad things, Kevin. I don't mean to ever take things."

"You shouldn't do what you don't mean to," Kevin said.

Tears rolled down my cheeks. Stealing in front of my children filled me with shame. I became a catalogue shopper almost exclusively, not trusting myself in department stores with their bright, glittery things.

Life was a roller-coaster ride of pain, when I had so much I should have been grateful for. My children were bright, beautiful, and healthy, Dan was kind, our home lovely, and yet things were very wrong inside me. Dozens of times I picked up the phone to dial a psychiatrist, but always the fear of Emily, fear of all I could not explain, held me in bondage to my pain. I remember standing in the sunshine on a beautiful day and thinking, I only feel the warmth on my skin, the light and warmth aren't reaching inside me.

Sexually I was confused. Emily viewed sex as an angry gesture, my Marcia-self didn't like it. It was a big revelation to have my first orgasm at age thirty-five. Emily had had a few, but I never had. Dan and I had been to a party and I had several glasses of vodka-spiked punch. It was late and I was mellow and sleepy. Dan made slow, lingering love to me, focusing on my clitoris. I lay in a twilight zone of sleepiness, not feeling the usual anxiety. The plea-sure built and built to a peak of exquisite sensation until there was an explosion of feeling radiating and throbbing through me. It was one of the loveliest things ever to happen to me. Dan was thrilled I had a climax. After the lovemaking was over, I felt happy on the one hand that I knew what an orgasm was and sad that at age thirty-five it was a first and isolated experience. It was only on rare occasions after that that I could freely function; usu-ally the old anxiety crept back. I longed to enjoy sex as I knew others did. I felt arousal, but it was mixed with the undefined ten-sion.

So many years went by, years of being half alive. My life was punctuated by memory lapses, affairs, and times when I couldn't focus on anything. The darkness inside filled up my being. It was as though in my head there were many rooms. In each room lived a separate segment of my life. My children were in one room, Dan in another, other men in another. There was a separate room for Emily and at the center of the house in my head was the room that was black, the place that held the panic feelings, the wanting-to-die feelings. I couldn't articulate or define this black place, but it was there, always breathingly alive, waiting to encompass me.

I belonged to my family, yet I couldn't fully feel them or expe-rience them. I longed to turn to Dan and say, "Please see me, feel me. Ask me where I am going. Ask me where I have been when I disappear for hours.''

It was a deeply desolate moment to find myself pregnant from one of Emily's escapades. After the abortion, I lay in bed next to Dan, hoping he would not roll toward me wanting sex. My life was lies, so many goddamned lies. At that moment I hated him for all his neutrality and obliviousness. I didn't want him to know about the abortion, but I thought as I lay there that I could bleed, cramp, grieve, and wish to die and he wouldn't pick up on any of it.

There were times I think I wanted to get caught, just to have the lies stop. My arrests for shoplifting were terrible, traumatic episodes, but even then Dan believed that I didn't mean to do it, and he let the issue drop. I wonder how often my behavior cried out for help, and, just like when I was a child, the protection wasn't there. Dan looked away from my pain. He was saying he didn't really want to know me.

A couple of times I tried to go back to work, just to find relief from the merry-go-round of splitting, promiscuity, and inner pain. But working was more stress than I could deal with, on top of being a mother and wife. I would work a short time and have crying jags and get so depressed that I would quit. I didn't know why.

Somehow I muddled along. Life wasn't all terrible. There were the happy wrestling-on-the-floor, tummy-tickling times with the children. I loved them and they knew it. Dan was a consistent, loving father. I knew all that I was missing, all the failure, was in my own head.

There were days that I contemplated ways of killing myself, certain of the fact that everyone in life would be better off without me. The thing that stopped me, the only thing, was always visualizing my children getting the knock on the door from a policeman, as I had been notified of my father's death. I didn't want to inflict that kind of pain on them. So many memories of childhood were blocked, but I could always vividly reexperience Dad's death.

When the mental pain became too great, I sought out doctors. I actually did have abdominal pains that were terrible, probably from stress, and I made up other complaints, hoping without understanding why that they would operate on me, cut me, hurt me. After two hospitalizations, I convinced the doctors I was in acute enough pain to warrant having my gall bladder taken out. The biopsy came back normal. I had another exploratory surgery for acute abdominal pain. I could step back from hearing myself lie to a doctor, wondering why I was doing that, but unable to stop my quest for pain. It stopped the splitting and the Emily-running for a while.

"Goddamn, I hate you for scarring us up with operations," Emily shrieked.

"I'll do anything I can to stop you, you whore!" I shouted back. "Why can't you leave me alone?"

"Look, princess lady, I have just the fuck as much right to our body as you have. At least I know how to have a good time while you do the dutiful things taking care of the brats and that spineless jellyfish of a man of yours."

"At least I don't run around like a slut getting pregnant with anyone's baby."

"You're so damn self-righteous. Tell me how you're so much better than me when you know you lie to doctors to have operations. You fucking choose pain! Tell me how that makes you so goddamn wonderful."

The internal dialogue between us was exhausting and unresolvable.

My dissociation created problems in the family. The children picked up on my inconsistent behavior.

"Mommy, you really act weird a lot of times. Your face and voice changes and you don't act the same," Cindi said.

"Do I upset you?"

"Sometimes you scare me when you don't act the same," Cindi said shyly.

"Oh, sweetie, I am so sorry that I'm not always regular. No matter what I say or do, I hope you know I love you."

"I know that, Mom." As the kids got older, they were accepting, even protective of me, for they knew I was fragile. Kevin had more angry times than Cindi when I got "wigged out." More than anything, they both hated my noncommunicative crying episodes.

Dan noticed how erratic my behavior was, saying things like,

"Last night it felt as though I was making love to a completely different person. You certainly are changeable."

Kevin and Cindi were in junior high in 1982 when I was sitting one morning at my kitchen table, drinking a third cup of coffee, when the phone rang. The instant familiar adrenaline rush hit my system on hearing Mom's voice. "Marcia, please come right away. Grandma Marie is sick, and with all your medical background I need your advice."

"What do you think is wrong with her?" I asked.

"I'm quite sure she has had a stroke," replied Mom.

"Poor Grandma. Tell her I'll leave right now." It was always the same. If my mother asked me anything I did it like the obedient slave.

I grabbed my purse and sweater, left a note for the family and drove the two hours to Mom's house. I hadn't seen her in months. I couldn't handle the anxiety of seeing her, so I made every excuse to keep from going, but when Mom commanded, I still jumped.

Grandma Marie was eighty-three, but still a beautiful woman, with perfect peach skin and penetrating blue eyes. She lay with a gray pallor against the sheets as I greeted her. Her eyes looked a hundred, and far away. I had never gotten to know her well, but in her later years she had been generous to Dan and me and had made the effort to get to know my children.

Mom was flapping about, tugging at Grandma's blankets and speaking rather incoherently. "She's had a stroke. I'm certain it's a stroke. She can't walk anymore. We mustn't let her suffer."

Grandma turned to Mom and said, "Please bring us some tea, Gisela."

Mom left the room and Grandma reached out and took my hand. "She is trying to kill me. Your mother tried to smother me with a pillow last night. It's true that I have probably had a stroke. Nothing on my right side moves."

"Let me call an ambulance and I'll go with you to the hospital," I said.

"No. I won't go to a hospital."

"Then please, Grandma, let me take you home with me. I can see Mom is getting crazy."

"Yes, she is going to kill me. Maybe it's best. I'm old and have outlived all my usefulness."

"For God's sake, don't talk like that, Grandma! Please let me at least call a doctor."

"No, he'll make me go to the hospital and I refuse to do that," Grandma said as her head slipped back against the pillow. Beads of perspiration were on her forehead from the exertion talking.

Mom entered the room with a teacup-laden tray. I gently lifted Grandma's weak head to help her sip the hot tea.

"We mustn't let her suffer," Mom kept repeating.

Those words set off a chain reaction of anxiety in me and flashes of scenes—rats, dogs, birds.

We three sat drinking tea, and I pleaded with Mom to let me call a doctor.

"No. We mustn't let her suffer. It's cruel to let things suffer."

Again there were voices inside my head, fractured pieces and flashes of memories. I excused myself and went to the phone to call my brother, Bobby. I couldn't reach him; he was out of his office. I called Dan. "Honey, Mom is going to kill Grandma."

"Don't be ridiculous, Marcia. Where are you?"

"I'm at Mom's house. I think Grandma has had a stroke, and Mom is talking about ending her suffering. Can you come?" I pleaded.

"No. I've got a class to teach and two parent-teacher conferences. Just call an ambulance."

"I can't do that. Grandma won't go to the hospital."

"So don't get involved. You know your mom is weird."

"I can't just leave. What will I do?" I was beginning to cry, regressing into the helpless-child state.

"If it were me," Dan said, "I would just call an ambulance whether your grandmother likes it or not."

"I wish you were here. I don't even know why Mom called me to come. It's awful."

"You'll just have to do the best you can. Bye." I clung on to the receiver as if waiting for help on the deadened line.

I stayed in the house as Grandma slipped in and out of sleep and Mom paced. I sat there virtually useless and had visions of the yellow room and my week of hell at the hands of my mother.

I feared for Grandma, yet I was the terrified child, afraid of offending Mom.

There was a fracturing of voices in my head. There was the crying sound of a small child. There was the Emily voice that said, "Run." There was an angry voice. It was confusion of thoughts and emotions. I couldn't deal with the scene.

Mom went into the bathroom and took a bottle of sleeping pills from the cupboard. I couldn't imagine what kind of stupid doctor would give my mother a prescription for sleeping pills. They were red Seconals.

With great deliberateness, she emptied the white powder out of the gelatin capsules and shook them one at a time into a teacup. She went into the kitchen and put cocoa and sugar in the cup, then added milk and stirred it. The powder kept floating to the top, so Mom took a little wire whisk and beat it until it was mixed.

Mom walked with the cocoa into the room where Grandma was resting.

"No, Mom, no. Please don't give that to Grandma."

Mom pulled a chair over to the bed and held up the teacup.

"Grandma, don't drink that." I was crying. "Do you know what Mom's doing?"

"Yes, I know," Grandma said. "It's probably for the best."

"Let me take you to the hospital, please, please . . ."

I lay my head on her soft breast and stroked her hair with my fingers. I could hear her heart beating slowly and regularly, as I looked at Mom, the source of terror, holding the lethal dose of sleeping pills. I became distanced from the scene as though this was an act from a play. Grandma looked at me kindly and squeezed my hand. Somewhere in my haze of consciousness I took it as a surge of life.

I raced to the phone and dialed 911. "Hello. This is Marcia Cameron. Please send an ambulance immediately. My grandmother is about to commit suicide because she's had a stroke. My mother has the pills."

I gave the address as Mom tried to rip the phone from my hand.

"We'll be there in a few minutes," said the operator, just as Mom clicked the phone dead.

"Get out! Get out of this house. Don't you see I need to do this. She stole everyone from me just like you did."

Crying, I screamed back, "Grandma, don't let her do this! An ambulance is on the way. I love you, Grandma. I'll come see you in the hospital."

Mom was tearing at me, shoving me toward the front door. She grabbed my purse and threw it at me. As I stumbled down the front steps, tears pouring down my cheeks, I could hear the ambulance in the distance.

I have no memory of the rest of the day. I escaped into Emily and remember only getting home late that night. I cried and cried as I told Dan about the day.

It was close to midnight when Bobby called me. "Grandma Marie died tonight. Mom just called me."

"Did she die at the hospital? Was it a stroke? I just left her this afternoon. I called an ambulance because Mom was going to give her sleeping pills."

"Jesus!" said Bobby. "She died at home."

"Bobby, I think Mom killed Grandma. Why didn't the ambulance take her to the hospital? They were arriving when I left."

"I heard about the time Jimmy called the police when Mom tried to kill you after the meningitis. She probably pulled that German aristocrat bullshit and convinced them everything was fine. The body is already at the mortuary. Mom has ordered a cremation."

"I'd turn her in if I knew for sure it was murder. Maybe Grandma Marie took the pills by her own choice."

Bobby said, "Being sick and weak didn't give her much bargaining power. Even if it was suicide, it shouldn't have happened."

"The whole day didn't have to happen. I hate Mom! I hate her! I hate myself for standing by and not knowing what to do. I should have carried Grandma to the car and brought her to our house."

I hung up the phone and felt angry with Dan. "God, Dan! I called you. You weren't there for me when I needed you. I can't deal with Mom. I never could. I get helplessly terrified around her."

"There's no doubt about the fact that your mom is nuts. She ought to be locked up."

"She never once told Grandma she loved her. She never cried. Should we call the police?" I asked.

"I don't think so. It's better to leave it as a suicide," counseled Dan.

A deep depression draped itself over me in the following days. It wasn't only a sense of mourning over Grandma; we hadn't been that close. It was the experience of her death, the nightmares, the flashes of images and scenes in my mind, a fracturing of reality.

Emily came strongly to life and dominated my actions. Increasingly, I unraveled, seeming less able to control her demands to leave home. My closet got more garish with provocative dresses, and new cosmetics appeared in my bathroom. I tried to keep track of my money to see if Emily was buying or stealing things. Often objects were stolen.

The more dissociative I became, the more depressed I got. It was a downward spiral. I felt lost to myself. Flashes of Grandma frail and lying in the bed mixed with visions of my own experiences. The more upset I got about Emily the more power she had.

I hated Dan for accepting my lies at face value. I lied about the clothes in my closet, the hours away from home, the miles on the car's odometer. My life was filled with lies. I constructed great scenarios to cover my lost hours, wishing Dan would see me, really see me and take me in his arms and say, "You need help." I ached to have him see into my pain and my charade. Emily loathed Dan for the fact that he never tuned in, never held me accountable. I could get home at nine at night and make up some story about where I had been and there would be no cross-examinations, no recriminations for not fixing dinner. I wanted him to grab me and hold me, make me feel safe and stop the running. It was as though he loved only the fantasy of who he thought I was.

Mom called me on the phone one day, and just hearing her voice made Emily take over. I watched as Emily hung up the receiver and slowly got dressed in one of the outfits she had bought, which had a plunging neckline. She put on makeup and blue eye shadow and teased our hair into a wild bouffant style and then she drove off. Miles from home, Emily went into a bar, not an elegant one but one of those little places that play juke box music, have pool tables and fake leather stools held together with black electrical tape. There were Mexicans drinking beer in the bar, and Emily joined them, ordering a beer with lime and salt like the men were drinking. The beer split me even further, for I have no memory of what came next. I only know it was hours later and I was naked in bed with a young Mexican who spoke almost no English. The hotel room was about as cheap as one can get. This man was touching me gently and I knew we had already made love. The familiar wetness inside me made my heart sink. Emily never used birth control. The man was trying to arouse me, but I felt a rising sense of disgust. His beer breath next to my face made my stomach turn, and I rolled out of the soft bed and raced to the bathroom to vomit in the toilet. I quickly dressed, escaping this half-drunk man and the tacky motel. Fortunately, my car was parked outside.

The next two months were horrible. Emily drank and I got sick, she left and I had to make up excuses. I missed appointments, got behind with housework, and the kids were upset at my erratic behavior.

Every day I waited for my menstrual cycle. By the time I was two weeks late, with swelling, tender breasts, I knew I was pregnant. My loathing of Emily reached a new intensity.

I made the appointment to verify my pregnancy. A Mexican stranger! God, I was depressed! The test was positive, and I made the date for an abortion. There was no way I could have this baby, nor did I want it, but I pictured a sweet, tiny, brown face surrounded by black hair.

I went through the abortion by myself, no friend, no confidante, no hope, no self-love.

That night, I lay in bed next to Dan hoping he would not touch me or reach over for me. My cramping was painful and I was bleeding heavily. Lying within touching distance of the man I married, I was filled with sadness. I had cheated him, myself, a strange man, and an unborn baby. I had made victims of so many. I felt Emily was to blame. I wanted her dead. There is no greater empty feeling than after an abortion. The very core of me felt vacuumed away. There seemed nothing left, no more hurt I could feel, no more capacity to sit idly by while Emily did disgusting, irresponsible things.

The black place at the center of my being enveloped me. It was like a spreading hopelessness that I couldn't fight. I couldn't stop Emily. I couldn't control my fears and my panics. I felt everyone would be better off without me. I couldn't even predict when I would be home for my family and when I would be in some sleazy place with strangers.

Forgetting my responsibility of motherhood, the pain became all-encompassing. I had to make the pain stop. I prayed to the God I did not believe in. My depression was so profound I did not even leave a suicide note. I got in my car and headed for Malibu Canyon. Oblivion, peace, nothingness was what I needed. There were no thoughts of the process of dying, no fear, no deep contemplation of consequences; there was only pain, the hallucination of blood everywhere, and a driving need to make the pain stop.

Chapter 9

"We're not dead," I whispered to Emily.

"I swear to God, you're the biggest fuck-up on the face of this planet. If *I* had tried to end it, we'd be feeling the flames of hell licking at our feet."

"I wonder if one of us could go to heaven and one of us to hell?"

"Listen, sweet one, you're not entirely squared away. We've both rather majorly failed at living the good life. You fail as a neurotic, pent-up prude, I've at least failed while having a hell of a good time."

"I wish we'd died," I said, pulling the pillow over my face to cry. Every inch of my body hurt. My skin was turning purple, blue, green, and the broken bones sent out electric shocks of pain when I moved.

Emily said, "This pain gets to be your pain. I'm not the one who got in the car."

"The pain has always been mine—and the humiliation, the grief, the failure. You've always gotten off scot free."

"Tough shit! No, that really isn't true. I don't think any of us in here can take much more. It probably *would* have been better if we had died."

Coming home after the long hospitalization was awful. The already fragile family unit we had was blown sky high by my suicide attempt, which we all called "The Accident." All time references in the family were B.A. (Before Accident) and A.A. (After Accident), as though we had had Camelot before and I had chosen to ruin it. With pain and depression I barely focused on the kids as I spent hours in bed recovering. When I wasn't doing physical therapy or seeing Scott Williams, my physician, I was deeply isolated in depression. I didn't read or watch television. I lay in bed and listened to my breathing and watched the white ceiling over me move in wavelike motions. I would concentrate on trying to make my heart stop beating.

Cindi cooked all the meals and took over the household. At the age of twelve, she became an adult in a matter of weeks. Kevin, who was fourteen, was angry. I don't think anyone talked about the accident as being a suicide attempt, but he knew. He came into my bedroom a few times, crossing his arms and leaning into the wall, away from me, as far away as he could get in the same room.

"I'm sorry I can't take you to the beach," I said.

"I'm trapped here," he said. "Life's supposed to be fun when you're a teenager. This stinks."

"I'm sorry. Hopefully, I'll be able to drive again soon."

"Why would I ever want to drive with you? You can't even stay on the road." His angry face was accusing me of what I was denying. I'd again ruptured the trust. He had been abandoned.

Night after night he came in late. Dan and I could smell alcohol on his breath, then Dan found marijuana under his mattress. When confronted, he denied it all but maintained his uncommunicative sullenness.

Dan was overwhelmed by the chores he now had to do since I was incapacitated, and by health insurance hassles. He and Kevin would shout at each other, Cindi would slam doors and cry, and I was saving my stockpile of pain pills to try to kill myself again.

This went on for about six months. Kevin had turned fifteen and had grown to six one. I was sitting in the rocking chair in the living room trying to teach myself to knit. It was hopeless. My fine motor skills since the meningitis were not very good. I was rocking and swearing at the ugly uneven stitches and the yarn was all in tangles. Kevin was doing homework at the kitchen table.

"Kevin, could you please bring me a Pepsi?" I asked.

"Get it yourself."

"My leg hurts. I'd appreciate it if you'd get it for me."

His chair screeched along the floor. In a few seconds, he was across the room and threw me a can. "What do you know about hurting, Mom? You just sit around like a queen and make all of us your slaves. I only have one more year until I can drive and I'm leaving this place."

"Come here, Kevin." I lay the knitting down in the bag. "Sit!" I pointed to the floor next to me. He hadn't touched me in six months.

He sat cross-legged in front of me; his long, skinny legs looked like a grasshopper's. His face was getting strong, manly features. He scowled at me.

"How can I make things right with us?" I asked.

"Nothing's wrong with us." I reached out to touch his light-brown hair. "You used to have such cute blond curls."

"Cut it out." He scooted back out of my reach.

Suddenly, I was overcome by sadness for the pain I'd put in his eyes. I burst into tears. "I'm sorry I've been such a failure as a mother! I've tried so hard and I haven't been able to do it. I'm all crazy inside! I don't know why I do what I do. The only thing I know for sure is that I love you and Cindi and your dad. I love you and I'm wrecking your life." I had meant to have a mature talk, and I was sobbing. "I wish I could just die and get it over with. All of you might do better without me."

Suddenly, Kevin burst into angry tears. "Don't say that, Mom! Don't you know how awful it is for us not knowing if you're going to commit suicide? For years I never went to camp or on trips with my friends because I thought without me you would do something stupid. You're right—you *are* crazy. But if you died, I'd want to die, too. I love you so much." He got on his knees, lurched over to me, then pressed his head against my breasts and put his arms around me. In spite of not wanting to remember, I saw my dad in the boat with his head on my lap when I was twelve. I clutched Kevin around his head and hung on to him, sobbing. "You are very special to me. I love you so much. More than anything, I want to be a good mother and I'm not. What can I do?"

"Just don't leave me!" Great sobs shook his skinny body. "Don't die!"

I stroked his curls and we both cried some more, then I cupped my hand under his chin and lifted his face. "I won't leave you, my sweetie. I'll find a way to get better. I promise I'll try." Then I kissed each eyelid and cheek and then his nose, just as I had when he was little. He kissed me back.

"I know horrible things happened to you when you were little, Mom. I'm still a kid, but I know Grandma is giving you a message of wanting you to die when she sends you the knives. Just don't talk to her. Don't open boxes from her."

"That's a good idea."

"I'll help you, Mom."

"But I'm supposed to be the one who helps you," I said.

"I can handle you being weird. I just couldn't handle you being dead."

"That's a deal," I said, kissing his eyelids one more time.

Kevin asked, "Do you remember when I was little and you'd lick the peanut butter off the knife while you made sandwiches and then kiss my eyelids before I went to school?"

"Yeah."

"You made my eyelashes sticky until I could wash them at recess. I liked that because it was like carrying your kisses around."

"Shall we seal our love with some peanut butter kisses right now?"

"No. I'd settle for the car keys."

"In your dreams, buddy."

We had our son back. There was no more alcohol or marijuana.

It took another eighteen months of surgeries, the affair with my physician Scott Williams, the aborting of his baby, and the wild behavior of Emily to crumble the resolve to keep my promise to Kevin. When I finally made the call to Dr. Naughton, my first psychiatrist, in the fall of 1984, it was for my children's sake. I wanted to die, but I didn't want my kids to be the inheritors of pain. I decided to give therapy a try, because there was nothing inside of me anymore. When I dialed the phone at the age of forty-three, I had run out of options.

That was the beginning of a journey, not an immediate resolution to the pain. I wasted time and money defending my secrets, the Emily twin.

Therapy with Dr. Naughton wasn't easy. He was passive and silent, never responding with any emotion to all I said to him, though he seemed kind. His bearded face was gentle, yet therapy was punctuated by feelings of anger and abandonment on my part. Having never been to a psychiatrist before, I had no expectations of what it should be. It was months into therapy when I burst into tears one day and said, "I think I want you to be warm like a father, but you just sit there passively listening."

"If you don't like my style, you can go find another psychiatrist" was his icy reply.

I wanted to please him. I brought him flowers for his office, and cookies. Sometimes he would seem pleased and thank me, other times he would say, "You're trying to make yourself special to me. You shouldn't bring me things." The messages were never clear. He could be almost severe in his comments one session and warm the next time.

My relationship with him seemed less important as the drowning realities of my childhood began to emerge. I would lie on his couch and sob at reliving the pain, the burnings, the broken bones. It was excruciating to experience the intensity of my childhood of abuse and then, after the forty-five-minute session, wipe my eyes and dripping nose and leave his office without any warmth from him. But I kept going back. I held the hope that there was help. Once I had begun to recall my childhood I needed him too much to quit therapy. I was sure if I stopped I would kill myself.

Dr. Naughton tried to give me Haldol, a major tranquilizer, but I broke out in a red rash and could hardly breathe. He questioned my capacity to handle therapy. I questioned his. I felt needy and small, like the tiny monkey clinging to the cloth surrogate parent. I felt safe with him but angry at his emotional neutrality and ambivalent messages to me. I feared my trust in him, exposing my vulnerable jugular to a man who only watched as I bled in front of him.

I was reduced to primary emotions. All the polish and finesse was gone from me. I panicked. I cried. I ached. I had a vivid dream that I was full of holes, leaking from every orifice, and I kept trying to patch the gaping wounds with bandages but they kept popping off. Therapy was like that—all the containment of self was gone.

I was oozing my pain around like cytoplasm with no boundaries. I withdrew from all the contacts with friends, not even returning Scott's calls. I felt isolated, unable to tell Dan about all I was remembering.

At times I didn't believe what I was remembering was true. How could such terrible things have happened to me? I called Bobby and asked if I could go see him. Over a weekend of tears he validated my memories.

"How could you have let me go through my whole adult life without talking to me about our childhood?" I demanded.

"I thought the meningitis must have wiped out your memory and that blank spaces were kinder than the truth."

"Don't you know how I've suffered not knowing? There have been no explanations for the fears, the pain that drives me."

"I'm sorry. We all thought you were better off not knowing."

"Oh, Bobby, you must have suffered, remembering it all and having no one to share it with."

We both cried, holding on to each other. Bobby choked out, "I'm not sure it's a pain that can be shared; it's a huge burden. I'm sorry for leaving you like I did after Dad died. That haunts me."

"We were both kids doing all we could do to survive."

It was healing to be able to talk to Bobby and know it wasn't just terrible fantasies or rampant insanity that was in my head.

On a hot August day, I drove myself to the home I grew up in. The big estate was surrounded by a tract of houses where the orange groves once stood, but the huge house remained in isolated dignity against the sea of ticky-tacky homes. With trepidation I knocked on the front door. A sweet-faced older woman opened the door. I explained how I had lived in the house as a child and wondered if I could see it again. My face must have looked honest, for she invited me in. I felt overcome by the flooding of memories. The vast living room was as huge as I remembered it, with the big brick fireplace at the far end. The kitchen had been remodeled. The butcher-block table I had been tied to was gone. There was no blood, no sign of the screams or the terror that had occurred years ago. I walked up the stairs to my old bedroom with its connecting bathroom. The needles, the enemas, the summer locked in the room came pounding back. I fought to contain the tears that pooled in my eyes, blurring my vision. Walking slowly downstairs, I noticed that the red velvet wallpaper was gone. I needed to see the closet under the stairs. The dark, secret closet behind the closet. I asked the woman if it was all right to see the closet and she said, "There is no closet under the stairs, we have a bathroom there."

My heart gave a flip-flop. Maybe I was crazy. Maybe the tiny closet was some terrible dream that just seemed real.

The sweet lady said, "There used to be a closet here with a door at the back opening to a smaller space under the stairs. I don't know what happened in there, but it had such a terrible odor that when we bought the house we ripped it all out and put in this powder room. Rats must have lived in there."

I was swallowing my sobs as I thanked the lady and quickly left. I cried for the two-hour drive to Dr. Naughton's office. I sat in his waiting room for three hours, overcome by the reaffirmation of the memories that seemed suddenly alive. He told me he had no time for me, so feeling abandoned and overcome by more memories than I could contain, I dissociated. Emily took the wheel of the car as we careened toward home, or destruction. Whichever came first didn't matter. Emily lost control of the car and we ended up in a ditch, unhurt, and the car intact but stuck in soft dirt. Some young guys in a truck helped me get the car out.

At my next session I told Dr. Naughton about being upset and losing control of the car, and he tried another new drug. It made me feel dizzy and nauseated. Much to his dismay, I stopped it after two days.

———

My experiences and feelings were in chaos inside me. I began writing my feelings down, trying to organize my thoughts. It became a helpful tool. I sent Dr. Naughton copious epistles of pain. Some he read, others he was too busy for. Again I got the mixed messages. Some sessions he would say he was glad I was writing, other times he said I was avoiding bringing things into a session by sending it to him in letters. I didn't know if he wanted me to write or not, but I kept doing so to untangle the pain.

Just as I questioned the heinous crimes against me as a child, I felt Dr. Naughton was uncertain as to whether I was telling the truth. I got him hospital records of X-rays and asked Bobby to call him to verify all I had revealed. I think he appreciated my wanting him to know I was neither fabricating great tales nor was I totally looney.

At the worst possible moment in therapy, when I was remembering getting tied up and having my right breast carved open by my mother, a box arrived in the mail. Opening it, I found knives from Mom with a cheery little note saying, "I couldn't wait until your birthday. I knew you would love to have these."

It was too much—the pain, the therapy, the memories. I went to Dr. Naughton's office and gave him Mom's letter and the knives. It was the first honest emotion I remember seeing him express. He was angry and wanted to call my mother and the police. He said he wanted to let her know he considered sending knives to be a death threat. I begged him not to call. I was terrified at the idea of inciting her wrath.

Dr. Naughton suggested a civil suit against my mother. "Take her to court for damages." Mom had no large estate to sue and I had no ability to face her in a courtroom. Just her voice over a phone could disintegrate me to a frightened, small-child state.

"Why don't you return the knives?" Dr. Naughton suggested. "At least don't let her get away with this."

I finally decided to leave them with Dr. Naughton and told him to throw them away.

Anger began to rise in me at all I was remembering. For months I relived unbelievable mind-twisting abuse. Often I felt angry at Dr. Naughton, but then I realized I felt angry at my mother. How dare she have abused me! My anger terrified me. I vividly remembered my childhood anger when I got my labia sewn shut or a wooden spoon stuck inside me or when I was hit against a wall. Anger made me dissociate. Emily knew how to be angry, but now I was beginning to feel it.

Emily said, "It's about time you got angry. Now you know what has made me furious all these years. You should take the knives and use them on Mom. I'll help you."

"I'm still afraid of my anger."

"It's a good thing you have me."

Without being able to reach Dr. Naughton for advice because he never returned calls Friday through Monday, I got in my car one Saturday and found myself driving toward Mom's house. I wished I had the box of knives with me, but I had a few of the guns in a metal case to return to her. I drove erratically in my upset state. As I got near her house, I felt my anger dissipate at the idea of confronting her. Perspiration sprang from every pore, and my face went white.

Parking in front of Mom's house, I got out quickly, before I could change my mind. My hands shook as I rang her door bell. I wondered if she would be home, for I hadn't called to let her know I was coming.

The door opened and there was my mother, as regal as always with her hair swept up in a bun, curls escaping like a little halo around her face. It was a beautiful face even in old age. "What are you doing here?"

"I have to talk to you," I said.

Mom opened the door, and I walked past her into the immaculate living room. Without sitting down, I blurted out, "Mom, I'm seeing a psychiatrist. I'm remembering. I'm remembering it all." My voice was quivering, my anger gone. "Why, why did you do those things to me?"

Mom became agitated and paced back and forth in front of the flowered blue sofa.

"Why did you hate me, Mom? What did I do?"

"You took your father away from me. He loved you more than me."

"For God's sake. I was a child!"

"You laughed and charmed everyone with your blond curls and blue eyes. You stole everyone from me."

"You're crazy, you know. I was a tiny defenseless child."

"You are a Jew," she almost spit out at me.

Mom was beginning to get that faraway agitated look in her eyes that sent terror shooting through my veins. My adult veneer was crumbling.

"I wanted to love you," Mom said, "but I couldn't. You are a Jew!" There was no look of sorrow on her face, it was a look of hateful accusation.

Realizing there was no point to my being there, I shoved the box of guns at her and said, "I don't want any more knives or guns. Don't call me anymore."

Through a mist of tears, I barged past her and stumbled out the door to my car. I jerked the car in gear and drove around the corner where I had to stop, open the door, and vomit in the street. I wanted to kill her, just as she had killed so much of my life. The anguish of the tortured years overtook me and I slipped away to a safe, dissociative, quiet place inside. I do not remember any of the drive home.

I told Dr. Naughton at our next session about what I had done. "You should have talked it over with me before you did anything that impulsive," he said.

"How the hell can I talk things over with you when you are out of town three days out of seven and don't return phone calls?"

"You could have waited to discuss it during our sessions."

"I'm sorry," I said, "but my life doesn't seem to be able to stay on hold for you." I was angry. I had done something upsetting and important and all he cared about was the fact that I hadn't asked his advice, like I was supposed to be a goddamn puppet. I wanted him to hold me, to make me feel safe, but there was always anger that came between us.

I left Dr. Naughton's office feeling fragmented. I was being swallowed by the vividness of the abuse I was remembering. It was close to impossible to stay functioning. I began to regularly call the suicide hot line. The kind voices at the end of the line were reassuring during my bad moments.

About a week after seeing Mom, a box arrived in the mail from her. I opened it and broke down in deep sobs. There in the box, with a note on the top, saying, "I thought you would like these to show your psychiatrist," was the ice pick, the blue kerchiefs that still had my blood stains, the sharp rectal thermometer, the old pewter nut cracker, and various other objects of my childhood torture.

Feeling totally broken, I went to Dr. Naughton's office and, between patients, handed him the box from Mom. He registered no emotion. "I don't have time to talk with you now. What do you want me to do with the box?"

"Throw it away," I sobbed, and left his office crying.

At the next session, the box was sitting on his bookshelf as though it had no significance whatever. "How can you leave the box there?" I said, bursting into tears.

"It's not for me to throw away. It's yours."

I got up and threw it in his wastebasket. I was sharing this journey to hell with a man who was incapable of showing human compassion. I wondered why I kept coming back.

To make matters worse between Dr. Naughton and me, we kept bumping into each other socially. Our town was small, and Dan taught his daughter in school. Our children were becoming friends.

At the next session, Dr. Naughton said he had given the matter a great deal of thought and he felt I should have another therapist, preferably a woman, since the core of my problems revolved around my mother. I was in shock. I had spent more than a year with Dr. Naughton, and as difficult as our relationship was, we had a lot of hours invested in each other. He said he would give me six weeks to get established with another therapist.

In subsequent sessions I begged, sobbed, groveled. "Please don't abandon me," I pleaded. It was too much to take, with all the newness of the childhood memories and my confrontation with Mom. Now Dr. Naughton wanted to get rid of me.

I kept appointments with four other psychiatrists. After one session, each told me they were too busy to take on a patient as complex as I was. I was getting rejected by new therapists and was being abandoned by the only one I had a relationship with.

I was coming apart with the feeling there was no help anywhere. Crying day and night, not being able to eat or sleep, I toyed with ideas of suicide.

Dan called Dr. Naughton—one of the few times he got involved in my therapy. They both decided I needed a mental hospital.

"Of anyone I've ever met, you have earned the right to go to a hospital for a while," Dr. Naughton said. "I'll make you a deal. If you go to the hospital I arrange for you, I'll continue to be your therapist when you get out."

That was an easy decision. I would have walked through hot coals to not be abandoned by Dr. Naughton. I was beyond coping and he was the only thread to sanity I could hang on to.

The hospital was a white, sterile monolith in a sea of single-story tract houses. The town had developed around this psychiatric hospital.

Dr. Naughton called and made all the arrangements for me. I entered in a sobbing, disintegrated state. Dan brought me there, carrying my suitcase, and as soon as he had deposited me in the hands of the admitting nurse, he turned and kissed me good-bye, and dashed off for his escape from the strange place—and possibly from me. I wanted to clutch on to Dan and say, "Hold me. Please don't leave. If you love me, just be with me for a little while," but words never came.

I felt the familiar abandoned feelings I had experienced as a small child when the nurse took my suitcase from me and went through each item in my possession, checking for drugs and sharp or dangerous objects. My jewelry was taken off me and put in an envelope which I signed over to the hospital safe.

I was led to a cream-colored room with two beds and a dresser. Stale cigarette smoke filled the air and permeated the blankets. Anxiety made me feel I couldn't breathe. I felt blackmailed into this admission to the hospital. If I left, Dr. Naughton would never be my psychiatrist again. I loved him and hated him at that moment. Everything was threatening and unfamiliar.

The nurse brought me a gown to put on for the admission

physical. Shivering more from emotion than cold, I waited for the nurse to return. She entered my room with a chart, pen, stethoscope, and urine bottle. She took a detailed health and psychiatric history, but I was almost silent, and my replies were a thousand miles from the reality of my life.

Next came the physical assessment, looking in my hair for lice and slipping the gown off me for observation. With minute attention, this nurse asked me about every single scar I had, measuring them in centimeters with a ruler.

"Why do you measure and count my scars?" I asked.

"Because they often relate to a psychiatric problem," she responded.

"How did you get this round scar in your side?"

"I was stabbed by my mother."

"How did you get all the scars on your legs?"

"Most of them are burn scars."

"How did you get the long scar on your breast?"

"My mother cut me with a butcher knife."

"Just a minute, please," said the nurse quietly.

In a few minutes, she returned with the young resident psychiatrist. He looked like a kid who had grown a beard to pretend he was mature.

The nurse went over the growing list of my scars, and the young doctor asked me the same questions. I felt uncomfortable and vulnerable discussing my mutilation with strangers. They were trying to act clinical, but I felt like a specimen, reminding me of my meningitis days. I finally said, "I don't see that it's anyone's damn business how many scars I have or when I menstruated last."

"I'm sorry," said the doctor, "but physical assessments are important. Just seeing these scars helps us understand some of your problems."

I was beginning to weep again, thinking they really knew none of my problems.

The doctor prescribed some Xanax to help me relax. I lay on my bed and hardly cared that my new roommate had entered the room. She was petite, blonde, and spoke very softly in a lilting southern accent.

"I'm Billie-Jo," she said.

"Hi. I'm Marcia. Have you been here long?"

"About two weeks. How come you're here?" she asked.

"I guess the admission form says depression. Why are you here?"

"I tried to commit suicide with aspirins."

I was sorry I asked. I'd forgotten this was the land of crazies—and being in the hospital meant I was one of them.

"I hope you will be better soon" was all I could reply.

"This is the fourth time for me in this hospital."

She's not a very quick learner, I thought.

"I'm sorry," I said.

Billie-Jo lit a cigarette, which made me want to gag. I always overreacted to cigarettes. Now that I had remembered the burnings, I knew the source of the anxiety, but just knowing didn't take away that sense of panic and revulsion. I got up and left the room.

There was a sitting area filled with smoke, and several patients watching television.

Emily said, "This was a mistake. We have to leave this place."

"You know, Em, this is probably the first time in your life you are right."

I couldn't relax. The other patients seemed strange, the nurses like aloof, crisp, linear people. I was profoundly alone in an institution full of people. I wanted help, but I trusted no one. My Emily-self needed protecting, yet she was angry at feeling caged. I wasn't certain I could maintain the status quo in a locked-up situation.

That first evening and night were horrible. I paced the halls like a caged coyote. I would walk to the locked door on the ward and fight the dark closet panic. Back and forth I walked until about three in the morning when the night nurse gave me some kind of pill to calm me down. My anxiety and fear weren't rational, but they were real. I felt as if I were in a tight place without air. It was a claustrophobic, panicky feeling. The dam of anxiety finally burst and I sobbed and sobbed, with my face pressed into the stale mattress to keep from waking my roommate. I did not want to be in a hospital getting exposed to the scrutiny of strangers. I missed Dan, the kids, and all that was familiar.

In the morning, a new psychiatrist came to see me. He said he would be my doctor while I was in the hospital. After a year with Dr. Naughton, it offended me to have to reveal myself to a stranger. I struggled to be polite, but I cried my way through the session.

I worked to keep my composure during the group therapy session with the other patients. I had regressed to a dark place way inside myself. Everything was too much—therapy, my guilts, the knives, my mother, the years of abuse that I remembered all too vividly. What I needed at that moment was a warm, nurturing place. A soft touch and a quiet voice reaching into my fathomless pain were what I craved. Instead, it was endless noise, cigarettes that reminded me of the torturing times, locked doors that reminded me of the closet.

"Run," Emily said. "You have to get me out of here. I can't be locked up. I can't breathe."

My emotions raged in a hundred directions until it ended in another crying jag.

A bossy nurse insisted I join the occupational therapy group, literally dragging me with my tear-reddened eyes to a crafts room.

It seemed an activity for preschoolers to be given a hunk of clay. The assignment was to make the animal we would most like to be and the one we would least like to be. I sculpted an elephant for the one I wanted most to be. The therapist asked me why, and I said, "Because they are gregarious, herding animals that nurture their young. They live a long time, communicate with each other and they don't have to kill to survive."

The one I least wanted to be was a bat. Asked again, I said, "Bats form no relationships, they live in black, closed places, drink blood and only live a few years." This plebeian sort of conversation seemed to hold great significance to the therapist, which struck me as odd. I could see from her face that she thought she could figure out the depths of me from pieces of clay. If I hadn't been so depressed, I would have enjoyed the challenge of jerking their probing minds around a bit. But basically at that moment I didn't give a shit about them or even myself.

They gave me the Minnesota Multiphasic Personality Inventory test. I lied in response to the obvious questions like, "Do you hear voices in your head?" I may be crazy, but I'm not an absolute fool! The questions were blatantly obvious—the reality-testing questions and the ones for mental illness, such as, "Do you think people are following you?" What idiot would say, "Sure, I'm paranoid!" The more middle of the road questions I didn't care about; I was honest. It didn't bother me that the test would show I didn't trust women or that I had nightmares. I just didn't want to stay in this place for twenty years. It occurred to me that the game must be played their way for me to get out.

The second night brought more pacing, and again the feeling of panic. A male nurse was on duty, which brought all the rapes to the forefront of my mind. The ward was locked and this male night nurse was not anyone I knew or trusted. When he entered my room because I was crying so much, I cowered in my bed and cried, "Don't touch me. Please don't hurt me." The past was getting mixed up with the present. Emily was looking around the room for something to kill us both with. It was too much, it was all too much.

The resident psychiatrist came in and talked to me, and I told him about the rapes at age eighteen. He was sympathetic and had me talk with him and the night nurse, then he gave me some pills.

Instead of being a healing experience, this was a disintegrating experience. I had entered the hospital in a deep state of disarray. Instead of music and quiet and gentleness, I got probing, regimentation, and other sick patients, all of which were driving me closer to the abyss. I could look over the edge into the dark nothingness in the center of myself.

The third night, Emily took over. She found a pen and paper and wrote a suicide note.

> I hate this place. I hate Marcia for putting me in here. I can't breathe. I can't sleep. The walls are moving in on me. I am trapped because I cannot let anyone know that I am here.
>
> Why can't we just end this charade of life? Let's quit. Dying would be deliciously comfortable. Dying would be damn easy. How much pain can we experience in a lifetime? Even inside we are not comfortable. Others have the world beating them down. We got the short straw—we beat at each other, trapped in the

same body. Marcia, face it; it is all shit. From start to finish it is shit. Life sucks! This place especially sucks!

Get away from all those nurses. Don't let them touch us. Don't you remember anything? Marcia, you are so goddamn stupid! How did Dr. Naughton talk you into this? You know I can't handle confinement.

Get me out of here. Someone, anyone, help me!

I am suffocating with cigarette smoke, questions, and fingers. I hate fingers.

Emily grew wild with terror and anger and tried to break the glass in the room, hoping for some shards to stab us with. I stood by in my twilight state watching as the nurses subdued Emily and gave us a shot. The sleep was deep.

The next morning it was hard to function. All I wanted was more blank sleep, a place away from people and a mind that felt splintered from pain.

In group therapy that morning I listened with a drug haze in my brain but growing hostility at the trivial things the patients were upset about. One woman wanted to commit suicide because her husband asked for a divorce. When it was my turn to talk in the group, my anger turned into tears, which was my only way of dealing with anger, and I laid on the group the whole long collection of my life of trauma. It wasn't kind. I did it because I was angry at them, at the hospital, and the pain. I gave them my pain to inflict pain on what I viewed as their shallow egocentricity. I had everyone in the group crying.

The psychiatrist had his session with me and told me I should be put on a major tranquilizer like Haldol, but I told him Dr. Naughton had already given it to me and I was allergic to it.

"We'll try something different. You need some help now, Marcia. You seem to be disintegrating."

At least someone noticed.

That night Emily was out of control. She was threatening to kill us both. Even with the threat of death I couldn't tell anyone about Emily. My struggle over which one of us would retain control was exhausting me further. I went to the nurses' station and asked to use a pen and paper. I went back to my room and wrote this suicide note, which like Emily's letters, comes from Dr. Naughton's file.

Dear Dan, Kevin, and Cindi,

I'm sorry to all of you who I have loved so dearly that I have failed to survive. I didn't want to die. I know none of you can understand this, because I have never talked to any of you about this—there is another voice, another person in my head, a twisted person who is demanding escape from life. I don't think I can stop her. I wish I could have told all of you about her, but I couldn't. I fear it is too late for both of us.

Dan, Kevin, and Cindi, I love you deeply. I'm not leaving you by choice. I am leaving because of a sickness inside that I can't change and I can't stop. As I write in this cold hospital room, I am crying for your pain. I am crying for my failure. I am crying because I fear you may never know how deeply I loved you.

My precious, treasured babies. My leaving will pain you and scar you. Remember it was not you I would ever leave by choice. You two are my most treasured gifts. Both of you possess the most that life can bestow on anyone. You have the gifts of laughter, warmth, intelligence, depth, sensitivity, creativity, beauty, and the ability to love. You have a wonderful father. You have a mother who has failed you, but who loves you even past life.

I would not leave you if I knew of any other way.

My dearest ones, in time I hope you will hold on to the memories—the loving, the laughter, the touching we shared.

> I love you,
> Mom

If there had been a means of killing myself that night, either Emily or I would have done it. I was at the rock bottom of life. I couldn't cry any more, feel any more, maintain any more. I don't remember the rest of the night for I dissociated, but in the morning I was still alive, with the suicide note in my bedside table. I don't remember being glad; I was numb. I lay on the bed, missing breakfast, feeling empty.

It was about the sixth day of this ghastly experience that I told the psychiatrist, "I want to go home. I'm not getting any better in this place. I hate it. I hate the locked doors, the cigarettes, the group therapy sessions, the whole rotten package deal."

"Marcia, I think you should stay in the hospital for a few weeks and let us get you on some kind of medication. You're not doing well."

"There is no way I'll stay here, and you certainly can't commit me against my will. I'm not that crazy," I said.

"I won't force you to stay," said the kind, tired-looking psychiatrist, "but your leaving is against my better judgment."

"I'll make you a little deal," I said. "Give me a month in my own home where I can rest and read and cry by myself and if I can't pull together a bit better, I'll let you hospitalize me and give me any kind of drug you want."

"I'm not sure you are well enough to function at home. I wish I could get you to stay."

"You can't, Doctor. Thank you for your time and caring, but I am leaving right now. Please sign me out." I felt better just taking control of my life enough to leave.

It felt wonderful to be back in my own bed with sheets that smelled sweet and my symphonies playing on my stereo. I didn't want to see Dan or the kids. The time away had traumatized me to the end of my reserves. Just cooking dinner overwhelmed me to the point of tears. It took an enormous effort to buck up for the family. When the kids went to school and Dan went to work, I luxuriated in the stillness of my home. I lay in bed for hours just drifting, trying to process the months of intense therapy, the remembered abuse. I took the phone off the hook in the daytime.

I called Dr. Naughton to let him know I was a mental hospital dropout. I told him I was hurt that in a hellish week he had not called me or come to see me. He had simply turned me over to the hospital psychiatrist. I felt abandoned and angry again. Those feelings came up too often in our therapy. I told him I needed a month alone. I couldn't talk or cry or feel anything more. He said that was fine, just call him when I was ready to see him.

It seemed odd to me that he had felt I was so off the wall the week before that he demanded my hospitalization and now just passively accepted not seeing me for a month. I think I wanted him to say, "Please call me to let me know how you're doing. I'll be here if you need me." Nothing. Nothing warm came from him. He was always detached.

I hung up the phone and wept. I wanted a warm, nurturing daddy. He wouldn't be that.

Baking bread seemed to comfort me. I spent hours pounding and smashing dough and then lovingly molding loaves, thinking of Grandma Bernice.

Gardening was another source of solace. The black, rich soil wafted its scent into my emptiness. I felt a need to have my seeds sprout, their very germination a sign of hope.

Every day I cried as I remembered more abuse, more horror. There were days I was so overcome by the pain that I would sit in front of the television and not hear a word. An hour could go by and I would realize a program had ended and I hadn't noticed any of it.

A strange thing was happening as I remembered and cried— Emily seemed to be getting sick. As I began to experience angry feelings, she seemed to grow weak. She told me she remembered all the abuse I had chosen subconsciously not to remember. Slowly, the thought evolved that Emily and I might be more closely linked than I had thought. It was an odd connection; but once I noticed it it seemed glaringly clear.

I went to the library and looked up "Dissociative Personality" in a psychology book. As I read, I realized there was a possibility that I was a multiple personality. Emily could be a piece of myself that I had split off from. She was angry and I was not. She had remembered the abuse that I had not. This was only the dawning of awareness, not yet on an emotional level, but an intellectual one. I opened my mind to the possibility I was not some genetic freak twin, but a person of psychologically split-off selves. Still it was too weird an idea to accept, really. My familiar scenario of my "twin" was easier. I couldn't be Emily. She was too heinous. Yet the idea had planted itself in my mind.

As the days wore on, I often went to the telephone to call Dr. Naughton. I wanted to tell him about Emily. I wanted to be helped, to be free of her tyranny over me. But I still wasn't ready. I had protected her existence for too many years.

I tried to set a structure to my days, just to hold myself intact. Crying continually, I forced myself to wash the clothes, vacuum the house, clip coupons. I was at the limit of what I could cope with. Looking back on those days alone after the hospital, I feel deeply angered at Dr. Naughton for never phoning me, checking on me, or offering me any help when I was in a state of deep need and exhaustion.

I made an appointment with Dr. Naughton just before Christmas. After not seeing him for five weeks, my heart was thumping with excitement at being with him again. He grinned and clasped my hands in both of his.

I had brought him a wreath I had made of pine cones and dried flowers. In the middle was a big candle. I had been working on this—I went over to the candle and lit a match and held it to the wick. I could do it. I could light a match without panic. It seemed like a tiny step forward, but I knew Dr. Naughton would be pleased. He was.

"That's wonderful," he said.

He wrecked my good mood by saying, "Well, you've gotten your way. You managed to disrupt the hospital and leave, and you have my word that I'll still be your psychiatrist."

"You make it sound as though I was upset on purpose at the hospital." I longed to tell him about Emily, but still I couldn't. I think he thought the out-of-control times were some kind of manipulation on my part.

"I don't think you gave the hospital a chance."

"Why can't you just be glad I'm better?" I asked. "You're just wanting me to measure up to some elusive standard of patienthood that I don't understand. I get the feeling there are rules to this game and I'm not picking up on what they are."

"You're doing fine," Dr. Naughton said, standing up to signal the end of our session but leaving me with the eternal sense of walking through a mine field in this office. There was no constancy to our relationship, no defined boundaries.

"I'm leaving to go skiing over Christmas for two weeks. I'm glad you're doing better. I'll see you after the New Year," Dr. Naughton said.

I left his office weeping. The five weeks without contact or therapy had been too long, and now I would be alone for another stretch of time. I resented my sense of dependency on him.

A wonderful thing happened over Christmas that year. I didn't lose my voice. Ever since the age of ten, when my mother stabbed me for singing, I had gone hoarse over the holidays. I never knew it was psychosomatic. I thought the loss of my voice was due to an allergy to Christmas trees. I'd even been to a doctor to see if he could solve the mystery of the holiday hoarseness. It made me wonder how many symptoms and fears were all connected to my childhood. I still carried iced tea with me everywhere. If I got in a car, I would take a diet drink. I had a tremendous fear of thirst and hunger. It was a big moment when I decided to go to bed without a glass of water on the bedside table. At first I went back and forth to the bathroom for sips of water, but after a few days I finally went to bed without the thirst panic. It seemed important to break that one phobia, for Dan always teased me about my need to drink and I resented his constant reference to it. I was able to tell myself that I was not locked in a closet, I was not going to die of thirst. Plugging into the sources of anxiety was the key to the resolution.

Food was another thing I was anxious about. My cupboards looked like a squirrel's nest just before winter. I often compulsively bought food. I nibbled constantly. My kids used to tease me, because for even short trips in the car I would bring a thermos of juice and snacks. Dan said it was amazing the whole family wasn't fat the way I focused on food. Knowing I had a high state of anxiety over eating, I tried very hard not to pass on my neuroses to my kids. I never forced them to finish what was on their plates. I never withheld food from them. It was never used as punishment or reward. I tried hard to not be dominated by my fears. It helped when I began to remember back to the closet days, the days locked in my room and the intense, gnawing hunger of my childhood. Even remembering did not resolve the focus, the compulsions, but it did help and at least gave me an explanation.

When I began therapy, I assumed I had a poorly functioning bladder. I needed to urinate about every thirty minutes, partly from the enormous volume of fluids I drank and partly out of a deep anxiety that gave me cramping pain if I tried to hold in my urine. So much of my life was spent in a preoccupation with food, drink, and voiding. In theaters, I made Dan sit on an aisle with me so I could get up during a movie and go to the restroom.

Dr. Naughton picked up on all of this right away when I began therapy. I would bring glasses of water or coffee into the session. Often, in the middle of talking, I would have to leap up to run to his bathroom. When he suggested I try to wait to the end of the session, I could barely speak from the anxiety I was experiencing. Gradually, it got so I could hold my urine longer. It was the anxiety I experienced in the closet, holding my pee until I thought my bladder would burst. Remembering didn't magically resolve symptoms, but it helped. I could understand why I was feeling the way I did and I could talk my way through some things, but it was an uphill road.

Every day for years I had five or six bowel movements. As I thought about the enemas I had lived through as a child, I realized the source of that tension. It was a nice discovery to realize I had no major illness. Most of the symptoms were in my mind, not my body. It gave birth to hope.

I don't remember what upset me. I think it was a phone call from Bobby talking about Mom. Emily got stronger and took over. The next thing I was aware of was being arrested for stealing another damn bear. It was an expensive stuffed bear that the security officer was taking away from me. I was booked for shoplifting and given a court appearance date. I was devastated.

I had been in therapy for eighteen months and still had not told Dr. Naughton about Emily and the other voices I sometimes heard in my head. I wanted to tell him, especially since I was confused about why she was sick.

I tried dozens of times, but I didn't know how. I had rarely spoken to anyone about Emily. Even during arrests I simply took responsibility for her. It was not an easy conversation to initiate. Now I tried by asking, "Dr. Naughton, do you believe in multiple personalities?"

"I don't use that term. I think all parts of a person are accessible to them," and so he would waltz around my questions.

I wrote a story about there being another part of me that didn't seem like me. This part stole things. I sent it to Dr. Naughton.

At the next session he said, "I think you are trying to tell me you have a problem stealing things."

That was not the real message I was trying to give him. I wanted him to know about Emily. He wasn't understanding the magnitude of my inner pain. "Yes, sometimes I steal things and I don't know why." I said nothing about Emily. I was humiliated enough to admit I stole.

Everything churned inside me—anger at Emily and the idea that she was not a twin but a part of me. It was an ugly thought because if Emily was truly a part of me, then *I* stole things, *I* had sex with strangers, *I* was angry. One part of me was moving toward this rational conclusion but my feeling self couldn't accept it. How could I steal when I would not? How could I be promiscuous when I was a moral person? Emotionally I rejected the whole idea that Emily and I were all just pieces of one self.

I was ruminating on all these issues when I went to the next session with Dr. Naughton. He said, "You wrote me a letter and pretended it was from someone named Emily. It is just your way of trying to tell me about things that are painful to discuss."

"Emily wrote to you?" I asked in shock.

"No. You wrote to me."

"I didn't. Emily is not me. She said she would never tell about us. We had this agreement."

Dr. Naughton read me the letter from Emily.

Dear Dr. Naughton,

Marcia is a lying bitch. She promised she would never tell anyone about me. I try to leave her out of my life, she should leave me out of hers.

Marcia sits in your office like a Miss Goody-two-shoes trying to get help, knowing full well I am there, too. She refuses to remember the great times and great fucks we have had. I love how she sits and says Scott and Dan have been her only lovers. She chooses to forget things because she holds on to the sweetness and goodness crap. I have taken her on some great cocksucking adventures. The damn bitch keeps getting sick on me.

Marcia thinks she is so intelligent, but it is me who has the smarts. At least I don't go around forgetting things.

My life has turned into a torment since Marcia tried to kill herself. She deliberately cut up our great bod. Did she tell you that she had the back surgery on purpose, lying to the doctor about her pain so she could put me out of circulation? Just to get revenge I steal things. I have stolen hundreds of dollars worth of things. I love to see Marcia cry and try to figure out how to return them. You should have seen her when they handcuffed us at Sears.

I roared with laughter when Marcia started writing a journal. I told her it was a sort of half-sided venture, that I deserved equal time. Actually, I get very little time for anything. Marcia keeps me boxed in with all her ailments and boring dutiful things. She is an incredible drag. I don't even talk to her much. We have nothing in common and I certainly want no part in the hausfrau bit.

You made me angry this fall with all the mind-jerking crap. I told Marcia that I was going to check out if I had to go through all of this shit. I decided, what the hell, she seems to care about life, so I would give her a sporting chance. I have been telling her why I'm angry and what the witch of a mother did to us. Marcia uses words like, "remembering," but it's me who is telling her. We are communicating civilly for the first time in years. She didn't even believe me when I told her that she made our body sick on purpose.

I make no sense of the connectedness of our memories. As Marcia is remembering, crying, and getting angry, it is making me sleepy and lethargic. The other day I saw a great necklace and didn't even have the energy to take it. All the zest is leaving me.

Marcia would like me to die and not have me take her with me. If she can figure out how, it's okay with me. She knows I've wanted to die for years. A couple of times I almost did it, but Marcia is so upset about leaving her children, I back off.

I'm finding I actually want to help Marcia, because we have both suffered too much. She made me read the book, *Sybil*, with her. I told her if one of us has to go, I'll be glad it is me, but it is for her to figure out how. She is older and loves all the intellectual bullshit.

I am eighteen. You have already met me, but you didn't know it. Don't ask me to sit and visit with you, because I won't. I know everything that goes on with Marcia and she knows most things about me. We are not like the stories where Sybil doesn't know the others. Marcia and I can occupy the same place at the same time. So, does that make us Siamese crazy, Doctor? Marcia is there with me, she just forgets on purpose. She is a sweet slob. Let's both give her a chance, since she is the one with the family.

It's not as if I saw any future possible for me in a body that is covered with scars and getting older. Mondo boring!

I'm not going to help Marcia if she keeps lecturing me on how I'm just her bad side and that we are the same person. That is crap, because I'm writing this while she is sleeping. I'll put this in our neighbor's mailbox before she wakes up. Old sweetness and light can't handle reality too well. Don't tell her about this letter; we usually don't do things behind each other's backs.

If Marcia bugs me too much, I'll have to tell her about our fun-fucking times. Maybe I'll tell her about the sweaty gardener we screwed in her own bed. Actually, Doc, I had fun until Marcia started making us puke. The prude thinks everything I do is bad. Up hers!

I'm writing you because I want you to know I'm trying to help.

Oops! I just thought of something. Since you do not know me, you might think this letter is a joke, so I'm enclosing this demand of restitution notice from the Broadway. It's one of many I've made Marcia pay. (Hee-hee, I always use her name in public.) You must know the Virgin Marcia would never steal anything! She still hasn't figured out it is a screw and be screwed world.

If you have doubts about what I'm writing, get the surgical report on Marcia's fusion. The physician knew it was unnecessary. Get the pathology report on the perfect gall bladder the doctors removed and the healthy uterus. Marcia gets sick on purpose to wreck my life, and the damn doctors don't question her. She won't even go in stores anymore. She shops by catalogue.

You can check out the abuse stories with the scars. You can undress us slowly in your office (Marcia would die!) or you can send to the psychiatric hospital for the admission physical where they measured and documented all the scars.

Marcia is wanting to get well, but she is giving you only half the story. There sure is a crock of shit to wade through.

> Toodles,
> Emily

"Don't make it worse on yourself, Marcia. You can say the truth in here. You are safe."

"You don't understand. There is a twin inside my head. I

think we have different brains. She is not at all like me. She is irresponsible, childish, and angry."

"You just make therapy more painful for yourself when you lie about it not being you who steals and does angry things."

He just didn't get the picture. I spent the rest of the session trying to explain to him how maybe Emily was a piece of me, since she got sick when I remembered the abuse but maybe she really wasn't me, since we were not alike at all. Dr. Naughton listened with his accusatory eyes focused on me.

At the next session, I felt angry that he didn't believe what I was trying to tell him. I told him I was angry and he said, "You always seem to be angry with me. Maybe it is time to stop therapy. You have had a year and a half and you have learned a great deal about yourself. Maybe we should end our sessions and you can take all you've learned and work with it on your own."

Here I had finally told him about Emily and he wanted to end therapy with me. I broke down and sobbed and sobbed on his couch. I couldn't win with him. He was warm one session and abandoning the next. I said, "I am telling the truth, there is an Emily and I hate her."

"You are saying you hate yourself."

"Yes, I hate Emily and I hate myself. Please don't send me away."

"You must tell me the truth if you want me to be your therapist."

"I'm trying to, but you aren't hearing what I'm saying. Maybe I'm crazy, maybe I'm a multiple personality, maybe I'm a freak of nature, but Emily seems real to me. There is another voice in my head. We can talk and argue. We can take turns with my body. I don't know what is real and what isn't, all I know is what seems real to me."

I left Dr. Naughton's office deeply depressed and feeling hopeless about ever resolving who or what I was. I questioned what kind of a psychiatrist would want to end therapy just as a patient finally gets honest.

"Why don't you go to Dr. Naughton's office at our next appointment and let him know who you really are?" I asked Emily.

"And get us locked up forever? Besides, I think the guy is a jerk. Can't you see how he manipulates you?"

"I guess if you go see him, it will just complicate things."

"I don't even feel well. The more you remember about Mom, the less energy I have. It's totally weird."

"Writing him without telling me was a rotten thing to do," I said.

"Believe it or not, I'm really trying to help you. I know things can't go on as they are."

"Thanks. That's probably the nicest thing you've said to me in years."

After that confrontation we seemed to do better in our sessions, Dr. Naughton no longer suggested I stop therapy. He wouldn't let me talk about Emily, though. He insisted that there was no possible way I had a second functioning brain in my head, so I must be just one person; therefore, Emily did not exist. Wanting to keep seeing him, I never referred to Emily by name, I sort of talked around it. When Dr. Naughton questioned, "Why do you suppose you steal things?" I wanted to protest that Emily stole things, not me, but instead I meekly answered, "I don't know."

So much of what I worked through was away from therapy. Things were said that made me mull ideas over and over. It did become clearer to me that Emily was a split off part of me. She had held the memories of abuse that I hadn't been able to deal with. She was the anger I had been punished for possessing. Emily acted on the pain that was trapped inside.

In the spring, Dan surprised me with tickets to Mexico—a week away just for the two of us. I was thrilled but apprehensive. It meant getting on an airplane—another damned confined space filled with smoke. Emily was sick. I could hear her breathing in a rattling way. The thought struck me that if she was just an imaginary piece of me, then the breathing I heard was imaginary, too. It was a simple but enormous concept to grasp.

Emily said, "Go. Just get on the fucking plane and go. If I die, I die."

Dan said, "Honey, we need to get away. I don't understand all of your therapy, but you have cried enough. Mexico will give you perspective. We need time together."

This was a first, Dan reaching out to me to try to improve our relationship.

With Xanax, I survived the flight and we stayed in a beautiful hotel in Cancun. We slept, ate, snorkeled, and talked. In the quiet moments alone, I shared in an oblique sort of way the horrors of my childhood and the running and splitting that I had done in trying to escape the pain. Of course I did not tell him of the affairs; it would have served no purpose.

Dan did not display any depth of emotion, but he did take me in his arms and say, "I don't understand everything you're saying, but I do know in spite of it all, I love you."

I let that be enough. My pain and tears belonged in therapy, not in my marriage. But I wished just one person could know the horrors of my life and weep for me.

After ten days away, I felt pleased to see Dr. Naughton. Entering his office, I swept into his arms in an embrace. He returned the hug, and I felt the energy flow between us. It startled me to view him as a sexual being. He had seemed neutered, with his passiveness and lack of energy. That hug was the beginning of others. They complicated our relationship further.

Therapy continued with my searching and delving into who Emily was. She became sicker as I felt the anger and abandonment of my childhood.

Emily sent Dr. Naughton another letter.

Dear Dr. Naughton,

I'm writing you because I am worried about Marcia. She thinks she would be better off without me. What she doesn't realize is how much I do for her. Marcia is wrong when she says she is the wiser, stronger twin. I am the strong one. It was me who learned to escape the pain and torture. When Marcia can't deal with pain and stress, it is me that takes over for her.

I am writing because I feel that I am dying. Please do not feel sad for me, because it is what I want. As much as I detest Marcia, I worry she won't be able to cope without me. She sees herself as so goddamn competent. She doesn't even realize the burden of pain I have carried for her. I have always known when she has reached her limit and I take over for her. She is always angry when I take over, never even realizing the service I do for her. If I die, how will she deal with our mother, or Dan's black moods, or all the painful memories? I hope you will be able to help her when I'm gone. Personally, I think she is going to unravel if I die. She doesn't deal well with pain or anger.

This is the first time in my life that it is me who is sick. I feel so weak I can barely get up and write. Even holding this pen is a supreme effort. I do not know what is happening to me, but I have a strong premonition of my death.

I have seriously thought of telling Marcia all the things I did on the escapades that she does not remember, but I think it serves no purpose. It is enough that she is finally remembering our childhood. I've tried to tell her about it before, but she refused to listen. I guess she is finally ready to remember it all. Jesus! I'm certainly willing to leave all the crying that has gone on for months now. When I die we should rule it a goddamn drowning. I never cry. I am the tough survivor. It has been Marcia who was the invalid and had the accidents and surgeries. I never once thought it would be the fragile sensitive twin that would survive.

Please help Marcia, Doc. She has no idea what I have done for her. She listens to you and believes in you, although I'll be damned if I know why. Anyone who puts people in hospitals where they can't even breathe isn't high on my list. But what the hell, it isn't me who has to stick around. When Marcia unravels without me, it will be your problem and her problem, not mine. I almost wish I could stick around out of curiosity, to see how she manages without me.

By the way, Marcia doesn't know how to tell you this, but I am not the only other one here. She personally doesn't know the others like she knows me, but she knows they take over. Because she can't explain it, she refuses to think about it. Complicated, ain't it!

Good Luck!
Emily

P.S. I don't know why, but I think what you and Marcia are doing in your office has something to do with my dying. That makes you an accomplice to murder. Thank you, you may consider it a mercy-killing. My life has only been pain.

In early summer, I felt with alarming certainty that Emily was dying. Logic told me that it was only because I remembered my childhood now and felt all of Emily's feelings that she was melting away. But it felt like a death. She could only speak in my mind with a hoarse whisper and couldn't take over anymore.

"I'm dying, toots. I actually feel sad to be leaving you," whispered Emily. "You've needed me more than you know. Just think how endless those closet hours would have been without me. We had some happy adventures. Don't you realize I was your anger for you?"

"I want to live life without your torment, but I'll miss you. I've never been alone."

Frightened at the thought of Emily dying, I called Dr. Naughton every day for a week. It was so fixed in my mind that Emily was another person that I feared when she died that I would die, too, like Chang and Eng, the Siamese twins.

I became sick, running a fever of one hundred and one degrees, and aching all over. It didn't feel like the flu, it felt like impending death.

Dr. Naughton reassured me I was hysterically causing Emily's death, that he was absolutely certain I would not die if she did. I didn't believe him. If I was two separate people, then Emily's dead cells would poison my system, and if I was hysterical, then I knew I was profoundly hysterical, like the Indians or aborigines who lie down and die at some witch doctor's prediction. Either way, I figured I wasn't long for this world.

It was a sunny Sunday morning when Emily died. I heard the death rattle in my mind and the silence of the voice that could no longer speak. When her breathing stopped, I panicked. I lay in bed waiting for my death. It did not come.

After a few days, I realized Dr. Naughton had been right, I was not going to die. My fever went away and I began to feel better. I wrote letters of grief and sorrow for my departed enemy. I had hated Emily but didn't know how to deal with the quietness in my head. There was a vulnerability to being devoid of my twin. I grieved for the familiar duality I had lived with. I felt drained and empty. There was no sense of liberation.

In Emily's death, I felt I had fully opened the door to the black place inside me, feeling all the pain of the tortured childhood.

Unprotected and alone, phone calls or letters from Mom left me with suicidal impulses. It was after a telephone call from Mom that I again had a memory lapse and lost time. Much to my alarm, I found I could still dissociate, but I hadn't wanted to face the existence of the other selves.

One afternoon, I got a phone call with a man's voice asking for Muriel. When I said, "I'm sorry, no one by that name lives here," he became rather insistent.

"I'm certain of this phone number."

"What does Muriel look like?" I don't know why I asked. Phone calls like this had happened many times before.

His description was me to a tee. "Actually, her voice is like yours," the man was saying, "but she spoke with a bit of an accent. I think she's English."

"I'm not only crazy," I thought, "I'm creatively crazy."

I lost more time, and it was five hours later that I found myself at a gas station near Mom's house. I called Dr. Naughton.

"Do you think I'm capable of dissociating and killing my mother?"

"It's possible" was his unreassuring reply. "Do you want to kill your mother?"

"Yes" was my response, feeling the anger of all the lost years. "Maybe you should lock me up for a while. Everything inside my head feels crazy. Emily wasn't the only twin. There are others, but I'm not entirely certain who they are or what they are capable of."

"They are all just parts of you," Dr. Naughton said gently.

"But I don't know these parts," I said, sobbing long distance from the gas station as a radio from a nearby car blasted over the noises of the pumps.

"Try to get control and don't go to your mother's house. Come back immediately."

I did, but spent the next couple of weeks crying my way through therapy. I wrote endless epistles of pain to Dr. Naughton, who said he would have to charge me for the time it took to read the letters.

Not having any more money, and knowing my insurance wouldn't cover charges for letter reading, I decided to give him the diamond ring I had from Grandma Bernice. It was worth at least a thousand dollars. With a letter of thank-you to Dr. Naughton and the ring in a beautiful velvet box, I went to his office. He was in a session with another patient, so I left the letter and ring in his mailbox. I turned to a woman sitting in the waiting room and said, "Please tell Dr. Naughton I left something for him."

"I'll be glad to," said the woman, who went back to reading her magazine.

After work, I called him to see if he liked the ring, hoping he would be touched by my generous gesture.

"I got your letter, but no ring. There was only a letter in my mailbox."

"I left you my grandmother's diamond ring," I said, describing it in detail, then I began to cry.

Angrily, Dr. Naughton said, "That was stupid to leave a ring in my mailbox. I couldn't accept it and, furthermore, how do I know one of your other personalities didn't come and take it back?"

I was devastated. Sobbing, I said, "I know when I lose time, and I haven't lost any time today. There can't be anyone on the face of the earth who is more conscious than I am of the hands on a clock. I did leave you the ring. I wanted you to have it as a thank-you for all the time I have taken and trouble I have been."

"Well, you were foolish. I will not accept your story. I'm sorry." Abruptly, he hung up.

I cried for days, for the lost ring and the fact that someone I was sharing my deepest self with didn't believe me.

Dr. Naughton was in the middle of changing offices. He had left his partners and taken a beautiful two-room suite in a high-rise building to carry on his practice alone.

His secretary normally booked appointments. I was regularly scheduled on Monday and Thursday mornings at ten. Arriving at his new office at my usual time, I waited. There was another woman waiting with me. Dr. Naughton came out of his office and looked at me with surprise. "You didn't make an appointment with me."

Incredulous, I stammered, "But I always come at this time."

"Well, you didn't make an appointment and I no longer have a secretary."

"But you didn't tell me I needed to make appointments with you!"

"I told all my patients that. I'm certain I told you."

"You didn't. Will you at least put me down in your book for my usual time starting my next session?"

Flipping through his book, he said, "I'm really sorry I don't have any openings until next month."

"A month? You can't be serious!"

"I'm very serious. I'm sorry, you will just have to wait until next month for time with me."

I stumbled out of his office feeling like the small child who had been left in a closet again. It had only been weeks since Emily died. I was still dissociating, upset at the thought of being a multiple personality, deeply involved in therapy, and Dr. Naughton said to wait a month, with no offer to work me into his schedule.

I came apart. I called him every morning to see if he had cancellations. I begged for his lunch hour, offering to bring him food. I began to lose track of the hours, disappearing to unknown places, putting unconscious miles on my car. The abandonment seemed beyond my ability to cope. I called an attorney and said, "I want to sue my psychiatrist for malpractice."

"Why do you want to sue him?"

"Because he has abandoned me. In the middle of therapy he has said he won't see me for a month."

"I'm sorry, but that doesn't sound like grounds for a malpractice suit."

I hung up the phone feeling angry and suicidal. I took pills that I had collected, pain pills of all varieties and doses, and made little piles of them, calculating how many it would take to kill myself. I called the suicide hot line and had the paramedics sent to my home. I talked them out of hospitalizing me. I called Dr. Naughton crying, and said, "I can't take this kind of abandonment. I want to die. I have the pills."

"Stop trying to manipulate me. I have told you I have no time for you. If you feel suicidal, go to the hospital." With that, he hung up.

I took a few of the pills, but something in me refrained me

from taking the rest. I think it was the certainty of the pain I would be inflicting on Dan and my children. I would be passing on the legacy of pain if I took all the pills. Even the deep sleep from being drugged couldn't take away the terrible pain of abandonment. I stole things from department stores, and my thoughts got splintered and fuzzy.

After another call to the suicide prevention hot line I think they gave Dr. Naughton a call. "I will give you an appointment in a week," he said.

When I saw him, he hugged me warmly and acted as if three weeks of hell for me hadn't existed. I hated him at that moment. I hated the emotional hold, the bondage I felt with him. This man was jerking me around like a dog on a short leash.

It took a month of tears and anger to get over the hurt of how he had treated me.

It was a complete surprise to me when Dan quit his teaching job. There was no great soul-searching or job-hunting, just the sense of finality in his mind that he had walked into his last classroom. Over the summer he had a hundred different career ideas, each one infusing him with enthusiasm.

By the end of summer Dan had found a job with a small company up in Marin County, north of San Francisco. With great delight, he called a realtor and put a "For Sale" sign on our lawn.

The idea of ending therapy with Dr. Naughton seemed a greater loss than any aspect of moving. I could leave neighbors and friends, but therapy had become my lifeline.

Dr. Naughton became warm and affectionate when I told him we were moving. "Have you thought of telling Dan you are not ready to leave therapy? You could stay here and get an apartment. We are in the middle of important work together." That seemed an odd statement when he had so casually stopped therapy for three weeks.

Divorce loomed as a serious consideration at that moment. Dan shared so little of me. He didn't understand me as I longed to be understood. I wanted him to be a part of all I was going through. I had repeatedly asked him to come to therapy sessions with me, but he always refused. The whole time I had been in therapy, he asked no questions as I walked around the house red-eyed. We had both kept up a civilized, gentle-voiced exterior for each other, but it wasn't real.

My attachment to Dr. Naughton seemed greater than my attachment to Dan. Another thing that added to my indecision was that Kevin and Cindi were both leaving home for the first time to college.

For a month I wrestled with the option of staying with Dr. Naughton, who seemed envelopingly warm, and going with Dan, who was filled with excitement about a new beginning in life.

Finally, I decided to go with Dan. We had a lot of years invested in each other, years he had stayed through my depressions and suicide attempts. I not only loved him, but I owed him. I felt grief at all I had failed to be for him, all the years of running from the pain that haunted me. Dan couldn't put love into words easily, but he was there when I woke up with nightmares, and was kind about my neurotic fears. He was distanced but accepting of all that I was, and couldn't be.

In thinking of moving, it surprised me to realize that Scott Williams was not even an issue in my decision. Four years of an affair and an aborted baby between us and somehow we had simply drifted apart. The intensity of remembering my abuse had consumed me to such an extent that weeks went by without my even calling Scott.

I saw him more clearly with therapy. I still loved him, but I saw him with all his warping and imperfections; he was no longer the perfect, safe daddy.

Saying good-bye to Dr. Naughton was to experience both a relief at leaving the confusing relationship and a deep grief at losing someone who had become precious to me. He was the first person I had let into my pain-filled center. In the two years together I had found a childhood, a ghastly one, but like a connect-the-dots picture, my life was beginning to make sense to me. I had answers to why I did things. Emily had died, although there were other selves. I had not learned how to stop dissociating, nor was I past feeling suicidal. I really was at the beginning of my journey in therapy, but I wasn't certain I would ever try it again with anyone. Dr. Naughton had made it a supremely painful experience, casting me away, then reeling me in—the coldness, then the warmth.

It was just as I was leaving him that I read in the newspaper he was being sued by a former patient for having a sexual affair with her. The town vibrated from the gossip and it added to my sense of confusion over his urging me to stay and get an apartment.

Dr. Naughton settled out of court with his patient for an enormous sum of money. I felt jealous he had not slept with me.

Chapter 10

Getting settled in Marin should have been a joyful new adventure, but the loss of therapy and all that was familiar to me felt suffocatingly lonely. For a month I lay in bed, unable to do the simplest things. I missed my children with the teenage mess and laughter. I ached to hear Dr. Naughton's voice. I called him several times, but he was abrupt. "You have moved, so get up and get on with your life. You've learned a great deal in therapy, now get on with living." His words fell like stones into the void in me. I felt lost and hopeless. I bought a plane ticket to fly back to him, wanting to beg him to be the safe daddy, but I canceled the ticket; I didn't have a place to stay and I was afraid of flying.

In another phone call, full of my weeping, Dr. Naughton gave me the name of a psychiatrist he had known years before. "Call Dr. Hambler, he's a good man."

"I only want therapy with you. You know me."

"But you aren't here. You need to make some effort to adjust. Give Dr. Hambler a call."

"Okay," I said, hanging up the phone like I was severing a

piece of my life. In a way it was, for I began therapy with Dr. Hambler the very next week.

Dr. Hambler was in his mid-forties, an immediately likable man. He was totally into his psychiatrist image, with his full beard, longish red hair and baggy corduroy pants. His eyes were bright blue, steady, and had the concentration of an intellectual introvert.

The first session I sat and did nothing but cry, spewing out a very confused tale of my childhood, the death of Emily, and my sense of loss of Dr. Naughton.

He was probably sitting there thinking, What the hell is going on here?, but he was very kind and said he would give Dr. Naughton a call and made an appointment for the following week.

I resented the hours it took to tell this quiet man about my life. The pain of the torture years surfaced in the retelling. There was so much to reveal to get comfortable with a new psychiatrist.

Tipping backward in his chair, always fidgeting with his pencils and the quarters in his ashtray, Dr. Hambler kept his eye contact steady and said very little. After two years of uncovering the locked-away horrors for myself, I was able to give him my childhood in vivid sequence, but after these graphically painful sessions, he would rise from his chair and simply nod at me and say, "I'll see you next week."

"Don't you feel anything?" I sobbed one day.

"That is not the purpose of therapy" was his cold reply.

We spent hours trying to untangle my mixed feelings about Dr. Naughton. I grieved for the loss of him, felt angry at his inconsistencies, confusion at the intimacies. He was six hundred miles away but still a part of my mind and its turmoil. It made me suspicious of a new relationship with another psychiatrist.

It was a clear, crisp autumn morning when the telephone rang. My adrenaline was always jump-started by the sound of Mom's voice.

"Marcia, I am going to kill myself."

Dead silence on my end—there was no obvious response to that statement.

"I have nothing to live for anymore. I called you to say goodbye."

"Don't be ridiculous, Mom. You're in perfect health and you have a lovely home. Don't do anything. I'll come to see you right now."

I hung up the phone and called Bobby. "Mom just called me saying she's going to commit suicide. What will we do?" I asked.

"I'll meet you at Mom's," Bobby said.

I flew into some clothes and jumped into the car and headed for the airport. I didn't question why I was going. I simply did what I did, like a lemming heading for the sea.

I arrived at Mom's house before Bobby. Suddenly, I did not want to face her. Why had I come? I rang the doorbell.

Instead of a disheveled, distraught woman, I found Mom beautifully dressed, as always, with the regal bearing, the hair as perfect as a wig.

As usual, I regressed to feeling like a small, helpless child in her presence. I stood there feeling the pain that separated us and was unable to speak. A feeling welled in me at the sight of Mom, a yearning so intense that I wanted to hug her, once, just once, to feel her arms around me. I wanted my hair stroked gently. More than anything, I wanted her face to light up when she looked at me. I should have hated her but all I wanted was a moment, just a small moment when I would be affirmed as a valued person.

Mom ignored me and began speaking in total self-absorption about killing herself. "No one loves me. No one has ever loved me." She was pacing in her long velveteen jumpsuit and black leather pumps.

I wanted to grab her and shout, "For God's sake, Mom, I'm here. I exist. I'm your daughter who you should have nurtured. Please see me. Feel me for one moment."

Just then Bobby arrived. Bobby could deal with Mom. I began drifting into a dissociative state, which was the only way I could deal with the complexity of emotions ricocheting inside me.

Bobby did not have his emotions confused; he hated Mom. "Goddamnit, stop the fuck talking about suicide!"

"Don't speak to me that way. I am still your mother!"

"Only by the donation of an ovum," snarled Bobby, forgetting the purpose of our mission.

Mom got more agitated and melodramatic, saying we were incapable of gratitude for all she had done for us and how no one had ever appreciated her.

Bobby went to the phone and called her doctor. "She says she's going to kill herself. No, I don't see any pills or guns. Yes, she seems coherent, but totally self-absorbed as usual. Doctor, I personally don't give a shit about what she does, I'm leaving this in your hands." Turning to me, Bobby said, "The doctor will make a house call tonight or tomorrow morning."

In a more pulled-together state Mom rustled about making us tea in her sterling silver tea pot and set out a platter of cookies. We sat around the mahogany table with its hand-crocheted tablecloth as we struggled to make conversation. Bobby and I spoke of our children and Mom talked about the spring bulbs she had planted in the garden. "It's a shame I won't be here to see them," she said.

We talked for about an hour, Bobby and I feeling the strain of our memories. Mom seemed oblivious to her heinous crimes. There were no kind words from her, no looks of sorrow or longing, merely the self-pity of a person who ceases to exist beyond her own nose.

She asked me to go to the market and buy groceries for a "Last Supper." It was as though we had entered a black comedy. Mom tried to convince Bobby to stay for her final dinner here on earth.

My nerves were frazzled, and I began to weep. "I can't stay for dinner, Mom. You certainly must understand why."

"It's because you don't love me," Mom accused.

"That's probably right," said Bobby. "Look. Killing yourself is ridiculous. Just wait until the doctor comes and he will give you some medication. Do you want us to take you to a hospital?"

"No. I'm not crazy. I won't go to a hospital."

"Well, we definitely are not going to be manipulated into your little theatrical production any longer. You can do whatever you want with your life," said Bobby rather severely. "Let's get out of here, Marcia."

A war raged inside me. My adult voice told me Mom was serious about the suicide threat. The child voice in me couldn't cope. It was as though I were rooted to the floor and all the wounds of my recently remembered childhood were oozing blood. I looked at my hands, expecting them to be covered in blood, with little Popsicle sticks taped to broken fingers. I had to leave. I walked over to get my coat.

"Won't you stay with me? Don't you love me?" Mom pleaded.

With all the years of agony reverberating through me, I looked at her and said, "No, Mom. I guess I don't. Good-bye." If I'd stayed any longer, I would have either gone into an angry rage or knelt before her, pleading to be loved. I wasn't sure which, but I knew I had to go.

In the morning, Bobby called me. "Mom's dead. She overdosed on sleeping pills. The doctor found her fully dressed, lying on her bed with candles lit and her last will by her bedside. I wonder if we should have taken her to the hospital. Well, we did what we could."

"We didn't do a damn thing except call her doctor," I said.

"Even that was more effort than she deserved." Bobby was always clear about where he stood. No tears from Bobby.

"Can you please call Jimmy?" I asked. "We should have called him yesterday." Jimmy had moved back to the West Coast.

"Sure. I'll call him, and I called the mortuary. I've ordered Mom's body cremated. I'll talk to you later."

Hanging up the phone, I began to shake, and went and flopped down on my bed, curling up in a ball. The moisture in my eyes gave way to sobbing. I wasn't crying for Mom. I was weeping for all that I had longed for and never had. I sobbed until my bed was damp and I could hardly catch my breath. The loss was so profound, it was beyond the tears I was shedding; they were useless tears. Some tears cleanse; you can feel relieved and go on. My tears felt like drowning tears, without end, without resolution. Lying there, I wished I'd kissed her soft cheek. I wished she had taken me in her arms before her death to say, "I'm sorry for all that I did to you." My heart ached leadenly for that.

She had stolen my childhood and my adulthood as well. Selfishly, I lay there weeping for myself instead of Mom.

———

Dr. Hambler asked me why I hadn't called him when Mom had called me, or why I hadn't called him from her house for advice. There was no answer to his queries. I guess it was because we were too new to each other to have a relationship that I depended on. He seemed a polite stranger.

That night after Mom's death, Jimmy called me in a rage. "How come you didn't phone me from Mom's house?" he demanded. "You both knew she was planning suicide and you left her!"

"Bobby tried to call you but couldn't reach you." That was a lie; we hadn't even thought of Jimmy. "I'm sorry, Jimmy. Maybe we should have hospitalized her. She's threatened suicide before, so we looked at this as another cry of wolf."

"Goddamn it! You don't just casually walk off if someone threatens suicide."

"We called her doctor."

"Fuck off," Jimmy spat out at me and, choking into tears, he hung up.

I felt like shit. Our minds were too mixed up to act in a logical, rational way. I wasn't certain I was sorry, I just felt confused at all that had happened.

Bobby called me up and read me the will. He and Jimmy got everything. I was left nothing. "That sort of validates everything we knew she felt about you, doesn't it?"

I couldn't even answer—I was crying. Even in death she managed to twist the knife one more time. Why did I always expect there would come a time of restitution? I should have been used to it, but it hurt so much.

"Will we have a memorial service for her?" I asked.

"Who the hell would come?" asked Bobby. "I couldn't be two-faced enough to pull off the grieving son bit. Just what could anyone say about her at a service?"

"I wish we could bury the past and the pain with her ashes," I murmured.

"We can try," said Bobby.

A week later I arrived home with a trunkload of groceries and noticed my front door was wide open. Puzzled, I entered the house and gave a gasp. Our home had been ransacked. Cupboards were open, drawers dumped out. My first assumption was that I had been robbed, but when I checked the house odd things were missing—only family things. My photo albums were gone, my framed picture of Dad, a ceramic dog, the afghan Grandma had crocheted. Then I knew Jimmy had done this to me. I called him, sobbing as I dialed. "Why, Jimmy?"

"You don't deserve anything of Mom's. You killed her."

"You're crazy," I said. "Bring my things back. You had no right to take my stuff."

"Mom willed Bobby and me everything."

"Not what was in my house. You took things that were mine."

"You walked off and let her die."

"For God's sake, please talk to Bobby. He was there, too," I said helplessly. Instead of being assertive, I was crying. "Besides, I am not sure I owed Mom anything after all she did to me."

"Go to hell." Jimmy slammed the phone down.

Bobby's wife, Nancy, called me, saying, "Your mom's ashes are in a jar rattling around the trunk of my car because Bobby can't face doing anything with them. What shall I do?"

"Why don't I fly down for the weekend. I need to talk with Bobby. This whole experience has been awful."

Nancy said, "Bobby isn't sleeping and he's having crying jags."

"Me, too," I said, not letting on that I was feeling intensely suicidal.

Seeing Bobby helped. We sat and rehashed all that we might have done or should have done that last day with Mom. "I keep crying," said Bobby, "but I don't think it is out of guilt or sadness at Mom's passing. I just feel overwhelmed at the life she gave us. I keep having flashbacks. If evil exists, then Mom was an evil person. How can we be expected to feel sad when she dies?"

"Like you, I think my tears are for what we lost and never had as children. We're weeping for ourselves."

"What shall we do with Mom's ashes?" Bobby asked.

"Let's go to the lake and feed her to the ducks."

We did just that, except that neither one of us wanted to open the jar, as if a huge omnipotent genie would appear and smite us with an avenging sword. We passed the jar back and forth to each other until the absurdity of it all made us begin to laugh. It was a black comic moment when we approached a total stranger to open the jar. When the jar was opened and we stood unscathed, we rented a rowboat and chummed for ducks and fish with pieces of bread. When we had a churning swarm of life around the boat, we began to sprinkle Mom's ashes in the water.

"This is for the pets you killed," Bobby said, throwing ashes behind the boat.

"Here's to the spoons, knives, ice picks, and needles," I said, releasing the gray powder in the ripples. The ducks made the ashes disappear.

We kept letting go of bits of Mom with pieces of poison from our hearts. We shed no tears, for with each ash and each memory, the anger built in us. When we finished, we both sat there feeling our rage at what we had lived through. We spread no flowers nor did we say kind words. We were trying to purge the pain, but we knew it was futile.

"I have this terrible fear that instead of drowning her in muddy duck water, we have released Mom to her cosmic evil forces," confessed Bobby.

"I know. I have nightmares of her coming back to hurt me. It doesn't seem that anyone as powerful as Mom could actually die."

Back at Bobby's house, sipping a good cabernet wine, Bobby handed me Mom's jewelry box. "I know Mom didn't leave you anything in her will, but I want you to have all her jewelry. Some of it was Grandma Bernice's, too." I noticed that he didn't offer to divide the proceeds from the sale of her house, but it was a big gesture nonetheless. There was probably ten thousand dollars in jewels sitting in the case—pearls, diamond rings, a sapphire brooch.

"Thank you. I think I'll keep only the things from Grandma and sell what was Mom's to help me pay for therapy. I don't know if psychiatry holds answers for me, but it's the only hope I have. All that we lived through has left me deeply scarred."

"Maybe finding the generosity to forgive Mom would free us."

"I can't," I said. "I wish I could, but I can't forgive having so much of my life stolen from me. It would be a lie to say I could release the load my heart carries. Certainly Mom was mentally ill, but she was accountable, and calculating. If I had power I would damn her instead of forgive her."

Jimmy never returned the things he had stolen. He quit another job and went to Europe for six months. None of us heard from him. I felt sorry that he was suffering and had no one to help him with his pain.

I turned increasingly to Dr. Hambler, feeling more and more dependent on him as our relationship grew. My telephone calls to him increased after Mom died. There were mixed-up feelings about her death. It was more painful than I anticipated, having never resolved the years of abuse with her.

"How could you have loved someone who repeatedly hurt you?" asked Dr. Hambler.

"I guess I always felt that I was bad or wicked, somehow deserving the treatment I got. All my childhood I viewed Mom as the beautiful, untouchable lady."

"Where was your anger at what was done to you?"

"I guess Emily and the others held the anger I was not allowed to express. I didn't let myself feel it."

Dr. Hambler said, "I'm not sure I understand your grief now."

"I should be glad she is dead, that I can't get hurt by her anymore, but I feel an enormous sense of loss knowing there will never come a day when she will open her arms to me, never look at me with love in her eyes." Strange as it seems, tears welled in my eyes. That hope had never died.

At other sessions, I told Dr. Hambler that I felt Mom was somehow still alive; I felt the hate messages surrounding me, like a strong thought transference, saying, "Die. I want you to die, you wicked Jew."

Dr. Hambler told me it was ridiculous to believe Mom was some kind of evil ghost out to get me. Instead of feeling reassured, I felt isolated; he didn't understand the haunting I felt.

After Mom's death, time again became fragmented for me. I found myself in odd places having a total loss of memory as to how I got there.

Dr. Hambler told me he got a letter from Sunshine, the six-year-old personality. It upset me not to know who I was being when I lost time.

One Saturday in the late afternoon, I found myself at the bottom of a dirt embankment lying in a heap with my hands bruised and my knees all skinned up. I had absolutely no idea where I was. Instead of getting up, I just flopped onto the soft, rich dirt and lay there in defeat. A hiker found me and helped me up to the main road. I was almost to Mendocino, three hours north of my home. It took me about an hour of walking to find my car. With bleeding knees, I drove to a little bed and breakfast inn and called Dan. Crying, I told him, "I drove north and just kept driving. I guess I'm really upset about Mom's death. It's late, so I think I'll spend the night here in Mendocino."

"That's okay. If you're too upset, maybe you'd better come home. It might make you more depressed to be in a hotel room alone."

"I need some time to myself, I'll be home in the morning."

I wanted Dan to hold me accountable for my lost hours, but he didn't. He was always sweet, but never truly tuned in.

Watching the orange sun slip into the ocean in a spectacular light show, I felt I couldn't keep going. There was no hope or life in me. My knees burned and oozed, and my mind was in turmoil, haunted by Mom and the whispering of other selves. I went down to the darkening ocean and almost gave in to the impulse to slip into the icy sea and just swim out to the pink-and-purple sky and let the exhaustion and cold take me away from the pain. A carload of teenagers driving by kept me from doing it.

Returning home the next day, I telephoned Dr. Hambler's office, crying into his answering machine. As always, he never returned my calls.

"Marcia," Dr. Hambler said at our next session, "I can not and will not call you between sessions. I have my private life to protect and my own needs to meet. If you feel suicidal you should go to the hospital or call the suicide prevention hot line."

I tried to understand what he was telling me. My adult head understood, but my child mind felt abandoned.

Mom's suicide brought up an array of memories that I choked out with sobs in therapy. Dr. Hambler listened attentively and made very little comment.

"Don't you feel anything when I tell you about what happened to me?"

"It is not my place to feel. I am your therapist. Your pain belongs to you. It isn't my pain."

Cold words. Hard words. Therapy was deteriorating between us.

Inside, I was screaming, "Someone please ground me to life, hang on to me for a little while."

Angry feelings emerged toward Dr. Hambler. He became like my untouchable mother. There was nothing I could do to move him or have him respond with any warmth.

"How about a smile, just one," I suggested one session.

"You are trying to be inciteful" was his angry response. I didn't have a clue as to what I had done wrong.

I tried to warm him by bringing him cookies, which he told me not to do.

One session I was especially disintegrated, for I had read an article about a badly abused child and my memories were overcoming me. I graphically and painfully described what it was like to hear Mom's footsteps coming, knowing I would be hurt and having no one, not anyone who could save me from the torture. I relived having my labia sewn together with the needle piercing through me while I thrashed against my bonds. Overcome by the intensity, I got on my knees like a small child, and, seeking refuge from the pain, I crawled over to Dr. Hambler, putting my head against his knee. He pushed me away, saying, "How dare you be so manipulative!"

The harsh angry words cutting into my pain seemed a repetition of my begging, needy relationship with Mom; now he was the angry abandoning parent. Today I know that was transference on my part, but then all I knew was the feeling of abject grief. He was not my friend.

Feeling absolutely alone, my dissociation got worse and my suicidal ideas were more constant. Dr. Hambler put me in the hospital for a while. It helped. I got on a more even keel, but my relationship with him was beyond restoration. He did not know how to be warm or nurturing.

Trying to pay for therapy, which was no longer covered by any insurance, I sold Grandma's and Mom's jewelry, all the beautiful heirloom pieces, gone for the hours spent with a man who seemed to be magnifying my illness.

As I began to run out of money the second year with him, I dropped to once-a-week sessions. It seemed hopeless. Therapy would open the door to intense memories of pain, or frightening new ideas, and then there would be no contact for a week to help me deal with the raw feelings. I was alone with my dissociative selves. Once a week was not a life raft for me in my inability to cope. It was more like an anchor, sucking me further down. I would call Dr. Hambler's answering machine just to hear his voice. "At the sound of the tone, please leave a message . . ." My sense of abandonment was intense. I was giving him the very depths of myself and getting feedback that lacked even a shred of humanity.

Without either of us knowing how it was happening between us, the relationship became worse.

I cried my way through every session, feeling anger and rejection. I fought panic feelings at his inaccessibility and a sense of loss at the end of our sessions. He never explained anything that I was experiencing, he merely listened and stood up at the end of the session. Once in a while, he would ask me questions or talk about transference but never explained it so that I understood it.

I offered to pay for another psychiatrist to come counsel both of us.

"I do not need help. The problems are yours."

"But I think the pain of my life is making you feel angry at me," I said.

"You just perceive anger because that is what you were given as a child" was his accusatory response.

"Your coldness and aloofness make me feel like you're angry with me. Can't you ever be warm?"

"Warmth is not what you need. You need someone who will

be firm with you to control the IT that is inside you and just goes off."

He always talked about the part of me that was the IT. I never knew what he was talking about—whether it was the dissociative parts of me, or whether he honestly viewed me as some subhuman life form.

Ever since Mom had tied me up and written "Recipes of Marcia" on her stenographer pad, I had an inability to talk when someone wrote in front of me. Dr. Hambler knew that, but he would pick up a pencil and doodle on a pad and I would be unable to talk. "Please don't write in front of me," I would choke out. "I know it is my problem, but I can't think or talk when you write."

"You'll just have to work on that, won't you?" he would say, continuing to doodle.

In fairness to him, I have to say he did have kind moments when we seemed to communicate. He was an attentive listener. How much of his coldness was my misinterpretation of his shy, introverted personality I don't know, but there was no mistaking the absence of helpful therapy.

The real end for both of us came the day I was especially upset and Dr. Hambler began playing with his cigarettes. "Please don't play with cigarettes in front of me," I said. "It reminds me of being burned." In what seemed to me to be a deliberate, calculated gesture, he took the cigarette out of the pack and wound it around and around his fingers, just watching me.

Something snapped in my head. I got out of the chair, lay down on the floor and screamed at him, "Just do it! Do whatever it is that you want to do to me. Just get it over with and stop this torturing. I won't tell anyone. I promise I won't tell anyone. Just do whatever you are planning."

I lay there and sobbed and sobbed and he didn't say anything or do anything. At the end of the session, I was still shaking with sobs. I felt humiliated by how I had acted and very angry that he was playing with my mind.

I called him and told him maybe we should end therapy, that I was getting angry, violent feelings toward him.

It was one of the few times he called me back. He said, "I need two weeks to think things over."

For two weeks I cried, wrote him letters of apology, promised I'd be better in therapy, begged not to be abandoned. At the end of the two weeks I brought my puffy-eyed self into his office. He could barely look at me.

"Marcia, I think we *should* end therapy. I don't think either of us knows why things have gone bad, but it is clearly not in your best interest to continue with me. Our work together is finished." He went on talking about transference and countertransference and our unconscious selves. It became a blur of monumental rejection in my mind.

"Please give me time to find someone new before you end therapy with me," I begged.

"No. This is our last session. We can do no more together. It will only get worse."

"Can you call someone for me? Can you find me a new therapist?" I was crying so hard I could hardly see.

"You'll have to find your own new psychiatrist. I have no one to recommend. You can look in the phone book."

That last statement made it clear to me he truly was abandoning me. After eighteen months of therapy, he was essentially saying, "Get lost. I have no further interest or responsibility for you."

I stumbled out of his office feeling like a monstrous failure. The hours, the money, the dashed hopes came crashing down on me. The ever-present voice was saying, "You wicked Jew, I wish you were dead."

Having given Dr. Hambler the core of myself in therapy, the rejection was devastating. The days in the closet, the feelings of being forgotten, permeated my mind. There was a thread of rational thought that said the therapy was twisted, it was a sick relationship that would not get me well, but the young voice in me screamed in the agony of being cast away again. I would never measure up, never be enough.

I felt broken inside, as though there was no more damage that could be done to me. I had begun to trust, only to be hurt once more. I longed to die, to have the hurting stop. There was a new feeling, an angry, enraged feeling of wanting to kill Dr. Hambler.

He had reenacted with me the role of my mother and in the end became the abusive, abandoning parent while I became the traumatized, hurt child. I wanted his balls cut off. I wanted to tie him in a chair and torture him with a knife just like I had been tortured. It pleasured me to visualize him squirming, begging me not to cut off his fingers or poke his eyes out. My rage was free-flowing. I wrote him angry letters threatening a law suit. An attorney listened to me spew out my anger against Dr. Hambler and even thought we might have grounds for a malpractice suit. I seriously considered it. The bastard had no right to call himself a doctor. I loved him and hated him. I called the ethics committee of his Jungian Institute only to get the verbal runaround about there being no law or contract that binds a psychiatrist to treating a patient. There ought to be some laws. I had become a puppet, getting my strings jerked and pulled in that office, then, in a sweep of scissors, left in a nonfunctioning heap. All the wrath I hadn't felt brave enough to express to Mom came pouring out of me in vitriolic, passionate anger toward Dr. Hambler. I contemplated killing him, then committing suicide before I was arrested. I gave this idea some intense thought. I knew I was getting crazier and becoming dangerous. My most logical thought was to find another psychiatrist before I ended up in jail for what I felt would be justifiable homicide, or a big splatter of my parts as I contemplated which building in San Francisco would be the best to jump from. The other thought was that after almost four years of therapy, I was still fucked up: dissociative, suicidal, overly emotional, and running in so many directions from inner pain. It made no sense to go on. I'd given it the old college try. The jewelry was gone, the money spent on a mind-twisting jerk of a doctor. It all seemed a waste.

My relationship with Dan and the kids seemed pale and meaningless in the turmoil I experienced. I felt they would be better off without me. All semblance of control vanished from my life; I cried continually. I would dish up dinner and sit and weep at the table. Dishes and beds were left undone. Hours disappeared unaccounted for and the hours I was aware of were filled with pain. Kevin got so worried about me he talked to Dan about quitting college and moving back home for a while. Dan talked him out of quitting school and suggested I get hospitalized for a while. Dan was livid that Dr. Hambler had dropped me as a patient for no apparent reason. It was one of the few times Dan got upset at my weird behavior. He had lost the security of being able to say, "Go call your psychiatrist."

"We have no insurance that covers mental health anymore. Don't you remember how much it costs to be in the hospital?" I asked.

"Don't you have any drugs you can take?"

"Nothing seems to help. Maybe I should just die. You'd be better off if I did."

"Don't be ridiculous," Dan said, walking out of the room. Leaving was always his way of dealing with me, or rather, not dealing with me.

Going into the bathroom, I took all the pills I could find and put them in little colored stacks. I looked at them, counting them for the hundredth time, feeling the urge to take all of them, to find the ultimate dissociation from pain in death.

It is odd how little things can stop a major event. I went to the phone and called a young psychiatrist, Dr. John Buchner, who had been kind to me after my last hospitalization, trying to get me started on a drug that would help me get on "a more even keel," as he called it. Dr. Hambler had sent me to him to regulate my drug dosages. He had tried me on Tegretol and other drugs, only to find out, as Dr. Naughton had, that I had allergies to nearly everything.

Reaching this doctor on the phone, I sobbed out my feelings of hopelessness and abandonment at the loss of therapy.

"Come to my office and we'll talk" was John's kindhearted reply.

He gave me an hour of his time, not even charging me, and told me leaving therapy in which I felt like a victim was a positive step, not a negative one.

"Please take me as your patient. I like you," I said.

"Marcia, I'm sorry, but I don't think I am the right therapist for someone with needs like yours. I'm certain you will do well with someone else. I know your history and I feel you need another doctor. I like you and I have thought of treating you, because I knew you were not doing well with Dr. Hambler, but I am not the right psychiatrist for you. Please trust my judgment on this."

His eyes were so kind and his expression so caring that I knew this was not just one more rejection. He had thought about my request.

"I have the name of the two best psychiatrists I can think of in San Fransisco. Call them and see which one you like and see if either of them can take you as a patient. You're going to do well, I'm certain of it. Don't give up. If you feel suicidal, give me a call and I will help get you admitted to the hospital."

Responding to his warmth, I said, "I think we would work well together. Please think about taking me as a patient."

"You'll just have to trust me and call these two other doctors. One is Dr. David Leof and the other, Dr. Ira Steinman.

I left Dr. Buchner's office feeling as though this was a little bit of firm footing out of the quicksand.

At home, I dialed Dr. Leof's number. He called me back within minutes and I asked for an appointment. I don't remember much of the conversation, except his pleasant voice and my sense of shock that he charged one hundred and twenty dollars a session. After Dr. Hambler's eighty dollars an hour, I couldn't even imagine the leap to one hundred and twenty.

I think I mumbled something about not being able to afford him. He spent a few minutes on the phone with me and said kindly that if I needed help in finding someone to feel free to call him and he would assist me. It was one more tiny step out of the bog. He wished me well and we hung up.

I dialed Dr. Steinman and got a slow, quiet voice saying, "Yes . . . ?"

"I would like to make an appointment with you."

"I have a full schedule, but let me ask you a few questions. Are you feeling suicidal?"

"Yes," I said.

"Have you been drinking?"

Offended, I answered, "Of course not!"

There was a low chuckle at my response, "Just checking.

Sometimes when people drink they make phone calls. Can you make it until tomorrow night at seven to see me?"

"Yes," I said.

"Here is my home phone number. Call me day or night if you need to see me or talk."

I couldn't believe it. Here was a total stranger who knew nothing about me giving me his home phone number and offering help. In four years of therapy, my psychiatrists had never given me a home phone number or said to call if I needed them. I forgot to ask what he charged.

The next day, I wandered around San Fransisco hoping I wouldn't dissociate and miss the appointment. I arrived early at the old Victorian house on Scott Street and walked up the stairs that smelled like mold and eucalyptus leaves. I sat in the waiting room feeling chilled in the night air and taking in the array of Picasso and Rousseau prints and stacks of magazines on an old library table.

The clock ticked toward seven-thirty and I was beginning to wonder if I was in the right place or if I'd been forgotten when heavy double doors opened and a patient walked down the stairs.

A tall man of about fifty introduced himself. "I'm Dr. Steinman. Please come in my office." It was a big room filled with the oddest array of artwork. Statues of humans contorted in pain and dozens of pictures hung on his wall. There were many chairs, an antique couch against the wall, a desk piled high with papers in disarray, and a tennis racket in the corner. In the evening darkness, it was scary to sit in the big leather chair across from this strong, stern-looking man. Dr. Steinman had a wonderfully Semitic face with an impressive nose, intelligent eyes, and a smile that crinkled with humor and understanding. He had an air of authority about him that overwhelmed me.

Beyond the first impression of him, I have almost no recollection of our session—I cried my way through it, telling him about failing at therapy with Dr. Hambler. I do remember he said kind things like, "Patients don't fail therapy, it's the doctor who fails."

I don't think I told him I was a multiple personality. Dying and Dr. Hambler were the only things on my mind. Thinking back to how disheveled and emotional I was, I wonder why he was even kind to me.

"Unfortunately, I'm going to be out of town for five days, but Dr. Leof is covering for me."

Through my tears, I laughed. "I've already talked to him. He charges a hundred and twenty dollars an hour."

"So do I," Dr. Steinman said.

"Then I can't afford you, either."

"Right now let's not worry about the money. Let's get you better."

It made no sense to me to see someone I wouldn't be able to pay, but inside I was so splintered that nothing mattered. It was as though I had been free-falling through space and had suddenly landed in a safety net.

"I'm sorry I'm so upset. If what I said doesn't make sense, please feel free to call Dr. Hambler. His view of reality will be better than mine. I think I'm a bit crazy."

"If you are crazy, we'll try to make sense of it." He shook my hand and gave me a tired but genuine smile.

Keeping myself together only lasted two days. With Dr. Steinman gone and feeling intensely suicidal, I again took the pills from the cupboard. I had swallowed a couple of the pills before the faces of Cindi and Kevin fixed in my mind. I visualized them weeping over my grave. Picking up the phone, I called Dr. Leof's office.

"I think I should die, but I'm trying not to," I sobbed.

He talked to me patiently and after calming me down said he would call me again in an hour. True to his word, he telephoned me back and talked some more. The words weren't as important as the gesture at that moment. I was a total stranger to him but he found time in his busy schedule to talk to me, and he gave me a time to come see him. I saw him twice and instantly liked him. He was like a warm-hearted bear, big and fuzzy-bearded. His extroverted people-loving personality seemed enveloping and safe after Dr. Hambler. As though I were someone of great concern to him, Dr. Leof telephoned Dr. Hambler to find out what was going on. At our next session, he spent time trying to make me see how this move away from Dr. Hambler was a good one. "You are very lucky to have Dr. Steinman willing to take you as his patient. He is the best."

"I think he scares me," I said.

"Give him a little time. He has a reputation of being able to help people other psychiatrists have given up on." The way his face glowed as he talked about Dr. Steinman I knew they were close friends. By the time Dr. Leof finished telling me about Dr. Steinman, I suspected my new psychiatrist could walk on water.

Chapter 11

For every deeply mentally disturbed person who finds the road to recovery there is a love story behind the healing. That, of course, is just my own unsubstantiated theory. Dr. Steinman would probably just smile and say, "I'm only doing my job."

The love I speak of is not a romantic one, but a love defined by deep mutual valuing, respect, and caring. Our relationship did not begin this way. In the first couple of months I did not have any hope. My life was a deep valley of suicidal despair. I wept through each session, feeling angry to begin again with yet another psychiatrist. Inside, I vacillated between my desire to get well and my desire to die, just to end all the failure and pain. My anger at Dr. Hambler was beyond containment. One day, soon after I'd begun therapy with Dr. Steinman, I dissociated and found myself outside Dr. Hambler's office. I don't know how long I'd been there. My death wish for him was so strong I panicked, thinking that maybe I was capable of violence. After all, I was born and bred in the arena of violence.

Telephoning Dr. Steinman, I sobbed, "Do you know if Dr. Hambler is all right?"

"As far as I know he is." He gave a little chuckle at my panic. "Why do you ask?"

"I don't know if I've hurt him," I cried. "I lost time again and found myself at his office. Do you think I could hurt him in a dissociative state?"

"You tell me, do you want to hurt him?"

"Yes, I'd like to stab him and see him bleed. I want to cut him just like my mother cut me. He has no business being a psychiatrist pretending to care and then, when I was beginning to trust and feel safe, telling me to go away. I hate him."

"It sounds to me like you're transferring your feelings about your mother on to Dr. Hambler," said Dr. Steinman.

At that point I really didn't understand transference. I only knew I was angry at Dr. Hambler.

"What was the last thing you remember before going to Dr. Hambler's office?"

"I had the left-alone feelings of being locked in the closet."

"How old did you feel before you dissociated?"

This was a whole new thought for me. "I guess I felt small."

"How old?" insisted Dr. Steinman.

"Why does it matter?"

"It's very important that you begin to catch yourself and watch what causes you to dissociate."

"I felt little, maybe about six."

At our next session, Dr. Steinman said, "Dr. Hambler called me and said someone named Sunshine called him making threats. He said that was one of the aspects of you."

Depressed, I said, "Yes, Sunshine is one of my others, but I don't know her."

"Well, you'd better get to know her, because you can't go around threatening people," said Dr. Steinman sternly, shaking his finger at me. "Do you really want to kill Dr. Hambler?"

Inside, the honest answer was "yes," but I knew if I said yes, I would probably get locked up in a psycho ward. "Not really," I said. "I feel angry at how he played with my mind."

"Marcia, look, so the guy wasn't able to help you. Do you think he deserves to die? Why don't you try expressing your anger in here?"

"I don't know how to be angry," I said.

"Why?"

"Because I learned when I was very little that if I got angry I would be hurt worse."

"We'll have to work on getting in touch with your anger."

At the end of the session, Dr. Steinman said, "Call me if you need me." At that point I didn't dare call him for fear he would reject and abandon me as Dr. Hambler had done, but I was awed just by the fact that he said I could call.

I spent weeks and weeks talking about my abuse. The tears would flow and all the raw pain that lived close to my surface became excruciating in the retelling.

Dr. Steinman said, "You don't have to tell me everything if it is too painful for you. I have a good idea of what we're dealing with."

It felt like a rejection of my pain. "I just want you to know me." I couldn't see how we could do therapy without him deeply understanding my childhood, the rapes, the failures.

Looking back, I think he intuitively knew I was slipping further and further into thoughts of death as, session after session, I relived the horrors. There was no ability to distance myself from the pain.

"You must tell yourself that the pain is in the past, it's not now, not here," Dr. Steinman said.

But it felt like intense, present-day pain to me. I regressed to the fearful, hurt child just in the telling. Dr. Steinman listened attentively, and insisted that I keep the control; that I was the adult and the pain was way in the past. I felt he didn't understand me, yet he would do remarkable things that let me know he really did. After a sobbing, traumatic session he would very often call me at home and ask, "How are you doing?" I couldn't believe he would care enough to find out how I was.

At suicidal moments, which were many those first months, I began to call him as he had asked me to do. He was usually kind, sometimes stern, and always instructive. "Try to stay forty-seven," he would say. "Keep control of your thoughts. Take a deep, slow breath, now let it out slowly. Why don't you call me back in an hour?"

Often there were several phone calls in a day. Instead of feeling abject abandonment as I had with Dr. Naughton and Dr. Hambler, I felt supported and embraced by his caring and commanding presence.

Once when I was overwhelmed by therapy, I begged Dr. Steinman to help me make my suicide look like an accident, for the sake of my children. He got very serious and said forcefully, "That is absolutely not acceptable. You are much too crazy to make a decision like that. You'll just have to stick it out in therapy with me until you stop being meshuga. Dying is against the rules of therapy." He was so domineering at moments that to disobey was untenable.

Several times in the beginning I called up, saying, "It's hopeless. There is no point in having therapy. I'll just fail at it again. There's no way I'll ever be normal, so why don't we just quit?"

"You're being excessive," he would say. "If you quit now you'd miss all this fun." He could get me laughing even in the middle of my tears, turning my distorted thoughts around in a few short minutes.

After an extremely painful revelation about my childhood, he would say kind things like, "I am very sorry that happened to you. You've had a terrible, painful life." It was the first genuinely human response I had ever gotten to my pain. Dr. Naughton and Dr. Hambler had been as warm as cigar-store Indians, and my anguish had been treated as though I were saying I had no date to the spring prom in high school.

My past psychiatrists had said very little. Therapy with Dr. Steinman was a penetrating crash course in understanding myself and my dissociative selves. At first I missed the quietness of being able to get in touch with my own feelings. "You don't need to get in touch with your feelings. You know what you feel. What you need is to learn some control over them," he said.

Therapy at moments seemed disjointed. The phone rang often. Dr. Steinman would get up from his chair and rummage through the mound of papers on his desk, looking for his prescription pad. He seemed too energetic and dynamic to just sit still and listen. He would pour us both hot tea, or share oranges with me. Even then he seemed attentive. He intuitively knew when to sit absolutely still and focus completely on me. He gave me the feeling of being deeply "there" with my pain. His responses were warm and human. Weeping one day, I said, "I've never had anyone be sad for me before."

"I'm very sorry for what you have lived through."

It made me cry harder, just to have one person look at me and see my pain and be able to say, "I'm sorry."

It was the little things that touched me, like the way he smiled as I came in, as though he were really seeing me as a person; even one he was glad to greet.

With all my anger, dissociation, and suicidal ideas, he remained calm, steady, gentle, and his responses to me were always positive: "We'll have to work on getting you well."

Dr. Naughton had said I was the most damaged human being he'd ever treated. All of Dr. Steinman's statements were affirmations of my ability to use my good mind to get well.

It took me about an hour to like Dr. Steinman, eight months to begin trusting him, and a year to deeply love him. Slowly, like a snail creeping out from under its shell, I began to let myself feel safe with him. It didn't just happen. Repetitively, I would burst into tears: "When are you going to tell me to go away?"

"I'm not even thinking of getting rid of you. Have I done anything to make you think I would abandon you?"

I don't know how I could have mistrusted him; the phone calls became nearly daily, the reassurances were always patient.

"I'm sorry for being a pain in the ass," I said. "I don't mean to be."

"You're no problem. I'm glad I can help." He would smile and wave his big hand slowly as though discounting my need to apologize.

When I began therapy, I was too sick to be a "good" patient. I tried, but I was like a leaking sieve with parts of me spurting out. I wanted Dr. Steinman to like me, wanted to be the model patient, but it wasn't in the realm of my control. Yet nothing was too much for this giving man. Rather than dreading appointments as I had with Dr. Naughton and Dr. Hambler, I began to look forward to my sessions.

The dilemma of my dire financial straits became distressingly clear. Dan was struggling in the new business and I was in no condition to work; the pain from my surgeries limited my functioning and my dissociative states further crippled me. "I think I will have to stop therapy," I sobbed to Dr. Steinman. "I can't afford to pay you. All the money from the jewelry was spent with Dr. Hambler."

"That's ridiculous. You can't quit therapy. Just pay me what you can now, and someday when I get you well you can find a way to pay."

"But what if I can *never* pay you?" I said through copious tears.

"Don't worry about that now. I'm not going to abandon you."

I was deeply moved that he would care about getting me well more than he cared about the money. When I couldn't pay Dr. Hambler, he had cut back the hours. "You are my business," he had said.

Dr. Steinman's magnanimous gesture dissolved me into tears for a whole week. It was like having the first person ever in my life since my father bestow value on me. He didn't treat me just for the dollars; he was a human being finding something worthy of being saved in me. That generosity of spirit should have instantly healed me. It didn't, but it opened doors to my dark, locked-away, hurting places.

It wasn't one single thing, but a multitude of little things that made me aware of the phenomenal commitment Dr. Steinman had to our therapy. He could be emphatic and even domineering at moments when I was acting unraveled, but he was never judgmental. Slowly, I began to feel safe, deeply safe, with him. I told him my failures, things I had never revealed to anyone else. Gradually, I began talking to him about the others in my head, the whisperings, the missing minutes from the clock. At first, I felt guarded and tense talking about Emily's death and my fear that she was not the only other person in my head. Dr. Naughton hadn't believed me when I had spoken of Emily, and with Dr. Hambler the dissociative self was called, "the IT that you must get control over." Our relationship had become so negative that I stopped telling him the deeper, disturbing parts of my life.

Dr. Steinman asked, "Who are these other aspects of you?"

"I'm not sure. I don't know them very well. Before she died, Emily told me a little about the others. Sometimes, when I have lost conscious awareness for a span of time, people tell me I call myself by different names and I do really stupid things."

"Why don't you get in touch with them? You must get to know who they all are."

"I don't want to know them. I don't like them. I know they must be pieces of myself, but they don't *feel* like pieces of me."

"You must get completely familiar with them so they can become integrated into you."

"I don't want to be like them, so why should I even want to know them?" My only knowledge of them was social humiliation when I would find myself in an odd place, or wearing an outfit that I normally wouldn't put on.

It took me weeks before I could tell Dr. Steinman about Joey. I had never breathed a word about him to the other psychiatrists. The terrible fear that I was a homosexual kept me from talking about him. If all these other people were truly only me, then how could I have a masculine personality? Did it make me even more twisted to not be all the same gender? So many things boiled around in my head. It was a struggle to make sense of it all, yet Dr. Steinman made it all seem easy.

"Who is Joey?"

"I don't really know. I only know what Emily told me about him, but it's not as though we talk."

"Well, start talking to him. Get to know him."

"How?"

"All these aspects of you are just creations of your own imagination, so I want you to go home and imagine what each of the other aspects are like."

"Why don't you hypnotize me? Maybe my subconscious mind will know more."

"We don't need to do that. It's all accessible to you."

For weeks and even months, nothing in my mind clicked with

what he was saying. I could hear Dr. Steinman's words, but I couldn't do what he was telling me to do.

I was highly dissociative, having many episodes of memory lapses.

Dr. Steinman would question, "What were you thinking of just before you dissociated?"

Almost always, my answer was either anger I couldn't face, a trigger of painful memories, or a feeling of needing to run away.

"How tall were you in your mind just before you dissociated? What did you visualize wearing? How were you feeling? How old did you feel?"

There was no escaping the scrutiny of this taskmaster. I wasn't allowed to merely report I had lost time. I was held accountable for each episode.

"Notice your breathing. Did it change? Do you focus your eyes differently?"

There were many questions to be answered that no one had ever asked me before, an often uncomfortable inquisition but one in which I began to see a pattern, a correlation to things. I began to see how I did often have the brief moment of time when I felt the desire to escape reality, where I had in my power that moment of choice. It was the awakening of the idea that I was not just the passive victim of dissociation, but an active participant.

With the patience of a saint, Dr. Steinman asked me the same things over and over. "You must stay the adult. You must not allow yourself to dissociate."

Those words often made me angry, as though this whole thing was easily under my control. It used to annoy me that he made it sound so damn simple. Nothing was simple for me, because my mind had been splintered for my whole life. The pieces didn't just fall into place. I didn't wake up one morning and say, "Gee whiz, of course this is how it all works." It was gradual, infinitesimal steps forward.

After I arrived for my appointment out of breath from racing three or four blocks after a ten minute search for a parking space, Dr. Steinman would say, "We have time. Relax."

I would sit quietly, snuggled into the big leather chair, with his kind eyes comfortably watching me, and I would travel into my

own head, questioning the voices, seeking the elusive identification of my mystery "others."

His accessibility was also a help in identifying my dissociative
selves. When I had lapses of awareness, I called him and always
within a span of two hours he returned my call with the insistence
I examine my feeling state, my thoughts, the pictures in my mind
just before I dissociated.

After what felt like the hundredth time of asking me, "How
old did you feel before you dissociated? How tall were you?" and
on and on, I began to have a very clear picture of the others in my
head.

Sunshine was the youngest of the others. She was six and had
the same parents I did. She printed letters in bold print that I had
seen before, begging to be taken care of. She tried very hard to be
good and always wanted a bear. She had big blue eyes. Dr. Steinman would say in his office, "Let Sunshine come out. What are
all the feelings?" I would let all the hurt, tiny-child feelings surface
and could visualize myself in the closet, or wishing, desperately
wishing, for someone to save me. Sunshine was the sweet, crying,
needy child who tried very hard to please. In talking about Sunshine, it was easy to see how she split off in my early years. Sunshine was the name my father had called me.

Sophie was my sixty-five-year-old Jewish personality, capable
of comforting warmth and deep sorrow. She had been in the concentration camps in Germany and often sat slowly rocking in sadness in the big rocking chair in my living room. She was plump,
and loved to cook and eat. She had long white hair which she
wore in a bun, twinkling blue eyes, and always wore an apron.
Sophie was creative, enjoying gardening, flower arranging, and
cake decorating. She had come from a happy childhood with
warm parents. It had enabled her to help me with the whispers of
how to care for my own babies. She was warm and nurturing. It
was a pleasant surprise getting to know Sophie. It didn't take a
vast amount of intelligence to figure out she was the best parts of
Grandma Bernice. She had split into being when I had wished for
the comforting of Grandma Bernice during my locked-up times
and she had grown stronger when Grandma Bernice died. After

my humiliation of Emily, it was nice to realize if Sophie was an aspect of me, then I had nice parts, too.

Getting to know Camille was embarrassing. She was a pale-skinned Christian, with long blond hair, and was blind. Camille was precise and neat, needing to stay organized to find her way around when she couldn't see. She believed God wanted her to suffer. Like Sunshine, she was very sweet and wanted to be taken care of. She liked hospitals and patiently waited to get hurt. She was a perfect victim, yet she was still a virgin. It was a struggle for me to identify with this personality. When I told Dr. Steinman about her, I said, "I don't think she is a part of me. I don't even like her. I'm not like that."

We argued about my ownership of this personality.

"Maybe she came into being when I had my meningitis?" I questioned. I couldn't plug into this personality. Way inside, I was convinced she couldn't be a part of me, she must be someone else. My intellect, with Dr. Steinman's insistence, told me I was a multiple personality, but emotionally the splitting was so complete that I kept slipping into denial.

It was Muriel who first began having conversations with me in the way Emily used to. Muriel was my age exactly, but she didn't have my parents. She had been born in an artist's loft in England. She was extroverted—a party lover, a lover of life. She wore bright clothes and red nail polish. She could be bossy and knew all the other personalities. She could be the advice giver to the others, and although she was flamboyant, she was a mature personality, deeply moral, wanting to do the right things, and, like Camile, she was still a virgin.

It was Muriel who told me that Camille began in the terrifying days when Mom threatened to blind me with the ice pick. The terror had been so great that I had created a competent blind personality.

Muriel, sort of the mother hen to the group, had often called my psychiatrists when I was suicidal, or when one of the "others" was endangering us. She wanted to live and was rather chummy with my therapists.

Joey was the Jewish, fourteen-year-old boy personality. He was about six feet tall, had big hands and feet, and brown eyes. He was an angry, often self-destructive character. He was a leader. He could be extroverted or brooding and sullen. He liked hot Mexican food and Indian curries, and enjoyed loud music. He resented the interference of Muriel, but he had liked Emily and was sad she was dead. Joey resented the intrusion of Dr. Steinman into his anonymity, angry at the exposure therapy was demanding of him.

It seemed that the more in touch I got with my dissociative selves, the angrier Joey became.

The message in my head that he wanted to die became loud and clear. That self-destruct message was an exhausting theme. The message seemed to come both in Mom's voice wishing me a slow, painful death and the Joey voice urging me to end our fucked-up life. I felt in constant jeopardy. It was as though Mom's ghost was whispering, "Jump off the bridge. Drive your car fast, faster, faster, into a concrete wall." Joey's voice said, "I can't take this crap anymore."

The other selves whispered among themselves in dialogues I became increasingly aware of.

Dr. Steinman would ask, "How are you today?" With a twinkle in his eye, he would say, "And how is Joey? What does Muriel have to say?"

As embarrassing as it often was, I did become aware of the multiple dialogues.

Joey became a significant force to contend with. He wanted to die. One day I was in my car after losing time and found a box of .38 bullets in the car seat next to me. I called Dr. Steinman and told him Joey wanted to shoot me with Dan's gun.

I don't fully recall the conversation, but Dr. Steinman was like a trumpeting elephant, commanding me to take the bullets back to the gun shop and insisting I make Dan lock up the guns. He said if my behavior continued in this manner, he would hospitalize me. I was frightened enough to think that was a good idea, but we had no insurance to cover a hospitalization.

It was as though two processes were going on; there was the learning and reorganizing and there was the constant theme of self-destruct. I had good days and terrible days. I don't know why

Dr. Steinman never said, "For God's sake, if you're going to kill yourself, why don't you just do it and save me a few hundred hours!" He never did. It was always the command that I stay the adult and not allow myself to regress into the black place that said I should die. I was not to allow myself to dissociate, and he always wanted the checklist of what triggered the impulse. Just as with my apology at dissociating, I felt deeply sorry for letting myself get into a suicidal frame of mind. It wasn't as though I sat around and planned how I could dissociate and have Joey kill me. I was like one of those blind fish that swims in black pools in the bottom of deep caves. Or as Dr. Steinman said, "You are like a committee with no leader." He had said that humorously one day, but it really seemed true. I was pulled in many directions, all seemingly without my commands.

At Dr. Steinman's request, I made a great effort to communicate with my "others." I talked to them as though they were a group of familiar friends, coaxing them into communicating with me. They seemed even more alien to me than Emily, since I didn't even know them.

I was afraid of Joey. As I began to plug into who he was, it became clear that he had some of the characteristics of Bobby. In a way, he was the replacement in my life for the tragic loss of both my dad and Bobby. It was reassuring to realize that I was not a homosexual, that Joey was just a piece of me that had split off in anger. Acknowledging the anger was different than feeling it, or owning it.

"Joey feels so angry," I would say to Dr. Steinman.

"What is he telling you?"

"He's glad he's a boy and not a woman. He doesn't like blood and never wants to menstruate."

"Why does he feel that?" asked Dr. Steinman.

The little threads of conversations picked up from the "others" usually held extremely emotionally charged revelations.

I think it was Joey who remembered the ice pick from childhood. "I hate blood. I'll never be a woman," Joey said.

I spent a lot of time in therapy figuring out what the voices were saying and, like parts of a puzzle, fitting it into my life. Often the feelings that another personality would have, I vehemently denied sharing.

"They are your feelings because it is all you," Dr. Steinman said. "They aren't real people, they are aspects of you."

Over and over I tried to tell him they were real.

"I don't read Braille, like Camille, I don't like hot Mexican food like Joey. They are too different from me," I would say defensively.

"Yes, they are, and you'd better accept them and get to know them," reiterated Dr. Steinman. His messages were always simple, understandable, and extremely difficult for me.

"So why don't you just say, 'Be well'?" I fumed.

With a hearty laugh, he said, "What a good idea!"

His humor always defused my anger and made me less shy in talking about the "others" in my head. Dr. Naughton and Dr. Hambler had made me even more defensive, but Dr. Steinman made it seem entirely natural to talk about what Muriel was saying or to tell him how Joey felt. The more he let me talk about them, the clearer they became and the more I could see how I'd split those parts of me away. Yet even talking about them couldn't stop them. They seemed to have a life of their own that was completely unrelated to mine.

Dr. Steinman didn't buy that for a minute.

If Joey was angry, he made me look at what I was angry about. He insisted I listen to the mature Muriel and allowed Sunshine to come into his office for the caring I needed. Repeatedly, he explained my dissociative abilities to me, showing me how I had used a mechanism of the mind to run from painful memories and experiences. Emotions of anger and sadness got channeled into other personalities to relieve my pain. Over and over he helped me see that the "others" were split-off pieces of myself, developed in my mind at a very young age to escape the intolerable.

Everything that happened in therapy was a learning experience. When I began therapy with Dr. Steinman, I had only a rudimentary understanding of myself as a dissociative personality. He talked about every behavior I had that was regressed or inappropriate, making me see what I was doing and why I was doing it.

In spite of the closeness that grew between us, the sessions were painful, emotional, tearful, and upsetting for me. I couldn't get a firm grasp of the Joey-self. He was repeatedly suicidal and angry.

There were things that I revealed in therapy to Dr. Steinman that I had never told anyone and abuses I remembered as I got to know the other selves. What should have been easy for me to untangle, wasn't. I began to recognize the feelings of wanting to escape, it became easier to see how each piece of me came into existence. But every inch of gain was earned the hardest way possible—with rivers of tears and dark, depressed days. Dr. Steinman was my ally in my search for answers, but God, what a slave driver! He never let up for a minute. Some sessions he let me talk and go at my own pace, but others he pressed me to see, to learn, to pay attention to the dissociative selves.

He was teaching me to become guardian of my own self. He pressed me to watch my behavior, to stand guard over my thoughts, and not to allow myself to regress.

If I went on a crying jag, feeling depressed and overwhelmed, he would say, "What is the advantage in feeling this way? You can choose not to have those feelings." He made me see I allowed myself to regress to the helpless-child state. It sounds much simpler than it was for me. We went through the same things dozens of times. Repeatedly, I failed, but I was beginning to get the picture. I could think back to when I was small and tied with the blue scarves to the bed, waiting to be hurt, and would stare at the plaster ceiling, seeing imaginary faces in the cracks of the plaster. "I am not here. I will leave. I can't stay," I said to myself as I focused on the cracks. Sometimes that had worked. It was escape. I learned the escape so well that the pretend became real. I don't know at what age Emily and the others came alive in my mind, for I have no memory of it ever being otherwise.

All this was insight gained with Dr. Steinman's help. He guided the conversations, probed for insights, interpreted things for me. He kept a wonderful balance between being a listening, empathetic parent and a teacher who allowed no escape from the lessons. I was a slow learner, hearing his words, understanding the concepts, having totally new definitions of myself and my behaviors, yet still failing. It was only my own sense of failure; Dr. Steinman was always supportive of my growth and success.

Each time I regressed and dissociated we would reexamine thoughts, and I would grasp another tiny concept as my own. It was as though he were giving me tools that I could hold but didn't know how to use. I felt like a monkey being handed a fountain pen and being told to write. But with simple yet profound directions, Dr. Steinman was determined I would learn.

About eleven months into therapy, Dr. Steinman said in four weeks time he would be leaving on a three-week vacation. That shouldn't have been a big deal, but it became a catastrophic event in my life. Joey was in a self-destruct mode, and I was feeling ambivalent about life, too.

"Are you going to fly in an airplane?" I questioned.

"Yes."

"Please don't die," I foolishly begged.

"I'm certainly not planning on it. I think you are worried because your father died in a plane crash. You are transferring your feelings onto me."

I hated all that "transference" talk. I only knew I felt tiny and safe with him, and he might die. I could understand his words in my adult-mind, but there was the child-mind that couldn't get control of the panic. I wanted to die before he did, so I wouldn't be left alone. Joey got crazier, talking about suicide. I wrote Dr. Steinman a farewell letter telling him I was sorry I'd failed therapy. Days and nights blurred in tears and pain. The feelings of his impending death made me relive my childhood abandonment even more intensely than I had with Dr. Naughton or Dr. Hambler, because Dr. Steinman was emotionally closer to me than anyone had gotten before. I loved him.

In all this craziness, a new memory surfaced, in which I was about eight and had all the broken fingers and bruises, and the principal of my grammar school had come to my house. It was terrifying to see Mr. Donovan come up the front steps to my big house. Bobby opened the door that threw its rainbow of lights from the prisms of glass around the room.

"I'd like to speak with your parents," Mr. Donavan said.

It must have been a Saturday, since Dad was home. My parents sat in the living room and talked with him. We children had been sent out of the room, and I hid at the top of the stairs, getting only hints of the quiet, serious-sounding voices. In a while I heard my name being called. I wondered what terrible thing I had done now. Would Mr. Donovan punish me, too? Slowly, I went down the stairs, fighting the desire to flee, to run past all the adults and go hide somewhere outside. Quaking, I entered the room to face three very serious adults. Mr. Donovan reached out his hand and pulled me close to him. He wore glasses and had bad breath. Leaning toward me, he said, "Marcia, how did you get your broken fingers and your bruises?"

My heart was pounding in my chest. I looked over at Mom who returned my gaze with a noncommittal look, as though she knew nothing. I looked at my father who was returning my gaze with a look that made me think he was angry. More than any terror of these adults was my terror of the Gypsies.

"I'm just not careful," I muttered. "I'm sorry I'm not careful."

"Has anyone hurt you?" asked Mr. Donovan.

"No," I lied. "I just play rough with Bobby." Tears were escaping down my cheeks. I wasn't lying very well.

The conversation probably only lasted a few minutes, but in my terrorized state each word had the weight of stones and the half-life of uranium.

Mr. Donovan rose to say good-bye.

I waited for Daddy to ask me more, secretly wishing he would sweep me into his arms and tell me he would take care of me. He said nothing.

Later in their room, I heard a terrible fight; I heard my name, and shouting, then my mother crying.

Shivering from the trauma of the encounter, I waited for the shouting to subside. Later, Daddy came down the stairs, banging his suitcase on the bannister.

"Where are you going, Daddy?" Fear clutched me, then a tiny rise of hope. He would take me away, far from Mom to be safe.

"I have to leave for a while, Sunshine. I'll be back soon. I love you." He put down his suitcase and scooped me into his big arms, kissing my nose and my cheeks, then rested his face in the nape of my neck. He put me down and walked out the door, leaving me behind.

It was a moment of heart-wrenching abandonment, for way inside I knew that Daddy knew I was being hurt. I heard him yelling at Mom, and he was choosing to leave me. "Daddy! Daddy, don't go. Take me with you."

Reliving this scene made me know where Joey was born. He was the anger I couldn't feel at my father, my perfect Daddy with the long legs, scratchy whiskers and the big, safe arms. Marcia's daddy was perfect. He was safe. Only Joey felt the rage at being left to be hurt.

Suddenly I felt I was losing my father in a new way, for reliving this scene with the principal brought back the questions about what Daddy really knew about my abuse. What did he see but refuse to acknowledge until I was twelve? Now when I thought about that day I told him everything, I didn't know if he cried for me or for his own guilt. I was overcome by feelings. It was a confusion of anger, grief, loss, longing, and it got all mixed up with Dr. Steinman leaving me to go on a trip. Wasn't he being like Daddy, seeing that I was in pain and choosing to leave me?

Dr. Steinman kept making me see how I was confusing him with Daddy, but it was all too emotional to sort out. It made me want to die. The loss of my perfect father image hurt more deeply than I could stand.

Emily had held the anger at the abuse, and Joey held the anger at the abandonment of my father. Now I knew that Daddy had known. He didn't save me. He didn't protect me. He didn't keep me safe.

Dr. Steinman was unbelievably patient with me as I acted in a regressed manner. I called him daily, couldn't leave at the end of my sessions; I was being a total jerk. The closer he got to his vacation, the more disintegrated I became. The last days before he left, I felt I was wishing him farewell forever, going into a deep state of grieving. He called me twice every day, giving me the message to stay the adult, that he wasn't going to die, that it wasn't abandonment. He told me to see Dr. Leof while he was gone if I couldn't manage my feelings.

It got so I wasn't even sure what I was crying about—Dr. Steinman's vacation or the remembered feeling of my father's abandonment. In all the confused process, Joey got sick. All the anger that Joey felt became my feelings, and he grew weak, just like Emily had, when I felt her feelings of the abuse. All the "others" were sick. My mature mind told me it was from the months of plugging into who they were, the familiarity growing between us until the boundaries were becoming fuzzy and blurred.

Dr. Steinman said they didn't need to be sick or to die, I could just integrate them and have them cease to exist. But it didn't work that way.

By the time Dr. Steinman left for his vacation, I'm sure he was wishing I would seriously consider making good on my suicide threats. (He vehemently denies feeling this.)

After he left, I couldn't do what he told me, to stay the adult and use my rational mind. I grieved for him, crying my way through each day, imagining my life without the stability and comfort he gave me.

In a deep state of mourning, and without even understanding why at the time, I listened to the inner voice that taunted, "You wicked little Jew. I wish you were dead." Going to the kitchen drawer, I got the ice pick out, and with tears of pain and loss, I sat down on a chair and plunged the pick deep into my leg. The pain felt right.

Later, as it got swollen and throbbing, I cried at my stupidity. That was such a regressed, dumb thing to do.

Arriving at Dr. Leof's office, I begged him to call me when Dr. Steinman died. The thought of showing up for an appointment and having him gone was more than I could bear. Dr. Leof was gentle and kind, reassuring me he had spoken with Dr. Steinman, who was fine. To this kind stranger I babbled on about it, feeling like I had when my father left me. Instead of saying, "Just wait for three lousy little weeks," he said, "Let's make some appointments. I'll find time for you." My involvements way inside with the sick others and my loss of Dr. Steinman made me dump my feelings on Dr. Leof as though we were old, established friends; I carried on about Joey and Muriel as though this were an everyday sort of conversation. Crying and grieving, I called him between sessions, with all the grace and social skills of the average two-year-old. Like his friend Dr. Steinman, Dr. Leof treated me with warmth and graciousness as though what I was experiencing mattered to him.

After the millenium, when Dr. Steinman returned, I could hardly refrain from covering him with kisses.

"I didn't do very well while you were gone," I confessed.

"You'll do better next time," he replied with his always generous appraisal of my failures.

"I don't think I'm ready to stop therapy with you. Please give me more time."

"Of course you need therapy. I'm not going to abandon you." We had to have this same dialogue at least once a month.

A warm relaxation spread over me in the presence of this caring man. He had come back. All the frail "others" became sicker, instead of getting well.

"Maybe they are sick because I trust you and don't need them so much when I have you."

"They don't need to be sick, you know," Dr. Steinman said as he smiled.

We talked for more sessions, rehashing the origins of each personality, what feelings they possessed, how I felt about them, why I needed them. We discussed all the trigger thoughts that made me dissociate. I was finally beginning to see how I, in a split second of consciousness, could will myself away from reality. I came to understand the mechanisms of dissociation that I used, the change of focus of my eyes, the mental picture that I was physically changing, the willed desire to flee. Our repetitive conversations about my other personalities made them familiar, less distant from me. I had made the decision to claim the pieces of myself. I dug at all the split-off feelings, or, to be accurate, Dr. Steinman dug at them, refusing to allow me to view them as anything but myself. He always called them my "aspects."

As my adult mind was coming to understand them, they were dying.

It was almost exactly a year to the day I began therapy with Dr. Steinman that Joey, Muriel, Camille, Sophie, and Sunshine "died." They died in the same hysterical way that Emily had died, with the hours of death-rattle breathing and a feeling of sickness in me. Dr. Steinman made a comment about me being dramatic, and he was correct, but at that moment it was absolutely real to me. I guess if my mind was capable of having the pretend selves seem real for all those years, then it wasn't incongruous that I would vividly have them die. They couldn't die until I felt them, accepted their emotions and anger, which happened long after I had intellectually claimed them.

I also knew that I chose their deaths. I wanted them to leave. It was a determined, conscious choice, for I clearly saw that the very mechanism that ensured my survival as a child was not a functional form of life as an adult. It was an indefensibly terrible way to live. Deciding to let the "others" die was probably not much different than an alcoholic deciding never to have another drink; it was connected to growth, insight, commitment to a new life. It was giving up a habit that shielded me from memory and pain—a decision to stand still and feel the pain, accepting all the parts and pieces of myself.

I make this sound as if it was all my own growth and insight. It was, but only after Dr. Steinman taught me, showed me, guided me to all this knowledge. Whose success is it when the monkey, after months of effort, picks up the pen and begins to write? Probably the teacher's.

Still, as determined as I was to reorganize, their deaths took me by surprise. It was a dreary Saturday when I was alone in the house feeling physically sick at their illness. It felt like a death vigil of friends, not a day of profound thoughts or psychological probing, a day of simply being, feeling them grow weaker inside me. There were no farewells. They did not die individually, it was a collective death, with a very clear moment when the breathing of all of them stopped. My own breathing halted in response to the deaths. I waited, lying on my bed, feeling a sense of loss descend on me. I turned my face into my pillow and wept.

It meant a great deal to me to call Dr. Steinman and tell him that my "aspects" had died. On a busy Saturday, he spent time talking with me, congratulating me on the progress I was making and being very understanding of all that I was experiencing. I think I called him several times that weekend.

In the days after they died, my sense of nonequilibrium made me feel like I was on a teeter-totter, airborne one minute and crashing into the ground the next.

Instead of rejoicing at my freedom from the tyranny of many,

I felt an upsetting quietness in my head, a profound loneliness. My fear escalated with the thought that I could no longer escape. All my life I had lived like an escape artist, darting away at the possibility of pain or danger. My head said I should be shouting for joy that I wouldn't have to lie to cover up for lost hours, do quick observational checks to see where I was and who I was with. My life had been run by random chaos, now there was only one in control, and instead of joy I felt the suffocating awareness that I was accountable and stuck. The necessity of staying around for whatever reality brought panicked me. I cried for days after the death of my "others"; tears of loss, tears of fear, tears at the danger I felt.

I walked endless miles, trying to sort out my feelings, often stopping at pay phones to tell Dr. Steinman he didn't know a damn thing, that he had done something dangerous with me and he had no understanding of what he had done.

The thought of pure, undiluted reality terrified me. Life had not been kind or gentle, so my idea of reality was just having to stay around for the torture.

"Why are you afraid?" Dr. Steinman asked.

"I don't know. I'm just sure I'm going to be hurt."

"Does anyone threaten to hurt you?"

"Only my mother," I whispered.

"She's dead. How can a dead person hurt you?"

"I don't know, but I feel her presence with an almost palpitating aliveness. I think she was so powerful and evil that she isn't truly dead."

"That's ridiculous," said Dr. Steinman in his emphatic way. "She is only alive in your mind."

"I think maybe you are wrong," I answered. "I can feel her when I'm in the kitchen, commanding me to pick up a knife and cut my fingers off. Or driving the car, I feel her demanding that I speed up, that I crash. I feel those messages of 'Die, you little Jew' in my head."

"In your *head* is exactly right. That's where those messages are coming from," said Dr. Steinman. "There is no outside force, no ghost, no spirit. Partly your belief in spirits is from your Bible upbringing and the terrible angel your mother talked to."

"How can you be sure she isn't around in a spirit form?" I asked.

"If you feel she is real, why don't you tell her to go away, to leave you alone. She doesn't have a body; she can't hurt you."

Whispering, I said, "She feels so powerful that even after death I feel the hate messages being directed toward me."

"Ask her to come see me at our next session. If you think she's real, I'd be glad to talk to her."

Over the next few days I silently talked with this onerous presence of Mom. I begged her to leave me alone. In the kitchen I could feel her taunting me to pick up the butcher knife. How could this presence that seemed as real as static electricity be in my imagination?

I asked Mom to come to Dr. Steinman's office so he could feel her. Just talking to her made me feel stupid and suspicious of my own sense of reality.

At our next session, Dr. Steinman asked if I had brought my mother's ghost. He had a difficult time suppressing his humor, his smile sneaking up at the corners of his mouth.

I could feel her in the room radiating the hate. Dr. Steinman's barely suppressed sense of delight frightened me for his sake. I felt he hadn't a clue of what kind of a force he was dealing with. "Do we need crosses or a wooden stake?" he asked with a grin. Seeing the fear in my eyes, he became serious. "Where is she?" he asked.

"Over there," I said pointing to the corner of the room."

"Tell her to sit in your chair."

Getting up, I offered it to my mother, and slouched way down in the big chair across the room. "Please be careful," I squeaked out of my terror-constricted throat. It was easy to visualize Mom materializing and hacking us both up with a knife. "Talk to her," I whispered.

Dr. Steinman not only talked to her, he yelled at her for all that she had done to me, shaking his big fist in the air in angry defiance.

As I sat shriveled in the chair, I had two entirely different processes going on in my head. There was the thread of logic that said most likely Mom was not truly in the room, that I was imagining her presence. The other far more emotionally real thought was how wonderful it was for Dr. Steinman to risk his life to stand up to her for my sake. I listened to his tirade and, on a child-like level, I had for a brief moment the adult I had looked for all my childhood who would rescue me. I loved him intensely at that moment.

"What shall we do with her?" asked Dr. Steinman.

"I don't know," I said between tears.

"Let's put her in this box," he said, holding up an old cookie tin.

"Please be careful!" Sweat was pouring out of me.

Grasping at the invisible presence, he asked, "Do I have her?"

"Higher. A little higher." I could feel her pulsating hatred as he grabbed her and shut the box on her.

"Is she in the box now?" he asked.

"I think so. Don't open the box. Please don't let her out."

My logic told me I was being foolish, but I felt an irrational sense of relief to have her in the box. Dr. Steinman could keep her.

"Where will you put her?" I still couldn't get control of my crying.

"I'll put her someplace safe, maybe in a couple of other big boxes."

In his usual calm, rational way, we discussed what he had done, and Dr. Steinman said, "Your mother exists only in your mind. You want someone to stand up and protect you from her. No one has done that in your life. This is what I have been doing."

I left feeling better, but still not fully understanding why.

My feeling of liberation from the ghost of Mom lasted about a week. I slept deeply, without the usual nightmares. It was nice not to enter my kitchen and feel the taunting to pick up an ice pick to poke my eyes out.

Then doubts crept in. Maybe Dr. Steinman had opened the box. Maybe she escaped. She was more powerful than any container.

I questioned what reality was—Dr. Steinman's view that she existed only in my head, or whether she was like the ghosts one reads about who travel the earth after a suicide.

On the Golden Gate Bridge driving to my therapy appointment, I again felt the evil presence commanding, "Stop the car.
Jump off the bridge." I fought off the voice, trying not to listen to
the self-destruct message, but it upset me. I burst into tears in Dr.
Steinman's big, safe office. Walking in there had become like a
haven, a port of safety. Mom wouldn't dare touch me in this
strong man's presence.

"She wants me dead. Mom wants me to kill myself."

"Yes. She did want to kill you when you were little. She tried
enough times, but not now. She is dead. Didn't we even role play
putting her spirit in the box?"

"Do you think she is in the box?"

"No. I know she is dead. With one hundred percent certainty
I can tell you she is alive only in your mind."

I went on to explain to this nonreligious Jew how people
didn't just cease to exist when they stopped breathing. I told him
I feared she was too evil to just dissipate into nothingness.

Dr. Steinman asked, "Even if she does exist in some spirit
form, how can she hurt you? She has no substance."

That was a new idea for me.

He continued. "If you let yourself regress inside to the helpless child, as you were when you were little and being hurt, then
the presence of your mother has power, but if you stay the adult,
you will know it is only the past hurts that make the voice seem
real."

I could hear Dr. Steinman's words, but I couldn't make them
seem as real to me as my mother's omnipotent presence was real.
I felt haunted and desperately missed dissociating.

For several sessions Dr. Steinman listened to my fears about
Mom, asking me for specifics about the times Mom spoke her
death wishes and the times of torture. It was easy to see how that
message became deeply embedded in my mind.

He said, "Be gentle with the child in you, but at the same time
use your mind to tell yourself that this is only a message from
your childhood. It is not now. Your mother is dead."

One morning, standing in my kitchen, my most dreaded
room where the voice of destruction seemed the strongest, I
heard "Get the ice pick. Stab yourself. Pick up the knife and cut
yourself." Suddenly, all that Dr. Steinman had been saying for

weeks clicked in my head like gears engaging and moving forward. It was obvious to me. I could hardly wait for my therapy session.

"I figured it out," I said elatedly. "It doesn't matter if Mom is a ghost or if she is truly, totally dead. If she has no protoplasm, no material body, how could she possibly hurt me? The self-destruct message, whether it comes from an ethereal presence or only a deep recording in my mind, has power only if I act on it. Mom can't kill me, it would be *me* that kills myself. I have the power!"

"Good for you!" Dr. Steinman said. "You're finally getting the picture."

It was a simple realization, but it made a great deal of difference to me. I didn't need to be the tiny victim waiting to get annihilated. I could feel this presence and say, "I refuse to listen to this message from my childhood."

With the new awareness of my own power, I felt angry at the haunted feelings. "Fuck you, you evil witch," I would fume as the thoughts crept in. Once in a while I slipped back to being the fearful child wanting to beg for mercy from my perceived ghost. It was an hourly, even minute by minute, task to fight my own mind, my own fears, and stay in control. "I have the power," I murmured over and over to myself. Severe childhood abuse definitely took away the sense that I had control or power over my life. These were new concepts. It sounds odd, but it felt as though I grew a little just with this realization. I would only be a victim if I let myself be a victim. There was no Joey, Emily, or Mother who could kill me. I was in control.

I had actual dialogues with my distorted thoughts. "Mom is not in my house. These messages are not real. Go away, evil presence." To stand up for myself took an unbelievable amount of effort. Each time was a little easier than the time before.

With all the growth and insight, suicide shouldn't have even entered my mind, but it still played its theme song to me. Depression descended easily, for there was the pain that wouldn't go away and my own sense of failure about my life.

"The more you can manage to stay the adult and not slip back into a regressed state, the easier it will be for you," said Dr. Steinman.

"I feel that I am only pretending to be forty-eight. A huge portion of me still feels stuck in some child state."

"Then bring the child part of you in here in therapy, but try to
be the adult the rest of the time."

Easier said than done.

It was easy to be young with Dr. Steinman. Sometimes on the
way to my sessions, I could feel myself shrinking, visualizing my
little patent-leather Mary-Jane shoes, a big lace collar on my
blouse and a neat ponytail. My attachment to him was childlike. I
wanted him to smile at me. I had to fight the desire to leave my
chair during a session and sit at his feet, putting my head in his
lap. I wanted my hair stroked, or just to touch his big hands. The
most difficult part of therapy was the rule of no touching. Dr.
Steinman said that was a definite, unbreakable rule. My adult-
mind understood it, but my child-mind ached with longing. Very
rarely did adult sexual feelings surface. My fantasies were young;
I wanted to curl up next to him and put my face on his naked
chest to feel the warm, soft hair as I had with my father. I wanted
to have a lullaby sung to me, or be hugged tightly, envelopingly,
to know for a moment I was safe. No one can know the sense of
endangerment that was my constant companion. It made the dad-
dylike safety of therapy seem compelling. Dr. Steinman managed
to give the nurturing parent-loving without touching. It was in his
smile, his twinkling eyes, his attentiveness, his accessibility. He
nurtured in the way he brought the fullness of himself into therapy. One day in my usual weeping way I said I wished he could
sing me a song, and he did; a lovely, silly song he'd sung his children. After one particularly painful session, I stood close to him,
begging for a hug, tears pouring down my face, needing desperately to be comforted. Unlike Dr. Hambler, who backed away
and became angry, Dr. Steinman shook my hand for a moment
and with great depth of compassion said, "We don't need to
hug."

"I think I'm going to love you too much," I said.

"That's okay. It's all part of therapy."

"I think I'm like one of those stupid cocker spaniels; smile at
me, or be nice to me, and I'll follow you anywhere. I want to
touch you. I want to be with you."

"We can be here together in your therapy sessions."

"But I only feel safe when I'm with you. I don't feel safe when I leave."

"The endangered feelings are just from your childhood. You will have to learn to deal with your fears."

Not being able to pull myself back to the mature adult-self, I stood sobbing, asking him, "Can I have one of your old sweaters to hold when I leave here?" It felt like grief to leave the safe room with the strong, safe, paternal man who could put life in a logical pattern for me and keep Mom's evil presence in abeyance.

He thought about my request for a minute. "I'm not sure it's a good idea to give you something that reinforces your regressed state. It's healthier for you to be the adult."

"But I don't feel like a grown-up. I'm not even sure I know what being an adult means."

"How about if I loan you a sweater on the condition that it's only for three months, and you must tell me what you do with the sweater and how you are feeling, even if it embarrasses you."

The next week he gave me an old Shetland wool sweater, fuzzy and full of holes. It was comforting to just hang on to it when I felt the panic rise up, when the voice in my head whispered the self-destruct messages. I pretended he was in the sweater and I would wrap the sleeves over my shoulders, like a shield of warmth against the coldness of my fear. At times when I could not talk to him, the long days when it was not my turn to belong to him, I could take the sweater out of the drawer and rub it softly on my face, easing the loss of the safe room, the warm man.

It touched me that Dr. Steinman seemed to truly see me, to know me. I'm certain giving me a sweater to hold rather flew in the face of all the psychiatric training that would not encourage infantile behavior. Yet he knew the emptiness in me. He could see into the darkness that was my childhood and he knew there was healing in going backward for a little while.

After that we occasionally talked about the sweater, less often with time. I wasn't being evasive, it's just that the longer I went without dissociating, the stronger I became at standing up to the voice of Mom's destruct messages, the less often the sweater got taken out of my drawer, where it lay nestled with sandalwood soap. I recognized the sweater has no more power than the feather

Dumbo the elephant held, just as the ghost of Mom has no more power than I am willing to give it.

The effort to keep from dissociating, to keep from regressing, to keep from listening to the suicidal thoughts took a toll that was exhausting. It was as much effort for me to control my thoughts as it must be for any alcoholic in need of a drink. It was a depressing discovery to realize that even though I didn't dissociate into another self, I still was a dissociative personality. My mind had compartments, completely isolated storage places. I could be a happy, functional person one minute and then something would trigger the pain thoughts—television, books, newspapers, conversations, a memory—and just like uncorking a vacuum bottle where the air rushes in, I'd get sucked into another room in my head, the place that holds the pain, where I am young, and feel helpless, waiting to be hurt.

Just before Easter at my Friday session, Good Friday, I sat again in Dr. Steinman's office letting the tears flow, remembering how all the Christian holidays were times of pain and torture. I remembered when Mom killed an Easter Bunny someone had given me, keeping it with its slit throat in a shoe box and showing it to me over and over as it stiffened and finally began to smell. I sat weeping.

At the end of the session, I was unable to leave. Huddling on the sofa in his waiting room, tears leaked out.

Dr. Steinman's next patient was late, so he said, "Why don't you come back to my office for a few minutes."

"I hate her. I feel angry at my mother for what she did. How dare anyone do what she did! It's not fair!"

"I'm glad you're angry. Bring that anger in the next time you come."

I felt empowered by my rage. How dare she!

That afternoon, I heard a screech of tires outside my house. The doorbell rang. My neighbor, shaking and looking ashen, said, "Oh, Marcia, I feel awful. I just ran over your cat in the street!"

Running out, I saw Blackie lying dead on the asphalt, blood oozing from his mouth and rectum. In a state of shock, I scooped him up and told my neighbor something to the effect that accidents happen. As though reliving what I had just hours ago cried about in therapy, I put Blackie in a box.

Crying and crying, I held the box as inside me grew the certainty that Mom was getting revenge for my anger.

Sobbing, I called Dr. Steinman and told him of the death. "She's doing it again. She wants to kill the things I love."

"I'm very sorry about your cat," he said, sounding genuinely sorry, "but it's a coincidence. Your mother did not kill your cat."

"Are you positive?" I sobbed over the phone.

"One hundred percent positive."

Hanging up the phone, I cried more, feeling the loss of this companion and terror at Mom's powers.

Needing more reassurance, I called Dr. Steinman again.

"You don't think she can hurt me? Are you absolutely sure you're not just saying it to make me feel better?"

"I'm absolutely certain it's coincidence, a bad time to lose your cat, but it wasn't the doing of your mother. I'll be home all weekend. Call me if you need me."

Working at recouping adult feelings, I sat and damned the presence of Mom. What would have in previous times made me escape to another self, a different state of reality, was not an option I allowed myself. With conscious effort, I said to myself, "I will stay. I will feel my feelings." It meant crying more, but it was progress.

The next day, I went out and bought myself two kittens, a black one and a fluffy gray one.

On Easter Sunday, I stayed the mature adult, not letting myself slip back into the past of horrors.

For every two steps forward, there was a step backward, a time of regression, times of black feelings and tears. I still had my suicidal thoughts that tangled my mind like an octopus twisting its tenacles around in my head. Dr. Steinman was always reassuring, persistently optimistic. He never let me wallow in guilt at my backward slides.

One rainy Saturday, when there was no one home and no reason in the world for me to create my own little crisis, I just fell down the hole, like Alice in Wonderland, to my own private hell.

Everything mushroomed inside—the abuse, my failures, a sense of hopelessness about life and myself. I think I called Dr. Steinman three times that day sobbing how I wanted to die. During the third call, I was lectured in that severe, commanding tone he could get when I was over the edge. "Either pull it together or I will call the paramedics to come put you in the hospital. You are allowing yourself to regress, to feel the pain. Take a deep, slow breath and visualize yourself a mature woman. You are not allowed to regress until you are in my office. Do I make myself clear?"

He was right. Without making a conscious choice that I was aware of, I nonetheless had allowed myself to fall down the chute of despair.

Contritely, I walked into his office at the next appointment waiting for a tirade on what a pain I was. Instead, I got a big, warm smile as he said, "Well, are you better today?" I had been expecting him to give me reasons why he couldn't be my psychiatrist anymore.

As I repetitively fell over the edge, or "regressed," as Dr. Steinman called it, I began to be able to say to myself the things he would say. His messages were simple. "Stay the adult. Don't allow yourself to regress. The pain is in the past. Not here. Not now. You're doing great." His maddeningly simplistic statements had power when I demanded of myself that I follow his words. It took a significant effort to visualize myself a tall woman, a grown-up. It was far easier to go with the thoughts that pulled me back into the mire of childhood pain.

When I slipped backward, Dr. Steinman said, "What advantage was there to letting yourself experience all those negative feelings?"

There was none. Losing a whole day or two to weeping, when I was rendered useless by my regression, had no redeeming features whatsoever.

Developing a vigilant guard over my feelings was a priority. My whole life had been spent running from my feelings. To stand still and own all that I felt and remembered was a major step toward victory. Demanding of myself that I stay the adult let me function more effectively, for only by staying the adult could I distance myself from the deeply recorded messages of trauma.

Dr. Steinman said all my other personalities were "integrated" into me. I don't agree with that word. They felt dead. I was alone and lonely without splitting and running. My sense of vulnerability was exquisite, rather like standing stark naked in an open field during a lightning storm. Over and over the terror would rise at the thought that I could not leave anymore. Somehow, after figuring out that the others were just pieces of myself, splitting would just be a self-deceptive game. It was sort of like when you're a child and you reach the age when you look at your doll and realize it can't really talk to you. You could still pretend, but it is never the same again when the magic is gone. It was the same after my "others" died. They could certainly be resurrected, but it would only be a pretend game, for I had plugged into who they were.

When they died, I did not inherit all the traits or likes of the "others." I could not have a multitude of parents, histories, memories, and opposing characteristics. As the days went by, I felt a new kind of power—I could pick and choose what characteristics I wanted to take from the "others" to be my own. I wanted Sophie's love of cooking and gardening. I rejected Camille's desire to be the victim, for I could see where it came from. The extroverted manner of Muriel intrigued me; that meant I had within me the capacity to be outgoing and even aggressive. Her ability to be the objective, mature adult seemed elusive to me, but I would think, how would Muriel deal with this situation if she were still around? Even after their deaths I thought about them as though they were friends and enemies, not as though they were truly me. What was integrated, if one chooses to use that word, were the feelings of the others. The most important feeling I struggled with was anger. Joey and Emily had cornered the market on red-hot, livid anger. To me it was as slippery as Jell-O, sliding away the minute I tried to grab it, but it became clear that it was my best ally to the small-child feelings that would leave me in a terrified state.

Dr. Steinman was supportive of my brief angry episodes. There was no shocking him as I graphically described the agony and torture I wished I could inflict on my mother.

"I want to tie her in the blue kerchiefs, just as she did to me, and I want to cut her slowly, watching her blood ooze out. I want it in her pants and in her hair, just as it was in mine. I want to poke her eyes out with the ice pick and watch the jelly ooze out of them and see just bloody sockets. I don't want to kill her quickly. I want to watch her scream and suffer."

"What would you say to your mother if she were here?" asked Dr. Steinman.

"I don't think there is one damn thing I could say to her. There are no words that could heal the years of torture. Words would be lost on her. Anyone that calculating and terrible wouldn't understand words. I want to torture her. I want to tie her up and hurt her."

"Yes, she deserves that."

"I feel angry because there is no pain worse than a child's pain. My rapes, my adult pain, can't match the intensity of the pain I knew as a child. My mother! My own mother! It was a be-trayal of my very sense of self. Of all relationships in the world, the one with my own mother should have been safe, and I spent long nights awake and in pain, thinking she would come in my room and kill me. I hate her! I hate what she did to my life!"

I liked it that Dr. Steinman never made me feel guilty for my anger as Dr. Naughton had, saying, "I'm sure your mother was mentally ill." Dr. Steinman could let me be wicked in my anger and agree that whatever I thought of was too kind. Even with his encouragement, anger seemed elusive. The tiny victim mode of thinking came more naturally. Panic feelings were more familiar than anger. It was a big step forward to begin to experience the rage at the abuse and not dissociatively run away from the feel-ings. Each time I let the anger surface, the stronger I felt at con-fronting the haunting presence of Mom.

It took about three months of grieving, panicking, and calling Dr. Steinman for reassurance before I finally began to feel com-fortable with the singleness of being. The wonderful sense of lib-eration from being a multiple personality began to dawn on me as I became more functional.

Dan noticed the changes in me. For the first time in my life I was dependable. There were no more days I couldn't account for.

I functioned better, even giving a few dinner parties. Dan became more affectionate as he noticed I was more emotionally even and willing to try new things.

Kevin and Cindi immediately picked up on the changes in me. "You seem more stable," said Cindi. "You don't get the blank look in your eyes and then get weird."

"I'm hoping my weird days are behind me."

"With as much as you have lived through, you've still been a good mother."

"That means a lot, Cindi. I haven't been consistent, or a constant for you as I should have been, but I've always deeply loved you and Kevin."

"I know, Mom. I've always felt that, even when you said you wanted to die. I always felt loved, even when our roles were reversed and I had to take care of you, as though I were your mother."

"I'm sorry for all I could not be when you were growing up," I said, giving Cindi a big hug as tears sprang into both our eyes.

"That's okay, Mom. We both made it, we made it just fine."

With a new constancy of existence, I began to have what I called "joy days." It had been an enormous burden to live a life that had no predictability; now I could plan my days and was infinitely more functional. I could go for days at a time without tears or needing to hear Dr. Steinman's voice over the phone.

I felt like a newly emerged butterfly, with wet wings still folded around me, teetering and clinging to the chrysalis. Life still seemed precarious but full of new possibilities. Flying was not as much the focus as feeling the relief of standing on the outside of the cocoon, the place where I had been wrapped in pain and blinded from insight.

The full impact of the revolution that had happened inside me hit me about three and a half months after I stopped dissociating, less than sixteen months after I had begun therapy with Dr. Steinman. Dan woke me on an early Sunday morning and said, "Let's go for a hike." We quickly dressed in our old jeans and sweatshirts and drove north, away from bay fog and houses, to find woods. We stopped at a bakery and got coffee and warm cinnamon rolls. We turned on a symphony and were sipping our steaming espresso, and snuggling next to Dan in the chilly air, I suddenly knew things were going to be different. We drove on a new stretch of highway and looking up at the sides of the hill that had been gouged away for the new road, I saw a single poppy plant laden with swaying orange flowers.

"I know it's silly, Dan, but would you stop the car for a second?"

He pulled over, and the sight of that plant clinging to a rocky bank moved me. Identifying with the blossoms reaching toward the morning sun, I thought, sometimes against all odds, nature springs forth with abundant life from the most barren of places. Please, let this be me.

written in the fourth year of therapy
with Ira Steinman

PART
TWO

Chapter 12

"One . . . two . . . three . . . four . . . five . . . six . . . seven . . . eight . . . nine . . . ten . . . Uncle Whoa Bill . . . don't cry." I remember being about five when I heard on the radio that I should count to ten and say, "Uncle Whoa Bill" when I was hurt, and if I didn't cry I was a good child. I counted as my finger was crunched in the nutcracker. I was silent as I was lifted off the floor by my braids. Now I'm into my fourth year of crying with Ira Steinman. All the tears I never shed as a child are flowing out. I have left soggy spots on his Oriental carpet after sessions of lying at his feet, sobbing out the abuse. Recently I brought him six boxes of Kleenex to replace a bit of what I've used.

Everywhere I turn these days there seem to be accounts of child abuse leaping from the television and glaring out of magazines. So often the accounts end with the implication that there is a magical healing that takes place simply in remembering the abuse and claiming the experience. That isn't true; that is just the beginning of the long, uphill climb to mental health.

I am making great progress, but it is with concentrated, enormous effort and commitment to therapy. I am sane enough now

to see the true tragedy of my crazy mind. Sometimes I cry thinking of the genetic perfection I began life with, just as most babies
have, and the twisting and warping that was done to my mind.
Anger at Mom, tears in a psychiatrist's office, will never give back
to me the lost years, the lifetime of inner agony. It's pointless to
focus on that. There is only today, another sunrise that gives me
one more opportunity to deal with the panics, the still distorted
thoughts.

There are other moments when I feel wonderfully impressed
with myself and my growth, and I brag to Ira about my progress.
"It's because I have such a good psychiatrist."

He smiles. "No. You've been working very hard in therapy."

The truth is, we both are.

Our relationship has evolved over time. I now call him Ira instead of Dr. Steinman. It took me a long time to do that. He
seemed so paternal and awesome. Now it is completely comfortable; safe enough to be angry at him. I've stopped fearing he will
tell me to go away. I still love him more than anyone in the world,
but anger and loving are not mutually exclusive. The other day he
said an emergency had come up and we would have to meet for a
shorter time. It shouldn't have sent me over the edge, but it did. I
sat fuming in his waiting room, trying unsuccessfully to gain control of my abandonment feelings. I waited for an hour and a half,
realizing I got thirty minutes and his other richer patients get double sessions. After his patient left, I stormed into his office yelling
that I wouldn't be a second-class citizen, that I wouldn't take the
leftovers of therapy and he could go to hell. Of course, in my
usual, stupid, all-or-nothing way, I escalated the whole scene into
wanting to die. Looking back, it was all childish and theatrical,
but when I'm in the middle of those feelings it has a seemingly
rational, logical progression of thought. I stormed out of his office, slamming every door I could find, trying to suppress my desire to break all the windows in his office. Driving home, I
thought of various angry death plots. Dying on the steps of his
office and letting my blood splatter his stairs seemed a satisfying
scenario.

Ira called me at home.

"Fuck you!" I raged. "You give me thirty minutes and give

some rich society lady an hour and a half. I won't be less than your other patients." Then I was crying, "It's just like when I was little. I got my dinner taken away before I was done. I didn't get to have toys. It was only me who got put in the closet!"

Then I calmed down and could see the transference. Ira is great because he doesn't let the craziness escalate. He calls right back to work things through. He can put things in perspective in a few minutes. After a good cry at what Mom had done to me, I realized again what an enormous gift he is giving me. He never once said, "You owe me a great deal of money, I can cut short any sessions I want." He keeps the issues to the real issues: the transference, the childhood pain which gets confused in therapy.

Ira always insists I keep some kind of calm, rational overview of things. I can't always do that. At moments it is like the old memory of being tied up; the more I wiggle and squirm, the deeper the rope cuts. I get breathlessly stuck. My emotions have the instability of a small child. One minute I can be laughing and the next, crying. I think I know one source of this horrific liability—I wasn't allowed to express my feelings as a child. All those feelings got divided and given to my "others." Now they are all congregating in only me and I don't know how to put perimeters around those feelings. There is anger and sorrow and grief and rage and longing and loving and needing and more anger.

I am still capable of splendid episodes of hysteria. I can magnify everything and panic over little things.

Sometimes I feel like I am failing Ira. I'm not dumb. I understand the concept of how to remain calm and rational. I get angry when Ira thinks sometimes I'm deliberately letting my mind get out of control. Control is easy only to one who is capable of control.

What happens to a child's mind when a child is not allowed to cry, be angry, play vigorously, or is kept for long days in a black closet? I see the faces of the Romanian orphans and I see my own deadened, passive child's face waiting, waiting. The child was not allowed to cry, so Sunshine cried. The child was not allowed to be angry, so Emily took the anger. In all the abuse and the splitting, my child-self didn't learn to deal with my emotions. They ooze, flow, hyperreact; they take control of me. Why can't I learn not to give energy to my feelings? My feelings lie, and they are magnified as a result of ice picks, needles, and blue kerchiefs.

In therapy, I'm beginning to learn what to do with this new feeling self. I'm trying to learn to identify and understand my thoughts and not just be this reactive piece of protoplasm zinging around like an oblivious protozoa.

I get Ira all mixed up in my learning process. Some sessions are like warm schmoozing, as we sip tea, laugh or talk quietly. Other times I'm a weepy, mascara-streaked mess. I get Ira mixed up in a hundred ways. He can be the mother, the father, or the best friend, depending on the interaction of the day. Once in a while I get angry just because he is so damn smart. I feel like a bird being outmaneuvered by a cat. No matter which way I go, Ira is there ahead of me, explaining me to myself. At other moments I feel like he is a lion trainer and all his patients are jungle cats, which he keeps in line by doling out just enough attention to keep us all sitting on our little pedestals.

That assessment of Ira is so unfair! I am jealous. I want him all to myself. I suffer with the time constraints of only two forty-five-minute sessions a week. There is often not enough time to deal with the intensity of the issues I face. My adult mind understands, but my child-self resents that he is a daddy who must be paid for. My adult mind is deeply grateful for his generosity to me, when I am paying him for less than one session a week. I hope soon I will be well enough to work full-time and pay him all that I owe him. But I could never do that. How can you repay someone for a life, for the very sense of self?

There are days of depression when I wonder if I am wasting the time of a valuable psychiatrist. I regularly offer to quit therapy so he won't be saddled with a hopeless, flightless albatross like me forever. He won't hear of it. At one point I offered to take out a life insurance policy and make him the beneficiary so whenever he needed to get paid, we could make my death look accidental. Ira laughed and said, "Absolutely not. People with a history of suicide attempts can't get life insurance anyway." At the time I was serious, but now I see what a completely ridiculous offer that was. That was one of my depressed days.

Occasionally I view him as Simon Legree, pushing me harder

than I can go. He is more than a quiet listener; he presses me for growth. It would be easier to remain the hurt child and let him take care of me, but his goal is that I take care of myself. He wants me well, but there is part of me that would relinquish all functioning to stay enveloped in the safety of his presence with the warm tea, fresh flowers, the kind, attentive eyes offering caring to my destitute child-self. I don't like to admit it, even to myself, but for his attention I would stay regressed if he would let me.

I love him so much that I feel guilty when I get sucked into transference issues and get angry. Anger is such a difficult emotion for me to deal with that he grins when I get mad at him and says, "Good, now tell me how you feel. Try yelling at me." I've only shouted at him a few times. It upsets me to be angry, for when I am, I still fear Mom is hovering around or whispering her self-destruct messages in my head, taunting me, commanding me to die. I'm sure Ira is right, that it's imaginative reactivation of my childhood experiences, but it still feels real.

At times, the boundaries of the psychiatrist-patient relationship seem almost cruel. I have been made to feel safe, protected, and nurtured, yet I must stay in designated time frames. I open up, showing Ira the exquisite hurts, and then must leave without touching him. I can let my child-self cry out in agony and then I must gather myself together, and when the cool San Francisco fog hits my face, I must regain the role of adult.

There have been times after emotional sessions that I have walked miles, weeping as I pass the old Victorian houses, oblivious to the tourist faces staring at me from cable cars. I often go to a little sushi bar, where the owner pretends he doesn't see my red-rimmed eyes and the small pleasant man behind the bar hands me my favorite Maguro Sashimi and a warm washcloth to wipe away my tears. The progress is that I am staying together with my pain. I don't slip into another persona, an Emily, and enter a bar or pick up a man to stop the hurting.

Therapy holds power over me because there is no one else in the world who would be willing to listen to this much pain. My family, my children, don't want it. It can't be part of my daily life. Sometimes it feels that the only thing in my life that is truly real is therapy. Conversations with neighbors or friends strike me as inane and superficial. I feel as if I am put on a hold button until I

can be back to Ira. He is gracious, or intuitive, enough to know
how much I need him, how imperative it becomes to hear his
voice between sessions. Ira has never once told me not to call, or
that I was a bother. He has a phenomenal capacity to carry people, be there for people, yet the limitations are obviously part of
psychiatry. I cannot belong to him. He has a life that I am not part
of. It hurts deeply, for the child-self has been seduced to the
safety, the gentleness, and for the child that was hurt clear down
to the very soul, the limits and boundaries are difficult to maintain. I don't do it, but sometimes at the end of a session, I want to
throw myself at his feet and beg, "Please, don't send me away." I
want to cry, "Please, don't belong to anyone but me. Don't make
me leave the only place in the world where I feel truly safe." But I
must leave at the end of my sessions. Occasionally, I have retreated too far back into childhood horror and have gone into his
waiting room to curl up on his couch. Just leaving becomes too
much separation to deal with. Then Ira becomes stern and says I
must go. It feels like a great hunk of me shears away from my
core, to be left lying in trust with him, as my shadow walks out to
the sidewalk.

Memories keep surfacing. I wish they wouldn't, but Ira says
that is part of the healing process. I function well for weeks on
end, and then something will trigger a memory.

I don't even know what triggered the memory of one of my
worst experiences. I began to see blood everywhere I looked. I
knew it was not real, that it was only in my mind, but I began to
disintegrate into crying jags and feeling like a small child again,
calling Ira often and having suicidal thoughts. All his probing for
causes and reassurances didn't seem able to reach me. At night, I
had nightmares, and my days were filled with a paralyzing anxiety, an almost panic. The voices began whispering in my head, the
dissociative other selves trying to run from the pain. It seemed as
though Mom was in my house again, whispering, "Jews are meant
to suffer and die." In a completely regressed, terrified, removed
from reality state, I went to the kitchen drawer and with a big
carving knife slashed my arm deeply and watched as the blood
flowed down.

The next day I had a session with Ira. I thought he would yell at me for doing such a stupid thing, but he never yells, he just quietly tried to get to the bottom of what was going on and why I was regressing so badly. I didn't know. I left therapy still all weepy.

It wasn't until I got home and entered my bathroom and changed the bloody dressing on my arm that the images came clear in my head. Suddenly, I was tiny again, probably about five, and I was reliving horror I couldn't deal with. I called Ira hysterically begging him to let me die, saying I didn't want to remember the dead baby. I couldn't stop crying, so he ordered me to take a tranquilizer. I had three days to wait for my next session; three days spent in bed crying, reliving more than I wanted to, three days of phone calls to Ira vacillating between hysteria and depression, begging him to let me die.

I came to the next session too unraveled to even sit in his leather chair. I curled up on the floor and just cried and cried and told him of the horror that was in my mind.

Bobby was in school and I was almost five, but I was still at home. Jimmy was a small child, for I remember he awoke from his nap and Mom was not around. I hauled him out of his crib and we looked for Mom.

I opened the bathroom door and stood transfixed at the sight of blood everywhere. Mom was hunched over, and there was blood slithering down her legs. In the sink was a bloody ice pick, the ice pick I knew with terror, and there were towels drenched in blood.

My eyes went to the toilet and there, rising out of the water, was a little, miniature, perfectly formed bloody baby, floating with the terrifying purple-black placenta and the crimson blood everywhere.

"I had to kill it," Mom whispered. "It was a Jewish baby, just like you."

I don't remember where Jimmy was. I tried to crouch down and make the scene go away. Mom ordered me to get newspapers, and I got them and she took the baby out of the toilet. It was a little girl baby and it had ice pick holes in the top of its head. Mom wrapped the baby in newspapers and she grabbed me by the neck. "You must help me," she said as she walked bent over, leaning on me. We walked out back to the big red brick incinerator in the backyard. She ordered me to get sticks and she put the baby on the sticks and squirted the newspapers with the lighter fluid in the can.

Mom grabbed my braids, immobilizing me, and took my hand, placing a match in it. "We must burn the baby." I tried to draw my hand away. I was shaking uncontrollably, but Mom put her hand over mine and made me strike the match and set fire to the newspapers. I tried to wriggle free of her grasp. I was sobbing, but she made me stand there, made me look as the newspapers were gobbled up in flames, exposing the baby that burned. The placenta popped in the fire and the sweet smell of burning flesh gagged me as I watched the baby turn black in the flames. I remember the tiny, blackened, curled fingers against the yellow of the fire.

I can remember Mom's pale ashen face looking into mine. My cheeks were hot from the fire and tears. "I wish I could put you in the fire to burn, but you are too big and everyone would ask where you are. If you tell anyone about the baby, I will burn you, too."

I sobbed and sobbed as I recounted this memory to Ira. It took a full forty-five minutes to stop crying, and I think I repeated the story several times, each time remembering something more. I regained some control, but it took about three weeks of intermittent crying, lying in bed, and talking to Ira to work this to a point of manageability in my own mind.

Ira kept saying, "It is in the past. You are not that five-year-old." Yet, it felt like I was five. It felt like it was happening all over again with the same intensity that it was remembered.

As with so many of the terrible memories, I felt I needed some sort of validation that this wasn't an imaginary episode. If Emily could be imagination, how can I trust what is real? I phoned Bobby, my reality tester, and asked, "Was Mom pregnant after Jimmy?"

"Of course. Don't you remember when I was in first grade and Mom was going to have a baby at Christmas, just about on your fifth birthday? I remember she was enormously pregnant at my Halloween carnival."

"What happened to the baby?" I asked.

"I don't know. She said she lost it. It died. Dad was on a trip, and I remember she was in bed at Thanksgiving, or maybe it was just after Thanksgiving."

"Did anyone bury the baby?"

"I don't remember anyone talking about that. Why?"

"Just wanting to know. I'm remembering more things in therapy."

"I don't even want to know what you're remembering, but everything else you've remembered has been true."

"Thanks, Bobby."

After crying and talking for weeks about this episode, I decided to go see my aunt, my mother's sister. I asked her questions about Mom and the family history. She was warm and chatty as we drank Earl Grey tea. I said, "Did you know I was hurt by Mom?"

Tears welled in her eyes, "Yes, I knew it. So many people knew it. I thought of trying to get custody of you, but I was in an abusive marriage and I couldn't trust my own husband." She took my hand and patted it, as though I was still a child. "So many people failed you. Your mother was a very sick woman. Once she asked me if I would take you."

"Do you remember her being pregnant when I was about five?"

"Of course, dear."

"What happened to that baby?"

"My secret fear is she aborted it. There never was a funeral. She must have been about eight months pregnant. She never went to the hospital, but I know she was very sick in bed for several weeks."

"And nobody ever investigated it?"

"Your mother was a very manipulative woman. She always did exactly what she pleased."

"Even murder," I murmured.

After that visit, I guess Bobby went to see her, too. My aunt began to get very depressed. She called me several times crying and apologizing to me. A few weeks after this, I got a call from my cousin; my aunt had taken an overdose of sleeping pills—another family suicide. I'm so glad I was polite and gentle with her so I don't have to live with guilt.

Shortly after remembering the baby, I was watching one of the daytime talk shows on TV and there was a woman telling of her severe abuse as a child by a satanic cult. She claimed that as a teenager she was forced to have babies which were ritualistically sacrificed, but neither she nor her psychotherapist, who was sitting comfortably next to her, offered any validating evidence. As I was sitting there watching, having just given Ira the grisliest of memories, I suddenly thought maybe he was as skeptical of my abuse as I was of this woman's.

When I had my next session, I was very upset. I told him, "I'm going to get documentation that what I'm telling you is true. It never crossed my mind until now that you probably think I'm making up wild tales."

"No. I figured out quite a while ago that what you have been saying is true. Even if it weren't, it wouldn't change how we do therapy."

"What do you mean it doesn't matter if it's true or imaginary? I've gone through hell, and the one person I'm sharing it with doesn't think it matters?"

"You're not understanding what I'm saying," Ira said. "It doesn't matter in the context of therapy."

That seemed like a complete negation of my experiences to me. I was crying and ranting. "I'll get you proof. I'll call Bobby. It may not matter to you, but it matters one whole hell of a lot to me that I was hurt."

"Of course it matters. It must have been terrible. I do believe you were badly hurt as a child."

That reassurance wasn't good enough. I didn't want him to have doubts. I went home and called Bobby and told him to get in touch with Ira and tell him it was true. I sent to the psychiatric hospital for my records. I called Dr. Naughton for the box with the blue scarves, nutcracker, and knives. (He called me back saying he had thrown them away! He even had destroyed the two letters from my mother.) I brought in the long list of doctors and hospitals I'd been in as a child. I gave Ira a list of physicians who had treated me for all my many real and imagined ailments. Next

I called my internist and made an appointment. When I went to see him, I brought paper and a measuring tape. "I want you to please look at all my scars and document where they are and how big each one is. I want my psychiatrist to know that for every experience I've told him about, I have the scar to verify it."

"That seems like a strange request. Do you want me to call him?"

"You can if you want, but I'd also like you to do this for me." We were both embarrassed as he held up the measuring tape. "This is my idea, not his," I said.

The doctor sent Ira the verification of scars. At my next session after the letter arrived, Ira tried to discount its importance, but to me it was enormously important. I didn't want him ever to listen to me cry and be as distanced from me as I felt from the satanic cult baby breeder.

There have been other incidents of abuse to remember. Sometimes I get physical symptoms as the memories surface. A few months ago I was vomiting and vomiting and had a terrible headache for days, until Ira helped me remember having my head held by Mom in Dad's big vise in the garage and squeezing my head so hard in the big metal clamps that I had a brain concussion. As my head was getting squashed, I looked up at the saws and was afraid Mom would take a saw, like Dad did to things in the vise. I screamed in pain and thought my head would split open to the popping sound of a watermelon. The next day I remember vomiting on the playground at school and having headaches as I tried to read and concentrate. The headaches lasted a long time and I remember my eyes hurting.

Unfortunately, I haven't gotten to the place where I can step back and just say, "Oh, yes, just one more incident to remember." The memories are highly emotionally charged experiences.

Each new ghastly memory becomes one more puzzle piece that gets fitted into the frame to help explain the fears, the panics, the nightmares, the hysterical physical symptoms, and the multiple personalities.

I always thought my panic reaction to barbeques stemmed from my fear of fire. Now I know it is from seeing a baby burn. It explains the times I see blood on the walls and floor when it isn't really there. The time Emily took a piece of liver and smeared it on the walls or times I have dissociatively cut myself and wiped my own blood on the walls have been a reaction to the memories that lay buried but affecting me.

There have been sobbing times in therapy that I have begged Ira to send me to a neurosurgeon to cut out the portion of my brain that holds the horror. He has gently and compassionately told me that it isn't that simple. That my conscious mind has to hold these memories seems a high price to pay for becoming functional, yet I wouldn't go back to my crippled, dysfunctional world. The running from what the unconscious knows, holding the conscious as hostage, was even worse. Life is much easier with conscious awareness. Even a little thing, like being near a fire, is easier when I acknowledge my experiences to myself, do some deep breathing to control the rising panic, than to simply operate on the dissociative level I did before of blanking out to another personality and losing a whole evening of time.

I can go weeks at a time now when life seems good and I am a functional person. I've had to be, for I'm a grandmother now. Our whole family has been captivated by the fast currents sweeping Cindi through life. In the last two and a half years she has gotten married to an outgoing chemistry teacher, finished college, and had twins. Every spare bit of time I have, I rush to her house to squeeze and rock a baby. It tickles me to hold these little tykes who look like their handsome Jewish father and know Mom is probably screaming in hell about what has happened to her Aryan genes. These babies feel like my chance to experience again so much of what I emotionally missed with Kevin and Cindi. I'm not anxious around these babies. I get to sing lullabies and give them leisurely walks to the park where I push their round, wobbly bodies in the baby swings. I wish I could sustain the completeness I feel inside when Eric has his warm, fat cheek against my neck when I hold him and my nose feels alive with baby lotion smells, or when Sam grins his four-tooth grin as he grabs fistfuls of my hair.

I have been doing all the office work for Dan's new custom-cabinet business. He started it a year ago and we have gotten closer as we have waded through California's business regulations and struggled in this learning stage. I do all the billing, and answer phones and handle many of the details. Dan has noticed how much more functional I am. It has continued to hurt me that he never wants to discuss my therapy or to talk about deeper things. I have cried my way through therapy, and on the really dark days he has quietly made dinner or gone marketing but has asked no questions. He has been preoccupied by all the business challenges, and the pleasure of taking rich grained woods and turning them into beautiful cabinets. The oak rolltop desk he made for a Napa vintner recently was exquisite.

The other night I lay next to him, watching him sleep as the moonlight played shadows across his face from our big window. I don't think I've ever done that before. For the first time I think I'm experiencing the little moments, catching the nuances of life.

I curled myself into his back to feel him breathing, and I wished I could have back the lost years when I didn't know his breathing was comforting. I wished I could give him a lifetime of fidelity. I wished I could tell him to his face that I'm grateful that he has stayed with me for so many years. Why was I so crazy that I didn't see his kindness and his patience? He has taken me each day as I am. He shouldn't have, but he did.

One of the most exciting things to happen is that I'm beginning to have orgasms. It's great! I have used the same methods in bed with Dan I use to avoid regressing and dissociating. I have to talk myself through the first part of lovemaking, "I'm not small. This is not Mom. I'm safe. There are no spoons, or ice picks, or enema bags. Relax. This is pleasure, not pain." This all sounds rather silly but before whenever my clitoris was touched, I physically tightened and mentally froze.

Dan has been a generously willing partner, going slowly, stopping when I begin to tense, backtracking to gentle cuddling until I relax, making love romantically and softly and not being overtly passionate. I have to be the world's most boring sex partner when we work on my orgasms, but Dan was so thrilled when I finally had one with him that he made love to me every night for two weeks. Now I'm the one who initiates the lovemaking, knowing what I've missed for all these years. Dan laughs and says, "Give me a break! I'm getting old. I can't do this all the time."

Dan came home from a garage sale with an old yet wonderful-sounding piano not long ago. I've begun taking piano lessons. I have zero talent, but love trying. My piano teacher is about my age and very supportive of my progress. Sometimes I tense as she sits next to me on the piano bench, our shoulders touching as she reaches over to show me something.

I am becoming more social. I don't just instantly retreat in my mind when someone enters my personal space. I'm even able to go out to lunch with some new women friends. "What do women talk about over lunches?" I asked Ira.

"Probably just regular, everyday things. Don't worry about it, you'll do fine."

I hardly slept the night before, but I *did* do well, even though I was nervous.

The little increments of progress make me feel pleased with myself. My social skills are better. I like it that I am becoming stable in terms of staying myself. Social connections were anxiety-producing when I had no certainty I'd stay intact if I got tense. To see me on the street, or meet me casually, I doubt anyone could guess at the monster I fight in my mind, the fears that still engulf me. It is a happy feeling when I overcome one more hurdle and Ira is proud of me. He isn't the gushy sort; his compliments are hard to get, but I know he is pleased with my progress.

My family thinks all my progress is terrific. I don't talk about my childhood or therapy. They know I have days of tears and days of cheerfulness, but my trend has been toward more constancy. I do infinitely more than I used to. I'm able to be mentally stimulated and involved. My concentration is better. I rarely read books or could follow a movie plot when I was dissociative. Everything would trigger flight in my mind. Scenes of blood or people shouting would send me into instant retreat in my mind and I could miss half the movie. Now I can go to a show and have the inner dialogue going, "This isn't my childhood. This is not Mom." This may sound like trivial progress, but it has added a qualitative difference to my life.

My growth is in a staccato rhythm—forward, forward, backward. There's no grace, no style, only jerky efforts.

A recent grandiose falling backward happened when Ira decided to take me off the small dose of a major tranquilizer he had me on for a while when I was integrating my "others." I was beginning to get side effects and he felt I didn't need any drugs. Even gradual weaning was horrible. Nightmares stalked my sleep, my thoughts raced around, always landing on the abuse. Childhood torture is like having a wound in the mind; any slight imbalance and the thoughts dart right to the wound, touching it, probing it, reactivating the bleeding, rolling around in the wound to test the intensity of pain.

I lived through three weeks of hell that affected even my relationship with Ira. My adult mind understood what he wanted to do and was grateful to have a psychiatrist who wanted me fully functional. I would be a more manageable patient if I were heavily drugged. I'm certain most psychiatrists would do that to me. I could grow old with a sweet smile pasted on my face, with all the cognitive functioning of a toadstool and hands and feet twitching and jerking from side effects. Ira wants more for my life than that.

In my child's mind with all the speeding up of thoughts, the nightmares, the nervous system irritability, I began viewing him in a distorted way as the abuser. I dangerously regressed: not getting out of bed, not wanting to go to sleep because of the nightmares, thinking more and more frequently of suicide. New memories surfaced. I could see myself standing naked in front of a mirror and Mom cutting my finger and making swastikas all over me in my blood. The jaggedness of my nervous system left me with no coping ability for new memories. To add to the problem, I made a stupid mistake of going to see the movie, *The Silence of the Lambs*, about a psychiatrist who eats people. With a mother who repeatedly threatened to cut me up, cook me, and feed me to the family, my mind zigzagged out of logic. Ira slipped into the role of torturer as he tried two or three new drugs on me which had ghastly effects. He says it wasn't the drugs, it was my hysterical reaction to them. He's always right, but I only know it was like being in hell.

My adult mind could step back from the chaos and understand everything on a rational level, but I couldn't sustain it. There were no voices in my head, no mother taunting me, but to stand alone at the epicenter of my inner self and be the sole container for all that was done to me was too much.

The one thing that reached me profoundly and deeply was Ira's constancy during those days. He was warm and patient and always accessible. His commitment to my recovery was obvious even to my regressed mind. He was firm but gave me autonomy in making choices. Even in the craziness my adult mind could see he was my friend.

My child's mind held him in great suspicion and I said to him, "I think when you go home, you laugh about me with your wife. I think anyone who would sit and listen to this kind of pain must be getting sadistic pleasure from it. You're not normal."

"Don't you see the transference that's happening? I wonder who in your past was sadistic?" He demanded I look at the thoughts that were getting convoluted.

I viewed the time limitations with him as a form of torture specifically designed to make me suffer. I even made him angry with me as he gave me a lecture on my regression, my transferences, and my ingratitude. One minute I viewed him as my friend and the next minute he was my enemy plotting the terrible drug reactions to make me suffer.

At seven in the morning, I woke up crying and couldn't stop. At ten, I called Ira telling him I was going to end my suffering. He firmly told me to be at my appointment at noon. I kept crying and wrote a suicide note and for probably the hundredth time tried to figure out the best suicide method. I had enough pills to put me to sleep and was going to put a plastic bag over my head and tie it at my neck. The phone rang again. It was Ira. "How are you doing?"

I couldn't stop crying. I don't remember what he said, but he reached into the lost child's heart and held on to it. I heard his voice of warmth, the voice of sanity, the voice that had the commanding assurance I would come see him. I left the house and have no memory of driving to the city. I cried in his waiting room and flopped on his floor when he opened his door. I cried for the child covered in bloody swastikas, cried for the mind that had been hurt, cried for the potential of what I could have been. For forty-five minutes I sobbed. At the end of the session I was still sobbing, but felt better. I wanted to go to Ira and cling to him like a broken child. He leaned forward in his chair, his pale face radiating compassion. I saw his eyes fill and glisten with unshed tears for me. In that moment I knew he knew my closet. I knew he felt my swastikas and was with me as I'd watched a baby burn.

We decided together I would go back on a small dose of a major tranquilizer for a few months while I tried to work through my new emotional intensity. I think this small amount of drug probably has more of a placebo effect than an actual one. Recovering from the suicidal ideas had much more to do with crying, talking, and feeling enveloped in Ira's caring.

It is upsetting to me to realize after all this therapy, I'm still capable of getting that regressed. I lost three weeks out of my life. My houseplants died. My family was traumatized once again. I must live with Dan calling me from work to check on me and his constant questioning, "Are you sure it's all right for me to leave you to go to work?" I wish I could reclaim those days, live them differently. I wish my own pain didn't cost anything to the people who love me. When I'm in that world of inner pain, that's all there is; my whole sphere of existence is as confined and dark as the closet under the stairs.

I feel especially grieved that I believed Ira was somehow tormenting me in trying to help me get off drugs. He is overly generous. "Transferences are part of therapy."

"I'm sorry. I'm truly sorry."

"Being sorry is not the issue. You have to catch it before, catch the regressions, the transferences." Ira taps his forehead with his long finger, saying, "Use your mind."

For months I can go with no memories rising to the top of whatever dam I have in my brain that holds the pain from spilling into my conscious mind. I begin to hope there is nothing more I have to reexperience, then therapy and the talking with Ira makes all the hidden things begin to migrate and rise.

The experience that I'm still crying about as I write this is too new for any level of coping with it.

I was sitting in Ira's office during a couple of weeks of upsetting therapy. I couldn't identify what was wrong.

Ira said, "Take two long slow deep breaths. What is it that the child in you is remembering?"

"I see teeth. I keep seeing teeth. Maybe it was from Mom biting me. I remember her bending down over me and I thought she was going to kiss me. I wanted so much to be kissed, but she bit me."

We had this session the day after Mom's birthday. I didn't see how any of that could connect.

My time was up in therapy. I was still upset, but the clock is the all-powerful dictator in therapy. I left feeling agitated. Getting stuck in the eternal San Francisco traffic, I sat in my car in a congealed mess of vehicles, and the memory started to surface. I turned up my stereo, to blasting sound, trying to make the now vivid scenes in my head go away.

Arriving home, I phoned Ira, shrieking, "I don't want to remember this. My teeth. The hammer." More crying.

His voice was saying, "I'm with someone now. I'll have to call you later."

I was alone in my house, walking back and forth sobbing, and remembering. I was in third grade, because I remember Ernie, the new little boy in my class, had just moved to our town. We were both behind in math. I'd missed the three months, with my fractured skull and broken arm. Ernie and I would practice our multiplication tables together. He was cute, with huge brown eyes, prickly black hair, and a dimple in his left cheek. I agonized over being behind in arithmetic, but he didn't care, he just giggled all the time.

On a Saturday, he came to my house and knocked on the door. My mother wouldn't let him in, but he handed her a box to give me. Mom shut the door in his face and threw me a little smudgy box. Inside was a love note saying he would love me forever, and in the bottom of the box was a golden bracelet with little red hearts. It thrilled me. It meant I had a real boyfriend. I ran down our long hallway trying to conceal the bracelet from Mom. She chased me down the hall and grabbed it away from me. She read the note and ripped it up. I was angry, and for the first time in a long while I talked back to her.

"It's mine. Ernie gave it to me."

She grabbed me by both arms and literally slammed me into the closet under the stairs. It was nightime when she let me out to go upstairs to bed. The next day was Mom's birthday, for she said, "My present to myself is not having to look at your face all day." She locked me back in the closet for the whole day without food or water. Instead of retreating into my pretend world, I sat there and fumed and plotted my escape. I was almost nine, and I knew now that other mothers didn't do terrible things to their children. I wasn't going to let her hurt me anymore. I would run away to Grandma's house. I had no money, I wasn't even sure where she lived, but I knew I was leaving. That night when I was finally let out, I was too weak to leave. I staggered up to bed feeling the hunger of twenty-four hours without food. In the middle of the night I sneaked quietly down the back stairs into the kitchen and gorged myself on cornbread. Taking a grocery bag from under the sink, I went back upstairs. I don't remember packing anything in the bag that was practical, just a notepad and pencils, some underwear, my pearls in case I needed to trade them for food, and my secret tiny treasures.

Early in the morning I crept out of my room, tiptoeing down the stairs, trying to miss the squeaky steps in the middle. I made it to the front door when Mom caught me. All the agony of my life turned inside me to violent anger. Mom grabbed me, and I struggled to get out of her grasp. I bit her arm with all the strength my terror generated. I had to get away. She screamed at me and picked me up as I thrashed, kicked, and bit her. Mom was enraged.

I don't remember the time frame, but I think she put me in the closet until everyone had left the house. Then Mom dragged me to the back porch, where she got the rope that always sat in a box on the bottom shelf and began tying me up as I fought and screamed, "I hate you! Mothers aren't supposed to do what you do! I'm going to run away and never come back! I hate you!"

Mom trussed me like a pot roast, the rope going around and around me until I couldn't wiggle. She hauled me into the kitchen and laid me on the cold linoleum, having my anger ebb into the tiles as I realized the punishment for my anger was about to be dealt. Mom had left the room and my terror mounted as I waited for her to return. Would my punishment be just to be tied up for a while? Mom came back into the kitchen and straddled my body with hers. She dangled Ernie's bracelet over me. She lifted up her dress, exposing herself without underpants, inches from my face. "Smell my German scent, you little Jew. Jews aren't supposed to be pretty. You steal everyone from me. You already get trinkets from boys." She spit the words out at me. Then she took a roll of heavy, wide tape and pulled off a long length of the tape and put it over my forehead and down onto the floor. I couldn't move. I was cemented down. The tape pulled my hair as I tried to move my head.

In a last fighting moment, I glared up from my immobilized viewpoint and yelled, "I'm going to leave here and tell Grandma what you have done to me. They will take you to jail."

Mom put her face inches from mine. "If you ever tell anyone what I do to you, I will give you away to the Gypsies and I will kill Grandma. I will kill whoever you tell."

Mom took a hammer and pulled up my lip. "Bite me! You damn little Jew." She swung the hammer at my top teeth. The sound crashed in my head, the pain shot through my whole body. She didn't hit them hard enough the first time. She kept tapping them with the hammer harder, harder, until my front teeth broke. The teeth were on my tongue and blood was pouring down my throat. I couldn't scream or breathe. I lay choking until Mom ripped the tape off my head so I could turn my face to the side to spit out my teeth. The pain was excruciating.

I have no memory of the rest of the day. I think I went into shock, or just dissociated myself away.

The next day Mom made me go to school. I didn't want to go. I cried looking in the mirror at my three front top teeth all broken and jagged. My tongue bled from the razor-sharp edges. I couldn't eat or drink with the electric pain of exposed tooth pulp.

I tried to cover my mouth with my hands as I sat in my desk at school, but all the children saw my mouth, for I was crying from the pain. A few kids laughed at how awful I looked. I have no memory of how I got to the dentist, whether it was Mom or the teacher who took me, but I do remember the three root canals that were terrifying and painful, then the ugly temporary plastic caps on my front teeth.

I remember sitting in front of the mirror at home rocking back and forth, looking at my ugly teeth, crying at what Mom had done to me. It took a few weeks for the porcelain jackets to be made.

Something happened to me with that experience; a piece of

me died. It was clear in my mind that if I went to school without my teeth everyone would know Mom was hurting me. I felt my teeth were a glaring announcement of my life of horror. It wasn't hidden like the abuse to my vagina or arms or legs or the needles in my feet. This was a drum-rolling announcement—and no one saw. No one saved me. When anyone asked me how I broke my teeth, I said I crashed my bicycle and the handlebars knocked them out.

I waited for Daddy to say something. He just looked sad and said he was sorry about my teeth. I wanted to tell him, but I knew Mom would kill him. I believed her. She had killed and burned a baby.

Something in me gave up with that experience. I was beaten by the omnipresent, omnipotent, evil mother. My anger became Emily's anger. My feeling self fragmented away.

This is one of the first episodes in therapy where I deeply felt my anger. I sat crying and yelling out my anger at what was done to me. As with all my more intense memories, I fight the desire to escape them, to die.

In high school I had surgeries, scraping the infections out of my bone, from the abscessed root canals, before I finally had my teeth extracted in my twenties.

In sharing the pain with Ira, I took out my teeth, saying, "I want you to know what I'm saying is true."

"You don't need to do that. I've never doubted your memories for a moment."

It still seems important to me to validate my memories; after all, I've not been a pillar of stability or sanity.

I called Bobby again. "Do you remember when I lost my front teeth?"

"Yeah. I think you were in third grade."

"Do you know how I lost them?"

"Marcia, please don't keep making me do this. I can't handle these phone calls. You're lucky enough to be in therapy. You dredge up the past for me and I get depressed for days."

"I'm so sorry, Bobby. Just tell me this one more thing and I won't ask you for any more memories."

"You know how you lost your own teeth. You never told me

how, but I can guess. I saw blood all over the kitchen floor and pieces of your teeth. I saw the rope." Bobby began to choke up with tears, which made me begin to cry all over again.

"Why did Dad let this happen?"

"I don't know. For one thing, he was never home. I think he slept with every woman within a hundred miles. His mind was on his business and his cock."

"I loved him so much, but he really failed us."

"You've got to let it all go, Marcia. What good does it do to dredge up all this terrible stuff?"

"If I had a life of any quality I wouldn't be doing this. You're lucky you can function without therapy."

"Maybe being a man I just pretend to cope. I've got the nightmares, the flashbacks, just like you."

I was still crying. "God, Bobby, how could she have done all that to me, to us? How could she have gotten away with it for years and years?"

"I think a lot of people knew. They had to. I'm sorry, Sis."

"You mean so much to me, Bobby. I begin to remember things, and I think that it can't be possible. Nobody would do that to their own child. Thank you for at least reassuring me I'm not completely crazy."

"I can't guarantee your sanity, but I can tell you that all the things you remember are real. They did happen. From now on, trust those memories and please stop dragging me into your therapy. You're making a wreck of me."

"Thanks for your help. I'll stop calling you about the memories." We were both on the phone crying into our receivers. "It was hell, wasn't it, Bobby?"

"It was worse than that."

"It means a lot to me to know you were there sharing it. I love you so much."

More crying . . . "I love you, too. Bye."

This memory is so new I cry as I brush my teeth. I cry intermittently through the day and I'm not sleeping well at nights. I feel the child's feelings that got shut off for over forty years. I'm reliving my anger, the terror, the pain, and the betrayal of all the adults in my life for not rescuing me when I was the child with the broken teeth, making my announcement of the abuse.

When I'm in the middle of working through another horror, I have a longing to be held, to be rocked. I want to live my childhood all over again, only this time have it be gentle and safe. Tears keep welling up in me for what I lived through; this little blue-eyed, blond child who loved her grown-up teeth that had come in so straight and pretty. I cry for the breaking of the mind that broke with the teeth.

When I have retreated into my childhood world, the clock slows down. The longest days in the history of the universe are my days between therapy sessions. I become panicky and feel an intense need to be with Ira. I phone him often. I beg him for extra sessions, but I am just one of many patients. There is no extra time for me, although he is generous with his telephone calls.

My flailing child-self knows no concept of waiting with the pain. My new integrated self does not know how to deal with the intensity of the memories. I still have the desire to flee, to separate from the pain. Wanting to die becomes a primary thought. If I die I won't ever have to be on the floor getting hurt. The reality is that I won't even if I live, but it is a child's state of trauma in which I reexperience it. The need to leave the pain was the core of the multiple selves. My need feels equally compelling now, and I haven't learned yet how to accept these painful memories without the overwhelming desire to run. Ira lets me run to him. He lets me need him, knowing I truly do need even the two-minute voice contact with him over the phone. When he is busy and can't talk I flop on my bed at home, holding the blankets over my head, making my outside world become as black as my inside world.

When the childhood experiences are revitalized in my mind, my heart beats fast, my breath comes in short gasps. I need the black quietness of my bed. There is so much inside my mind, I'm not capable of interacting with anyone. Noise seems irritating and lights seem glaringly bright.

I don't understand why making the world small, quiet, and black under the covers is something I would seek, when so many hours and days were spent in a closet as a child. You'd think I'd throw open the windows and turn on the stereo when the images begin to play in my mind.

It's still very new and overwhelming to be the sole container for the memories. It takes a lot of determination not to restore my "others" to life. It would be so easy to fragment and place this much pain into several containers. Joey could be angry, Sophie could cry, and Sunshine could suck her thumb. My mind could be busy with the other selves to distract me from the memories.

When my turn for therapy finally comes, I sit across from the big, solid man with the gray eyes looking kindly at me and I begin to talk, then cry and blurt out all my pain. Ira is the daddy who is finally listening, the adult who is not turning away. I don't know why it works, but giving the agony to someone else in words does help. Crying alone isn't the same as crying and being heard. It is the feeling of not being alone with the pain anymore. It becomes manageable.

Ira's empathetic eyes have a way of making my abused child-self feel as though I am being snuggled and held. He says all the right things. Even if it's just for forty-five minutes, the child has been recognized. The profound message, "You matter to me" has been given.

I am defying the Gypsies. I'm telling the daddy, finally break-ing the silence of a lifetime. A silence that was so complete it needed several selves to hold the secrets. The revealing and the crying feels good in a way I can't describe. For the first time in my life it is truly connecting me to another human being. When I give Ira the explosion of thoughts and emotions, it's like letting a crack of light come into the secret darkness at my core.

With this memory of the missing teeth, other memories sur-faced. Each thing seemed interrelated to something else. Over a period of a week I was remembering things. I was crying all the time, trying hard to function; pulling things together for an hour, then crying for an hour. It had been several days since I'd seen Ira, and I went to his office even though it wasn't the time of my ap-pointment. He wasn't there. I sat in his outer office for about an hour and a half, weeping and lying on his sofa. He never returned, so I began walking the streets of San Francisco, crying, locked in the images of bloody Kotexes getting dumped on me when I was thrown down the laundry chute in our big house, getting trapped in the blackness with the smell, another time getting hung by my braids from the clothes hook in Mom's walk-in closet. As I walked, I could smell the perfume of her closet, I could feel my braids screaming at the roots. I walked off a curb in front of a truck and didn't even realize it until the driver yelled at me. I called Dr. Leof, the kindly psychiatrist who has adopted me when Ira is away. He couldn't be reached, either. As I walked, I was back in time re-experiencing the traumas.

I'm stuck on the floor. The tape has me trapped. What is she going to do with the hammer? My head. She will crack open my head. My brains will be all over the floor. Maybe she'll just break my bones.

Stop this! You aren't the child. You're fifty. You're not on the floor.

I can't breathe. The hammer. What will she do with the hammer? My hair pinches. I smell her. I hate her smell. Brown hairs. Straight blond-brown hairs and her smell like old cheese. Her legs are over my face. Why doesn't she wear underpants? Everyone wears underpants. I hate her. I'll bite her if she gets closer. The hammer—where will she put it? It's too big for my holes.

Take deep breaths. Count to ten. You're not nine. You're not in third grade. That was long ago. This is just a memory. You're not there anymore.

Tap. Tap. Smash. The pain. I'm not here. I'll go away. Can't leave. The pain. My teeth. My teeth. Choking. Can't breathe. Gurgle. Can't scream. My teeth—stuck in my throat. I'll die. Good! I'll die. Far away. I'll go far away. Tape is ripping. My head—rip! Choke! Gag! Spit the blood and teeth out. My teeth are gone! Oh! My teeth! Tongue feels cut, sharp edges. Electric pain. Is my face gone? Is my whole face smashed in? I can't feel my face. Maybe no face. I can see. Do I have a nose? Emily come back. Take this face and run away. We'll hide in our room forever. Too ugly to be seen. Maybe we can die now. The pain. Oh! It hurts!

Stop crying. You're not the child. You've grown up. This won't happen again. You're regressing.

I taste my blood. Blood everywhere. My blouse is red. The floor is red. My teeth! How will I chew?

Deep, slow breaths. Call Ira again. He doesn't know what this is like, he never had his teeth knocked out. Yes, he'll know. He understands everything. He's gone. I need to die. I can't remember any more. Life isn't worth this. How to do it? Lots of ways. No! Breathe deeply. Shit on breathing deeply! No teeth. Maybe I should call Bobby. Of anyone, he remembers. He says not to call him. He's as fragile as I am. I'm alone, so alone. There is Ira. He knows.

I'm in the laundry chute. The stink. It's all too much. There's no way out.

I thought of the Golden Gate Bridge. There would be no more torture to remember in the blue, cold water of the bay. I kept calling Ira's office from pay phones around the city and then walked some more. There was still the merest thread of an objective self fighting the panic and death impulses. This once-removed third eye standing away from me knew I was in serious trouble. I think the rational voice was Ira's in my mind. "This will pass. Time will give these memories some distance. You can work through this, just look at the progress you've made. You are an adult now, not the child."

This Ira-infused voice in my thoughts took me to a crisis clinic in the heart of the city. Entering, I immediately knew this was a place I didn't want to be. A huge black woman was screaming obscenities on the telephone while lifting her shirt up over her torn bra, then pulling it back down. A dirty man with a stubble-beard was hunched over in an alcoholic stupor, one young guy was being hauled away in handcuffs because he was on a violent PCP trip, and an obviously schizophrenic man sat down next to me, leaning alarmingly close to me and saying lots of words which meant nothing.

I sat crying on a torn, grimy chair and some crisis counselor asked me what I needed. "I just need someone to talk to for a few minutes. I'm trying hard not to die today." They had me wait for about an hour as a colorful assortment of people came and went. Then the young black man with a goatee asked me to come into a private room so he could get information. Instead of asking me why I was crying, he asked me for my name, Social Security number, and what kind of health insurance I had. It scared me because I felt I was suddenly entering The System, but I was crying so much I gave it to him, then blurted out, "Can I just talk to you a few minutes?"

"Sure," he said, "but I just process the applications for the psychologists."

I didn't care. He was a warm body with ears. I could probably have talked to a wall and it wouldn't have mattered.

I babbled out all about the hammer and teeth experience, the laundry chute, other things boiling in my head. I probably cried and talked for twenty minutes to this polite stranger.

"You definitely are in a crisis" was his sage assessment of me. "Our psychologist can help you. It will be just a little while."

"Thank you, but you are the one who helped me by listening. I'm going to go now."

"The doctor might want to hospitalize you."

"That's what I'm afraid of. Bye."

When I got home, Ira called me. He was back in his office and had listened to all my chaotic messages.

"I waited for you today. It was an awful day," I said. "I just keep remembering things."

"It must have been terrible for you. We'll have to talk about it when you come in."

"Now that I'm all cried out, I don't want to die. I just fall into the pain and I can't get out."

"I know. You regress when you remember things."

"I'm sorry. I don't mean to. I really don't mean to."

"I know," said the kind, low voice. "You're doing better all the time. Even with progress there can be times of going backward for a little while."

"I love you so much that I don't really want to die because then I wouldn't see you anymore."

"That's right."

"Ira, tell me I can work through all this." I was crying again. "It feels like it's too much."

"You'll get through this. Look at the other memories that aren't as intense as they were. Just think of how well you have been doing with your job and the fun you've been having as a grandmother. There will be more babies to get well for."

"I forget all that in the bad times."

"You'll have to work harder on that. Take extra medicine if you can't get control. You should catch yourself sooner."

"I feel like Mom killed me. Sometimes I can't even find myself."

"You're definitely there. You'll get stronger."

"At the clinic today I felt fortunate to have you as my psychiatrist. I love you so much for being there for me."

"Call me if you need me."

"I need to cry about my teeth when I see you."

"Of course. You need lots of time to cry."

"I love you."

"That's okay. It's all part of therapy."

"Probably the part that's keeping me alive through all of this."

"I gotta go. Bye."

After we'd hung up, I realized how much of our dialogue had played in my head even when I was in a panic state. I'd been objective enough to seek help, not just let that state totally control me.

"I don't ever want to leave you," I said to Ira when our session was over the other day.

"You can take me with you, inside yourself when you go."

It's a nice feeling to realize I'm beginning to do that. Maybe someday his voice will become my voice and there won't be any more Mother.

After remembering the episode of my teeth, in the course of just a week, a two-year period of my life, from nine years old to eleven, came careening into my consciousness. I thought the abuse just magically stopped after Mom had stabbed me with the fire poker. The abuse was certainly less with Ruth, the housekeeper Dad had hired, who was in our home a good deal of the time, yet it continued every chance Mom had to get me alone.

My anger the night I tried to run away and bit Mom was not isolated anger. As I got older, I got smarter, stronger, and furious at the ongoing torture.

As I entered puberty, Mom would tie me up in my poster bed

with long lengths of clothesline ropes. When my first pubic hairs began to come in, she plucked them out with tweezers. As the months progressed, she was focused on stopping my physical development. She would come into my room at night and try to bind my little budding breasts down with cloth wrapped tightly around my chest. When she'd leave, I'd rip it off in anger.

Emily raged during the beginning of the hormonal roller-coaster years. I was no longer the docile victim. I'd read books. I'd been to other kids' houses. My world went beyond the boundary of my own home. But I still lived in the silent terror of the Gypsies and getting anyone killed if I told about the violence.

Mom tied me up naked and shaved my whole body with a straight razor. "We can't let you have hair like a Jewish whore." As I got stronger, I fought, kicked, and scratched as I was subdued into submission. I thrashed against the ropes and hated Mom as she stuck things in my vagina, saying she was teaching me what to do with my "Jewish cunt."

It angered me to be physically inspected by both Dad, who was probably looking for abuse, and Mom who was trying to think of nonvisible ways of torture.

One time Mom tied me up and took sandpaper and rubbed my nipples raw, then started rubbing it between my legs. I let Emily lie in the bed as I drifted away. When I was untied, my Emily-self leapt at Mom with unsprung hatred. I slammed her against the wall of my room. I hit her in the stomach, then grabbed her throat. I squeezed with my child's hands as hard as I could but she overpowered me and threw me to the floor. Her hands were at my throat, squeezing, squeezing, until I lost consciousness. I remember flashes of lights and colors before everything went black.

During the days these memories were surfacing, I had angry feelings and crying jags. I found myself in my kitchen with my hand splayed out on my cutting board. In a trancelike way I took one of my big knives and was stabbing back and forth between my fingers with the knife. I cut my finger with the knife and was smearing my blood droplets around on the counter and the walls. I was reenacting what I was remembering. Mom used to do that with my hands on the big cutting board. Then I remembered when I was almost eleven creeping down to the kitchen in the

middle of the night and taking the knife she used to terrorize me
with out of the kitchen drawer. The old mottled carbon-steel
knife was in my hand as I went quietly upstairs to Mom's bedroom. It wasn't Emily, or Sophie, or anyone else, it was *I* who was
going to kill her. I went in her room and saw her sleeping like a
beautiful queen with her hair in soft curls on the pillow. I hated
her. I wanted her dead. I went over to her bed with the knife
clenched in both fists. I stood watching her breathe for a long
time, my knife poised over her body, wanting to plunge it into
her. I don't know why I didn't. I began to shake, my bare feet cold
on the hard wood floor. I tiptoed out of the room and put the
knife back in the drawer. I lay awake for hours thinking of all the
places I should have stuck her.

The enemas, the castor oil followed by bouts of diarrhea continued. The invasion of my maturing body continued. I think I
was eleven when after an episode of sexual violation my Emily-
self went down to Dad's library, the forbidden room which was
off limits to the family. It was a huge room with a big carved oak
desk, two walls of books, and at the end a big brick fireplace. On
another wall was his glassed case filled with guns. I opened it and
took out his heavy, long-barreled shotgun. I knew he kept all his
bullets in a box behind some of his books. Bobby had showed me
once how to load his guns. I hoped I was taking the right bullets as
I fumbled with the various sizes.

In an Emily rage I found Mom in her room and jammed the
barrel of the gun into her stomach. "I hate you. I hate you for all
the things you do to me. I'm going to kill you so you never hurt
me again!"

"Please don't. Put that gun down."

"I'm going to kill you because you won't stop. You'll never
stop. I don't want you to hurt me or touch me ever again." I was
screaming and crying at the same time, my hair sticking to my
tears and in my mouth.

I felt powerful as I stood almost eye level with Mom. I'd blast
big holes in her.

"Please, I promise I won't touch you anymore. Don't shoot."
Her hands went over her face as she stood crying, cowering in the
corner of the two flowered walls. I remember wondering what

Mom's parts would look like on the wall. Brains on the walls. Her smeared, red, dripping brains on the walls was what I wanted.

"You're a crazy person! Mothers aren't supposed to hurt kids! I hate you!" I was poking the gun so deeply into her that part of the gun seemed swallowed up.

"I promise I won't hurt you anymore. Just don't shoot."

I stood there wanting to pull the trigger, but felt suddenly frightened. What if I had the wrong bullets or put them in backward? It was not compassion that made me lower the gun, it was fear of the gun. Yet it was a power struggle Emily won for me.

This was not a victorious memory. I felt it somehow put me on an even plane with Mom. She had reduced me to her level of violence. I was like her.

Ira said, "Good for you. What a wonderful memory to be able to hang on to."

"But I don't want to be like Mom! I don't want to know I've got that violence in me." I was sobbing at the concept that I could ever be like her.

"You're not like your mother. You did what you were driven to do."

"I hate her! I hate therapy! Every time I get a definition of who I am, I get a new memory and it changes my view of myself."

"It's part of therapy. It will be healing to have these memories. Your anger is healthy. You aren't like your mother."

"But I became the whore she said I would."

"Not anymore."

"You're a goddamn optimist. I'm remembering more than any person ever should, cutting myself as the memories surface, crying about my teeth getting knocked out, and now finding out I'm an angry person who almost killed my mother.

"That's how therapy works. There can't be too much more to remember. You're getting better."

"I'm exhausted. I don't know how you can be a psychiatrist and go through all this with me."

"It's nothing."

"I swear to God, I think you're as crazy as I am." It was my first laugh in a few weeks. It felt good.

*written in the fifth year of therapy
with Ira Steinman*

PART
THREE

Chapter 13

I t's been ten months since I've been off all drugs and eight months since any new memories of abuse have surfaced. I've been impressed with my improvement.

There are a few key things that have happened in therapy which helped turn me in this new direction. One incident happened several months ago. Ira told me he would be going to India for a month. At that particular time, my home life was full of stress; Dan was working twelve-hour days trying to get a big contract for an office building finished and Kevin had moved back home from Grad school with hepatitis. My anxiety level escalated to great crying jags. I was certain Ira was going to die. I began hearing Mom's voice in my head again telling me to kill myself. The closer the time came for Ira to leave, the more I disintegrated. I even began dissociating again, losing time, but not knowing who I was being. Ira said I called him as "Margaret" a couple of times. That upset me because I thought I wasn't going to come apart like that anymore. I didn't know who this "Margaret" personality was. (I still don't know her.) Mom's angry, threatening presence was all around me. A few days before Ira left, I told him I was sure Mom would find a way to crash his plane because I loved him.

With a shaking of his long index finger he said, "Your mother is dead. You're acting like a child who is about to be locked in a closet. The odds are clearly in my favor that my plane won't crash. You know, Marcia, your regressions are only making things more painful for you. You are not even trying to stay together. Make an effort!"

There was the rational thought that agreed with him: Mom was not some powerful entity ready to dash his plane from the sky and all these feelings were reawakened abandonment feelings. Yet, inside me the voice, the presence, of Mom was ominously there. All the things I'd loved that she had killed were in my mind. I felt I'd jeopardized Ira by loving him. I'd had enough therapy to know I was probably just having crazy thoughts, but there was a compelling energy and "otherness" to the voice of Mom in my head.

Ira called me and said Dr. Leof would see me while he was in India. That was reassuring, for I liked Dr. Leof very much. The closer it got to the day of Ira's leaving, the worse I got. I couldn't get a grip on my thoughts, which became increasingly disjointed. All the past abuse was playing in my head in a montage of images, sounds, and smells.

I called Dr. Leof for an appointment and he told me he was too busy to see me while Ira was away. "But Ira said you'd see me!" My panic was escalating. I cried and begged him to see me, that I'd only take a little time. His rejection was firm.

I called Ira and said, "Dr. Leof won't see me."

Ira said, "You called him a few days ago and asked him for Chinese herbs to help you kill yourself, that you wanted it to look accidental."

"I don't remember doing that! I must have dissociated." I had no reason to believe Dr. Leof lied. I'm certain I did do it, but now I was being rejected once more for something I had no memory of.

"You have to take responsibility for your own behavior. Dr. Leof doesn't want to take the time to deal with this kind of disorganization."

"But he promised me if he was ever in town when you left, or if anything ever happened to you, he would be my psychiatrist. It was a promise!"

Even though I'd only seen Dr. Leof a few times, it felt like abandonment. He knew me. We'd liked each other, and I'd shared my pain with him. Those few people I did share my past with all managed to disengage from knowing me. My crazy, dissociative behavior turned even those I liked and trusted from me. Ira was leaving. Dr. Leof rejected me, even with my pleading and tears. I called him again and sobbed into the phone, "I feel like I'm six and I've shown you the blood in my underwear. You're just one more adult turning away." Then I went on to tell him something to the effect that psychiatrists are like all adults, they just learn to fuck you in a different way.

Dr. Leof was kind enough to call me back, but clear about being too busy to see me. In my unraveling mind, his broken promise was the repetitive abandonment of all the adults of my childhood, who had to have seen the casts, the bruises, the blackened eyes, and never helped me. Mom's voice was intruding, ricocheting, "See! He wants you dead! Everyone wants you to burn. We'll watch as the skin peels off your face." In my off-the-wall state I knew Dr. Leof wanted me dead. I wanted to die. Such a monotonous theme, yet compelling when the intense feelings of childhood overcome me. I wanted to die before Ira died. I *knew* I was distorting reality, yet I couldn't get control of my thoughts.

Ira was leaving at ten the next morning. He called and said, "I'll come to the office early. I'll meet you there at six."

It was eerie driving over the Golden Gate Bridge in the dark. When I arrived at 5:45 A.M., Ira was already making phone calls. At six, he asked me to come into his office, which was cold and filled with shadows from the streetlights outside. I sat across from him, and all I thought about was the gesture he had just made by seeing me at that time in the morning when he was getting ready to be gone for four weeks. After all the kind words, the many phone calls, the attentiveness of four years, there is nothing that reached me more deeply, or made me feel more loved, than sitting across from Ira before the sun was even up and having him pour us both hot tea as though this was exactly what he wanted to do with his time. I think the gesture profoundly reached me because my behavior had been abominable. Here was Ira acting cheerful and warm toward me. Suddenly, in the face of such unwavering commitment, I was overcome with a sense of responsibility for getting well. I don't think there is anyone in my life, except my dad on the day he took me away from my mother, who made me feel as valuable a person as Ira made me feel that morning.

We sat and talked about how I would cope while he was gone. We discussed my going in the hospital, but I had no insurance or money. I asked for medication, but Ira said that I didn't need all the regression and histrionics. He said he'd talked to Dr. Hambler, who agreed to see me while he was gone.

"Dr. Hambler! I can't see him! He abandoned me and our therapy. I couldn't see him without you being here!"

"I think you've both changed in four years. I think you'll be surprised at your own growth. Right now you don't have a lot of choices, unless you choose to pull yourself together and not see anyone while I'm gone."

He got up and phoned Dr. Hambler while I was there, arranging for me to see him.

Ira wouldn't let me hug him good-bye. I left his office as the newspaper truck drove by in the gray early light. I walked up the street to my car and looked back at his big white office building and the light shining out of his window. Mom cackled with glee, "He's going to die. Just you wait. He's going to die." I vomited into the gutter and drove home crying. But there was a new strength, a determination I would be worthy of the gesture of love that had been given me.

I vomited and had diarrhea all morning, and when ten o'clock came I was shaking all over, almost like the state of shock I was in as a child after an attack of violence. I called Ira just as he was headed out the door. "I'll be fine while you're gone. Have a happy trip. I love you."

"Thanks. Go look in the mirror and concentrate on seeing the mature woman you are. Stay that way. I gotta go. Bye." The voice was warm. I hung up and didn't even make it to the toilet before I threw up again; bile-green on the bathroom floor.

I listened to all the news broadcasts for the next twenty-four hours, hoping not to hear of any airplane crashes. There weren't any. I wanted to lie for a month in a warm, black womb, hearing and seeing nothing, but I began to pull together, thinking about how much I wanted to honor the investment and caring Ira had given me for four years. It took me two days of lying in bed, bereft but fighting, really fighting all the crazy thoughts. The third day I forced myself to get up. Instead of just succumbing to the feelings of my childhood, I got dressed, and made myself put on my old blue apron, the one Sophie always wore. Feeling like every movement of my body was in slow motion, I began to bake bread. As though I were taking care of Ira by the gesture of baking, I kneaded and baked all day long. By evening, Dan came into the kitchen and laughed at the ten loaves of challah, the rich, twisted Jewish egg bread my grandmother used to make, lying on every countertop. There was a snow dusting of flour and sesame seeds everywhere. In my mind I was giving Ira a gift for all his time, for believing in me. In the process, I began to pull back together.

Every morning I gave myself a list of tasks to do so I wouldn't just sit like a zombie for a month. I called Dr. Hambler and made an appointment.

That next week I walked up the once familiar stairs to his office. In spite of my apprehension and desire to bolt from the room, there was an immediate warmth between us. We had shared a journey in therapy for eighteen months, so we were instantly comfortable. What was new was our ability to relate to each other. It was an odd experience, feeling I'd come full circle. Here I was sitting with Dr. Hambler, who had terminated our therapy, and we were talking and analyzing it like adults. I was returning to a place of trauma knowing I was no longer the same person I was four years before. In spite of the big regressions and even suicidal days I still had sometimes, the trend was toward a more stable self. I was able to talk about our emotionally charged therapy and remain intact.

With a comfortable ease Dr. Hambler talked about how our therapy had fallen apart. He said he had been overwhelmed by my pain and had put up a shield around himself to insulate himself from it. I had felt that and taken it as rejection.

"Why did you end our therapy so abruptly?" I asked. "You knew I was suicidal."

"I felt I was in danger. I thought you might come after me," he answered quietly.

I sat across from this sensitive, kind-looking man and began to cry. "I can't tell you that what you felt was wrong. I'm sorry if I was that crazy."

"I think we're both sorry for what happened. I'm just glad you're doing so well with Ira." Watching my tears of sorrow for what I'd put him through he said, "With all the terrible things that happened to you as a child, it surprises me that you still have so much humanity left in you." I thought that was a lovely thing to say.

I saw him twice more while Ira was gone. I stayed mature and controlled with him, enjoying my ability to be intact, delighting in the awareness of how far I'd come since the suicidal days with all the multiple voices in my mind.

We parted warmly, both of us knowing I was in therapy with exactly the right psychiatrist.

As I left I felt overcome with emotions, realizing the gift Ira was giving me, in taking someone as disturbed as I had been, and often still was, as a paitent. I drove to the Japanese Tea Garden in Golden Gate Park and sat drinking green tea by a quiet pond, my tears flowing soundlessly.

It meant a great deal to me that Dr. Leof later called me back and apologized for not being available to see me as he had promised. He had had several patients of his own in crises and didn't have even one more minute in his days. I went to see him for a session and realized once again how I repetitively bring my past into present relationships. He greeted me with a big bear hug and told me what important work Ira and I were doing together. He seemed genuinely pleased with my progress, saying, "Most psychiatrists wouldn't even have tried to do therapy with you, they would just have given you medication. You're lucky to have Ira." We mutually reinstated my being his adopted patient when Ira is gone. On a couple of occasions he has swapped sessions for applesauce cake. Ira is not the only extraordinary psychiatrist around.

When Ira got home, he called me. "There aren't any long, tearful messages from you on my machine, just a message from Dr. Hambler that you have done well."

"I'm so proud of myself! I really pulled things together. I've had a busy few weeks. I can hardly wait to see you tomorrow!"

It amazed me how suddenly shy I felt the morning of my appointment. I always struggle with my empty air, no face feelings, as though Ira woudn't recognize me.

He greeted me warmly when I arrived, but instead of sitting down to talk, he stood at his desk fiddling with his answering machine. "It's broken," he said.

"Please come sit down and talk to me," I said. Any change in our routine upset me. I get instantly small-child jealous, wanting his full attention. "I've waited forever for you to get back. Come sit down!"

"Just a second. I guess I'll need to buy a new machine. It's an important tool of my profession. It seems to me that possibly on one or two occasions you have left a message for me." I noticed his easy to smile face beginning to crinkle, his mouth lifting at the edges.

"Me? No! When have I ever bothered you, or called you? You must be thinking of some other paitent!" I grinned back at him, feeling the gift again at that moment.

A real turning point in therapy happened just a couple of months ago; one of those moments of epiphany that makes everything seem new. After all this time with Ira, I have understood on an intellectual level that the presence of Mom that comes alive during times of stress, or when the memories of abuse are reactivated in my mind, are probably just another dissociative voice. But inside, way in my interior self, I have so strongly felt the omnipotent, ominous power of Mom that I really have felt she still was alive in some evil dimension of life after death. The exorcisms, the discussions, examining the possibility of her presence with Ira, has not been able to take away the complete sense of "otherness" to the voice. I could accept being a multiple personality. I could agree that Emily, Joey, and the "others" couldn't actually be different selves even when they felt "other." But Mom whispering, "Die, Jew! Pick up a knife and cut yourself.

Jews are meant to suffer" couldn't be any part of my own mind. No matter how often Ira said that Mom was dead and it was not a real message, a real voice, I didn't believe he was right. I wanted to believe him. I wanted the voice to stop. It's impossible to convey the terror I've felt over the years at this voice urging me to kill myself. When Mom was alive, I thought it was mental telepathy. When she was dead, I considered her a ghost too evil to be allowed entrance to any afterlife, and most certainly too powerful to lie quietly in the ground and turn back into recycled molecules. There is no one more huge or powerful in the child-mind than the memory of the violent abuser. How could she be dead when she wrapped her dynamic, malevolent presence around me and taunted me to die?

Ira told me he couldn't see me at my normal time for the next session and told me to come at five o'clock.

"Then I will be on the bridge in rush hour traffic. I hate that. I always hear Mom's voice if I'm stopped on the bridge. She tells me to jump off."

"Those are just your own paranoid thoughts. It's your imagination."

We'd been over this dozens of times before. Now I really thought about it. Ira's word "imagination" stuck in my mind. If Mom's voice was just my imagination, maybe I needed to use my imagination to solve the problem. It certainly wasn't getting intellectualized away.

If I could invent a voice, why couldn't I use my imagination to find a way to stop it? I already knew that the death of the other personalities had been hysterical imagination, just a way of resolving what Ira had helped me to see; that they weren't real, merely aspects of myself. Maybe Mom was just another split-off part of my own mind . . . I still wasn't convinced, but I thought a lot about it.

For some reason I thought of a wooden apple puzzle I'd seen. It was a big round apple made up of three-dimensional jigsaw pieces that all fit together. I thought how the mind is like a puzzle. It was clear that all the pieces of me that should have formed a whole had been in disarray my whole life. I wanted some way to visualize the self back together, to conquer this ongoing terror. Why was the voice of my mother so definitely an outside force?

Ira had kept reinforcing that there was no evil, hovering mother, she was just my own mind bringing to life the terrorizing commands of childhood. I wanted to believe him, yet every time I heard the voice, listened to the taunts, I became a frightened young child backed against the wall, seeing the huge figure coming toward me, anticipating the approaching pain.

The next day Dan was at the hospital with Kevin, who was still sick, and I felt Mom's presence. I went in my bedroom and flopped down on the bed. I breathed deep, slow breaths like Ira had shown me. Closing my eyes, I began to think of the apple. I gave all the jigsaw pieces the names of Emily, Sunshine, Sophie, and all my "others." The biggest piece I labeled "Mom." I was the apple core, the solid center. I put the pieces into the puzzle one at a time, feeling them lock in place. The hardest part was taking this big, jagged, piece labeled "Mom" and pulling it in. I twisted and turned it to fit the hole in the apple. I made my apple core magnetized (which is ridiculous because my puzzle was wood, but this is my imagination—so what the heck!). It took an incredible visualizing effort to bring the "Mom" piece into the apple, but I did it. An amazing thing happened when I locked the piece in place. The voice stopped. The "otherness" was gone. I commanded there to be a central thought switchboard, and I had the controls. "All incoming thoughts must be monitored by me," I commanded the pieces.

It wasn't until that moment that I knew, really *knew* that the voice of Mom was just my own mind reactivating the terrorizing words from childhood. It wasn't Ira telling me, or some rational, linear part of my brain agreeing. I knew it way inside. If I could pull the voice, the presence of Mom, into my apple and have her disappear, then I had control over it. She was not a separate entity. Deciding I had power over her presence in my mind was vastly different from four years ago, for then I had still viewed her as an actual, real, evil force.

I doubt that Thomas Edison was any more excited with his incandescent light than I was with my apple.

My new sense of certainty that Mom is not really here waiting to annihilate me in some creative, torturous way has been one of the happiest things that has happened to me. "Hurray! Mom isn't here. I'm just paranoid!" I want to shout it to the sky. Who would ever understand that realizing I'm nuts is such a relief!

It is a thousand times easier now during the stressful times knowing that it's just my own mind unraveling a bit, instead of having the terrified, persecuted feeling that Mom was trying to find ways to kill me. It's easy now just to think, Oh, here are the crazy thoughts coming into my mind. Relax. Breathe deeply. Pull the pieces back together. Why did it take me so long to figure this out? Scratch all the bragging about my high intelligence! I'm probably about as smart as the average tree frog.

Now that Mom seems truly gone for the first time in my life I feel lighter, like a giant load is gone. I also feel embarrassed. I honestly believed it all—the other personalities, Mom stalking me— and I didn't even know I was crazy! I just made up my own reality. I think I read this somewhere in Carlos Casteneda's, *The Teachings of Don Juan:* "Reality is merely one explanation for the way things actually are." I was willing to live with the concept that I was just constructed differently. My inner pain was so huge that I honestly wasn't even concerned that my elaborate explanations of myself and my other personalities clearly couldn't stand up to the test of known external realities.

A curious thing happened with my apple trick. I began to visualize the other personalities with greater clarity. I'm recovering more memory of things I did and said while I was functioning dissociatively. Emily and the other aspects of me aren't dead. It was all just me.

I'm actually getting now so I recognize what is a crazy thought before Ira tells me. It's a big step forward when one recognizes one's own insanity. It has taken a deeply trusting relationship with Ira to have the candidness and honesty to let him enter all the mixed-up perceptions and try to rearrange them. I'm smiling as I write this, for Ira would not have given me the choice to stay crazy. I've had angry, shouting, door-slamming sessions with him because of my confused view of what he was saying. But he made it very clear he would not tolerate any other option but for me to get well.

The closer I get to being well the more embarrassing it is looking back at all I've said to Ira. During our sessions I've told him in total sincerity that Sunshine had done something, or that he was in danger of getting killed by Mom because she knew I loved him.

I'm in awe of the generosity that lets him sit graciously week after week with a patient as disturbed as I've been and go through the effort of repetitively bringing probing, rational discourse to thoughts that dip in and out of psychosis. Thinking about some of our conversations, I don't know how he kept from howling with laughter. It seems funny to me now.

I am less erratic, but I still get easily upset. So many things trigger the painful memories. I have an arousal button to the past abuses that goes off as fast as a booby trap hidden in loose sand.

Dozens of times a day there are visual, verbal, sensory stimuli that set off the feelings or memory of the torture. I'm finally getting to the point where I can stop the explosion in my mind that sets up the regressions or the mental shifting. Over and over as Ira has watched me regress into the tearful, childlike state, he has demanded I examine the trigger thoughts, the cues. I'm learning to pull a "STOP ACTION!" in my mind and think about what I'm seeing or feeling. I'm not always successful, but Ira was right—the more I practice and try, the easier it is getting to stay the adult.

The price I'm paying in not shifting to other personalities is that I have to stay with my pain and memories. I doubt my mind will ever be a comfortable place, but it is wonderful not to be fractured to the point of not always feeling disconnected from everything around me.

Recently, Bobby came to stay for a week because he was having marital problems. I was able to listen to his troubles and be supportive of him. I've been a good listener to Dan, who has the pressures of a new business. It's a new experience to be stable enough not to get sucked down by the problems of those around me.

There is a new, stronger self which is becoming attracted to life. The ongoing suicidal ideas are receding. I find myself looking forward to things, free from the ominous presence of the imagined mother, the shackles of being a multiple personality.

Learning to be the guardian of my own thoughts is an enormous task. It's still easier to be crazy than sane. Change has occurred because I decided to learn to change. It's also because Ira has the persistence of a pit bull. There are times when I'd like to regress and not cope, not exert the discipline it takes to constantly examine my thoughts. Other times my thoughts seem perfectly rational to me, but not to Ira. When we disagree, he makes me look at my thoughts or actions in a commanding way. With forehead furrowed, eyes narrowed, he says, "Sit down! Be quiet and listen!" Then he will address my disorganized thoughts.

There is an evolution way beyond the cognitive in therapy, for a whole spectrum of things is happening inside me that I can't define. The experiences I remembered just last year of seeing the baby burn and getting my teeth knocked out made me suicidal, and I cried for months. The other day I talked to Ira about my teeth, and I didn't even cry. There was a quieting of the intensity. There are some days now that I live completely in the present— whole, total days of being involved in the pleasures of the now.

There are times of pure delight just experiencing simple things. I am still the oral of Joey, the tactile of Camille, the fun-loving of Muriel. I'm certain in my coming together to a saner state, I feel a more intense pleasure at being able to fully participate in my external world. My greatest joy right now is being with my two grandchildren. I am fully with them in a way I wasn't able to be when Kevin and Cindi were small. I am giving the child in me free rein to throw bread to seagulls and go down slides on pieces of waxed paper. At the beach I make big sand castles with my two enthusiastic helpers, holding little plastic shovels, scooping mounds of wet sand onto our tower and in our hair and eyes. At the zoo we jump and hoot in front of the monkeys and leave scatterings of popcorn for the wild chickens that follow us. More than anything I am connecting with the little sticky kisses that get pressed on me. I love the warm, quick breaths next to my face as we lie on the carpet reading *Winnie the Pooh*. The little arms that wrap around my legs when I have to leave, and the sweet faces pressed to the window when they hear my car arrive are filling me, filling me.

I wish Ira was more a part of the new world of pleasure and wholeness I'm entering. I don't seem to bring him that, for he drifts away if I talk about grandchildren or an interesting book I've just read. I know there isn't time to share my joys when our minutes are preciously few. The pain demands a tithing in tears. It's getting so I can go between therapy sessions fairly well, but the thoughts are storing, the multitude of feelings are rising. We can't waste even a moment. Ira is the one person who will let me share my pain with him. I function better when I give time to the tiny young child who still lives in me. I curl on his floor, just inches from his shoes that I wish I could touch, and all the feelings, the hurts, rise up in sobs. I haven't yet left the pain behind. It seems self-indulgent to say I'm into my fifth year of crying about things that happened to me so long ago. The tears are like the little drops of acid my old chemistry professor dropped into the cloudy calcium solution to turn the mixture sparkling clear. The tears shed in the presence of Ira are causing a transformation way down to my center. If not an atomic one, certainly a psychological one.

It's as though I'm holding his hand and bringing the adult protector back with me into the closet, into the bed where the scarves bound me. My child-self is saying, "Let me show you the pain, the horror. Come back with me to the places that are so terrifying I can hardly breathe, but don't let go of my hand. Be with me while we turn on the light in that black closet and smell the stink with me." Each time I bring him back with me I'm a little braver, a little stronger. Maybe I'm not just bringing his adult presence into the terror, maybe I'm bringing my adult self back, too.

Even though I still cry with Ira, I'm getting better and better at leaving the pain with him. I can leave his office with rumpled clothes, hair sticking to my cheeks and my collar still damp from tears, but I feel better because I'm more able to return to being the adult.

Over the past years of therapy with Ira I have brought him pictures I've drawn, given him photographs of me, and written him things. I thought the only trace of my existence that he, or *anyone*, would remember, would be some concrete, physical item. I began this book for him, not to try to organize my experiences, but to give him words on a page so he would remember I have lived. Once when he left for a vacation, I asked, "Will you remember me when you get back?" He gave me a quizzical look as though it didn't even deserve a reply. But I remember my anxiety of feeling I was as vacant as a roomful of air. I honestly believed if people didn't see me for a few weeks it would be as though all trace of me would leave their minds.

I frequently said to Ira, "Thank you for treating me as though I were a person."

His response was always, "You *are* a person."

I'd hear his reply, but sitting in the chair across from him would be the many pieces, the inconsistent lump of life.

A few weeks ago, I asked Ira, "Do you think I have a soul?"

"What do you think a soul is?"

"I'm not sure. But I think I have one. When I sit here, I feel really here. When I leave here, I feel that there is a presence you'll remember. When the clock ticks, I'm all in one place. When I look in the mirror, I see just one face. Mostly, way inside I'm beginning to think I'm a person."

"You've always been a person."

"No. I used to be lots of people."

Ira smiled and said, "You still have that wrong. You've always been one person, you just thought you were several."

"Yeah, you're right. When I think back, it still seems like there were several selves, not just one. It's marvelous to not have other voices in my mind. I wish I could explain to you the evolution I feel inside."

"I think I understand it."

"I don't have to touch my face all the time to feel if it's there. When I close my eyes, I don't visualize all the skin burned off, or think the face is one other than the one I have now. I have a certainty that I actually exist."

"How long have you felt that inside, the feeling you have a soul?"

"It's new. Not until the voice of what I thought was Mom stopped. I guess it's been happening over time. It's as though I've gone from a liquid to a solid. What is that feeling?"

"What do you think it is?"

"Ira! You always throw things back at me." I thought for a minute. "It's an awareness of my own congregated energy. A feeling of my own presence. I guess it's a sense of self. I don't really know what is happening to me, but it's a happy feeling. When I visualized myself as the apple core in my little pulling-it-all-together trick, I realized I couldn't have done it without feeling the power of the core. It was the certainty of an inner substance. I'm beginning to be a definable being to myself. How have we done it?"

"It's what therapy is all about."

Sinking back into the cool leather chair, tears suddenly sprang in my eyes. I looked at Ira, with his gray, shaggy hair that he can't find time to cut, his scuffed shoes, and the world's most compassionate smile, and said, "I wish I could put into words all the things that are changing inside me. Even if I never progress past this point, it will have been worth it. Thank you for all you have done for me." Looking at Ira, I added anxiously, "But I don't think I'm ready to end therapy yet!" Suddenly, my emotions had shifted; I'd opened the door to abandonment feelings. In that second I caught the regression that was about to happen. I sat up straighter in the chair.

Ira was watching me with his steady gray eyes, which never miss anything. We looked at each other and we both knew I'd stopped myself from slipping into those feelings of childhood. He continued to hold my gaze. I gave him a big smile. "I'm making progress!"

"Yes, you are. Time to go. Call me if you need me."

PART
FOUR

Chapter 14

Soon I will begin my sixth year of therapy with Ira. What a long journey for both of us. We both know I'm not finished yet, but my progress is exciting. This last year has been one of the best of my life, except for a period of about five weeks when another memory surfaced. I don't think my mind has ever forgotten any of the abuse, it's just been compartmentalized, subdivided to hold it all at bay. My body remembered with the pain and physical symptoms.

For a period of weeks I was obsessed by food, thinking about it, planning meals, cooking, baking, filling my pantry like a squirrel getting ready for winter. This was a Sophie thing. I didn't completely dissociate into being Sophie, just the aspects of that subdivided side to me had a priority to it. I found myself putting on my Sophie apron and compulsively baking cookies and eating half the batch, feeling bilious and comforted when I was done. I'd sit in my Sophie rocking chair going back and forth in a glutted sugar high trying to block out the emptiness, the pain that still rises up.

I gained fifteen pounds in a period of just weeks and was upset at the compulsiveness of my behavior. I wasn't even hungry. It was psychological.

Ira wasn't very concerned about it. He chuckled as I brought him cakes and cookies, and asked me if I wanted to talk about it.

I would lie on his floor on the Oriental carpet and let the thoughts free-flow.

"People taste like sweet pork, Mom once said, only the fat tastes like lamb. She talked about eating me, sweet pork flavor. The first meal I had in the hospital after getting stabbed when I was ten was lamb chops. I didn't know why. I thought it was some kind of plan to fatten me, like Gretal in the fairy tale.

"Angry. Angry feelings at eleven and twelve. I wanted to be fat—gagging lamb fat all around me. I'd make Mom choke when she swallowed me.

"The picture of Jews in the concentration camps. Mom said the soldiers made soup of the Jews' bones. Would I look like a beef knuckle when I was boiled? Would the meat fall off the bones? My meat, where was my meat, I wondered when I was small. Would it be albacore pink or chicken white?

"Hungry. Lying in bed at night with no dinner. Daddy's gone, always gone. No dinner for any of us. Stomach growls. Hungry. Sneak down back stairs. Don't be heard. Don't get caught. If Dad was home we were safe. Refrigerator raids when we awoke at 2 A.M. Dog food was never noticed if it was missing. Rolled oats okay, box was never checked. No cookies. No cake. Mom would know it was missing. No fruit. She counted. A slice of bread okay if the loaf was big. Cream of Wheat mixed with water trickled in it. Eat it crunchy. Couldn't cook or make smells or noise to wake Mom. Crunchy Cream of Wheat. A few crackers if the box was full. Leave no crumbs. No trace. No box out of place.

"Sandwiches, half-apples, raisins in school trash cans. Crusts with clinging peanut butter. Brush flies off the can. Look nonchalant near trash cans. Check who's watching. Grab whatever the hand could get fast. Caught if I browsed. Grab fast. Eat fast. Stuff inside my sweater.

"Grandma's Haviland bowl with little pink flowers sitting on the sideboard always waiting for me with chocolate-covered raisins. Sometimes lemon drops. Abazaba bars in her kitchen drawer next to the napkins. Always black pumpernickel bread and sweet butter and heaped with raspberry jam. Homemade raspberry jam with seeds that stick in my teeth. Sugar cookies, flaky and eaten warm out of the oven. Reading books with Grandma, sucking lemon drops, leaning against her large, soft breasts, smelling the scent of lavender soap. Her hair was long and smelled of kitchen smells; no perfume like Mom wore. Cashew nuts in a bowl shaped like a turtle. Dried apricots. Grandma loved apricots. I love apricots. I was safe with Grandma. Safe and cookies. Safe and chocolate. Safe and full.

"I hate Mom. I want her to die in my mind. Out of my mind! Stop the conversations. 'I wish I'd fried you when you were tiny enough to fit in the Dutch oven. Your skin would be good crispy.' The baby was crispy in the fire. She didn't eat the baby, at least I don't think she ate it. Of course not, that's a terrible thought. But she talked about what King would taste like. Dog meat. Some people eat dog meat. When I read about cannibals in school, dark men with bones in their noses, I used to think they were Gypsies. Maybe they would eat me. Did Mom learn about eating people from Gypsies with bones in their noses?"

Sitting upright, I looked at Ira. "I have a lot of confusing, conflicting thoughts about food. But that's not explaining why I'm eating all the time. When I used to be Emily I sometimes ate and ate and then made myself vomit. I hate throwing up. Why am I eating so compulsively?"

"Do you think you're trying to choke down your anger?" Ira asked.

"I don't know. Maybe."

I went home and continued eating. Somehow it was connected to the nightmare I've had forever that reoccurs on a regular basis. I'm always being suffocated in an avalache. I was sleeping less and less, getting up to eat in the night when the nightmare came.

It was almost Easter, and I'm not sure what prompted the memory to surface. I was at home having trouble breathing, feeling anxious, trying to stop the anxiety by leafing through one of my hundred cookbooks, my comfort books. Then it all came back to me.

I was almost twelve and I don't remember what the situation was, but I remember being naked in my room and I was scream-

ing at Mom. She tied me around and around with a rope and I
was dragged down the stairs, banging on the steps. My shin
crashed against the sharp banister. Mom dragged me outside in
the twilight sky. Jimmy, who was nine, had been digging a swimming pool in the backyard for two days; about a three- or four-
foot deep hole and about six feet long. He had confided in me he
was building us an escape tunnel to China, but he told Mom it
was for a pool.

Mom hauled me to the mound of dirt at the edge of the hole
and dumped my tied-up naked body in the dirt pit. I felt the alarm
of falling without being able to put my arms out to stop. I landed
with a thud, facedown in the dirt. Mom climbed in, turned me
over. I was choking on the dirt in my mouth. She was talking to
her angel, something about Passover and the Angel of Death coming for me in the night. Then she put her finger in the blood from
my gashed leg and drew something on my forehead. The blood
trickled a few drops into my eye. I couldn't wipe it out, for I was
tied up.

Mom commanded Jimmy to come outside and shovel dirt on
top of me. "Bury her!" she commanded. "But leave her head out.
I don't want to go to jail for murder." He tried to break away
from Mom, but she had him by the T-shirt. "Shovel!" she commanded.

I watched him as he plunked the dirt down on top of me. He
was crying, and snot was running down his face. Then Mom was
on her knees above me throwing handfuls of dirt on me saying
things about the Angel of Death taking me away in the night.

As the dirt encased my naked body, it became more and more
difficult to breathe. I spit out little grains of soil and panted shal-
lowly as the weight of my grave pressed down on my chest.
Jimmy was sobbing as Mom hauled him into the house. The slam
of the back door had a finality to it.

More than anything, I remember the terror of not being able
to breathe deeply, just shallow gasps. I'm certain my panic added
to my sense of asphyxiation.

The memories of the night are disjointed. A cat came and
licked my face in the dark, a friendly cat, but it was frightening
that I couldn't get away from the tongue licking the blood off my
forehead. All the repetitive fears—my death, hunger, thirst, the

numbing, repetitive worries of a lifetime of abuse were there, and a fear of worms crawling in my vagina. That seemed horrifying, worms in my vagina. My female center had been host to too many objects already, but worms crawling inside made my breath even harder to get. I never screamed. Mom would kill me or kill Jimmy, I thought.

The next thing I remember was Bobby digging me out in the shadow of dark sky that was just bluing with dawn. He was crying softly and when he had me dug out and the rope untied, I couldn't move. I was so cold, and numb, he had to half carry, half drag me into the house and up the back stairs to his bathroom, where he put me into the tub.

"We have to tell Dad," he said. "We can't let this happen anymore. She's going to kill you one of these days."

"It'll just make it worse," I said, as I ducked my head under the water to wipe more of the dirt and blood off my face.

"Maybe we should kill her," Bobby said.

"But we might go to jail forever. I hate her. I hate her guts," I said.

It was that experience that led me the next weekend to tell Daddy all about what Mom was doing to me. Bobby said if I didn't tell Dad, he would. I remember the feeling of certainty that in telling Dad I was finally agreeing inside with all my many selves that this was the end, my death might as well come sooner than later. Telling Dad was a swan song. I had no more hope or fight.

Along with recalling this experience, there came memories of rage, the livid anger at the ongoing abuse. I was no longer the passive small child by twelve. I had experienced rage and been beaten. Remembering this burial brought back feelings of passionate hatred.

Unfortunately it was a three-day wait to talk to Ira. By that time I was angry at him. He was busy and only half attentive. "It's just another memory. There will probably be others," he said as he crunched the apple I'd brought him.

Everything about our session ticked me off. He wanted me to maintain a mature, objective view of this one more memory of abuse. He said, "It certainly can't be as painful an experience as seeing the baby get burned." He was trying to say how those intense feelings got more manageable with therapy and time, but to me he was qualifying and categorizing my experiences, as though I should just discount being buried in the ground and feeling the panic of not being able to breathe.

I told him to go to hell and slammed the door as I left. During the next four weeks, I failed to pull things together. I went to my sessions, but had diarrhea before seeing him, and in between sessions called him to say, "I'm quitting therapy. You're just keeping me in therapy because you want me to suffer." I regressed into Sunshine. He said I called him asking him to be my daddy.

Ira generously let me come to his office at the end of one day for an extra twenty minutes to talk about the transference, which didn't pull me together, for in my mind I was six and he wanted me dead. It was dark when we both left his office, and the next thing I knew it was the middle of the night and I was crouched by a big trash dumpster, about three miles from my car, with three black men in an alley talking and watching me. I was back to the present, and they were kind enough to tell me where I was.

I called Dr. Hambler several times. Once I was suicidal and decided to check in to a hotel to take sleeping pills. Another time I called him, sobbing that Ira wanted me dead. I wrote Ira long letters about how he had turned stone-cold toward me, that I knew I had ruined the relationship between us. I went to see Dr. Leof and asked him if Ira abused his own children. At the time, I didn't even see this as ridiculous.

As Ira later put it, "You were having a temper tantrum all over town. You were just projecting all the cold hatefulness of your mother onto me."

The closeness I'd felt with him broke down in me during those few weeks. I didn't tell him everything I was thinking and doing anymore. I didn't tell him that there were dissociative voices, Mom's voice getting louder and louder, cackling, whispering, "Jews are meant to die."

Ira was going to be away for the weekend, and it again became abandonment. My Friday session was canceled and I felt enraged, and without being able to step out of the regressed, convoluted thoughts I went home telling Dan, "I need time just to be alone." After a lifetime of my disappearing, he accepted it one more time, but there was a look of hurt in his eyes.

"Do you want me to go with you?" he asked.

"No. I don't know what's wrong. I just have to be by myself."
I threw random, irrelevant objects into my blue canvas sports bag.

"Don't you think you ought to talk to Ira?"

"No! He is so damn sadistic. I'm never going back."

"That seems rash to me," said Dan. "Especially after you have made all these good changes. Your feelings are excessive."

I was crying. I hated all the reasonable people around me. I hated Dan for wanting to pawn me off on Ira, for never once saying, "Can I help?"

I hated everyone because I couldn't make the voices in my head shut up, those damn "Jews should die" voices.

I drove up the coast and into the woods. I drifted around in my head, escaping to another place in my mind. It is humiliating to say, but I wanted the familiarity of craziness. I don't remember calling anyone for help, I was in comfortable madness, seeking a dirt grave. Ira says I called him several times as Sunshine and then as Emily, asking if he wanted his cock sucked. I have only a gauzy, distant memory of digging down in the dirt past the pine needles and little wildflowers. With bare hands I couldn't dig far, but I lay all night in these woods, smelling the forest-rich earth, hearing the grinding noises as two large pines rubbed each other in the breezes off the coast. It was damp sea air that chilled me to shivering. The dirt was cold, dark, hard, and felt familiar. It felt right.

By morning, the storm of memory, the babble of Mom's death threats, subsided. Rational thought seeped into my mind. Unlike the past, when craziness just bashed me around, I knew I'd let myself regress. In my distorted relationship with Ira, I hadn't been honest with him. I hadn't tried to get help when the craziness started. Once I'm really into the place in my head that holds the horror, I can't easily get out, but there were moments before when I could have taken medication, could have told Ira about the voices before he left instead of slamming the phone down on him.

I drove back down the coast with a new feeling of calm. The initial hurricane of feelings had blown through. I washed in the icy ocean just north of Bodega Bay, then lay in the sun, which still didn't warm me, for the air was cold, and let myself dry. I couldn't arrive home all wet. That night I apologized to Dan, who had been seeing my crying jags for the past weeks.

"That's okay," he said. "Are you feeling better now?"

"Yeah. I'm better. I'm really sorry, though."

Dan never pressed me for more. He's shared a lifetime of un-predictable behavior.

That next Tuesday I was back in Ira's office, back to seeing the face of the man who is my best friend. I felt overcome with sor-row and humiliation once again for the regression, the craziness, which days before seemed absolutely sincere and real. Ira pressed me about what I had done over the weekend, demanding details, and wouldn't let me be evasive. I felt a failure.

"I'm so sorry," I said. "After all this time and therapy, I don't know how I could have gotten everything so turned around in my mind. You haven't really been wishing I were dead, have you?"

"Of course not," he said. "You've been back into your child-hood, transferring all kinds of things on to me."

I sat crying again. "I really am sorry."

"Sorry isn't the issue. Learn to catch it. Don't allow yourself to regress," he said for the thousandth time.

For the first time I knew he was right. There had been the very small window of opportunity when the rational and irrational thoughts had been zinging around together, that sort of third-eye objective view when I knew I was progressing into crazy. There was even the humiliation of knowing I'd wanted the whispers, the cacophony of the voices, of Mom's voice. Terror, pain, death threats, cold dirt was familiar—sick, but familiar.

For the next couple of weeks I was still anxious, not sleeping well, and eating and eating. I said to Ira, "I know I've told you I don't think Mom is still alive like a ghost, but when her voice came back, it was too real. I heard her breathing. I think maybe you're wrong. I think she really is alive, that it's a real psychic presence."

"She's not a ghost. If you believe that, you're being psychotic."

"You just don't understand because you're not a psychic per-son."

Ira sat and roared with laughter.

Between sessions, I was trying to untangle all my confused

thoughts. After my pulling in the jigsaw puzzle pieces I was so sure she didn't exist, and now I'd backtracked to being unsure. I called Ira. "What if when I come for my session you sit really quietly with me and see if you can hear my mother?" I instantly knew I was being stupid. Ira affirmed that thought with laughter.

"She is dead. It's just your imagination, but I'll be glad to have you bring her in with you when you come."

When Ira ushered me into his office, he said, "Well, do you want us both to try to listen and see if we can hear your mother?" His eyes twinkled.

"Don't embarrass me," I pleaded.

"You're the one who keeps believing she is somehow alive."

"Yes. And I'm pissed, totally pissed at myself, that I can't keep her out of my mind and life. Being mentally ill is such a fucking waste of time! My mother and my childhood should be irrelevant to my life as an adult. I'm just completely pissed!"

"Well, since you have this rich imagination, why don't you imagine your mother here with us right now. Why don't you tell her how angry you are?"

"I can't do that," I said, my anger shriveling away as rapidly as dry ice in water. I was standing behind the chair as Ira was pointing to my imaginary mother.

"You look like you're about to bolt from this room. Come on. Tell her how angry you are right now. Talk to her as though she were right here."

I began slowly, feeling foolish, feeling frightened at the thought of ever being directly angry at my mother. I had done that before and gotten my teeth knocked out, been buried in a hole in the ground. That's powerful conditioning.

"I hate you," I said hesitantly.

"How do you really feel?" asked Ira. "Tell her."

"I hate you," I said loudly. My anger began to rise. "Mom, you had no right, no fucking right to do what you did to me. I was a child!" After a few minutes, I began to really feel the anger, feel my own strength. I began to shout. "Mom, if you're here, or a ghost, I dare you to hurt me. I dare you, you fucked-up witch!" I walked around the room with my arms outstretched, daring her. I screamed, "You can't hurt me because I won't give you the right. I want you out of my mind. Out of my life! You stole my childhood! You twisted my mind! I hate you!" Then I was storming around the office putting pillow figures in the chair, killing her, poking her eyes out, slitting her open. I'm sure my voice could be heard clear down the street. I never even cried. I was big and strong and furious.

After my killing rampage, Ira had me sit down to calm myself before I left the office.

"How do you feel?" he asked.

"Taller. Stronger. There really is a big difference between you being angry and putting her in a box like we did a few years ago, and me being able to be angry and kill her, isn't there?"

"A big difference," he said.

It was Easter, just after this incident when Bobby called me. Knowing I am in therapy and dealing with our childhood has brought us closer together. This was the first time he had called me wanting to talk about *his* upsetting memories.

"Happy Easter," he said, sounding as though he was choking. "Don't you hate Easter?"

"I always get upset when everyone else is dyeing eggs and buying chocolate bunnies. In fact, I've just been crazy over remembering getting buried."

"I remember how blue your lips were. You frightened me. You washed and washed after I dragged you up to my room. You were crying and asking me to look for beetle eggs in your hair. You kept carrying on about worms inside you. Every Easter that I can recall when we were kids was horrible. Do you remember the chicks Mom bought us that were dyed pink, blue, and green?"

"I don't think I do," I said. "Were they live chicks?"

"Yeah. We kept them in a little box with a light bulb for warmth and they kept walking in their bowl of mash." Bobby's voice cracked. "Don't you remember we were outside playing and Mom asked us if we wanted fried chicken and we all said yes? When we came in for lunch our little chicks were served to us on a plate, fried and lying there whole, with their fuzzy down all plastered with hot grease against their tiny bodies. Their little eyes were fried away."

"Now that you say that, I sort of hazily remember. I think I was expecting them to get killed, so I didn't get attached to them."

"It's strange how we all have different things we recall as terrible," Bobby said. "Even more than the chicks was the way Mom stood there, wearing that cotton dress with the blue fish design, waving that big spatula in her hand, laughing and laughing."

"I'm sorry, Bob. Here we are getting old and she still haunts us, doesn't she?"

"Like every day of my life," he muttered. He went on to tell me a few more things he remembered. I was glad he was finally talking about it.

"Do you want to come up here for a few days?" I asked him.

"No. I've got work to do. I just needed to hear your voice."

"Call me anytime. You know you're my hero. I can still feel your knobby little knees against me as I fall asleep sometimes. I remember you gave me your set of dominoes when I lost my first tooth and the tooth fairy never came. I would have died that summer in my room if you hadn't been there."

"I didn't do enough," he said. "I can't believe we lived all those years in silence. It's as though we lived in two worlds. There was our life on the outside, then there was a whole other world, past the orange trees and palms into the house of terror."

"We were just little kids. We did all that we knew to do. I think one reason I lived was that I always knew you were just beyond the door. I knew you loved me." I heard Bobby clear his throat and whisper good-bye. I always feel loss when he hangs up.

I looked at my arm with the tiny round scar and remembered when Mom was peeling potatoes and slashed at me with the paring knife. Bobby pulled me in the bathroom, took a razor blade and cut his own arm, then in an intense ceremony, he pressed our bleeding arms together and told me we were blood brothers for life. I remember his hair sticking out in a thousand directions and his nose sprinkled with freckles as we stood pressed together. I felt proud to have his blood going into my body, up my arm, pooling into my heart, which I imagined looked like a big valentine. Then he gave me his Hopalong Cassidy pistol.

I told Ira it depressed me that I couldn't make Mom stay out of my thoughts. "You know," I said, looking at him intently, "When I really think about it, it doesn't seem all that surprising that I would have the feeling Mom is still alive as a hovering, omnipotent being. I don't think I'm as paranoid as I am programmed. My God! She threatened me repeatedly, then reinforced it with pain. That's strong conditioning." I was getting impassioned, sitting on the edge of my chair, slicing the air with emphatic hand gestures. He was quietly attentive.

"There was her angel. There was Fritz and Frieda, who she created to terrify us. She dressed Jimmy in little soldier outfits, armed him with a toy gun, and told him he could make five dollars every time he told her when I did anything wrong. She paid him money when he shot me in the back with a BB gun. She reinforced the Gypsy threat with pain. I resent that you think it's such a great leap into craziness to think my mother is a spirit that haunts me!"

"Do you still think she is around?" Ira asked, not buying into my passion for even a moment.

"No. I think she's dead. Absolutely dead, and that her voice in my mind is a reactivation of the programming I got as a child. I was set up! I don't think this is a matter of silly mind tricks, like my wooden puzzle and visualizing pulling her back into place. I'm not being haunted. Mom isn't going to slay me in my sleep or grab the steering wheel of my car. I don't need little mind tricks. Just rational thought can make it obvious that I was powerfully conditioned by torture to view her as omnipotent. It's easy to see how my thoughts evolved to creating her haunting presence. She was the all powerful invader of my most private space—by that I mean my psyche." I was speaking to Ira as though I was telling him something he didn't know and I had to make him understand it.

He was kind enough to let me think I'd discovered something on my own. "I think it's very important you see that," he said. "You'll be less likely to believe her voice in your mind if you hold on to these insights."

"Ira, why didn't you just tell me all this a long time ago and save me all this agony of feeling haunted?" I was irritated with him, as though he had withheld vital information on purpose.

His face crinkled up in his slow smile that always makes him seem very alive. "I did tell you exactly that. You just hadn't made it yours yet."

"I'm without a doubt the slowest learner on the face of this planet!" I crossed my arms in disgust at my stupidity. When crazy thoughts get untangled into rational thought, the price is always looking back to where I've been with humiliation. "I'm incredibly stupid!"

"You're not stupid at all," said Ira. "Therapy takes time."

"You're generous with the face-saving remarks."

"The important thing is that you're getting it."

That all took place several months ago. Since then I've done better, having more good days, even happy days. Whenever I start to regress, feeling as though I were looking out at the world from eyes that are three and a half feet off the ground, I try to recapture the strength I felt when I killed my mother in Ira's office. I jerk myself up, saying, "I'm tall. I'm strong. I'm angry." Anger is a big emotion. I also know that rational thought can win over conditioned responses—but not easily!

It was at Ira's urging that I began writing in the early days of therapy with him. I had written a few things and he kept urging me to put everything down on paper. It has become a whole book. Repetitively, we have talked of publishing it as a way of helping others, but every time we discussed it, it felt threatening. Then the subject would be dropped.

For the first time in my life I'm having days and days go by without regressions, multiple voices, and multiple selves. There are days now filled with the sound of laughter I can feel inside, connections to people that penetrate into the new part of me where I'm able to respond to others, and feel them. The other day I said to Ira, "I want to publish my story. I'm going to do it."

"Are you sure you want to publish your story?" he asked, as he got up from his old leather chair, banged the lumps out of the bottom cushion, sat back down, then focused on me.

"Yes! Because there are no Gypsies who will carry me off if I tell. There is no mother who can hurt me anymore. I want to do it for the child in me who lied about the wounds, who hid, who kept the secret out of terror. I want to publish the book out of revenge. I'm going to tell . . ."

written in the sixth year of therapy
with Ira Steinman

EPILOGUE

Epilogue

I t tickled me as I typed the word "Epilogue" at the beginning of this chapter on my Jurassic period computer that I bought at a garage sale. It makes me feel magnificently completed. I'm not, but I'm well on my way. Since the episode of reliving being buried in dirt and killing off Mom, I think I've been mellower inside than I've ever been.

Fifty-two years is a long time to have lived in pain. The thought that thrills me is that whatever remaining years I have on this earth will be new years, time spent very differently from the agonizing lost years of my life. I am gaining control over fears, panics, my dissociative selves. For the first time in my life I am one with myself. There are no more occasions of finding myself in some strange place, with the hours of the clock having sped by in an altered state. I will probably always be capable of dissociation. The "others" that split my life and mind are not truly dead, for they never lived in any place but my fractured mind. There are stressful days when I hear the whisperings of other voices, the escaping aspects of myself, but I have mastered the mechanism of escape. I can catch myself willing myself away from reality, and with what is still an enormous amount of effort I can stay intact.

There were six other personalities who ran my life and even a few more who emerged in therapy with Ira who I still do not know. There could easily have been a hundred. There still could be, as quickly as it takes an imaginative mind to create one. What was in the realm of the unconscious is now accessible to my conscious mind. The victory is choice. Even now I cannot say I will never dissociate again, but I do know that if I ever look at a clock and can't account for the minutes that ticked away, I will not be the helpless victim; I will have made a poor choice. I will have allowed myself to regress to the panic state that I lived in when I was little, needing to run, needing to create an escape from the intolerable.

It is almost nine years since I began therapy; three and a half extremely painful years with the two psychiatrists who did not know how to deal with the severity of my problems, and over five with Dr. Ira Steinman. The years with Ira have been an intense period of reorganization of the very definitions of self. It has been exhausting, stressful, and nurturing in a deeply healing way.

What can I say to the man I owe my life to? Thank you seems laughably inadequate when I know if it hadn't been for Ira's caring, insight, and commitment I would have been a little type-set line in an obituary column. I wouldn't have enjoyed Kevin's wedding, or have been the proud mother watching Cindi get her college diploma, looking sweet and eager in her cap and gown, wearing her boxer shorts and Birkenstock sandals underneath. I would have missed her wedding and the birth of my adorable, effervescent grandchildren. There would not have been afternoons watching the fog rolling into San Francisco Bay and clearing to display the beautiful city. There would have been missed plays, restaurants, and family dinners full of laughter. I am glad I'm alive. I feel deeply indebted to Ira for the investment of his hours, even the essence of himself. Unlike Dr. Naughton or Dr. Hambler, he did not turn away from my pain. He took it and held it in trust for me, calmly watching me ricochet around dissociatively, always holding the picture of wellness for me. He cared more for my growth than for my pain. Maybe "loving teacher" are words to describe him.

It worries me that I love him too much, but it is a healing love. In the confines of that strange therapy room with its lovely flowers and odd pictures, the deep fathomless well of pain is getting filled drop by drop with the nurturing, the "thereness" of this surrogate parenting. Sometimes I'm still like a small child wanting to please him. I bake him cookies and bring him fruit. It devastates me when he has his tired days, when his eyelids droop from the exhaustion of giving so much to many others. I want to belong to him, to be special. He always makes me feel that I matter, but I fight a childish feeling of jealousy, seeing others enter our room, our place of closeness. I have had so little close human contact in my life. The brief times of joy in my childhood stand like beacons to hang on to. It is the same way in therapy. The minutes that I get focused on, the positive affirmations of my growth and insights seem the most precious of all the minutes in my week.

The long way I've come makes the concern of my loving Ira too much seem a moot issue. Maybe the loving is part of the healing. Maybe it is my strong attachment that lets me feel safe enough to open like a little flower bud that is at last getting exposed to gentle rain and sunshine.

Another new evolution is happening in how I view our relationship. It's been months since I've lain on Ira's floor, regressed into the pain. I sit in the chair opposite him and we talk. He doesn't seem so much the parent; I don't hyperreact to every little thing he says or does. There is far less anger in me toward him. I call him less. I'm able to work through a lot of things without being a clingy, needy, weepy woman. I'm able to bring rational thought into not only my relationship with him but also my other relationships.

I know it sounds silly, but he seems shorter and I feel taller now. When I started therapy with him five years ago, I could have sworn I only reached his waist.

I hardly ever ask him, "When are you going to stop therapy with me? When are you going to make me go away?" But when I do, his answer is still the same. "I'm not going to abandon you. That's transference. What made you ask me that today?" There are some conversations we've had so many times that we both begin to laugh when I bring it up.

I've always had easy laughter, but it was the dissociative laughter, just a sound, never a feeling—sort of like the Salvation Army
bell over the charity bucket at Christmas time. The sound is right,
but it's an empty sound. I've noticed when I was in the psychiatric hospital how mentally ill people don't laugh, and if they do it's
a meaningless noise. A person can cry and be somewhere in their
past, somewhere other than the here and now, but laughter is an
in-the-present experience. Not only do I laugh much more now,
but it's because I'm genuinely finding things to be funny. My
mind is getting rational enough to find the irrational funny. I
think it is a sign of mental health that I can distinguish what is off
center.

The other day Ira said, after our session of simple, quiet conversation, "Without all the histrionics and regressions, I think
you're turning bland." Then we both burst out laughing.

"Not a chance," I said.

The great emotional pendulum swings are arcing less radically. When I'm feeling distraught over something, I ask myself,
is the emotion truly in sync with the situation? Usually it is not.
I'm getting to the point that when I'm doing well I don't even
want to remember my childhood because to rehash the memories
wrecks a whole day. I doubt I will ever be comfortable with my
experiences, but I can consciously recall them now without having the desire to head for the bridge.

I think Ira would agree that this story is not at an ending, it is a
beginning. Years of torture and deprivation do not get healed
quickly. My thoughts get distorted easily. I feel danger that does
not exist. Self-destruct messages still play in my head. I do not
always perceive reality as it actually exists; it gets filtered through
a mind that was deeply hurt in its growing stages. I rejoice that I
have Ira to be my reality tester, my sounding board, my thought
reorganizer. I trust him more than I trust my own mind.

I have missed much, and experienced more than I wish I had.
My experiences did not make me tough, they made me fragile.
Since I am no longer dissociating, I feel even more sensitive and
vulnerable. I never stayed together long enough to fully experience all my own feelings. My new range and depth frighten me.
Maybe that is why I feel such intense love for Ira right now, because it is not getting diluted by splitting into separate selves. All

my feelings seem magnified. I see and feel my children as never before. My capacity to have a relationship has been radically changed by my ability to stay one person.

I'm still very close to my brother, Bobby. He is now a grandfather with a thick thatch of white hair. I have sought healing in therapy and he seems more at peace with prayer and talking about forgiveness. He has had a more functional life than Jim or me. He is now an executive for a large insurance company. I think he wants to be viewed as the stable achiever, but his wife Nancy has confided in me he has episodes of profound depression where he doesn't eat or sleep for days on end. He has not had psychotherapy, but his internist has had him on several different antidepressants over the years. Unlike me, he never repressed memories of the violence he saw. He still feels protective toward me, and other than Ira, he is the only other person who truly knows what life was like for me—and for him, when he would lie in bed with me and comfort me in his child's arms and we would plot our escapes.

As magnified and unstable as my emotions are, Bobby does not seem to have any range at all. He is charming and cultured, but what on first impression appears to be sophistication is actually a deadening of his emotions.

Jimmy's life, like mine, has been one of terrible inner pain. I will not write of his adult life, for that is for him to do if he chooses.

I feel grief for the little boy with the curly hair and big ears, who was forced to shovel dirt on me. I wish I could find a way to heal him. I wish he knew how much I still love him and how deeply I share his pain.

My relationship with Dan has changed in many ways during my metamorphosis. We still do not talk about the deeper things between us. He is willing to be my comfortable friend. We love each other in a growing way.

I owe him more than I can ever give him. He has stayed with me for all these roller-coaster years, seeing me through suicidal depressions, missing days, hospitalizations, and my disastrous attempt to end my life that has left me pain-ridden.

Sometimes I feel he loves me in the way one loves a cancer

patient—intensely, but with no talk or hope of a tomorrow. After a lifetime of failing him, it will take a long time to build trust.

I knew I had to let him read this book before I could ever send it to a publisher. Over and over I made overtures to him to tell him about me, about us, about therapy, and he always gave a reply like, "I'm not good at the emotional stuff. Let's not talk about this." He stayed warm, but always distant. It's that removal of himself from our relationship that kept me free to be crazy without creating the conflict it should have or getting me the help I needed. I don't think either one of us knew how to deal with my mental illness.

Finally deciding I had to give him this book, I told him he had to know me even if it meant divorce. I was certain it would, but I wanted an end to all the lies between us. For several weeks the manuscript sat in his office in the cabinet shop, covered with blueprints and sawdust. Then one evening he didn't come home from work. It was after midnight when he slipped into bed next to me and just whispered, "Good night."

He was up by five, pulled on his jeans and tiptoed out of the room. When I got up at eight, I found him hunched over the manuscript at the dining table. I fixed breakfast anticipating he would get up, pack his clothes, and leave me.

I said nothing as I fixed him his favorite Spanish omelette and brewed strong coffee. Out of the corner of my eye I saw him finish the last page and slowly close the lid on the box of paper. We were alone, and I placed the breakfast in front of him and sat down. The rain outside seemed to reinforce my sense of doom. His face was pale and indecipherable.

I couldn't be direct—we never have been with each other. Instead of asking him how he felt about me, I said, "Do you think I should publish this book?"

"Yes. I think it's an important book."

"Do you think people who know me will hate me for all I've done?" Tears sprang to my eyes.

Dan looked at me, reached across the table and gently clasped his big, rough hand over mine. "Of course not. Everyone will understand." Tears were in his eyes, too. We held hands for a few minutes, both of us crying softly. Then he got up without eating the omelette and whispered, "I've got to get to work."

I stood up, and he pulled me into his arms and squeezed me hard. "I love you," he murmured in a choked voice.

He has never mentioned it again. But it was a start. We have been closer even without words.

To Kevin and Cindi I am just Mom. Like Dan, they would rather sit on the worn blue bar stools in my kitchen and carve on warm brownies still in the pan and talk about their day, their plans, their hobbies and children than listen to my pain or my past. We never even talk about my being a multiple personality, although they know. I want it this way, too. Probably the biggest gift life has given me is two whole and happy adult children. They weathered their growing-up years with me. As they burst enthusiastically into our house with dogs, or new scuba-diving gear to show me, or sit and visit quietly and sip tea with me, I feel somehow life is saying, "Open your hand. Hold this gift. Let your heart see these are your pearls."

I'm amazed how Dan and my kids were able to see beyond my instability and understand I loved them. Our love for each other has survived. There are damages I've inflicted on both of them. They don't treat me like a fully competent adult. How could they? I'm only now becoming one. If they ever want to talk, or cry, or need me to help them come to terms with the traumas I've caused them, I will do anything to heal things. Lately there has only been their enthusiasm at my new evenness, their support of my therapy. Just as I am seeing my family with new eyes, they are discovering a new mom. I think when the one bird with the broken wing begins to heal and fly, the whole flock feels safer.

Our family dinners are noisy, silly affairs with Cindi's children the star attractions, blowing bubbles in the strawberry-flavored milk and giggling. Then the youngest goes from adult to adult giving Eskimo kisses. Kevin always has a funny story to tell. My son-in-law and new daughter-in-law are a precious part of our circle. I look at all the young faces and I wonder how I could ever have thought the pain was so intense that I should choose to leave them.

Anger is an emotion I am beginning to feel without the apprehension that I will be punished. There is a whole boiling, stewing volcano of anger that erupts at the memory of what was done to me. I could easily carve my mother into chunks if she were alive. My anger is helping me deal with the small victim feelings I have. To be assertive and angry is by far more difficult for me than to be the pale, frightened child, cowering in a corner waiting to be hurt one more time. But I'm practicing.

There are days even now that I waste in grieving for myself. With the insights of therapy, I can also clearly analyze the cost, the loss. My failures loom very large. I ache that I have hurt people, that I have not been a fully functioning individual. The positive side of the self-awareness is a new understanding of why I was the way I was—because that is all I was capable of being. Rather than judging and condemning myself, I am struggling to find a forgiveness, a new gentleness with myself. Ira's magnanimous acceptance of all my failures has helped me try to get past my mistakes. As he says with his twinkling eyes, "Hey, it wasn't your fault you were crazy."

It amazes me that with all my years of therapy, I still have no interest at all in reading about psychology or other multiple personalities. My suffering has been too intense and personal to even allow me room to care about anyone else's experiences. I have not joined any survivor or abused people support groups. I'm certain it is valuable for others, but I would be useless to any group, for other's experiences would turn me into a tearful blob. I have so little distance from my pain that in therapy I'm still working on how to move past it and how to function.

I have been appalled at the women I have seen on television who seemingly have been convinced by their therapists that multiple personality is a viable life choice. The women clutched teddy bears and spoke in children's voices as though we are to accept their dissociation and give sympathetic clucking noises to their regressive behavior. My impression is that the therapists and the patients themselves have become enamored with how many personae they possess and what their characteristics are. Ira was never interested or captivated by my other personalities. He said, "They are just flat characterizations made by your imagination." His objective was always for me to gain control of the dissociation. Our therapy was to figure out who and what these split-off pieces of self were to gain the intimacy necessary for integration.

I have a problem believing people who say that until therapy they didn't know they were multiple personalities. I fear these people are victims of inept therapists who are rewarding patients with attention for high drama, or even worse, who by hypnosis and suggestion are causing women to actually believe they are several selves. How could anyone "discover" they had other personalities as an adult? I don't get it. From my earliest memory there was Emily, the voices, the missing time, clothes in my closet I knew I hadn't bought, money I needed to pay bills for what Emily spent, abortions, VD, appointments missed, the lies, the infantile behavior humiliating me and my children—my dysfunctional list was endless. It is also behavior that others noticed. Everyone around me knew I was a multiple personality years before a psychiatrist gave it a label.

For me, dissociating was such crippled functioning that I can't imagine anyone choosing it as a creative life option. I'm glad Ira never listened to me on the five or six occasions I quit therapy, telling him I'd rather stay a multiple personality. He would call me up and say, "Sorry. You're in the middle of therapy and you're too mixed up to make that decision. I will expect you here for your appointment on Friday. Do I make myself clear?" At the next appointment, I'd slink back to his office. In the beginning, I tried to bargain for the number of months I'd give it before I could quit and die.

Living life in the chaos of my shifting internal states and time frames was extremely complex, to the point of filling my days and preoccupying my mind. Multiplicity for me was the construction of the ultimate house of cards. I was like a hummingbird in the wind, darting here, darting there to keep the whole delusional structure from crashing. No one knows the word stress like a multiple personality.

I question the therapy techniques of hypnosis. Before I began therapy, I went to a hypnotist out of desperation. I only told him of my depression and my fear of closed-in spaces. He did past-life regressions, and now I have a clear image in my mind of being an Indian by a stream bed grinding acorns in a metate when an avalanche rained dirt and rocks down on me, suffocating me! The hypnosis frightened me, so I didn't continue. Later in therapy, when I relived the experience of Mom burying me in dirt and had Bobby validate the memory, I realized my subconscious had recycled the trauma, just as in a dream. I'm glad Ira and my other two psychiatrists never used hypnosis. There were never any directives or suggestions as there were when I was hypnotized. It makes me realize what a malleable thing memory is. Even Bobby, Jimmy, and I, who lived in the same house, have a different memory of some things. I wrote that Mom locked me in my room for two months the summer I was nine. Bobby said he is sure it was about four weeks. He's probably right. The only memories I have that can't be validated by Bobby, Jim, scars, and hospitalizations are the earliest episodes of my labia being sewn, and the sewing needles used. Maybe I imagined it, but it seems real to me.

As suspicious as I am of the people on television claiming to be multiple personalities and others claiming horrendous abuse after recovering memories under hypnosis, I am even more skeptical of the False Memory Syndrome Foundation which is trying to disclaim recovered memories. The true science of how memory works is important to explore, and I hope this group and others are doing it, but there is one thing I know for sure; if my mother were alive today her index finger would be pressing the buttons on her telephone to the False Memory Syndrome Foundation and she would articulately, elegantly, and emphatically claim to be innocent of what I accused her of with my false memories. She would be doing that in the face of the irrefutable corroborating evidence of my abuse, as she did to the police after locking me in the yellow room. Jimmy has the faint scars at his temple where he got his brains sizzled by shock treatments because people who live in functional families don't want to believe that abuse is happening in their air space. The police saw vomit and feces on the floor of my room, me semiconscious—and they carted Jimmy away. Abusers can be pretty or handsome or wear jewelry, and just as victims have been terrorized to lie, the perpetrators, the betrayers of childhood lie, too.

What will happen to all the adult survivors, who like me, are defying their Gypsies and standing up to confront their abusers if repressed memory is suspect? What will happen to those who only have their memories of dark rooms and sexual violation, but have no scars to show? Vaginas usually heal to tell no tales.

I don't know how memory works. Fortunately, I only have my experiences to relate. For me there is a big difference between forgetting and remembering. I never truly forgot my abuse. It got terribly disjointed to the point of craziness. For years my mind kept fast dancing with dissociation, frantically holding the horror out of my mind. My body remembered with pain and symptoms, my nightmares remembered. I would have to say that I never forgot any of it, I just didn't want to remember it because it was beyond endurance. Even my conscious mind was aware of experiences that I denied or shoved away. I think all minds try to move toward stress reduction, and for me being dissociative and crazy was less stressful, in a convoluted way, than coming to terms with the violence. How could I for thirty years take my false teeth out to brush them and never think about how I lost them? When a new dentist would ask me, I would give some flip, casual lie. I didn't forget. I just couldn't acknowledge it in my conscious mind.

The times when I've said a memory was surfacing, the violent physical symptoms of vomiting or hurting myself were not from the shock of remembering. It was from the need to stand still for the first time and give it texture, chronology, and a place in the structure of self. The more accurate description of recovering repressed memory would be giving the correct emotional feelings to experiences that couldn't be processed when they first happened. In therapy, it wasn't hard to remember; the hard part was getting to the point of being willing to remember.

Therapy has given me the memory of my childhood. As heinous as it was, it gives me definitions and answers. Much that was unexplainable is now clear.

Extreme child abuse is like being given a road map to life that is all turned around. Therapy is going clear back to the basics of north and south and untangling all the misplaced road signs. When I began therapy, I had no geographical location on the road map of life. I was completely disoriented. As far as I still need to go in untangling the mess, I feel exhilaration at how far I've come. No one but another dissociative person could truly know how terrible it is to live under the tyranny of others in your own mind.

There must be a special place in hell for those hexed with multiple personalities. It is not funny, or fun, as is often perceived by others. In a way it's a form of self-abuse, although not out of conscious choice. Often these days I wake up and feel the deliciousness of knowing that the day holds my choices, not the civil war of disagreeing voices. There is no group consensus, no arbitration between warring factions, no fear of failing obligations or missing appointments because another piece of self has gone its separate way. Hurrah! I am one!

Not long ago I went to a shopping mall alone for the first time in four years. My fear of dissociating and having Emily or Joey steal something kept me away from stores. Freedom is the wonderful feeling of knowing I am in control. I went into the glittery, glitzy mall with its splashes of colors and felt the feeling of childhood deprivation overtake me, remembering the smashed dolls, the cut-up bear, the murdered pets. Instead of dissociating, I was able to say to myself, "These are childhood feelings that are rising. It is not now, not here." I still felt the desire to steal something, but I resisted the urge. I did something dumb, but it felt good; going to the toy section, I bought myself a Pooh Bear. It would never be the Pooh Bear I had in the closet to comfort me. It would never be the bear I cried for as Mom cut its eyes off with a knife and gutted it into cotton fluff, but it felt symbolically significant. I would listen to the crying child inside myself and not run away from all those feelings. I would own all the parts of myself, accepting the pain that came with it.

That Janis Joplin line, "Freedom's just another word for nothing left to lose . . ." strikes me as one of the world's faultiest statements. In my childhood days, freedom meant the time that the closet door would swing open and the waft of fresh air would whisper onto my face with the rays of light. It was the relief as the blue kerchiefs were untied. In my wheelchair-bound days following my meningitis, it meant walking and independence. My freedom was fought for with exercise, sweat, and tired muscles on parallel bars. Freedom was the moment the white-coated rapist was caught and smashed into the wall. In my adult life there was no freedom, only the tyranny of the multiple selves, the slavery to the inner pain and fears. Therapy has been the road to freedom

for me. It is as arduous a trip as any climb up Mt. Everest. Freedom is having choices. The word freedom reverberates through
my head like a clear, glorious sound. For the first time in my life I
have choices, I am accountable, I am responsible for all I do. The
thought invigorates me and terrifies me. I'm no longer the helpless little cork getting tossed by waves in the sea. I have known
every kind of pain that life can offer—confinement, torture, illness, physical handicap, surgeries—and I can unequivocally state
there is no greater pain than the pain that exists in the human
mind. A sick mind can make the trip through life into the voyage
of the damned. Physical pain goes away, but twisted thoughts per-
vert every waking moment, distort pleasure, isolate you in your
own netherworld. Now that I am getting well, I grieve for the pain
of my own mental illness. The cost! God, what cost! I cherish my
newfound freedom. Freedom's just another word for wholeness
of self. There are no redeeming features to the pain-locked life of
mental illness.

With my progress I can see how egocentric and self-centered I
have been. Psychological pain is an enveloping experience. It has
been a full-time job dealing with me, myself and I, I, I, I . . . I had
to spend so much energy dealing with the pieces of myself that I
have few meaningful friendships with others. I'm just beginning
to form bonds, make friends. I have a few new women friends,
the first in my adult life, now that I am able to disconnect my
mother from the half of the species who are female. My life has
been totally focused on male involvements, with my numerous
affairs. Most women still frighten me, but I find myself reaching
out, being willing to experience more.

Looking in the mirror it surprises me to see the middle-aged
face reflecting back. My graying hair and new wrinkles seem incongruous to how young I feel. The scars that once were vivid
signs of my abuse have faded into the softness of older skin. It is
only in my mind that the scars are livid. The abuse can, in an
instant, seem as intense as it was decades ago. It is an ongoing
battle not to get sucked back in memory, not to replay the old
horrors over and over in my mind. Often it takes the help of Ira's
calm, reassuring voice: "You can stay your adult, tall self. You do

not need to regress. Bring the hurts into my office, but only here." Someday maybe I won't need him, but the very thought of that makes me grieve.

It is less and less often that I get in suicidal, black states. Occasionally, I get sucked into the vortex of childhood pain and can't get out. My mother's threat still seems strong in the darkness of my pain-place. Sometimes I need Ira to help me, sometimes I can work it through myself, for there is the newer, stronger self that can step back, away from the blackness and say, Yes, this is a familiar place. It is the bleakness of my childhood, the abandonment of the closet, the repetitive pain and the death wish of my mother. But this is not my life today. These feelings seem real now, but there have been other suicidal times when I have fought through the despair and been glad I have made it through.

There are many times when Ira could have hospitalized me, times when we both knew I was a suicide risk. I feel touched and indebted to him that he would spend the time teaching me how to find my way back to a safer mental place, and not just lock me up in a hospital as the other psychiatrists did. He smiles that marvelous smile of his when I accuse him of being a gambler, a risk-taker. "No," he grins. "You were easy."

Tapping his forehead, Ira would say, "Use your mind. Stay in control." That's easy for him. God! How I struggle. But the more often I work through those suicidal episodes the more I feel able to use my logical mind to gain control.

As I get older the physical effects of my abuse seem more noticeable. In the mornings I need to work my fingers, sometimes kneading my hands under hot water just to be able to open and close them. The old broken bones ache from the arthritis that has set in. My hearing is worsening, especially in my right ear, from having been hit too often, slammed against a wall too many times. The doctor says one of these days I should consider a hearing aid. The worst pains are from my car accident, or maybe the pain only seems worse because of my sense of guilt that I would inflict this damage on myself. The pains in my femur ache when the weather gets cold, my back hurts. I get angry at the pain, the limitations, but like so much of my life I have to accept the reality of what is.

I'm trying to be kind to my aches and pains, not just beat myself up for what I can't undo.

The surprising thing is how many physical symptoms have been lessened by therapy. I no longer have bouts of diarrhea and the continual abdominal pains, I don't need to urinate as often. There are no days of blurring vision, which I now know were connected to my fear of having my eyes poked out with an ice pick. There is none of the blindness which was Camille's. Nightmares are still a part of my sleep, but they are lessening. I no longer pace the house at night like a caged jungle cat. I am able to say, "Yes, this is why I can't sleep," and plug the nightmares into the events that I now remember. My headaches are less frequent. There is no need to see any doctor, other than Ira, with an array of symptoms. I will never again seek surgery as I once did in the subconscious desire to re-experience pain.

Pride is a newfound feeling in me. Comparing where I was even two years ago to where I am today, the difference is as drastic as between a dark, dripping cave and a sunny, wildflower sprinkled meadow. I feel hope. I feel happy as I do the simple things of life. There has been such phenomenal progress at mastering my fears and panics that I am beginning to feel like a functional person. I don't steal things. There is no sense of foreboding that I will find myself getting handcuffed by a rough security officer for an offense I have no memory of. Never again will I walk the streets looking for the safe daddy or have hurtful sex with strangers. I do not carry water around with me or keep it by my bed at night. Hunger and thirst are still sources of anxiety, but not in a neurotically crippling way. Twenty pounds have slipped off me since my "others" have died. Eating in a dissociative state was a problem; now I can calculate my calories and know I'm the only one doing the eating. There is no sabatoge from the split-away selves.

Fire no longer panics me. I can light matches or sit next to someone smoking and not have to leap up and leave the room. It still arouses the feeling of the cigarettes getting pressed to my skin, but it isn't an overwhelming, irrational fear.

For the first time I can enter an elevator and not have my breathing get rapid and feel like my heart will burst through my chest as the blood drains down to my feet. Recently, Dan and I went on vacation and I didn't need to be drugged with Xanax to fly. Well, I did take one when the sides of the plane began to implode on me. I'm not a one hundred percent success yet.

With all the learning and therapy I am viewing myself as a person who was psychologically handicapped, and I feel an acceptance of my damaged self. My fears, my panics are not failure but merely the result of trauma. Like relearning to walk after meningitis, I have to relearn how to live. There is no defensiveness in me when Ira says, "That's a crazy thought." Those thoughts continue to sneak in, and probably always will. The important thing is learning to deal with them.

There has been a price to pay in giving up my dissociative "others." I now own my childhood, my history, all the memories of rejection and pain. But for every loss there is gain. I've lost my vehicle of escape, but I've gained accountability. I've gained the conscious experiencing of all the parts of myself. It is control. It is growing up. Reality is often harder than splitting and running, for what is familiar is always easier. I've been a gifted escape artist. Unfortunately, the escape became the trap.

Another new happy occurrence is the surge of creativity I have had since I've gotten better. After my mother stabbed me for singing, I lost my voice when I tried to sing. Now I play music at ear-splitting volume and sing and sing. I've joined a choir recently, my first group venture. My Beethoven tapes are nearly worn out as I absorb the transcendent music. I've never stayed still inside my mind long enough to simply experience an outside pleasure like music. That is hard to explain to anyone.

Gardening is another pleasure. Digging in the small yard around my house, I almost feel I am nurturing a piece of myself as I care for my flowers and fertilize my vegetables. The rich dirt crumbles in my fingers sending the aroma of life into my nose. I feel a gladness that I am here.

I am learning to have fun. To goal-driven workers like Dan that is not a statement of achievement. Two weeks ago, I woke up about seven on a Saturday. "You know what?" I said to Dan, who was lying next to me with the pillow over his face trying to block out the morning sun, "I've never seen snow."

"Consider yourself immensely fortunate," he muttered.

"I really want to see it and feel it. Let's go to Tahoe. We've never been. Get dressed and we can go right now. It'll be fun."

"Can't you just stay home and pull my fingernails out slowly?"

"Nope. Wouldn't it be fun to build a snowman?"

"Are you getting weird? Should you call Ira?"

"No. I'm getting normal. This is called enthusiasm. I'm going!"

"Okay, I'll go with you. You don't know how to drive in snow."

We went and had a wonderful day tromping through crunchy snow piles between big pines. We had a snow fight, laughing and getting our clothes cold and soggy. Then we warmed up at Caesar's Palace and won twenty dollars in the slot machines. Feeling rich and silly, as well as cold, we decided to spend the night. We sat in the Roman tub in our room, luxuriating in the bubbles, drank wine and then made love gleefully. I didn't even have the clutching anxiety as we rolled on that king-size bed.

Afterward, as Dan lay propped against the pillows and I snuggled against him, he said, "Do you realize you were in a smoky restaurant tonight and you went in an elevator and it didn't even upset you like it used to?"

"I'm getting to be like a regular person."

"Better than that," he said as he smiled at me. "Much better."

I have been a dependable employee in Dan's business for over two years now, which has been the longest period of employment in my life. I told him to watch out because I'm getting stable enough to get a better paying job. He grins and says, "Yeah, but the benefits are good. You can go to lunch with the boss."

Two months ago, I gave my first big dinner party for some of the contractors who have been working with Dan. Cindi came and helped me prepare for the occasion. She looked at the table all set, the house clean, flowers around and dinner under control, and said, "Oh, Mom. You've come such a long way! I'm really proud of you." She curled my hair for me, helped me make an apple strudel, then got ready to escape before the guests arrived. "Are you sure you can handle this? Are you actually going to light the candles you put around the living room?" she asked as she peeked back around the front door.

"Yes. Everything will be fine." I gave her a little grin. "I put the candles around so no one will see the streaks on the paint from where the roof leaked. Thanks for helping."

It was fine. It was even enjoyable. After the dinner was over, Dan was helping me with the dishes. He hooked the kitchen towel around the back of my neck and pulled me toward him as though I'd been lassoed. There were warm lights reflecting from his blue eyes. With the side of his finger he traced down the side of my cheek, then he said, "I'd say our party was a huge success. It brought us two new jobs, as well as an interesting evening. You were some hostess. Everyone loved your stuffed artichokes. We should do this regularly."

"Yes. I'd like to." I answered, feeling incredibly successful. I didn't even have to be Muriel to pull it off.

Cindi phoned at seven the next morning. "Mom, how did it go?"

I gave her a detailed account, including the fact that I lit the candles. Then I said, "You are so dear to be my cheering squad. It means a lot."

"I'm just so happy for all the new things you are able to do. I think you're wonderful."

It's like that with all my family; none of them wants to talk about where I've been, but they all are enthusiastic about where I'm going.

I'm fifty-two and new to life, new to myself. I guess this is a form of rebirth. I don't know if I will ever be wholly well. Ira is the eternal optimist and says, "Of course you can get well." This marvelous, wonderful turning toward health has not been a serendipitous happening. My struggle is profound and painful. I am determined to persevere. Actually, at this point I am so thrilled and intrigued by my progress I wouldn't quit for anything. It's exciting to think of living my life without Emily, without the voices. There are days when therapy seems painful, or I slip off the edge of logic, but I just have to think back to what life was like a short time ago and I see what leaps forward I have made.

I stand as testimony to the fact that the human mind has extraordinary capabilities. My integration of my other selves is clear evidence that psychotherapy works. If someone were to ask me what is the single most meaningful thing to have happened in my lifetime, I would in deepest honesty say, "It was finding Ira Steinman, the generous, caring, committed, psychiatrist who has given me my life." There is an enormous qualitative difference between existing and living. I am finally finding my life.

I'm more interested in the things going on around me. Instead of the inner running, I'm now into outer exploring. I go to the museums in the city, or wander into galleries to look at photo exhibits. I'm still pulled to the ocean, feeling a need to hear the waves and smell sea air with the wafting scent of drying seaweed. My happiest memories as a child were at the beach. In the early mornings I will often go by myself and take long walks along cold stretches of dark sand, listening to the breakers. I seem to need time alone. Still being in therapy, still reorganizing down to the core, I need the solitary processing time, not to run from memories, but to take time to search the inner changing landscape.

Recently, I joined a Chinese cooking class and had a delightful time wandering through Chinatown buying a duck for the next lesson. I found one hanging in a butcher shop. I felt adventurous as I sniffed curious herbs, then waited while my duck got wrapped for me. Dan was very impressed with the Peking duck dinner I fixed. Next is lobster sauce.

My neighbor Sylvia and I have been volunteering at the shelter for abused women in our town. We bake cookies and collect clothing for the hollow-eyed women. It makes me feel grateful to give back to others when all my life I've been the one needing the care.

That I can even experience joy is far beyond any expectation I had of life. When I began therapy, my greatest hope was that I would find a way of coping, just to survive and not traumatize my children with my suicide. In the early days with Ira I didn't believe I could achieve even that. I thought of that when I took my two grandchildren on a ferry ride across the bay recently. It was one of those crystal-clear mornings, and we three were leaning over the rails looking for sea lions. The children were jumping in excitement next to me, their blond curls whipping in the breeze, when I looked up and saw the Golden Gate Bridge. My heart clutched for a moment when I thought of the despair that made me sit perched on the railing, contemplating a leap into the dark water below, such a short time ago. Just then, several dolphins surfaced to swim beside the ferry. The sun reflected off the shiny black backs and made the wake of the ship a shimmer of dancing white foam. As little hands held mine, I knew I was no longer simply existing. I was experiencing the moment—and I was happy.